Therapist's Guide to Posttraumatic Stress Disorder Intervention

Therapist's Guide to Posttraumatic Stress Disorder Intervention

SHARON L. JOHNSON

AMSTERDAM • BOSTON • HEIDELBERG • LONDON • OXFORD • NEW YORK
PARIS • SAN DIEGO • SAN FRANCISCO • SINGAPORE • SYDNEY • TOKYO
Academic Press is an imprint of Elsevier

Academic Press is an imprint of Elsevier
32 Jamestown Road, London NW1 7BY, UK
30 Corporate Drive, Suite 400, Burlington, MA 01803, USA
525 B Street, Suite 1900, San Diego, CA 92101-4495, USA

First edition 2009

British Library Cataloguing in Publication Data
A catalogue record for this book is available from the British Library

Library of Congress Cataloging-in-Publication Data
A catalog record for this book is available from the Library of Congress

ISBN: 978-0-12-374851-5

For information on all Academic Press publications
visit our website at elsevierdirect.com

Typeset by Macmillan Publishing Solutions
(www.macmillansolutions.com)

Printed and bound in the United States of America

09 10 11 12 13   11 10 9 8 7 6 5 4 3 2 1

CONTENTS

Part II Treatment

Chapter 3
TRANSTHEORETICAL AND MULTIMODAL INTERVENTIONS

INTRODUCTION

THIS book has been written to serve as an essential resource in trauma intervention for therapists who want to enhance their skill in working with those who have posttraumatic stress disorder (PTSD). It also provides a review of the vast spectrum of associated theories and pertinent information. PTSD remains a controversial diagnosis, with numerous theoretical underpinnings attached. Even the American Psychiatric Association's Darrel Regier, MD, MPH, executive director for research and education, states, "It is very important to have a better paradigm than what we have been using to look at somatic presentations of mental disorders, and the relationship of disorders in other organ systems." This statement contributed to the author's belief that while somatic treatment may appear to be in the realm of "feel good therapy" its tenets offer useful information regarding the understanding of the patient's experience and belief system. However, it does not change the current standard of care for evidenced-based treatment: the first-line treatment for PTSD is cognitive behavioral therapy and psychopharmacology. It should also be recognized that gender and cultural issues play a role in the connection between mental and physical health in association with physiological characteristics, socio-cultural influences and personal perspectives.

This book is divided into three parts: Biopsychosocial Aspects and Diagnosis of PTSD, Treatment, and Skill Building. Most books on the topic cover one perspective of theory, knowledge, or treatment of PTSD, or several valuable pieces of information which the therapist (providing direct services) is able to utilize in their daily practice. This text is a transtheoretical review with a cognitive behavioral focus that incorporates physiology, body-oriented and emotional/relational theoretical perspectives and interventions. The reviews center on empirically based research and well-known national and international theorists, researchers, and clinicians. The goal for the expansion of information and encompassing renowned leaders in the field was to broaden the perspective of PTSD, which better suits the rich diagnostic complexities of the disorder instead of narrowing the field of understanding and interventions. It is acknowledged that the standard of care for PTSD will continue to change as scientific information and advances clarify all aspects of the disorder. This research will continue to result in an evolution of the diagnosis and treatment of PTSD. However, at this time, all of the major guidelines consistently identify cognitive behavioral therapy and pharmacologic intervention as first-line treatments, in conjunction with numerous beneficial second-line treatments.

This is a useful text for any therapist and was developed with consideration of the high level of demand placed upon those practicing to deliver effective treatment using outcome-oriented interventions. Not only has managed care significantly impacted the time frame of therapy, but consumers also demonstrate an elevated level of expectation for evidence of relief and recovery. On the positive side, the result has been increased collaboration in developing the treatment plan and increased responsibility on both sides of the partnership to fulfill the obligations laid down in the treatment plan. This requires that the treatment plan be clear, concise, and time-effective and that it demonstrates the medical necessity for treatment. Again, the premise is to evaluate the current situation to determine what is presently causing distress and to intervene in a manner which alleviates distress and improves coping.

For the most appropriate and effective utilization of the information contained in the *Therapist's Guide*, therapists should be professionally trained and licensed in their state or country. Typically training includes a graduate level degree, a clinical internship or its equivalent, and past supervision in the specific technique or approach employed. Any professional provider of interventions and/or treatment to individuals following the experience of trauma should be well-trained, experienced practitioners. The user of this book is responsible to consider their own expertise in providing services. In addition, to effectively access the information in this text it is recommended that the therapist familiarize themselves with the contents so that they are easily accessed.

Whether it is a traditional, terminal, or professional mental health program under consideration, there is a need to include education on trauma response and treatment skills across all mental health disciplines in accordance with the therapist's ethics, education, and training. This training should incorporate knowledge, supervision, and experience in the different types of trauma, trauma responses, and interventions (sexual/physical/emotional abuse, critical incident, and mass disaster which includes natural disaster and terrorist attack). This diagnosis is particularly vulnerable to more damage being done to the seeker of treatment if the therapist lacks necessary education, training and expertise.

The first section of the book covers a significant amount of distilled information in an effort to present the therapist with a user-friendly review and overview of PTS, diagnostic criteria, comorbidity, functional impairment, neurobiology, and accurate diagnosing of PTSD. It highlights the difficulties experienced in the clinical setting, which often lead to the diagnosis of PTSD being overlooked and how to take a more comprehensive approach to accurately determine this complex diagnosis, which often presents with diagnostic comorbidity. It discusses the range of PTS-related diagnoses for the purpose of conceptual understanding, but the focus of this text is on PTSD.

The second section of the book covers the transtheoretical treatment options and treatment planning. As previously stated, the aim was to include theoretical information from well-known national and international theorists, researchers, and clinicians because the information is valuable and allows for flexibility for individualized intervention even within the frame of cognitive behavioral treatment. The physiological experience is so fundamental to the diagnosis of PTSD it is not reasonable to disregard information because it is not within the parameters of traditional cognitive behavioral treatment. To do so, would be antithetical to the needs of patient characteristic individuality, and the need to meet the patient where they are in symptom presentation, skill level, resources, and belief system. The sophisticated therapist recognizes much of the information from their own first-hand clinical experience. It is actually validating to the seasoned therapist to see literature that addresses the complexity of information provided by those they treat with PTSD. The treatment planning segment is drawn from the central areas of PTSD diagnostic criteria symptomology in the form of goals with associated treatment objectives for accomplishing those goals. Cognitive behavioral interventions offer appropriate structure and are excellent for achieving stabilization, improving coping, and facilitating change.

The third section of the book offers skill building resources for increasing competence. The information in this section can be used adjunctively during therapy, as education, and/or homework. The information in this section and its presentation are designed to be supportive of a cognitive behavioral therapeutic frame. This allows for the goals and objectives to be easily understood and engaged. The more those presenting for treatment can be helped to understand how they have been affected by what has happened to them and the role they play in sustaining patterns or problems, as well as identifying recovery resources, the more they can be motivated to make the necessary changes via a variety of pathways offered by knowledge and skills development. These recovery efforts have a self-reinforcing quality. Again, even though the focus is on a cognitive behavioral frame it does not exclude the utility of deep personal searching associated with psychodynamic theory or dealing with physiological symptoms medically or by the use of somatic theory.

The patient offers the information about their experience, how they have been impacted, and their level of coping. In their effort to seek support and effective interventions to alleviate their distress they are depending on the therapist to be thorough, skilled and flexible in developing a treatment plan designed to meet them where they are and to use well-chosen skills necessary for facilitating desired change and eliminating or alleviating their experience of distress. This is the foundation of the individualized treatment plan.

PART I

Biopsychosocial Aspects and Diagnosis of PTSD

Chapter 1

Assessing and Diagnosing Posttraumatic Stress Disorder

The National Institute of Mental Health (2008) states that 2.5 million people are hospitalized each year having sustained injuries during a traumatic event. As the literature is reviewed, however, it can be seen that most research has been focused on combat veterans (predominantly Vietnam and the Middle East) and female adult survivors of sexual abuse/assault. When clinicians engage with those who have been exposed to trauma, they are challenged to differentiate posttraumatic stress disorder (PTSD) from other clinical problems. Sometimes symptom presentation is simple (such as depression and/or anxiety), in other instances symptom presentation demonstrates multiple layers of comorbidity.

PTSD is a complex and often chronic disorder that has been found to be comorbid with numerous other disorders. While exposure to a traumatic event appears common, only a fraction of those exposed to trauma develop posttraumatic stress disorder. The symptoms of PTSD are indicative of a disturbance of the normal capacity to resolve cognitive and emotional responses to traumatic events (Yehuda and McFarlane, 1995). It is a disorder that involves a traumatic stressor, intrusive recollections, avoidant symptoms, and hyperarousal. Earlier diagnostic criteria set acute stress disorder (ASD) and PTSD apart from all other psychiatric diagnoses by including the requirement that one of the factors should be outside of the individual: "a traumatic stressor." Some patients diagnosed with chronic PTSD develop pervasive and persistent incapacitating mental illness which can negatively impact all areas of psychosocial functioning (marital/family, social work/school). Van der Kolk (1996) highlights the most basic premise of the experience, stating that beliefs and cognitions give meaning to the emotion brought on by trauma. These thoughts activate the amygdala and trigger the emotions which, for many, become the central challenge of moving forward from their experience of a traumatic event. One of the potential consequences of trauma is that emotional memories of trauma get incompletely processed and are constantly being reactivated by triggers.

Therapist's Guide to Posttraumatic Stress Disorder Intervention

While the effects of psychological trauma have been acknowledged throughout history by mental health and medical professionals, PTSD was first suggested as a diagnostic category in the development of the third edition of the *Diagnostic and Statistical Manual of Mental Disorders* (DSM-III) in 1980. It was an extremely controversial diagnostic category at the time due to the required criterion for an external traumatic event. Nevertheless, the high rate of psychiatric casualties among Vietnam veterans inundating US Department of Veterans Affairs facilities helped to establish PTSD as a legitimate diagnosis. The diagnostic struggle continues, however, as researchers try to determine whether symptoms emerge only in relation to the trauma or are suggestive of a significant underlying psychiatric disorder(s).

Yehuda et al. (1998) emphasized the evidence of an abnormal acute stress response of a biological nature in those with PTSD. Many feel that the substantial experiential aspect of physiological effects have not been adequately considered diagnostically, which has limited and/or negatively impacted treatment as well as diagnosis. Darrel Regier, MD, MPH, executive director of the American Psychiatric Institute for Research and Education, states "It's very important to have a better paradigm than what we've been using to look at somatic presentations of mental disorders, and the relationship to disorders in other organ systems" (Regier, 2007). This illustrates the limitations of the tradition nomenclature of diagnostic criteria, highlighting the need to explore physical–mental associations, along with lifespan, gender and cultural issues.

Another view by Keane (2006) is that PTSD does not and should not describe all of the possible symptoms of the disorder, and therefore there is no need to expand the nomenclature to include complex PTSD.

Trauma is the consequence of exposure to an overwhelming and inescapable event which overcomes a person's coping ability, thus encapsulating the interaction between the individual and the traumatic event. In other words, no two people exposed to the same event will react in the same manner. The person's ability to cope with the traumatic exposure will be associated with factors, such as (1) their belief system, (2) prior experience(s) of trauma, (3) chronic stressful experiences, (4) level of support, (5) perception of their ability to cope with the event, (6) internal resources (coping mechanisms etc.), (7) genetic predisposition, and (8) other stressors in their life at the time of the event.

PTSD is a multifaceted and complex disorder which challenges the clinician in making an accurate diagnosis. Bearing in mind that there is significant controversy about the criteria written in the diagnostic nomenclature, this review will begin with the diagnostic criteria set by the diagnostic manual and expand from there to encompass the conceptual and practical challenges in evaluating trauma exposure. Currently, the fourth edition of the *Diagnostic and Statistical Manual of Mental Disorders* (DSM-IV-TR) foundation for the PTSD syndrome includes 17 symptoms within three symptom clusters:

1. Re-experiencing the trauma
2. Avoidance and numbing
3. Hyperarousal.

The first step in assessing trauma is to establish and identify exposure to an extreme stressor, Criterion A in the DSM diagnostic criteria. An extreme stressor is identified as having three elements:

- The type of exposure (directly experienced, witnessed, informed indirectly)
- Distinguishing traumatic stress from ordinary stress, i.e. the event presents a threat to life, serious injury, or threat of physical integrity to self or others.
- The event triggers an intense emotional response of fear, horror, or helplessness.

As can be seen, the subjectivity of this criterion is the basis of the controversy, either viewed as personally restrictive (what is traumatic from one individual to another) or that the criterion is too broad, which allows too many stressors to be identified as traumatic. Whatever the view, the gatekeeper function of Criterion A is important for setting a parameter or threshold of what is identified as an extreme stressor warranting the diagnosis of PTSD.

Once it has been determined that a patient has experienced exposure to trauma, the therapist can consider, based upon symptom presentation, which diagnostic criteria are matched. The continuum of diagnoses associated with exposure to a trauma are commensurate with the range of emotional and psychological reactions experienced and are shown diagrammatically in Figure 1.1.

The next step in assessing for PTSD is to review the constellation of symptoms used to determine if the patient has the necessary number of symptoms in each symptom category to differentiate a diagnosis from diagnostic features (fewer symptoms than warranted for a diagnosis) from a diagnosis of PTSD. There are several noted difficulties regarding this mission:

- The large number of symptoms that represent both overt and covert manifestations. A diagnosis requires:
  (a) at least 1 of 5 re-experiencing symptoms;
  (b) at least 3 of 7 avoidance and numbing symptoms; and
  (c) at least 2 of 5 hyperarousal symptoms.

- Some symptoms are vague in definition, leading to a lack of consensus as to what is exactly meant by the terminology. This leads to poor interpretation and significant variance in accuracy of symptom determination.

- Symptom overlap between clusters, which can lead to what is called "double coding" of symptoms, meaning that they are given diagnostic credit for essentially the same symptom in different symptom categories.

- Negative symptoms (such as emotional numbing or loss of interest) may be difficult to assess because the patient is focused on positive symptoms with notable associated distress.

- Are the presented symptoms within the normal range of reaction to such an experience or is the symptom representative of a pathological or clinically significant problem?

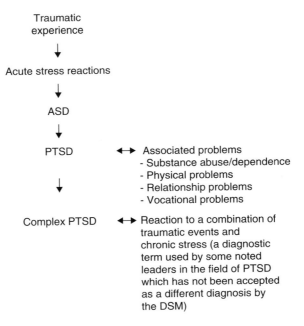

Figure 1.1   The range of emotional and psychological reactions following a traumatic experience.

- Patients presenting for assessment or treatment following a current trauma exposure that present with prior trauma exposure and/or previous posttraumatic stress symptoms must present a clear and distinct change from their previous level of functioning.

- Multiple practitioners are often involved. Often the patient may be referred from their primary care physician for depression or anxiety with an associated misinterpretation of origin or history of symptoms. This may result in an incorrect diagnosis.

With this brief review of potential diagnostic difficulties, one can see why developing diagnostic criteria for PTSD has been so arduous and factious. Just investigating one symptom can demonstrate the numerous questions posed that are often not easy to define by an accurate qualitative or quantitative answer. For example, Weathers et al. (2004) makes an excellent point in questioning the origin of a symptom such as amnesia in assessing for PTSD. If the patient is not able to recall aspects of their experience it may be difficult to determine whether it is the result of intense fear and associated avoidance, having been unconscious during part of the event, or poor memory which has another foundation (medical, function of time, etc.).

SYMPTOM CLUSTERS AND ADDITIONAL DIAGNOSTIC CRITERIA

In addition to Criterion A (defining the trauma exposure) there are five other criteria (B through F) and additional specifiers.

The *Diagnostic Manual*, DSM-IV-TR, describes the development of characteristic symptoms following exposure to an extreme traumatic stressor, through either direct experience, witnessing, or knowledge of an event that involved actual or perceived threat to life or physical integrity of self or others. In such a situation a person's response involves intense fear, helplessness, and/or horror. The symptoms, which cause significant distress or impairment in social or occupational functioning, must be present for at least one month. The diagnostic criteria or symptoms consist of three clusters (B, C, D):

CATEGORY B: PERSISTENT RE-EXPERIENCING OF THE TRAUMATIC EVENT (AT LEAST ONE SYMPTOM)

1. Recurrent and distressing recollection of the events (images, thoughts, impressions)
2. Recurrent distressing dreams of the event
3. Acting or feeling as if the traumatic event were recurring
4. Intense psychological distress at exposure to internal or external cues that symbolize or resemble an aspect of the traumatic event
5. Physiological reactivity on exposure to internal or external cues.

The patient experiences flashbacks, traumatic daydreams, or nightmares in which he or she relives the trauma as if it were recurring in the present. Intrusive symptoms result from an abnormal process of memory formation. Traumatic memories have two distinctive characteristics: (1) they can be triggered by stimuli that remind the individual of the traumatic event, (2) they can have a "frozen" or wordless quality, consisting of images and sensations rather than verbal descriptions.

Nightmares assocated with trauma exposure are generally classified according to being thematically related dreams (re-experiencing symptoms).

Contrary to general belief, flashbacks are not intrusive recollections but rather dissociative episodes in which the individual believes, or responds as if, the traumatic experience was actually occurring. This means that the individual is reliving, not just recalling, the traumatic experience. Additionally, flashbacks may involve hallucinatory perceptual disturbance (American Psychiatric Association, 2000). While dissociation can be a symptom of PTSD it is also a diagnostic category.

Trauma cues may be obvious or subtle and difficult to identify. For example, the survivor of a sexual assault finds the trauma triggered by sexual arousal. In fact, there is increased likelihood of such a trigger if they were aroused during the assault.

Recurrent, intrusive recollections and dreams are the most usual re-experienced symptoms (American Psychiatric Association, 2000). Intrusive recollections may also include other somatosensory experiences in addition to emotions experienced at the time of the trauma associated with taste, smell, touch, and sound.

There is some controversy as to the origin of somatosensory recollections. These bodily sensations could be body memory (van der Kolk, 1994; Rothchild, 2000), or manifestations of an individual's psychophysiological reactions to the trauma cue or other trauma stressors (McNally, 2003). According to Lanius et al. (2006), bodily sensations experienced during trauma might be triggered by a trauma cue at a later time and they are typically accompanied by conscious recollections of the trauma (therefore, not a body memory). Lindauer et al. (2006) reported results similar to previous studies on combat veterans, demonstrating heightened physiological responses as seen in civilians and police with PTSD when presented with trauma-specific stimuli. Regehr et al. (2007) concluded that prior trauma and decreased social supports were associated with continued psychological distress as well as physiological responses.

CATEGORY C: EMOTIONAL NUMBING AND AVOIDANCE

Persistent avoidance of stimuli associated with the trauma and numbing of general responsiveness as indicated by at least three of the following (which were not present prior to the trauma):

1. Efforts to avoid thoughts, feelings, or conversations associated with the trauma
2. Efforts to avoid activities, places, or people that arouse recollections of the trauma
3. Inability to recall an important aspect of the trauma
4. Markedly diminished interest or participation in significant activities
5. Feeling of detachment or estrangement from others
6. Restricted range of affect (i.e. unable to have loving feelings)
7. Sense of a foreshortened future (i.e. does not expect to have a career, marriage, children, or a normal lifespan).

The patient attempts to reduce the possibility of exposure to anything that might trigger memories of the trauma, and to minimize his or her reactions to such memories. This cluster of symptoms includes feeling disconnected from other people, psychic numbing, and avoidance of places, people, or things associated with the trauma. Note that patients with PTSD are at increased risk of substance abuse as a form of self-medication to numb distress and painful memories, or to feel alive and engaged in life/to counter flat affect (McFall et al., 1992; Breslau et al., 1997; Kilpatrick et al., 2003; Brady and Sinha, 2005).

The individual who experiences emotional numbing may not be able to experience feelings of love, joy, humor, or pleasure considered appropriate to significant relationships, activities, or experiences which previously elicited positive emotions. Some would describe this emotional experience as "feeling bad" or their range of emotional experience being restricted. They may feel like a spectator or experience a sense of unreality. Estrangements can result from the experience that others cannot understand what they have lived through. For example, when an individual makes an effort to explain their experience to others who are not able to understand they may experience increased feelings of alienation or isolation (Rothchild, 2007).

Lindauer et al. (2006) reports studies of the psychophysiological aspects of PTSD in which patients provoked by script-driven imagery reacted with heightened physiological responses and commensurate increases in autonomic and muscular activity. This physiological reactivity on exposure to external or internal cues resembles an aspect of the traumatic event, and they often develop into points of avoidance. Wald and Taylor (2005) state that physiological sensations that commonly occur shortly after a traumatic experience such as extreme hyperarousal (palpitations, shortness of breath, dizziness, etc.) may take the form of (symptoms) posttraumatic panic attacks. As a result, these sensations, become cues to avoid. It is worth noting that avoidance is not always a maladaptive response; for example, where avoidance cues are associated with potential danger.

CATEGORY D: HYPERAROUSAL

Persistent symptoms of increased arousal (not experienced prior to the trauma), as indicated by two or more of the following:

1. Difficulty falling or staying asleep
2. Irritability or outbursts of anger
3. Difficulty concentrating
4. Hypervigilance
5. Exaggerated startle response.

Hyperarousal is a condition in which the patient's nervous system is always on alert for the return of danger. This symptom cluster includes hypervigilance, insomnia, difficulty concentrating, general irritability, and an extreme startle response. Some clinicians believe that this abnormally intense startle response may be the most characteristic symptom of PTSD (Levine, 1998; Rothchild, 2000).

Insomnia can take various forms: difficulty falling asleep (initial insomnia) or difficulty staying asleep (middle insomnia) (Krakow et al., 2001).

Hypervigilance can take the form of being alert and vigilant (watchful). The person may place themselves carefully so that they can scan their environment for potential threat, or may display excessive worry/concern regarding the safety for those close to them, or engaging in checking rituals (doors and windows) associated with safety and security.

Difficulty concentrating might interfere with completing basic daily tasks, losing place in conversation, failure to complete tasks/activities. Difficulty with concentration could be associated with a preoccupation with intrusive thoughts or hypervigilance.

People with an exaggerated startle response often report that they feel "on-edge" or "jumpy." Understandably, this feature carries with it risk of exaggerated, over-responding, which can have negative social consequences (displays of over-reactiveness in social situations which in some way present cues/triggers) and safety consequences (such as exaggerated responses associated with driving environments, and for the demands and associated responses for first responders).

Irritability and anger may be easily provoked. It could be demonstrated as irrational, low frustration tolerance.

Matsakis (1998) described hyperarousal of the adrenal gland, which releases epinephrine (adrenaline), as being responsible for the intrusive symptoms of PTSD. The experienced consequences of hyperarousal are numerous.

CATEGORIES E AND F

Category E specifies that disturbance due to symptoms (B, C, and D) is more than one month. Category F specifies that the disturbance causes clinically significant distress or impairment in social, occupational, or other important areas of functioning.

Specify if:

- **Acute:** If duration of symptoms is less than three months
- **Chronic:** If duration of symptoms is three months or more

Specify if:

- **With delayed onset:** If onset of symptoms is at least six months after the stressor. Delayed onset is often triggered by a situation that has some semblance to the original trauma.

SUBTHRESHOLD PTSD

An overreliance on the diagnostic category model of psychiatric disorders has resulted in a lack of study of posttraumatic outcome that does not meet the diagnostic criteria. According to Marshall et al. (2001) "substantial disability and suicidal risk is associated with subthreshold PTSD" and a lack of information is associated with the examination of "the role of comorbidity in explaining disability and impairment in subthreshold PTSD." These researchers concluded that there was impairment, comorbidity, and suicidal ideation associated with subthreshold PTSD, which may be partially related to the presence of comorbid disorders. When major depression was controlled for in patients with subthreshold PTSD there was an evident increased risk for suicidal ideation:

Adjustment Reaction → ASD → Subthreshold PTSD → PTSD → Complex PTSD

Diagnostic clarity lies in the continuum of symptom presentation and severity, ranging from those associated with painful, but relatively common life events (death, loss of relationship, being fired, etc.) versus overwhelming trauma associated with ASD and PTSD. An additional complicating factor is that these ordinary life events sometimes reawaken prior trauma which result in the diagnosis of delayed PTSD or a history of trauma resulting in complex PTSD.

Van der Kolk (1988) points out that "traumatization occurs when both internal and external resources are inadequate to cope with external threat." In the case of PTSD, even though the threat is generally external in the form of a traumatic event, it becomes mentally and emotionally integrated into the person. To understand this, consider the web-like connections associated with PTSD:

- Pre-existing/coexisting disorder(s)
- How the mind impacts the body
- How the body impacts the mind
- How the past influences the present
- How the basic underlying personal constitution influences all aspects of the experience
- The psychological, cognitive and emotional interpretation of reality
- Ongoing social interactions
- Experiential meaning beyond the individual self, self in a social relational context, and of the world (search for meaning)
- Role of risk factors.

In addition to the aforementioned connections are the following aspects of intrapersonal and interpersonal experience which impact the outcome of traumatic exposure. In other words, exposure to traumatic stress has multiple effects, like the ripple of a stone thrown into a body of water. The multiple effects take into account

- Risk factors
- Protective factors (resilience)
- Dimensions of impact that are complex and interactive:
  – Physical
  – Emotional
  – Social
  – Spiritual/existential.

To simplify the picture, the factors can be seen as being:

1. Trauma factors (having magnitude, duration, and a type of traumatic exposure)
2. Individual factors (internal) or
3. Social factors (external).

Individual factors	Age and gender
	Physical health
	Emotional health
	Coping ability
	Spiritual beliefs
	History of losses
	History of trauma experiences, including childhood trauma/adversity
	History of mental illness
Social factors	Actual or perceived social support
	Concurrent stressful life events
	Presence or continuation of stressors
	Social environment where shame, guilt, stigmatization, or self-hatred are felt
	Availability of treatment and professional support.

COMMON REACTIONS TO TRAUMATIC EXPERIENCES

After reviewing the factors associated with the development of PTSD, the focus is directed to the range of reported experienced symptoms. Common reactions to a traumatic event(s) may be either cognitive, emotional, physical, or interpersonal, or have aspects of resilience:

Cognitive reactions	Feeling unsafe
	Confusion
	Disbelief
	Dissociation
	Impaired memory
	Intrusive thoughts
	Flashbacks
	Nightmares
	Memory impairment
	Concentration difficulties
	Shock
	Worry
	Avoidance
Emotional reactions	Anxiety
	Panic attacks
	Anger
	Emotional numbing
	Fear
	Guilt
	Grief
	Helplessness
	Hopelessness
	Sadness
Physical reactions	Fatigue
	Exhaustion
	Sleep disturbance
	Tremor
	Cold sweats
	Insomnia
	Physical pain
	Hyper-energy
	Hyperarousal
	Extreme startle response
	Gastrointestinal problems
	Rapid or irregular heart beat
Interpersonal reactions	Social withdrawal
	Poor impulse control
	Increased relational conflicts
	Sense of alienation and abandonment
	Sense of detachment from others
	Altruism (urge to help others)

A lack of resiliency is indicated by:

- Not bouncing back from experienced stress
- Loss of balanced routine
- Increased focus on physical distress symptoms
- Does not seek personal support or professional consult
- Changes in emotional balance.

The concept of dissociation is woven into many of the aforementioned symptoms, therefore warranting a precise statement describing what it means. The American Psychiatric Association (2000) defines dissociation as a breakdown in the normally integrated functions of consciousness, identity, memory, or perception of one's self or surroundings and is manifested by symptoms such as depersonalization, derealization, or psychogenic amnesia. Dissociative symptoms consist of and are manifest by a subjective sense of numbing, emotional detachment, absence or lack of emotional responsiveness, decreased awareness of surroundings, derealization, depersonalization, or dissociative amnesia.

PTSD AND QUALITY OF LIFE

When quality of life experience for those diagnosed with PTSD is compared with those suffering from major depression or obsessive compulsive disorder, those with PTSD demonstrated impaired vitality, mental health, and social functioning (Malik et al., 1999). This translates to:

- Negative work performance
- Social impairment
- Lower employment
- Physical limitations
- Decreased well-being
- Negative impact on personal relationships
- Negative impact on daily activities.

Interestingly, patients with PTSD are more likely to present in a primary care setting with symptoms of sleep disturbance, chronic pain, or gastrointestinal problems rather than a psychiatric setting for mood disturbance and/or acute emotional distress. In addition, they commonly have a history of trauma or violence but do not connect their past trauma with their current symptom presentation. It is also likely that they experience comorbid psychiatric disorders, including substance abuse.

THE EFFECTS OF TRAUMATIC STRESS ON THE BODY AND THE MIND

During a traumatic event the body, as directed by the brain and autonomic nervous system, evokes a defensive state which is the culmination of physiological changes such as heart rate, respiration, blood pressure, digestion, and internal temperature control. All of these changes are normal reactions to an abnormal event. In general, when the traumatic event has ceased, the nervous system will return the body systems to homeostasis. This return to homeostasis takes a few hours to several weeks. However, when the threat continues (real or perceived) the nervous system remains in the defensive state. The consequence for the chronic defensive stance is a physical and psychological disturbance which is known as PTSD. Symptom presentation demonstrates a change in level of functioning:

Physical	Chronic pain
	Migraines
	Vague somatic complaints
Mental	Substance abuse
	Depressive disorders
	Anxiety disorders
Behavior	Irritable
	Avoidant
	Anger/non-compliance
	High-risk behaviors (e.g. potential risk of harm, HIV)

This could be an effort to feel alive or the emotional experience "nothing matters" anymore.

There are multiple methods for obtaining a rich clinical picture. Traditionally, therapists conduct a thorough clinical interview which is individualized by the information and observations elicited during the interview process in addition to clinical hypothesizing and intuition. Another method recommended is the use of a clinician-administered structured diagnostic interview which provides a dichotomous and continuous range of PTSD symptoms. Numerous assessment instruments have been developed to cover the range and needs of the therapist.

ADDITIONAL DIAGNOSTIC CONSIDERATIONS

DIFFERENTIAL DIAGNOSIS

Differential diagnosis can be challenging because of the shared symptoms, premorbid level of functioning, and comorbidity. The most common diagnoses include depression and other anxiety disorders.

PTSD versus:

Depression

- PTSD may result in depression
- They may co-exist as comorbid diagnoses
- There is no significant symptom overlap between PTSD and depression. However, re-experiencing symptoms are only present in PTSD

  decreased interest

  estrangement/social isolation

  numbing

  impaired concentration

  insomnia

irritability

sense of foreshortened future

- Premorbid depression may play a role in vulnerability to developing PTSD following exposure to a traumatic experience

Generalized Anxiety Disorder (GAD)

- They may co-exist as comorbid diagnoses
- Symptom overlap includes

being on-edge

poor concentration

irritability

sleep disturbance

- Different origins of excessive worry

PTSD worry is focused on re-expressing trauma

GAD worry is generalized

Panic Disorder

- They may exist as comorbid diagnoses
- Autonomic hyperarousal is the distinguishing feature for this diagnosis
- Assess origin of panic attacks

premorbid

if unexpected and spontaneous Panic Disorder is a secondary diagnosis

related to trauma and trauma triggers

Obsessive Compulsive Disorder (OCD)

- They may co-exist as comorbid diagnoses
- Both PTSD and OCD have recurring intrusive thoughts
- OCD may develop with generalization (i.e., compulsive checking to avoid feeling fear/distress)
- OCD may serve as an underlying vulnerability that activates PTSD

MULTIAXIAL DIAGNOSIS

The multiaxial diagnosis allows for a global assessment of functioning, thus clarifying the impact on current social and occupational functioning versus highest level of functioning during the past year. It is also an opportunity to identify differential diagnosis, comorbid disorders, and the assessment of additional clinical problems such as impaired interpersonal relationships, affect dysregulation, survivor guilt, etc.

This is also where, until DSM diagnostic criteria change, symptom presentation complexity, or "complex PTSD" is diagnostically clarified. Currently, the clarification takes place via the diagnostic formulation and thorough documenting of symptoms and history. "Complex PTSD" is one of the highly controversial areas previously mentioned along with "Subthreshold PTSD." To date neither has been recognized as DSM diagnoses. However, their clinically relevant diagnostic criteria have been documented by numerous researchers and clinicians respected in the field of trauma research and treatment (Rothchild, 2000; Herman, 1992; Cook et al., 2005; van der Kolk, 2005, to name a few). It is also acknowledged by Foa et al. (2009), but viewed as an unneccesary change to the DSM nomenclature. According to these studies, complex PTSD is characterized by chronic and debilitating difficulties in numerous areas of emotional and interpersonal functioning, exemplifying the overall complexity of the PTSD diagnosis. Two of the most commonly identified patient histories associated with complex PTSD include child sexual abuse and an extensive experience of domestic violence (interpersonal trauma) (Dutton and Painter, 1981, 1993; Rothchild, 2000; Lawson, 2003; van der Kolk, 2005; Hedtke et al., 2008). This term, complex PTSD, is often used to describe those with a history of early interpersonal trauma exposure that was repetitive and severe.

As a consequence of significant variance in research and clinical view of PTSD, researchers (DSM-IV field trials) were not able to reach consensus on the inclusion of these diagnoses, the divergence of belief associated with the range of diagnoses associated with PTSD continues (Foa et al., 2009). Regardless, the term is frequently seen in much of the research published as describing a subset of patients diagnosed with PTSD which have a history of interpersonal violence/trauma. Interestingly, the outcome of the DSM-IV field trial demonstrated that patients with PTSD who had experienced trauma prior to age 14 were more likely to meet the criteria for complex PTSD. Other diagnostic features include (Herman, 1992; Gold and Cardena, 1993; van der Kolk, 2005):

- Impairment of affective regulation
- Chronic self-destructive behavior (i.e. self-mutilation and drug abuse)
- Amnestic and dissociative episodes
- Alterations in relationship to the self
- Distorted relationships to others
- Somatization
- Loss of sustaining beliefs.

Patients with complex PTSD were found to have an average of four or more DSM-IV comorbid diagnoses and an increased likelihood of meeting diagnostic criteria for one or more personality disorders. The next section will expand the diagnosis of complex PTSD.

COMPLEX PTSD

DEFINITION

As previously mentioned, there is significant conflict in the literature regarding the legitimacy of acknowledging complex PTSD as separate from the recognized diagnosis of PTSD. Although not currently included as a diagnosis and although many of the symptoms not accepted as PTSD criteria, the clinical significance of case complexity with those diagnosed with PTSD reinforces their relevance. Therefore, basic information about what has been designated as complex PTSD has been included in this section so that the reader is exposed to the breadth of information in a context to promote increased familiarity and understanding of major lines of thought and constructs associated with traumatology.

Complex PTSD may be the consequence of chronic interpersonal trauma (early, repetitive and severe trauma) associated with sexual abuse and domestic violence. Sometimes referred to as "type II traumatization," complex PTSD could be described as a reaction to a combination of specific traumatic events and chronic stress. Isolation also appears to be an important factor. Other diagnoses may have a root in complex PTSD such as borderline personality disorder, dissociative disorder, and other classes of severe mental illness.

The clinical presentation of complex PTSD and DESNOS involves (Rothchild, 2000):

- Impairment of affective regulation
- Chronic self-destructive behavior (self-mutilation, substance abuse, etc.)
- Amnestic/dissociative episodes.

Herman (1992) describes complex PTSD as a potential consequence of: "A history of subjection to totalitarian control over a prolonged period (months to years). Examples include hostages, prisoners of war, concentration camp survivors and survivors of some religious cults. Examples also include those subjected to totalitarian systems in sexual and domestic life, including survivors of domestic battering, childhood physical or sexual abuse, and organized sexual exploitation." While the information on complex PTSD expands, the conceptual foundation of trauma experience clinically significant clinical problems, it also carries with it increased subjectivity which complicates achieving clarity in establishing an accurate clinical designation and diagnosis. Nonetheless, anyone who has worked with victims of trauma and PTSD have been exposed to symptom presentations outside the current diagnostic parameters.

FEATURES OF COMPLEX PTSD

Alterations in affect regulation	Persistent dysphoria
	Chronic suicidal preoccupation
	Self-injury
	Explosive or extremely inhibited anger
	Compulsive or extremely inhibited sexuality
Alterations in consciousness	Amnesia or hyperamnesia for traumatic events
	Transient dissociative episodes
	Depersonalization/derealization
	Reliving experiences with intrusive PTSD symptoms or ruminative preoccupation
Alterations in self-perception	Sense of helplessness or paralysis of initiative
	Shame, guilt and self-blame
	Sense of defilement or stigma
	Sense of difference from others (specialness; utter aloneness; inhuman; no-one could understand)
Alterations in perception of perpetrator	Preoccupation with relationship with perpetrator
	Unrealistic attribution of total power to perpetrator
	Idealization or paradoxical gratitude
	Sense of special or supernatural relationship
	Acceptance of belief system or rationalization of perpetrator
Alterations in relations with others	Isolation and withdrawal
	Disruption in intimate relationships
	Repeated search for rescuer
	Persistent distrust
	Repeated failures of self-protection
Alterations in systems of healing	Loss of sustaining faith
	Sense of hopelessness and despair
Somatization	

Although this is not a text on the diagnosis and treatment of complex PTSD, inclusion of its diagnostic criteria are conceptually important.

SOMATIC MEMORY

Everyone is unique in their own response to trauma, including the way the body remembers the trauma or copes with the trauma, as the case of somatosizing. However, there are also some patterns of response that are not uncommon. For example, survivors of long-term trauma often experience the following physical complaints (Ogden, 2005; Rothchild, 2000; van der Kolk, 1994):

- Cardiopulmonary symptoms: Most often seen as anxiety/panic symptoms, such as racing heart, chest tightness, etc.

- Gastrointestinal problems: irritable bowel syndrome or diarrhea/constipation

- Autoimmune disorder: Fibromyalgia or chronic fatigue

- Chronic pain: No discrete source

- Sexual problems: Pelvic pain or recurring infections or discomfort.

Over time, images, sensations and behavioral impulses associated with a traumatic event may become disconnected to the context and understanding of that experience. Somatic memory (body memory) = implicit memory. Contextual cues (understanding) and concepts of the traumatic event = explicit memory (Rothchild, 2000). It is the nervous system that communicates this "memory" to other parts of the body.

State-dependent recall occurs when trauma memories stored as sensation are triggered by similar sensations. The body often remembers what the conscious mind cannot. This means that there is the experience of implicit memory (body) or trauma without the explicit memory (thought) necessarily making sense of it. In other words, various parts of the body may experience symptoms (such as pain) that are trauma-associated, but there is no conscious knowledge of how or even if those parts of the body were involved in the trauma. According to Rothchild (2000) "emotions feel different on the inside of the body" and this experience is unique to each individual. Trauma can generalize or amplify physical symptoms. A thorough physical examination by a physician who understands the impact of trauma is an important referral to rule out serious or contributing medical problems. Regardless, part of healing is allowing those symptoms to speak.

DIMENSIONS OF PAIN

Pain is both physical and psychological. According to Curro (1997) there are four dimensions of pain:

1. Motivation (the desire to avoid or escape pain)

2. Cognitive (personal experience with the memory of pain)

3. Affective (feelings a person associates with pain such as fear, anxiety or stress)

4. Discriminative (the nervous system's response to what causes pain, its onset, duration, intensity, quality and location) most often seen as symptoms of anxiety/panic attacks.

Rothchild (2000) and Curro (1997) state that if pain does not improve over time it tends to get associated with negative emotions such as fear and anxiety, which may result in decreased awareness of the body and body sensations. There may even be dissociation of chronic pain. When chronic pain is not based upon a medical condition, cognitive behavioral therapy (CBT) offers a way to work through the pain. CBT can challenge thoughts and behaviors that are destructive or maladaptive, using techniques of distraction, rational thinking, relaxation, and visual imagery. Grant (1997) views chronic pain as possibly being somatization of unresolved trauma. Therefore, when trauma is treated there can be a marked decrease in physical symptoms.

DEFINING TRAUMATIC MEMORY

Over a hundred years ago Pierre Janet (1889) published his first text, *L'Automatisme Psychologique*, on dealing with the challenge of how the mind processes traumatic experiences. Later, he would be the first to show clearly and systematically that dissociation was the most direct psychological response, or defense against overwhelming traumatic experiences. Janet believed that overwhelming emotions interfered with accurate appraisal and appropriate reaction. He asserted that this failure to effectively and fully experience the trauma leads to the dissociation of trauma memory and the return of the fragments of the trauma memory as flashbacks of memory states, somatic sensations, visual images, and behavioral reenactments. His dissociation theory went on to demonstrate the role of this phenomena in the wide range of posttraumatic responses. It is amazing that over a century later, Janet's theories continue to provide an integrative framework of the cognitive, behavioral, psychodynamic, and biological effects of human traumatization.

Janet's theory of dissociation is based on nine concepts (van der Kolk et al., 2005b; van der Hart and Horst, 2005):

* Psychological automatism
* Consciousness
* Subconsciousness
* Narrowed field of consciousness
* Dissociation
* Amnesia
* Suggestibility
* Fixed idea
* Emotion.

In traumatic memory:

* Emotions are strong and overwhelming, interfering with information processing at both verbal and symbolic levels
* Memories are not categorized (may lack context)
* Trauma is split off from consciousness
* Memories are stored as visual images, affective states, body sensations, or memory fragments (which can return in a state-dependent manner).

The differences between traumatic memory and narrative memory are summarized here.

Traumatic memory	Narrative memory
Inflexible	Flexible
Without context	Contextual
Fragmented/dissociated	Integrated
Autistic	Relational
ANS hyperarousal	Minimal arousal
Sensorimotor/non-verbal	Symbolic/verbal
Developmental context in which trauma occurred	Telling a story within a frame of reference
Somatic presentation	Identified emotional response
Regressed reenactments outside of conscious awareness	Requires core sense of self and relationship skills

STAGES OF DISSOCIATION

According to van der Hart et al. (1998) there are three stages of dissociation:

1. Primary dissociation: Classical amnesia. Dissociation of the traumatic memory state from the consciously available autobiographical narrative memory system.

2. Secondary dissociation: Here there is a lack of association within the traumatic memory system, i.e. compartmentalization or fragmentation of normal integration of behavior, affect, sensation, and knowledge memory (BASK).

3. Tertiary dissociation: This is the compartmentalization or fragmentation of the self-representational system. This is dissociative identity disorder.

Murray et al. (2002) asserts that evidence supports the prediction that higher levels of fragmentation are related to the occurrence of dissociative experiences. Gold and Cardena (1993) suggest that chronic dissociation is more likely to occur after repeated rather than a single experience of trauma. Victims of traumatic events are more likely to experience or deliberately use dissociation as a means of coping.

The important work of recovery is not necessarily correlated with the historical accuracy of the remembered information and details. Obviously, it is generally not possible to determine whether a recollection is true or false, however, it is likely that there is a mix of accurate and inaccurate memories presented by patients with dissociative identity disorder. Taking the perspective of this dilemma from Herman (1992), it is more important to acknowledge what the patient believes has occurred, and to deal with the consequences or impact that alleged experience has had on the patient so that they can find their own truth in their own voice.

PREVALENCE/FREQUENCY

The fourth edition of the *Diagnostic and Statistical Manual of Mental Disorders* (DSM-IV) (American Psychiatric Association, 2000) revised the definition of PTSD so that the event need not be outside the range of usual experience. The updated defining criteria state that the event can be direct to the individual, witnessed by the individual or something experienced by others that was learned or informed (such as the traumatic event of a loved one). The DSM-IV reports that community-based studies demonstrate a lifetime prevalence of PTSD ranging from 1% to 14%, with at-risk individuals (combat veterans/victims and victims of natural disasters revealing prevalence rates of 3–58%). This is in comparison with the predominance of the general population being exposed to a traumatic event during the course of their lifetime. According to Breslau et al. (1998), as many as 90% of the general population may encounter a range of traumatic experiences including, but not limited to, life-threatening accident, fire, flood (natural disasters), service in combat, rape, robbery, physical attack or witnessing the injury or death of another individual. Though the exposure rate to a traumatic event is very high, not everyone develops PTSD. Lifetime prevalence of PTSD among combat veterans is 22–31% (Prigerson et al., 2002). The lifetime prevalence of PTSD for women is 10% and for men it is 5% (Kessler et al., 1995; Solomon and Davidson, 1997; Breslau et al., 1998). Foa et al. (2009) asserts that while women demonstrate a lifetime prevalence of PTSD at twice the rate of males, and that women are four times more likely to develop PTSD when exposed to the same trauma, gender responses to treatment have yet to be thoroughly investigated.

Gender differences are likely associated with numerous mitigating factors. One of these is the difference in the types of trauma that men and women are likely to experience. Men more often experience physical assaults and women more often experience sexual assault. However, sexual assault, compared among both genders, is more likely to cause PTSD (Kilpatrick and Acierno, 2003). According to the statistics in this study 60.7% of men and 51.2% of women experienced at least one traumatic event. The study also states that the statistics presented represent only a small fraction of adults who have experienced at least one traumatic event, and that over 10% of the men and 6% of the women had experienced four or more types of trauma in their lives.

In addition, PTSD may have its onset and recurrence at any point in the life cycle. The most common trauma experiences identified were:

- Witnessing someone being badly hurt or killed
- Involvement in a fire or natural disaster
- Military combat.

So what does this translate to diagnostically for all of those exposed to a traumatic event (Kessler et al., 1995; American Psychiatric Association, 2000; Yehuda and Wong, 2001; Blanchard and Hickling, 2004; Bolton et al., 2006; National Institute of Mental Health, 2006, 2007).

1. Some people do not develop ASD or PTSD following exposure to a traumatic event.

2. Some people exposed to traumatic events did not develop symptomatic criteria to warrant a diagnosis of PTSD but did develop ASD which was resolved.

3. Symptoms, often in response to life stressors and triggers, re-emerge.

4. Of those that develop PTSD, >50% develop a chronic PTSD symptomology.

5. In at least half of all trauma survivors, complete recovery occurs within three months.

6. Hours or days following the experience of a traumatic experience most people have some symptoms of PTSD.

7. Some people (4–6%) do not develop PTSD until months or even years after their experience.

As with gender, according to Hein (2003) the breakdown for most frequently mentioned negatively impacting traumatic event was as follows:

Women:	Rape	Men:	Rape
	Sexual molestation		Combat exposure
	Physical assault		Childhood neglect
	Being threatened with a weapon		Physical abuse
	Childhood physical abuse		

- Women experience more sexual victimization than men.
- Women report more self-blame, suicide attempts, sexual dysfunction, and revictimization than men.
- Women with PTSD report more sexual victimization than men with PTSD or substance use disorders alone.
- Women engage in substance abuse for a shorter period of time than men before becoming substance dependent.
- Women with PTSD/SUD may be "triggered" in mixed gender group settings.

An overview of research on trauma/PTSD with substance use disorders draws attention to "converging developmental and neurobiological literature on the consequences of trauma on self-regulation." In contrast to the statistics of PTSD in the American population, the prevalence of PTSD in Australia was found by the Australian Survey of Mental Disorders and Well-being to be 1.33%, which is considerably lower (Creamer et al., 2001; Hall et al., 2002; Rosenman, 2002). Prevalence was higher among the never married and previously married, and lower among those over 55 years of age. For both men and women, rape and sexual molestation were the traumatic experiences most likely to be associated with PTSD. A high level of axis I comorbidity (anxiety, depression, and substance abuse) was also found in those with PTSD.

PROBABILITY OF DEVELOPING PTSD *RISK*

There is a range in the rate or probability of developing PTSD. Yehuda and Wong (2001) and Kessler et al. (1995) offer estimates of probability indicating that 40–60% of adults in the community have been exposed to a traumatic experience, and approximately 8% of those will develop PTSD (American Psychiatric Association, 2000). This confirms that there are variables beyond the traumatic experience that increase vulnerability to risk. Women are clearly identified as being twice as likely as men to develop PTSD. Therefore, just being of female gender becomes a risk factor. Likewise, social support, life stressors and traumatic exposure are associated with diagnostic variance. In addition, the experience of peritraumatic dissociation, which is seen as a defense mechanism or result of biological mechanistic disruption/dysfunction, is a significant contributor to the development of PTSD. Research suggests that this risk factor (dissociation) is the largest predictor of PTSD symptoms, and that those who dissociate have significantly greater likelihood of developing PTSD than those who do not dissociate. The risk factors that have been identified are the result of two meta-analyses (Brewin et al., 2000; Ozer et al., 2003).

Bryant (2003) states that while the studies focused on determining the predictive power of ASD (recent trauma exposure) leading to chronic PTSD did not yield a positive confirmation, a review of the biological and cognitive mechanisms associated with acute posttrauma may provide a more accurate means of predicting chronic PTSD.

Simmons and Granvold (2005) used a cognitive model to explain PTSD causal factors, with a focus on the greater risk of women developing PTSD. Cognitive function lays the foundation for a theoretical explanation of PTSD development. During the course of a traumatic event, cognitive functions combine the content, process, and structure of cognition to transform the traumatic experience into the individual's subjective meaning:

- *Content of cognition*—What the individual thinks, believes and values and has recorded in memory

- *Process of cognition*—Attention, interpretation, encoding cognitive elaboration and retrieval
- *Structure of cognition*—Cognitive networks, associative linkages and stored memory into which the event is internalized.

An important facet of the process of creating meaning from experience is referred to as "schemas." Schemas are internal structures that are relatively enduring and stored as generic or a prototypical aspect of ideas, experiences, or stimuli utilized to organize new information in a meaningful way. Schemas determine how phenomena are perceived or conceptualized (Simmons and Granvold, 2005). Young et al. (2003) postulated the existence of early maladaptive schemas, unconditioned beliefs about the self that are formed in life and play a role in emotional and psychological disturbance. This "self-knowledge" becomes progressively elaborated during the course of development and defines the self in relation to others and the world in which they live. Schemas are triggered by various stimulus conditions, and trauma is a highly activating function.

Information processing may result in meaning distortions. According to Simmons and Granvold (2005), the consequences are that the individual is highly vulnerable to cognitive distortions, the activation thresholds of dysfunctional schemata become lowered significantly, the voluntary control process becomes impaired, and the individual becomes hypervigilant and hypersensitive to "threatening" stimuli. The erosion in cognitive functioning leaves the individual vulnerable to extreme emotional responses and the activation of uncharacteristic or dysfunctional behavior.

Cognitive processing therefore plays an important role in differentiating those who develop PTSD following a traumatic experience from those who do not. Adaptive cognitive processes can act as a buffer against extreme negative consequences, contrary to maladaptive cognitive processing which increases an individual's vulnerability to develop symptoms of PTSD (Tolin and Foa, 2002).

Adaptive cognitive schemas	Strong coping abilities
	Resilience
	Trust in others/environment
	Thus resulting in a positive influence in the meaning of the experience, responses/activation, and recovery
Maladaptive cognitive schemas	Intense fear
	Incompetence
	Unworthiness
	Vulnerability/weakness
	Thus resulting in a negative influence on the meaning of the experience, past trauma, emotional, activation/body sensations and protracted recovery. Overall, acting as a liability contributing to the development of PTSD

Therefore, an individual's memory and belief about the trauma influences recovery from the trauma (or impact on emotions and behavior). Foa and Rothenbaum (1998) propose that there are two differences between trauma memories and fear structures:

1. The perception that the world is dangerous results in physiological (for example heart rate) and behavioral (fight/flight responses) reactions.

2. Trauma memory often includes the individual's response to trauma (for example freezing/screaming).

"Trauma victims who develop PTSD seem to interpret the responses during the trauma in a negative manner; this subsequently interferes with recovery from the trauma" (Foa and Rothenbaum, 1998).

Other associations with an individual's belief system include:

Frazier and Schauben (1994)
- Higher rates of psychopathology are found in trauma survivors who exhibit self-blame.

Bandura (1997)
- The perception of limited self-efficacy during trauma exposure may contribute to a lack of self-efficacy and corresponding reduction in the activation of post-trauma coping strategies (and thus symptom alleviation).

Basoglu et al. (1997)
- Feelings that they gained something positive from the traumatic experience are often associated with positive recovery (for example, when military personnel who have been captured and tortured believe that they in some way benefited from the experience, possibly with personal growth, or when a survivor of a motor vehicle accident views themselves as responsible for the accident thus demonstrating lower rates of PTS than individuals who blame someone else for the accident).

Delahanty et al. (1997)
- Feelings of empowerment over one's situation.

Dunmore et al. (1999)
- Suggest that the cognitive factors of mental defect, mental confusion, negative appraisal of emotion, and negative appraisal of symptoms impact the nature of the traumatic memory.

Brewin et al. (2000) and **Ozer et al. (2003)** in their meta-analyses demonstrate the PTSD risk factors of social support and life stressors following a traumatic experience and point out the following. Both of these factors play a role in the individual's ability to:

- process through the experience (expected non-pathological reactions to traumatic experiences
- resume daily function/structure.

Negative social interaction responses were found to have a direct negative influence on adjustment. However, positive interaction/responses from others have little impact on adjustment. Regarding the issue of life stress, this factor may consume the individual's coping and adaptive resources, resulting in increased vulnerability to PTSD.

In an effort to conceptualize the vulnerability of developing PTSD among individuals who have been exposed to similar trauma stimuli, Tolin and Foa (2002) outlined an emotional processing theory which is based upon four core factors:

- "PTSD is a form of pathological fear"
- "All fear is a memory based program for escaping danger"

- "The fear program can be construed as a cognitive structure consisting of inter-connected cognitive representations" which include information about
  - The fear stimulus
  - Overt, physiological and behavioral responses
  - Interpretive information about the meaning
- There is a difference between the fear structures of those who develop PTSD versus those who do not develop PTSD.

SPECIFIC RISK FACTORS

Foa (2000) asserts that the more direct and severe the traumatic experience, the more likely that the survivor will develop PTSD. She also cites other factors that can lead to PTSD:

- Previous psychiatric disorders
- An avoidant coping style
- Experiencing numbness or dissociation during or immediately after the trauma
- Fearing for their life during the trauma.

Though not everyone exposed to a traumatic event develops ASD or PTSD, the following factors may increase the potential risk:

- First-hand experience of a traumatic experience
- Severity of the trauma
- Duration of the trauma
- Proximity to the event
- Interpretation of danger (directly proportional)
- Repetition of the trauma
- Neurological soft signs (history of brain injury)
- Harm by another person (sexual assault)
- History of childhood trauma or abuse
- Lack of control associated with a situation/circumstances.

The American Psychiatric Association (DSM-III, 2004) and Foa et al. (2009) highlight various specific clinical features which influence variance in relationship to risk:

Age

The risk of trauma peaks in adolescence, however, the relationship between age and development of PTSD remains inconsistent. Development stage plays a role in the meaning of the traumatic material exposure. Threat to life may result in different concerns or meanings in association with age and developmental stage.

Increasing age is associated with the additional risk of developing comorbid medical conditions and associated medications which influence pharmacotherapy choices. PTSD may have its onset or recurrence at any point in the life cycle.

Kilpatrick et al. (2003)
- Age is a consistently identified risk factor, thus strengthening the association between age and mental health.

Heim et al. (1997)
- Genetic disposition coupled with early stress in critical phases of development may result in a phenotype that is a neurobiological vulnerability to stress and may lower an individual's threshold for developing depression and anxiety upon further stress exposure.

While it appears that early life traumatic exposure may be one of the most complicating factors, the risk of exposure increases over time (as a function of the more time the more potential for exposure), and there may be developmental stage amplification of risk (i.e. adolescence).

Gender

The overall risk of trauma is greater for males. Males and females differ in the types of trauma exposure experienced, and females demonstrate high prevalence rates of PTSD. In other words, while females demonstrate two times the lifetime prevalence rates of PTSD, they are four times more likely to develop PTSD when exposed to the same trauma as males.

Brewin et al. (1999)
- Female gender is twice as likely than males to develop PTSD.

Davis and Breslau (2000)
- Females with PTSD experienced some symptoms more often than males: (a) more intense psychological reactivity to stimuli that symbolized the trauma, (b) restricted affect, and (c) exaggerated startle response. This is also reflected by the fact that females experienced a larger mean number of PTSD symptoms.

Brady (2001)
- There are changes in the stress response during different phases of the menstrual cycle. The HPA axis stress response during the follicular phase of the cycle is less robust than the stress response during the luteal phase of the menstrual cycle.

Tolin and Foa (2006)
- Sex differences in risk of exposure can only partially explain the differential gender risk of PTSD.

Sukel (2008)

- The female menstrual cycle phase may play a role in activation of brain structures involved in the response to trauma exposure. Neuroscience research suggests that some gender trauma response differences reflect sex differences in the brain. For instance, when men and women are shown an emotionally graphic film, activity in the right hemisphere in the amygdala predicted how well the men would remember the film; for women it was activity in the left hemisphere of the amygdala.

Hoeft et al. (2008)

- Gender differences in the brain activation frequency require more research to increase understanding in underlying genetic differences.

With women twice as likely as men to develop PTSD, gender demonstrates an important factor to examine regarding increased knowledge and understanding of what contributes this PTSD determinant. A review of trauma experience and posttrauma functioning as per gender reveals that:

- Men are more likely than women to be exposed to traumatic experiences
  - Kessler et al. (1995): 60.7% men; 51.2% women
  - Stein et al. (1997): 81% men; 74% women

- Men are more likely to report exposure to multiple traumatic events than women
  - Stein et al. (1997): 55% men; 46% women
  - Breslau et al. (1998): 5.5% events averaged for males; 4.3% events averaged for females

- In a population of men and women where there was no demonstrated difference in amount of traumatic experience, women indicated increased frequency of PTSD symptoms than men, and were diagnosed more often with PTSD than their male counterparts (Breslau et al., 1992).

Wellman et al. (2005) examined gender differences in 733 college students and compared the following:

- Disclosure
- Social reactions
- Post abuse coping
- PTSD survivors of child sexual abuse.

Female versus male respondents in this study reported:

- Prevalence and severity of child sexual abuse
- More distress and self-blame immediately following the assault
- Greater reliance on coping strategies of withdrawal and trying to forget
- More likely to have disclosed their abuse to others
- More likely to have received positive reactions
- Greater PTSD symptom severity.

For women delaying disclosure was associated with greater PTSD symptom severity (for men symptom severity did not vary as a function of disclosure timing).

Considering cultural male/female differences associated with differences of reinforcement given to boys and girls:

- Women were more likely to:
  - display increased openness about feelings
  - use verbal processing of experience
  - seek help/support from others
  - express emotion (for example crying).

- Men were:
  - less open
  - displayed less verbal processing of experience
  - were less likely to seek resources
  - showed less emotional expression.

Tolin and Foa (2002) assert that while research suggests that women and men report different types of traumatic experiences this factor does not explain the gender variance for the development of PTSD. For example, in cases of exposure to natural disasters, women continue to demonstrate twice the rate of PTSD. This similar statistic for such a different experience of trauma exposure (the experience of sexual assault (child and adult) which is a form of intimately intrusive violence versus natural disaster) does not support the gender development theory of PTSD (Shore et al., 1986; North et al., 1999). This reinforces the importance of continued neurological research seeking the information that underlies the general gender responses patterns to traumatic exposure.

When attention is focused on self-schemas and world schemas (Tolin and Foa, 2002) female trauma survivors had an increased likelihood of viewing the world as dangerous, blaming themselves for the trauma, and holding more negative views of themselves than male survivors (issues of weakness and distrust). Breslau et al. (1998) reinforces the impact of negative self-schemas as being consistent with increased diagnosis of PTSD in women and a protracted length of pathology.

Krause et al. (2002) focus on the different socialization experiences of males and females as the factor that significantly impacts how trauma is interpreted, processed, and recovered from a gender perspective. According to a report in the *Psychological Bulletin* the type and prevalence of trauma experienced by men versus women did not appear to account for the doubled rate of women developing PTSD (childhood sexual abuse, sexual assaults/raped) versus men (serious accidents, physically assaulted, seeing people killed or injured). Once the type of traumatic event was controlled for (i.e. both males and females experience the trauma of sexual abuse or assault), PTSD appears to develop equally across genders.

Gender differences from a biological perspective may reveal more information regarding anatomical and physiological differences between the male and female brain. Krause's research demonstrated that male responses were more in line with action (fight/flight) and female responses were more demonstrative to the needs of the moment (tend and befriend). Whatever the revelation in ongoing research on gender differences there is likely to be a demonstrated influence by the neuroendocrine system.

Gender Differences in PTSD for Military Service Personnel

When the circumstances of service and gender difference in combat condition-related PTSD was reviewed, by Turner et al. (2007) the results from the National Vietnam Veteran Readjustment Study (NVVRS), they found that increased PTSD related to circumstances of high probability severity of war zone stress exposure in males who demonstrate a level of PTSD prevalence significantly lower than their female veteran counterparts. Murdoch et al.

(2003) reviewed the use of care for combat-related illness by veterans for both genders. It appeared that there was a gender bias that disproportionately favored males. However, the appropriateness of this bias was not clear as it was not explained by more severe PTSD symptoms or greater functional impairment.

According to Keane and Phelps (2008) "Fundamentally, trauma is about exposure to life-and-death situations. Trauma may also be secondary to exposure to events that challenge one's personal integrity or may inculcate shame or humiliation. For combatants, their experience in a war zone may transcend all of these experiences and exposure to these experiences often happens multiple times over the period of service. Combat is not exposure to a uniform, single, traumatic event. Rather, it often involves multiple types of life-and-death experience associated with strong and wide ranging emotional reactions in the context of a malevolent living environment that is estranged from the usual forms of family and social support. As a result, it's vital to conduct a comprehensive assessment of exposures to both in the war zone and prior to service in the war zone.

Ethnic and cross-cultural factors

Clinicians need to be sensitive to the importance of social and cultural dynamics, demonstrating understanding, knowledge and respect to culture, cultural meaning of symptoms/illness, social/cultural views, the impact of cultural norms on influencing the perception of trauma, cultural expectations and meaning of life, and the cultural context of the treatment frame. Treatments that may be effective for Western cultures may be contraindicated for some non-Western cultures (i.e. some South-East Asian populations and others from non-Western cultures).

Ethnicity, cultural values, and genetic issues may also be an important factor relevant to pharmacotherapy choices and developing an individualized treatment plan.

Tull (2008)

- African Americans, Asian Americans, and Native Americans tended to report having experienced fewer traumatic events as compared to European Americans and Latinos. However, African Americans, Asian Americans, and Native Americans were more likely to develop PTSD after experiencing a traumatic event as compared to European Americans and Latinos.

Dohrenhend et al. (2008)

- Elevated prevalence rates of chronic PTSD have been reported for Black and Hispanic veterans. There was no comprehensive explanation for these group differences.

Eikhoff (2008)

- Elevated rates of PTSD in minorities may be associated with expressiveness vesus a true elevation. Therefore, the increase rate may be an artifact, thus identifying the need for research and decreased stereotyping. Minorities are often misdiagnosed.

Ford (2008)

- The role of racism as a risk factor for exposure to psychological trauma requires careful study.

Medical and other Psychiatric Comorbidity

Physical injury is a common complexity in the ASD/PTSD clinical picture. Also, physical disorders such as cardiac or neurological disorders may mimic symptoms of ASD or PTSD, resulting in diagnostic confusion and an underdiagnosis of ASD and PTSD. This reinforces the fact that comprehensive treatment is in reference to the treatment team.

Both intensive care units and rehabilitation facilities could include the complex medical treatment plan which includes intervention associated with ASD or PTSD.

Patients with ASD or PTSD are more likely to have comorbid psychiatric disorder; somatization, depression, anxiety, substance use disorders, increased suicide risk, dissociative disorder, and personality disorders. Substance use may complicate pharmacological management and increase risk of overdose/oversedation.

Comorbidity of psychiatric and medical disorders may experience increased severity of symptoms and chronicity with an overall potential consequence in mental and physical debilitation necessitating a higher level of care.

History of Previous Trauma(s)

Exposure to prior trauma may alter vulnerability to ensuing trauma, influencing the development of PTSD and complicating treatment. While the current trauma may precipitate symptoms, they could actually be associated with prior traumatic exposure (sleep disturbance, hyperarousal, irritability, etc.). Treatment may be required to target integration of the precipitating trauma and the remote trauma.

Breslau et al. (1999)
- Those with a personal or family history of psychopathology or prior exposure to trauma are at increased risk of developing ASD or PTSD.

Regehr et al. (2007)
- Research on police officers concluded that prior trauma exposure did not increase risk of biological distress. However, prior trauma and decreased social supports were associated with continuing psychological distress, thereby identifying the cumulative negative effects of traumatic exposure as a concern on psychological health.

Emery et al. (2006)
- Veterans with PTSD demonstrated greater childhood stress associated with parental alcohol use and unemployment than did their non-PTSD counterparts. Perception of their experience also played a role.

Aggressive Behavior

Episodic, impulsive, aggressive behavior can be a part of the ASD/PTSD symptom presentation. It is referred to as "anticipatory bias" or increased readiness for aggression, as well as decreased sleep associated with ASD or PTSD which decreases ability to tolerate irritations, and potentially resulting in acts of aggression which are disproportionate to the infraction experienced. Currently, pharmacotherapy (selective serotonin release inhibitor (SSRI) antidepressants) may decrease this heightened aggressiveness. Aggression may also be associated with states of intoxication and withdrawal, emphasizing the importance of concurrent treatment for comorbidity.

This behavior ranges from self-mutilation to eating disorder behaviors and abuse of substances and may be associated with both acute and chronic responses to trauma exposure. There appears to be a significant relationship between these compulsive behaviors and childhood sexual abuse. In addition, those with PTSD have a greater or equal risk for developing a suicide plan (as compared with those with mood or other anxiety disorders). Note that anxiety disorders (including PTSD) have a higher risk of suicide in general. There is also greater risk during the early treatment phase before pharmacotherapy benefits are experienced.

Additional reported contributing factors increasing risk for developing PTSD are as follows:

Marmar et al. (2004, 2006)
- A greater level of terror, horror, and dissociation at the time of the event.

Saltzman et al. (2006)
- Cognitive factors such as lower IQ and coping ability.

Goenjian (2008)
- Research following the 1988 earthquake in Armenia revealed that 41% of the variations in PTSD symptoms were due to genetic factors.

Grohol (2008)
- Traumatic stress can alter both brain structure and function.

In addition to these, there may be vulnerability associated with personal situation or circumstance. For example, the person may be disenfranchised due to low socioeconomic status, low intelligence or low coping ability. In the National Comorbidity Survey (1990–1992) Kessler et al. (1995) cite the estimated lifetime prevalence of PTSD for those who live in economically depressed urban areas or on a Native American Reservation as 23%.

Norman et al. (2008) state that identifying the risk factors that lead to PTSD is the key to understanding and preventing it. They cited peritraumatic pain (pain experienced shortly after the injury) as an associated risk factor in developing PTSD. An increase in pain after injury was associated with a fivefold increase of PTSD at four months and an almost sevenfold increase at eight months.

PSYCHIATRIC RISKS ASSOCIATED WITH PTSD

Paykel (1978) asserts that in the month following a traumatic event the people involved experience:

- 6 times greater risk of suicide
- 2 times greater risk of developing a depressive disorder
- Slight increased risk of developing schizophrenia.

Kessler et al. (1995) state that survival analysis demonstrates more than one-third of those with PTSD fail to recover after many years.

Katon (2001) found that following the development of PTSD patients were:

- 26 times more likely to develop an affective illness
- 37 times more likely to develop GAD
- 6.5 times more likely to develop alcohol abuse.

He also noted that:

- 89.5% of affective disorders in men and 65.5% of affective disorders in women occurred after the development of PTSD
- 62.5% anxiety disorders in men and 50% of anxiety disorders in women occurred after the development of PTSD
- 62% of respondents in the Australian Survey (2002) with PTSD were found to have experienced suicidal ideation.

The relationship between phobic disorders, panic disorders, and depression was noted before PTSD was an acknowledged diagnosis (Horowitz, 1993). Additional risks associated with having a diagnosis of PTSD may include:

- Substance abuse
- Alcohol, nicotine, and other drugs
- Eating disorders or other compulsions
- Divorce.

With comorbidity the symptom overlap may increase the difficulty of achieving diagnostic clarity.

PERSONAL VARIABLES

Personal variables that may increase the risk of developing ASD or PTSD include:

- Gender (female)
- Age (youth)
- Temperament (shy/introverted)
- Family history of anxiety
- Early separation from parents
- Being part of a dysfunctional family
- Chronic illness/physically disabled
- Pre-existing history of psychiatric illness/disorders, such as: personality disorder (borderline, narcissistic, antisocial), anxiety, or depression.

Adams and Boscarino (2006) conducted a baseline survey one year after the attack on the World Trade Center. Analysis yielded the following increased likelihood of developing PTSD:

- Younger
- Female

- Experiencing more World Trade Center disaster events
- Experiencing more negative life events
- Having low social support
- Having low self-esteem.

Those cases where PTSD symptomology remitted following exposure to a community disaster and traumatic stress demonstrated fewer overall negative life experiences and an increase in self-esteem. This highlights the significance of the role of cumulative life stress and self-efficacy in whether or not an individual develops PTSD.

Zalin (2004) reports that alcohol abuse is associated with increased risk for a PTSD diagnosis in 20–40% of trauma victims.

Some people experience a negative reaction by their primary support system, including family, friends and peers. The impact of the quality of the primary support system on the development of PTSD has been a consistently identified factor.

OCCUPATIONAL FACTORS

Some career tracks expose workers to traumatic events. There is also the risk of these workers developing secondary PTSD known as compassion fatigue or a variation of burnout. Particular occupations associated with increased risk due to direct and vicarious traumatization results in clinically salient posttraumatic stress disorder symptoms in approximately 5–10% of first responders. Such occupational tracks include (Marmar et al., 2006):

- Military—The National Comorbidity Survey (1990–1992) (Kessler et al., 1995) estimates the lifetime prevalence of PTSD developed by Vietnam veterans at 30.9% for men and 26.9% for women. The lifetime prevalence of PTSD among Korean War veterans was estimated to be 20%.
- Police
- Firefighters
- Search and rescue
- Disaster investigators
- Medicine
- Psychotherapists.

Further individualized issues are also associated with occupational exposure:

- The worker's degree of empathy/sensitivity
- The amount and intensity of exposure to suffering victims
- Unresolved issues from the worker's personal history.

SOCIOCULTURAL FACTORS

In general, social structures that show higher rates of PTSD are those that are:

- Authoritarian
- Glorify violence
- Sexualize violence.

Low socioeconomic status and level of education (less education = higher risk) are associated with higher rates of PTSD.

The National Comorbidity Survey (1990–1992) (Kessler et al., 1995) states that the estimated prevalence of PTSD among victims of violent crimes is 58%.

Hedtke et al. (2008)
- Results show that lifetime interpersonal violence exposure was associated with increased risk of PTSD (and other mental health problems like depression and substance use disorders).
- The role of PTSD, depression and substance use disorder increased incrementally with the number of different types of violence exposure.
- New incidents of violence between the baseline and follow-up interviews were associated with an escalated risk of PTSD and substance use disorders.

MEDICAL FACTORS

Also at risk of developing PTSD are patients who have undergone highly intrusive and distressing medical procedures, such as a traumatic birth, hospitalization, intensive care unit/critical care unit, intubation, or a surgery where the patient awakened during a procedure due to insufficient anesthesia.

COMORBIDITY

Comorbidity of substance abuse disorders, depression, and other conditions can hinder or delay recovery in PTSD. Therefore, a central treatment goal is to prevent secondary disorders, accurately diagnose, and treat other concurrent conditions (American Psychiatric Association, 2004).

There is sufficient research to validate the acknowledgment of a significant overlap between PTSD and other psychiatric diagnoses. The overlap and complexity of comorbidity often clouds an accurate diagnostic formulation. In a report on the primary care treatment of PTSD for the American Academy of Family Physicians, Lange et al. (2000) state that up to 80% of patients with PTSD have a comorbid psychiatric diagnosis. This is reinforced by Spinazzola et al. (2005) in their review of the literature, "PTSD rarely occurs alone and has routine comorbidity rates of 80%." Foa et al. (2009) assert that in the United States epidemiological findings suggest that 80% of those with lifetime PTSD have depression, another anxiety disorder, or a substance use disorder. If there is a psychiatric disorder prior to experiencing a traumatic event there is increased risk for developing PTSD. Likewise, having a diagnosis of PTSD increases the risk of developing other psychiatric problems. The most common comorbid psychiatric disorders are listed below:

Axis I		
Depression disorders	Major depression Dysthymia Bipolar	Most likely to co-occur with PTSD. It is also clear that depressive disorders can be a common and independent diagnostic phenomena of exposure to trauma and having a previous depressive disorder is a risk factor for the development of PTSD once exposure to a trauma occurs
Anxiety disorders	Phobias	
	Generalized anxiety disorders	
	Panic disorder	
Eating disorders		
Somatization		
Substance abuse		Complex issue due to the development of a substance abuse disorder in response to an attempt to self-medicate the painful symptoms of PTSD, and withdrawal states exaggerate these symptoms
Dissociative disorder		
Atypical psychosis		
Intermittent explosive disorder		
Axis II		
Borderline		
Obsessive compulsive		
Avoidant		
Dependent		
Paranoid		
Self-defeating		
Antisocial		
Mixed types		

From a multiaxial diagnostic picture, general medical conditions (axis III) are a common treatment component for many traumatized patients and can be associated with major health consequences, such as:

- Physical abuse
- Sexual abuse
- Motor vehicle accidents.

With this multiaxial perspective (inclusive of medical conditions), two groups in particular that need to be assessed are: (1) first responders (law enforcement officers, firefighters, paramedics all have the potential for injuries in their work in the form of a medical crisis and chronic health issues) and (2) veterans (demonstrated potential for health crises and chronic health issues associated with injuries).

A comorbid psychiatric diagnosis should be treated simultaneously with PTSD as part of a comprehensive treatment plan. Understandably, there are some issues that may need to be prioritized in association with safety, basic needs and health. However, this does not disregard other clinical issues which are woven together in their cumulative impact. The reasoning behind this is that coexisting diagnoses and PTSD cannot be separated. It has long been known that patients with chronic depression and anxiety demonstrate an increased use of health care for medical illness. There is also evidence that patients with PTSD appear to be at greater risk of developing medical illness. Since individuals tend to seek medical intervention instead of mental health intervention following the experience of a traumatic event there is reduced likelihood of the constellation of presented symptoms being identified as PTSD. This information reinforces the importance of primary care physicians refining their interviewing, screening and diagnostic skills to include assessment of PTSD, which may be masked by misrepresentation of a physical or medical ailment.

Patients with multiple symptoms of PTSD are also more likely to experience poor social support, marital/relationship difficulties, chronic illnesses, work-related problems, and negative impact in terms of income and potential disability.

When reviewing PTSD and dual diagnosis the statistics are clinically significant, and demonstrate the need for a comprehensive diagnostic formulation. According to the National Institute for Mental Health (NIMH), of patients diagnosed with PTSD who meet criteria for a dual diagnosis:

- 80% have a dual diagnosis of anxiety (and the breakdown for anxiety disorders is 15% generalized anxiety disorder—female; 29% simple phobia—female; 31% simple phobia—male; 31% obsessive ompulsive disorder—female; 23% specific phobia—female; 7.3% panic disorder—female)
- 30–60% have a dissociative disorder
- 26–85% have a mood disorder or a somatoform disorder
- 40–60% have a personality disorder
- 60–80% abuse alcohol or narcotics to numb/avoid painful and distressing memories (men: 51.9% alcohol abuse/dependence; 34.5% drug abuse/dependence; women: 27.9% alcohol abuse/dependence; 26.9% drug abuse/dependence).

COMPLICATIONS OF TREATMENT ASSOCIATED WITH AXIS II DIAGNOSES

The statistics of dual diagnosis clarifies the significant association of PTSD with psychiatric comorbidity. Davidson et al. (1991) found that people with PTSD had:

- A higher risk of chronic medical illness such as bronchial asthma, hypertension, and peptic ulcers
- Twenty times greater likelihood of somatization disorder, schizophrenia/schizophreniform disorder, and panic disorder
- Ten times greater likelihood of social phobia, obsessive compulsive disorder, generalized anxiety disorder, and major depressive disorder
- One in five people with PTSD were likely to attempt suicide (15 times greater than those without PTSD).

According to Zalin (2004), in the United States each year approximately 2.5 million people are severely injured and require hospital admission. Of those admissions, 10–40% go on to develop PTSD symptoms. In addition, 20–40% of trauma victims have a history of alcohol abuse which plays a role in the increased risk of recurrent injury. Kessler et al. (2005a) report that the lifetime prevalence of PTSD, based upon the National Comorbidity Study Replication, is estimated at 6.8%. Regarding the variation in response rates for self-reports and the prevalence of PTSD, differences in rates will continue to be noted by researchers until sampling strategies and assessment approaches are consistent. Until that standardization is achieved, providers of services across disciplines must strive to improve identification of PTSD, appropriate referrals, and interventions.

Friedman (2005a), in a report to the Institute of Medicine, states that PTSD is not the only "posttrauma outcome," and that the following disorders should also be included in any diagnosis:

- New onset depression
- Other anxiety disorders
- Alcoholism
- Behavioral alteration.

Also, in a large nationally representative community-based sample of veterans from the Vietnam theater and other wars, the following was reported:

- Any combat veteran: lifetime prevalence of PTSD 39%
- Lifetime prevalence Vietnam veterans: men 31%, women 26%
- Current prevalence Vietnam veterans: men 15%, women 8%
- Current prevalence Gulf War veterans: 10%
- Current prevalence Afghanistan veterans: 6–11.5%
- Current prevalence Iraq veterans: army 13–18%, marine 12–20%.

Posttraumatic stress disorder (PTSD) is an anxiety disorder. Two significant points associated with PTSD are (1) that not all individuals exposed to a traumatic event develop PTSD, and (2) that women are twice as likely as men to develop PTSD. An additional, and significant, component of PTSD is the issue of comorbidity. Solomon and Bleich (1998) offer four alternative hypotheses to explain the significant degree of comorbidity found in PTSD:

1. Preexisting disorders could constitute a vulnerability to PTSD
2. Other disorders could be subsequent complications of PTSD
3. The disorders could co-occur because of shared risk factors
4. Comorbidity could be the result of a measurement artifact.

The National Comorbidity Survey (1990–1992) (Kessler et al., 1995) found a lifetime prevalence rate of PTSD of 7.8% and 88.3% of subjects to have one or more comorbid axis I diagnoses.

- Men with PTSD were 14 times more likely to have a second lifetime diagnosis
- Women with PTSD were 8 times more likely to have a second lifetime diagnosis
- The most common diagnoses with PTSD were alcohol abuse and major depression (each occurring in about half of patients)
- Although more men were exposed to trauma, women were more likely to develop PTSD.

A large epidemiological study in Australia, the National Mental Health and Well-Being Survey, examined whether PTSD precedes other axis I comorbid disorders. Regarding the survey subjects, it was found that:

- they were 26 times more likely to develop affective disorders
- 89.5% of affective disorders in men and 65.5% of affective disorders in women occurred after the development of PTSD
- 50% of anxiety disorders in women occurred after the development of PTSD
- they were 37 times more likely to develop generalized anxiety disorders
- they were 28.6 times more likely to develop panic disorders
- they were 6.5 times more likely to develop alcohol abuse.

Suicide ideation and attempts also appear to be a major risk following the development of PTSD (62% of the subjects in the Australian study experienced suicidal ideation).

In their review of the literature regarding the comorbidity of PTSD and other disorders Spinazzola et al. (2005) produced the following figures:

- Major depression 37–48%
- Alcohol abuse/dependence 28–52%
- Substance abuse/dependence 21–35%
- Simple phobia 29–31%
- Social phobia 28%
- Agoraphobia 16–22%
- Suicide attempts reported by 20%
- Obsessive/compulsive disorder 15%
- Mania 18%
- Severe psychopathology including bipolar disorder 56%.

Asmundson and Hadjistavropolous (2006) reinforce that PTSD frequently co-occurs with other conditions and symptoms which can complicate assessment and treatment. Of these, chronic musculoskeletal pain and related avoidance behaviors are among the most common and, unfortunately, most often overlooked. According to Oquendo et al. (2005) PTSD is frequently found to be comorbid with major depression. The co-occurrence of these two disorders enhance the risk of suicidal behavior. When cluster B personality disorder is added to this clinical picture it appears to be a salient factor resulting in further increasing risk for suicidal behavior. In comparison, when there is a history of major depression and no diagnosis of PTSD, the cluster B comorbidity suicidal risk is decreased.

SUBSTANCE ABUSE/DEPENDENCE

A SPECIAL CASE OF COMORBIDITY

Impairment of the patient with PTSD with a comorbid diagnosis of substance abuse disorder is complex. While a substance use disorder may develop as a result of attempting to self-medicate distressing PTSD symptomology, the withdrawal state both exacerbates and exaggerates the PTSD symptoms. There is often concern that the treatment of those with PTSD with a comorbid substance abuse disorder who are early in their recovery can easily be propelled or precipitated into relapse. This issue cannot be generalized, but should be evaluated in a case-by-case manner to appropriately individualize treatment based upon safety, stabilization, internal resources, and external resources. An essential aspect of an accurate diagnostic formulation requires an assessment of a comorbid substance use disorder.

In general, there is a significant association between substance-related and other psychiatric disorders. Kessler et al. (1995) state that 35% of men with PTSD demonstrate substance abuse/dependency compared with 15% of men without PTSD. The same review of women showed that 28% of women with PTSD demonstrate substance abuse/dependency as compared with 14% without PTSD. These statistics are elevated in the military population.

There is no drug preference for those who meet criteria for a diagnosis of PTSD. Instead, there appears to be marked variability in substances of choice—alcohol, marijuana, narcotics, stimulants, hallucinogens, etc. (Robbins et al., 1975). Khantzian (1985) and Lehman et al. (1989), in accordance with this hypothesis, view PTSD as the primary disorder and that substances are taken to diminish the discomfort of the anxiety-related symptoms. Research is not definitive on this topic because it does not provide the clarity which would be optimally useful with regard to direct extrapolation to a specific substance class or other specific associations. Perhaps the problem with the hypothesis is that the perspective of why a relationship exists should be modified. For those who specialize in working in the field of substance use disorders the importance of listening to the patient's reason(s) for use and how they believe they are benefited by substance use is fundamental. If the clinician lacks this basic information they are not going to have any success in motivating the patient toward harm reduction and abstinence.

Motivational interviewing and associated research on the topic of substance choice and perceived benefit has been used by clinicians for some time and may demonstrate the potential of the modifying the prevailing view by including the following:

Follette et al. (1998)

- Tension reduction. Substance use among trauma survivors may represent an attempt to avoid negative memories and affective responses.

Kosten and Krystal (1988)

- The euphoria produced by substances such as cocaine, opiates, marijuana (and to a lesser degree alcohol) may combat flat affect and numbness by restoring feeling.

McFall et al. (1992)

- Pronounced avoidance/numbing symptoms of PTSD result in affective blunting, which may be altered by substances that induce sensations.

Another point of view is associated with cases where there was substance use prior to the development of PTSD. This point of view asserts that this prior substance use is actually a predictor of substance abuse/dependence following PTSD (Hetzer, 1984). Research reinforcing this perspective includes the following:

Volpicelli (1987)

- For success in treating PTSD and comorbid substance abuse/dependence, both diagnoses must be treated individually.

Minkoff (1989)

- If PTSD is the primary disorder, when it is successfully treated, the substance abuse/dependency should ameliorate. Therefore, the primary–secondary relationship is unclear which indicated the importance of challenging both issues in the treatment arena.

Zalin (2004)

- Of the patients who are hospitalized each year having sustained injuries during a traumatic event 10–40% will go on to develop PTSD and alcohol abuse.

NIMH (April 2007, Clinical Trials.Gov, Identifier: NCT00270959)

- Each year 2.5 million people are hospitalized having sustained injuries during a traumatic event. In June 2006 a clinical trial was initiated to evaluate the effectiveness of a patient-centered collaborative care that combined behavioral therapy and pharmacotherapy as compared to traditional treatment following physical injury with the belief that it will decrease PTSD and substance abuse. Their program was structured whereby treatment will continue up to 12 months with subsequent phone reviews at 1-, 3-, 6-, 9-, and 12-month intervals. The outcome of this study will offer interesting treatment effectiveness information. For the clinician in the field, while research information associated with evidence based treatment is continually sought, it is often not feasibly translated to the continuum of care most desired due to a lack of resources afforded researchers via grants and other means versus the same resources being made available to all providers of services.

According to Chilcoat and Breslau (1998) causal pathways exist in the interfacing of PTSD and substance use:

- PTSD increases the risk of developing drug/alcohol dependence (4.5 times)
- Drug/alcohol dependence does not increase risk of exposure to trauma
- Drug/alcohol dependence increases the risk of PTSD after exposure to trauma.

Kendler et al. (2000), Bulik et al. (2001), and Nelson et al. (2006) studied childhood sexual abuse, substance use disorders and psychiatric disorders in women and found that:

- Abuse is positively associated with a number of disorders
- The strongest relationship is with alcohol/drug use
- More severe abuse increases risk.

Brady and Sinha (2005) discuss the need for greater understanding of the neurobiological interface between substance use disorders and other psychiatric disorders which highlights the four most common comorbid diagnoses with substance use disorders:

- Depression/mood disorders
- PTSD

- Attention deficit hyperactivity disorder (ADHD)
- Schizophrenia.

The comorbidity or interfacing of pathology of PTSD and substance use disorders considers the following:

- Risk factors
- Self-medication
- Cyclic interaction
- Common neurobiology.

Kendler et al. (2000) published the first co-twin study demonstrating a causal link between childhood sexual abuse and substance use disorders. Additional long-term consequences for female survivors of childhood sexual abuse are implications in the form of lower wages and work difficulties. Other research information on the topic of PTSD/substance abuse epidemiological data includes the following:

Cottler et al. (1992)
- Cocaine/opiate users are over three times as likely to report a traumatic experience.
- Physical attack (not combat) was the most frequent event reported by the population. Substance abuse preceded posttraumatic stress symptoms, suggesting that substance use is a predisposing factor to exposure to traumatic events.

Brady et al. (1994)
- Found that women with PTSD were more likely than women without PTSD to have experienced sexual and physical abuse during childhood. Both genders diagnosed with PTSD experienced higher rates of comorbid substance abuse.

Brady et al. (2007)
- The co-occurrence of substance use disorders and other psychiatric disorders is prevalent and heterogeneous. This interfacing of comorbidity between substance use disorders and psychiatric diagnoses (PTSD/anxiety disorders, depression/ mood disorders, ADHD, schizophrenia) will continue to be better understood by advances in molecular biology, neurotransmitter systems, and the neural circuitry involved in mental illness and substance use disorders.

Breslau et al. (1997)
- PTSD increases alcohol disorder risk.

Kessler et al. (1995)
- The odds ratio of developing alcohol disorders for those with PTSD is 2 out of 3 men and 2 out of 5 women.

Kilpatrick et al. (2003)

- Results suggest that those exposed to interpersonal violence early in their life (the population surveyed were adolescents aged 12–17) such as physical assault or sexual assault, or who witnessed violence, experienced an increased risk of PTSD, substance use disorders, and major depression.

Koenen et al. (2003)

- A co-twin control design was used to explore the association of PTSD and other mental disorders after adjusting for shared familial vulnerability.
- Combat exposure was significantly associated with increased risk for alcohol and cannabis dependence.
- PTSD mediated the association between combat exposure and major depression and tobacco dependence.

Simon (2003)

- "Combat exposure is directly and indirectly, through PTSD, associated with increased risk for other mental disorders."
- Comorbidity appears to be associated with the development and maintenance of PTSD symptoms. Although the nature of the association is unclear, hypotheses include:
  - The presence of comorbid conditions increases susceptibility and reactivity to traumatic stress.
  - Comorbid conditions are a complication of PTSD.
  - Comorbid conditions contribute to maintaining PTSD symptoms. Other predisposing factors of vulnerability include locus of control, substance use, and recent life stressor.
  - Patients with less severe injuries and less psychosocial supports were more likely to meet criteria for PTSD.

FUNCTIONAL IMPAIRMENT OF PTSD

According to Koch et al. (2005), PTSD demonstrates a high rate of spontaneous remission within the first year. However, "at least 10% of trauma exposed people suffer chronic distress." These authors further report that little is known about the course of PTSD beyond the one-year time frame.

There are numerous perspectives of functional impairment. Criterion F requires demonstration of clinically significant subjective distress, also known as functional impairment. Determining functional impairment means developing an understanding of impact on global functioning (multiaxial severity score) as a function of the combined impact of all presented symptoms affecting social and occupational functioning and/or coping.

According to Levine (1998), "A person's ability to cope depends on their ability to experience and follow their felt sense." A person will be traumatized if:

- Their body and mind perceives a situation as life threatening
- They lack the coping ability to respond effectively
- They are not able to discharge the energy associated with the freeze response.

Factors that affect the ability to cope or "copability" (Levine, 1998) include not only the event itself (the intensity of the threat) but also several factors relating to the subject:

- The context of their life at the time of the trauma
- Their physical characteristic (genetic resiliency)
- Their coping ability
- What the individual has learned from prior experiences of success or failures
- Self-perception of coping ability
- External resources of support
- Family, friends, connectedness with community and nature
- Internal resources
- How the event is interpreted and recorded by the body and mind.

PROFILE OF IMPAIRED FUNCTIONING

It is not uncommon for individuals who have experienced a psychologically traumatizing event to suffer from impaired functioning (even if they lack the diagnostic criteria of PTSD). Norman et al. (2007) reviewed the patterns of trauma-related symptoms in two independent community surveys ($N = 1002$ with 88% demonstrating functional impairment and $N = 630$ with 74% demonstrating functional impairment) which resulted in the following symptom profile:

- Intense recollections and/or emotional symptoms upon exposure to reminders (plus)
- One or more of:
  - numbing/detachment
  - avoidance
  - sleep problems
  - concentration problems
  - hypervigilance.

The reviewers stated that the identified symptom profile may be instrumental in helping clinicians to recognize traumatized individuals who may benefit from treatment. However, this recognition is not necessarily indicative of the constellation of symptoms required for the diagnosis of PTSD.

While not defined as core PTSD symptoms, self-destructive and impulsive behaviors (compulsive behaviors) are recognized as associated features of PTSD. These symptoms complicate PTSD treatment and require assessment of PTSD to consider other diagnostic issues for clarity in treatment planning. Therefore, while performing a clinical interview it is considered a standard to assess for a history of self-destructive thoughts and behaviors and substance abuse as well as many other clinical and potential medical issues necessitating an appropriate referral. In addition, there is significant variation among those with PTSD regarding:

- Symptom severity
- Associated life/relationship complications
- Comorbidity
- Complexity
- Coping ability
- Relative strengths and weaknesses
- Functional impairment
- Internal/external resources.

The Quality of Life Enjoyment and Satisfaction Questionnaire (Q-LES-Q), a patient-rating scale used by Brady et al. (2000), is another means of gaining an additional layer of clinical information to be considered in treatment planning and intervention. Such a questionnaire enables clinicians to measure a range of functional impairments and is especially beneficial when time and therapy resources are limited. The items measured include:

- Mood
- Social relationships
- Leisure time activities
- Ability to function in daily life
- Living/housing
- Ability to get around physically
- Ability to do work or hobbies
- An overall sense of well-being.

It is imperative that clinicians are able to understand empathically and conceptually how the experience of trauma has negatively impacted the daily life experience of those who have been traumatized. Empathy is used here in its most basic definition, "to try to understand what it is like in the shoes of another"—to understand their experience. If this humanity-based feature is missing in the clinician they will not be capable of truly meeting the patient where they are at. This feature separates academicians, theorists, and technicians from those who are honored by their work in truly making a walk of change in improving the lives of those they work with in the frame of the therapeutic alliance. This is the honored relationship in which healing has an opportunity to take place.

Therefore, as the clinician strives to create a useful model of functional impairment in association to the internal experience of the patient and how it extrapolates to external experience and coping, consider the following definition or outline:

- Lack of stability or inability to:
  – Tolerate distress
  – Self-soothe
  – Manage psychological defenses
  – Restrain from self-destructive behaviors
  – Identify and regulate emotion
  – Maintain present-moment awareness
  – Plan and follow through on meaningful daily activities

- Form attachments
- Manage between sessions
- Manage intense issues in a therapeutic relationship.

- Signs of decompensation (retraumatization) include:
  - Dissociating while in session
  - Freezing response (shock)
  - Becoming overwhelmed
  - Flashbacks
  - Anxiety
  - Panic attacks
  - Withdrawal
  - Dissociation
  - Increased suicidality
  - Regressive dependency
  - Regressive childlike behaviors
  - Unrelenting crises.

A DEVELOPMENTAL MODEL OF FUNCTIONAL IMPAIRMENT

A developmental model of functional impairments is viewed in terms of a reversal of gains along developmental lines (Parson, 1984; Brown and Fromm, 1986).

• Self-pathology	Self-esteem and self agency failure
	Self-inhibition and self-definitional problems
	Self-fragmentation
• Relational disturbance	Trauma bonding
	Disturbed power relationships
	Pathological introjects acquired during trauma
• Affect disturbance	Alexythymia
	Affect regulatory problems—feeling too much or too little
	Extreme numbing (affect experience problems)

Friedman (2007) states that common demonstrations of functional impairment for veterans of combat exposure include:

- Unemployment
- Being fired
- Unresolved symptoms
- Divorce or separation
- Spousal abuse.

FUNCTIONAL IMPAIRMENT AS A CONSEQUENCE OF CHRONIC DOMESTIC TRAUMA

There has been much research and many publications on the impact of trauma associated with child sexual abuse and children living in a chronically traumatizing environment with domestic violence. In addition, many adults experience the consequences of the socially significant and chronically traumatizing life experience of domestic violence.

Relational distubance has been of interest to many researchers, particularly domestic violence. Dutton and colleagues (Dutton and Painter, 1981, 1993; Dutton, 2008) explored the topic of what was referred to as Domestic Stockholm Syndrome and a traumatic bonding model with the following characteristics:

- Strong emotional ties develop in the context of intermittent marital abuse.

- The majority of battered women (87%) have not been abused in previous relationships.

- There are unmet dependency needs of both partners.

- Two common features are power imbalance and intermittent reinforcement. "When the physical punishment is administered at intermittent intervals, and when it is interspersed with permissive and friendly contact, the phenomenon of 'traumatic bonding' seems most powerful" (Dutton and Painter, 1981, p. 149).

- It results in a strong emotional attachment or trauma bond. Strong emotional ties between two people where one person intermittently traumatizes the other. For example, harasses, beats, threatens, abuses, or intimidates the other).

- There are cognitive changes such as introjection of self-blame and lowered self-esteem.

- The attachment bond can be described by an "elastic band metaphor." They pull or stretch away from the abuser and return to the known quantity, altering their memory for the past abuse and the perceived likelihood of future abuse in the relationship. It is difficult to leave—they may be isolated, have few if any resources, fear they are not capable of successfully living independently, etc.

Additional features include the following:

- In approximately 71% of all violent couple fights, women initiate the first violent act (this is a controversial statistic).

- Male to female acts of violence are approximately six times more likely to cause injuries to the woman, more health problems, stress, depression, and psychosomatic symptoms.

- A critical difference between men and women in domestic violence is that men are motivated to use violence as a means to terrorize and victimize their partners (i.e. violence is used as a means of controlling or dominating their partner), whereas women tend to use violence as an expression of frustration or self-defense.

Lawson et al. (2003)

- Approximately 1300 women and 800 men are killed each year by partners

- Once violence is initiated it does not cease without some type of intervention

- Previous violence by a partner has a 46–72% probability of predicting future violence.

Hedtke et al. (2008)

- Lifetime violence exposure is associated with increased risk of PTSD (and other mental health problems like depression and substance use disorders)

- The role of PTSD, depression, and substance use disorders increases incrementally with the number of different types of violence experience

- New incidents of violence between the baseline and follow-up interviews were associated with an escalated risk of PTSD and substance use disorders.

Montero (2000) states that the imbalance of power is not a consequence but an antecedent of the abuse. The trauma bond protects the victim's psychological integrity. Five stages in the development of the cognitive bond have been described by Montero (2000):

1. Trigger—initial physical abuse breaks the previous beliefs and security in the relationship. There is disorientation and an acute stress reaction

2. Reorientation—involving cognitive dissonance between abuse evidence and continuing to go along with the relationship (between intermittent abuse episodes), cognitive restructuring to decrease dissonance, and thoughts of self-blame

3. Coping—managing the abuse potential

4. Adaptation—an assumption of the abuser's beliefs and projection of guilt outside the couple's relationship

5. Full emergence of Domestic Stockholm Syndrome.

CODEPENDENCY AND SAFETY

An additional consideration around domestic violence is codependency and safety. This section is adapted from information presented by the National Conference on Codependency. Codependency is a relationship dynamic manifested as caring too much for another person who has dysfunctional behavior at the expense of one's own self. Codependent individuals are willing to put aside what they need and want as a means to gain approval, validation and self-worth.

In order to procure safety and security an individual may engage in codependent relationships. There are two levels of conceptualization with this phenomenon. The first is codependency defined as a pattern of painful dependence on compulsive behaviors and on approval of others in an attempt to find safety, self-worth and identity. The learned coping strategies characteristic of codependent behavior include:

- An overly sensitive nature, being concerned for the needs of another person

- Overemphasis on being responsible for others and not looking at the irresponsibility of one's own behavior

- High levels of guilt and beliefs that they are at fault for anything that goes wrong

- Enmeshment in a relationship with a chemically dependent, personality disordered, another codependent individual or power-addicted person

- Fear of abandonment by their partner, resulting in ignoring important issues, giving in and submissive behavior

- Pervasive lack of self-esteem resulting from inner beliefs of worthlessness

- Acceptance of the sick, martyr, or victim role

- Need for seeking gratification and validation from others but not from one's own self
- Shutting down of emotions and feelings resulting in emotional numbness
- Need to control others through passive aggressive behavior and manipulation.

FUNCTIONAL IMPAIRMENT AS A "LACK OF BALANCE"

In an effort to understand functional impairment from the initial condition where trauma creates a lack of balance, the interruption of self-stability and building resources of recovery, Levine (1998) asserts the importance of the therapist assessing the patient's range of resources. The greater the internal and external resources, the more positive expectation that the patient will be able to process and resolve the negative experience.

The fluctuation of instability versus stability or moving toward improved emotional health (symbolically viewed like a figure "8") is used as the source to build upon, as the therapist guides the patient in a slow, incremental progression through the trauma symptoms and states of instability as they are experienced, thus improving coping, and thereby, functioning.

DIAGNOSTIC CONFUSION ASSOCIATED WITH FUNCTIONAL IMPAIRMENT

THE CASE OF COMORBID PTSD AND BPD?

The high degree of symptom overlap can contribute to diagnostic confusion, resulting in underdiagnosis of PTSD where trauma histories are not specifically obtained (Brady et al., 2000). The most common comorbid diagnoses are depressive disorders, substance abuse, and additional anxiety disorders. Investigating the belief that borderline personality disorder may be a complex variant of PTSD (due to affective instability, anger, dissociative symptoms, and impulsivity) or that PTSD is the result of premorbid borderline personality disorder (because of increased vulnerability), Zlotnick et al. (2002) concluded that the additional diagnosis in either case does little to exacerbate the pathology or dysfunction when examining the needs of patients with either diagnosis. Therefore, while the diagnosis of borderline personality disorder increases vulnerability to the deleterious effects of exposure to trauma it does not necessarily exacerbate the impact of trauma. In another study (Heffenan and Cloitre, 2000), dual diagnosis patients with PTSD and borderline personality disorder (women with a history of childhood sexual abuse) demonstrated no difference in severity or frequency of PTSD symptoms and no comorbid borderline personality disorder. Zlotnick et al. (2002) noted among patients that have comorbid PTSD and borderline personality disorder:

- They have a pattern of PTSD symptoms similar to that in patients with PTSD and no borderline personality disorder.
- The level of impairment found may be unaffected by either diagnosis because both disorders are chronic conditions (PTSD is often chronic and personality disorders are pervasive and enduring) that have severe effects on function or impairment.

- They have a larger number of PTSD symptoms and avoidant symptoms (possibly because these symptoms are prominent in patients with borderline personality disorder as well as incorporating aspects of affect dysregulation and dissociation).

DIAGNOSTIC AMBIGUITY

Zimmerman and Mattia (1999) state that PTSD is under-diagnosed in both medical and psychiatric clinical practice. Instead of accurately diagnosing PTSD, many clinicians diagnose and treat anxiety or depression but many do not identify the constellation of symptoms commensurate with the diagnostic criteria for PTSD. This is likely due to the overlapping of symptoms among these diagnoses. The essential mechanism through which exposure to extreme stress and the consequences of physical health should be considered are in both medical and clinical professional environments (Schnurr and Green, 2004). The most common clinical environment in which PTSD is likely to be presented following a traumatic event is a medical office (natural disaster, witnessing an accident, or experiencing a sexual assault). When presenting in a medical office they are likely seeking intervention for:

- Musculoskeletal complaints
- Gastrointestinal complaints
- Pelvic complaints
- Neurological complaints.

A smaller percentage of patients will present with symptoms of depression, anxiety, or stress.

To increase early recognition, and therefore intervention, clinicians need to inquire about trauma and become more familiar with the diagnostic criteria of PTSD. The clinician's skills in this area may benefit from reading the histories of PTSD cases and the intermittent review of diagnostic criteria.

PROGNOSIS

RECOVERY

According to the American Psychiatric Association (2004), some people recover in six months, others do not exhibit symptoms until much later, and some exhibit a chronic course of PTSD. Thus demonstrating a significant range in the experience of recovery. The longer the symptoms continue, treated or untreated, the poorer the prognosis. PTSD can become a chronic psychiatric disorder that can persist for decades, and for some a lifetime. Patients with this longitudinal course of PTSD often demonstrate episodes of relapse and remission. Unfortunately, treatment for chronic PTSD is less successful.

With the poorest prognosis for recovery some patients do not respond to any treatment. Patients with delayed PTSD often present the most difficult and complicated cases. In general, has been found to alleviate core PTSD symptoms such as hyperarousal, affective symptoms, intrusive thoughts and rage.

Supporters of the implementation of critical incidence stress debriefing (CISD) believe that trauma survivors who receive CISD as soon as possible following a traumatic event have the best prognosis for a full recovery (Mitchell and Everly, 1993, 1995, 1996; Mitchell, 2005). Nevertheless, there are also numerous detractors who believe that CISD increases the risk of developing PTSD (Rose et al., 2003; Jacobs et al., 2004; Benedek et al., 2007). For those who develop PTSD, a combination of individual therapy, supportive group meetings, and, when necessary, pharmacotherapy to deal with core symptoms is often the best treatment plan. Treatment may require several years, and it is likely that the patient will experience episodes of relapse.

TREATMENT RESISTANCE

Treatment resistance refers to the patients who, although they might demonstrate some progress, do not demonstrate a degree of progress or benefit from first-line treatments. Treatment-resistant patients are generally identified as those for whom the course of PTSD has been chronic and/or complicated by comorbidity and the experience of pervasive dysfunctions (Foa et al., 2004, 2009).

Patients who demonstrate a less positive prognosis include:

1. Those who lack positive and adequate social supports

2. Complicated cases with comorbid conditions

3. Enmeshed patients.

In complicated cases with comorbid conditions the clinical picture may be complicated by comorbidity with borderline personality disorder and personality characteristics such as dependency/low autonomy, external locus of control, blaming, self-preoccupation and self-defeating behavioral patterns. Additional complicating clinical and medical issues include: organic brain damage, severe medical illness, substance abuse, and eating disorders. Patients in this category generally present with a long treatment history with negligible evidence of treatment benefit. Additional characteristics associated with poor clinical outcome include: age (older), severe family/marital problems, severe medical problems, complex PTSD, symptoms refractory to treatment, severe memory problems, and affect dysregulation. Out of necessity, treatment with these patients must move much slower and the potential treatment benefit is uncertain. Full fusion and integration may not be possible with this group of patients.

Enmeshed patients are the most difficult to treat. They tend to remain in abusive relationships and live a "dissociative" fractured lifestyle. Additionally, they may actively participate in self-destructive and/or antisocial behaviors. As a result, the therapeutic outcome for these patients is poor. The most beneficial interventions with this group would be to focus on symptom stabilization and crisis management.

DETECTION OF MALINGERED PTSD

PTSD is a diagnosis which can be easily malingered for the benefit of secondary gain. It is therefore identified as having the potential to be an expensive social problem, aside from the social expense associated with functional impairment and general dysfunction. Even standardized inventories may not pick up malingering (Sullivan and King, 2008). Hall and Hall (2006) state that PTSD is frequently claimed for financial compensation in personal injury and disability cases, and that the prevalence of malingering can range upwards of 50% of such respondents. Therefore, it is important for those who treat this disorder to understand all aspects of the disorder as well as the context and reason for seeking mental health intervention. Identified risk factors offer some insight into the dilemma of differentiating clinical diagnostic criteria from malingering. Since PTSD is regarded as relatively easy to fake, the following should be considered in assessing the potential detection of malingering (Hall and Hall, 2007):

1. Be cautious regarding symptom over-reporting as a feature of PTSD versus a true case of PTSD.

2. Use clinical interviews, psychometric testing, and the patient's physiological responses, such as:
    (a) the Minnesota Multiphasic Personality Inventory (MMPI) and subscales (infrequency (F), infrequency–psychopathology (Fp), and infrequency–posttraumatic stress disorder (Fptsd);
    (b) the Personality Assessment Inventory (PAI) malingering indices MAL and RDF (both designed to detect features of malingering). The RDF demonstrated superiority in detection sensitivity (Sullivan and King, 2008).

3. Compare information given on a symptom checklist against consistencies in their story or explanation of posttrauma symptom experience.

Sullivan and King (2008) highlight several reasons why there is such potential for malingering to go undetected:

- The format of some measures of psychopathology contribute to their vulnerability in not detecting malingering.

- The general level of community awareness for PTSD contributes to the increased risk of malingering success (associated with symptom knowledge and simulation). The plethora of information available could help potential malingerers, leading to symptom exaggeration, as well as: (a) coaching by attorneys and (b) information available in the media.

Overall, when attempting to rule out the potential for malingering use a systematic, multifaceted approach. Rosen (2006) reminds therapists, as per the DSM-IV-TR, that malingering must be ruled out when there are issues of financial remuneration, benefit eligibility and litigation. It is further suggested that until malingering has been ruled out, the risks of inflated rates of psychiatric comorbidity will enter the PTSD database.

According to Rubenzer (2005) estimates of malingering associated with personal injury range from 20% to 59%, and "even these could be underestimates." Ruling out malingering requires a focus on factual data and many therapists feel that it places them in opposition to patient interests. While Rubenzer states the importance of ruling out malingering he also states that the presence of feigning or poor effort cannot result in the assumption of malingering.

The four sources of information that play a significant role in determining the possibility of feigning include:

- Semi-structured interviews which cover the patient's life experiences

- Observations of the patient's characteristics of behavior during and outside of the interview

- Specialized psychological testing
- Collateral information from sources such as family, physician, witnesses of the traumatic event, and others who become identified who may contribute beneficial information in clarifying the clinical picture.

Koch et al. (2005) state that, "Research on functional disability associated with PTSD is in its infancy, but it seems likely that PTSD will account for only part of the variance in work disability. The role of forensic practitioners is to offer guidance for improving forensic practice, identify and encourage necessary research, and to advise the courts regarding limitations associated with forensic opinions.

A National Center for PTSD Fact Sheet (Baker and Alfonso, 2006) states that "Reliable and valid psychometric instruments should be used to determine whether an individual meets the symptomatic criteria for PTSD. However, data from psychometric tests should never serve as a stand alone means for diagnosing PTSD." The fact sheet further states that information obtained by the use of psychometric measures are best used as a supplement and substantiative tool combined with information gained from an interview assessment and additional informational sources.

ASSESSMENT INSTRUMENTS

A skilled clinician is the most valuable assessment instrument. There are multiple methods for obtaining a rich clinical picture. Traditionally, therapists conduct a mental status exam embedded in a thorough clinical interview which is individualized by the information and observations elicited during the interview process and reasons for referral in addition to clinical hypothesizing and intuition. The Institute of Medicine (2006) states that while screening and diagnostic instruments may be a benefit in the diagnosis and assessment of PTSD, these instruments are not a substitute for the evaluation by an experienced clinician. Keane (2006) suggests a multimethod assessment of PTSD which includes a clinical diagnostic interview, psychological testing, and neurobiological testing (reactivity measures). Another method recommended is the use of a clinician-administered structured diagnostic interview which provides a dichotomous and continuous range of PTSD symptoms. Numerous assessment instruments have been developed to cover the range and needs of the therapist.

THE CLINICAL INTERVIEW

How can clinicians improve their diagnostic acuity for PTSD? It is important to think about the areas which could yield the information useful for clarifying any diagnostic picture and need for referrals:

- Presenting problem(s). Question: "What has concerned you most since the event?"
- History of presented issue(s)

- History of deeply frightening experiences
- Current symptoms: Explore frequency, intensity and duration of symptoms
- Psychiatric history (including past and current medications)
- Risk factors
- Mental Status Exam (MSE)
- Functional status:
  - work/school
  - significant relationships
  - social functioning
- History of losses
- Anniversary reactions and trauma reminders
- History of traumas (physical, sexual, or emotional abuse). Question: "Have you had any kind of extreme stress or trauma that was very upsetting that might be causing these problems?" Validation: "It's not uncommon for people who have experienced extreme stress or trauma to have symptoms like you are describing," or "Posttraumatic stress is a biological illness that can be experienced by anyone who has had extreme stress or a traumatic event happen to them"
- History of substance abuse. Motivational interviewing (example):
  - Explore the pros and cons of drinking
  - The importance of change
  - Specific substance use goals
  - Action plans to bring about change
- Self-rated perceptions of self, support system, and life experiences
- Somatic symptoms
- Current medical treatment/medications (comorbidity needs to be closely examined due to its significant impact on treatment planning)
- Healthcare utilization
- Immediate needs:
  - survival
  - safety
  - security
  - basic needs (shelter, food)
  - sleep
  - medical care
  - mental health triage
  - release of information to communicate if necessary with appropriate collateral contacts, including family, friends/supports, professionals
- Acute interventions
  - acute symptom management
  - education, normalization and validation
  - social, spiritual support
  - medical tests/treatment
- Provide literature such as handouts for increasing the recognition of PTSD.

It is unfortunate, but there are some patients motivated by a secondary gain who will manipulate, falsify, or exaggerate their symptoms during the above process and use any information they are given to potentially improve their case. This adds to the importance of documentation regarding the clinical process and objectivity. The caring and objective therapist is able to skillfuly endeavor to clarify the accuracy of trauma response without invalidating the experience of those legitimately distressed and seeking clinical intervention.

SCREENING INSTRUMENTS

There have been several PTSD screening instruments designed to elicit diagnostic information in the brief time allowed in primary care settings. One is the Short Screening Scale (7 items) by Breslau (2005). Several adaptations of instruments have been provided to offer a framework for the type of information being sought.

BRIEF SCREENING SCALE FOR PTSD (ADAPTED FROM KIMERLING et al., 2006)

Have you ever had an experience that was so frightening, horrible or overwhelming, that in the past month, you ...

1. Have made efforts to avoid being reminded of the experience by staying away from certain people, places, or situations?
2. Have lost interest in activities that were previously enjoyable?
3. Have lost interest in activities that were previously important?
4. Feel more isolated and distant from people?
5. Are finding it difficult or uncomfortable to feel love for others?
6. Are finding it difficult or uncomfortable to have affection for others?
7. Feel that your life is going to be shortened?
8. Feel that there is no point in planning for the future?
9. Have had more difficulty than usual falling asleep or staying asleep?
10. Are more easily startled by common noises and movement?
11. Are jumpy and on-edge for no identifiable reason?
12. Are experiencing more physical problems or discomfort than usual?

As can be seen, even this brief interview instrument would have value, though it lacks a comprehensive symptoms review. The information it renders would offer pertinent avenues of further exploration, appropriate referral, and medical intervention.

Recognizing that the diagnosis of PTSD during a physician's visit can be challenging, direct questioning is required within a safe environment and a non-judgmental approach with expressions of empathy, genuine care, and interest. Direct questions to ensure that a diagnosis of PTSD is not overlooked would include:

- Have you even been in a severe accident?
- Have you ever been physically assaulted?
- Have you ever been emotionally abused?
- Have you ever been sexually abused or assaulted?

- Have you ever served active duty in a war?

- Have you ever been in a natural disaster?

- Many people have childhood experiences that they continue to think about that have affected their life. Do you?

- Did anything ever happen to you as a child that you were afraid to disclose?

- Have you experienced more than one traumatic event?

- How have you responded and coped, if any of these aforementioned events have been experienced?

Lange et al. (2000) acknowledge that PTSD symptoms can mimic depression and anxiety, thus requiring appropriate and effective screening. The clinical course of symptom development for sufferers of PTSD is a variable presentation. This is one of the major complicating factors that impedes accurate and timely diagnosing. The mnemonic DREAMS was designed to elicit pertinent details following a traumatic experience. The mnemonic should be used for each event.

D = Detached (alexithymia) from the event or in relationships with others. General numbing is a variation of manifestation

R = Re-experiences the event in the form of nightmares, recollections or flashbacks

E = The event involved significant emotional distress, with threat of death or loss of physical integrity, and feelings of helplessness or disabling fears.

A = Avoidance of people, places or activities that remind the patient of the event.

M = The symptoms have been present for more than one month.

S = Sympathetic hyperactivity or hypervigilance which may include insomnia, irritability, and difficulty concentrating.

For more detailed clinical information in an outpatient setting there are also numerous screening scales/assessment instruments. A composite of screening devices using the criteria defined by the DSM-IV-TR including a second part which is focused on general anxiety and depression criteria and followed by substance abuse screening is more comprehensive and clinically useful. The following is provided as a sample of combining several information gathering instruments to gain a comprehensive assessment:

THE PTSD SYMPTOM CHECKLIST

Part A

	None	Occasionally	Moderately	Frequently	Extreme
I feel irritable and on edge					
I have trouble falling asleep					
I feel angry or have angry outbursts					
I try to erase it from my mind					
I am jumpy and startle easily					

	None	Occasionally	Moderately	Frequently	Extreme
I have a loss of interest in activities I used to enjoy					
I avoid activities or situations because they remind me of the event					
I feel as if it didn't happen or it wasn't real					
Waves of strong feelings sometimes come over me					
I have trouble concentrating					
I feel like I am always on guard					
I have trouble remembering parts of what happened					
I have trouble staying asleep					
I feel distant and isolated from people					
My feelings about what happened are kind of numb					
I avoid thinking or talking about what happened					
I get pictures in my mind of what happened					
I fear I am losing control					
I sometimes act or feel as if I am experiencing the event now					
Reminders of what happened cause me to have physical reactions (trouble breathing, heart racing, break out in a sweat, nausea, diarrhea, etc.)					
I feel as if my future will be cut short					
I feel unable to have loving feelings for those close to me					
I try to not think about the event					
I stay away from reminders of what happened					
I have repeated disturbing dreams					
I sometimes feel like I am reliving what happened					
I am aware that I still have a lot of feeling about what happened to me					
I think about it when I don't mean to or expect to					
I try to not let myself get upset when I think about it.					
I don't seem to care about much of anything					

Adapted from Weiss and Marmar (1997).

The pattern of responding will clarify the diagnostic criteria experienced by an individual. Here is a symptom category list and the corresponding items:

- Avoidance subscale 4, 7, 8, 16, 22, 23, 26, 29
- Emotional numbing 6, 14, 15, 20, 21, 30
- Intrusions subscale 9, 12, 13, 16, 17, 18, 24, 25, 28
- Hyperarousal subscale 1, 2, 3, 5, 10, 11, 19

	None	Occasionally	Moderately	Frequently	Extreme
Fever					
Repetitive, senseless thoughts					
Repetitive, senseless behavior					
Fainting or feeling faint					
Tremors, trembling or shaking					
Seizures					
Easy bruising					
Skin rash					
Violent behavior					
Constant worry					
Irritability					
Tension					
Headache					
Feeling in a dreamlike state					
Fearful feelings					
Fear of losing control					
Jumpiness					
Restlessness					
Sweating					
Dizziness/lightheadedness					
Keyed up/on edge					
Agitation					
Nervousness					
Trouble concentrating					
Insomnia/trouble sleeping					
Decrease in sex drive					
Trouble making decisions					
Sad/depressed/down in the dumps					
Lack of/loss of interest in things					
Helpless feelings					
Fatigue–lack of energy					
Weakness					
Increase or decrease in appetite					
Increase or decrease in weight					
Frequent crying or weeping					
Frequent thoughts of death or suicide					

	None	Occasionally	Moderately	Frequently	Extreme
Worthless feelings					
Despair					
Excessive feelings of guilt					
Hopeless feelings					
Feeling life is not worth living					
Sleeping too much					
Frequent negative thinking					
Memory problem					
Fear of doing something uncontrollable					
Fear of dying					
Chills					
Seeing or hearing things that are not real					
Fear of going crazy					

Adapted from Bristol-Myer Squibb, Neuroscience Division.

This check off list is intended as a screening device for PTSD with associated depression and/or anxiety

10–27 Consider a diagnosis of persistent anxiety if patient checked constant worry and three other symptoms in that range

28–44 Consider a diagnosis of depression if the patient checked off six symptoms in this range

If the patient checked any symptoms in the range of 22–27 plus either 28 or 29 consider the diagnosis of depression with associated anxiety.

Part C Substance Abuse Assessment

In order to develop an individualized treatment plan for each patient, a therapist must endeavor to identify potential avenues for change that have provided some degree of self-mediated stress reduction to those who suffer from posttraumatic stress and PTSD. Trauma-focused work is generally associated with increased arousal. If substance abuse is an issue which is accurately assessed and appropriate intervention made, considerable emphasis should be given to anxiety/arousal management, since this is the problem most likely to be exacerbated by decrease or elimination of substance abuse to facilitate and reinforce adequate support and reinforcement for change. There are numerous well-known assessment instruments that can be utilized (Johnson, 2003).

To screen for the comorbidity of alcohol abuse there are numerous inventories, for example the Alcohol Use Inventory. Two brief screening devices are known as TWEAK and CAGE.

TWEAK (Russel et al., 1991)

T = Tolerance: How many drinks can you hold or how many drinks does it take to get high?

W = Worried: Have close friends or relatives been worried about your drinking?

E = Eye-opener: Do you sometimes take a drink in the morning to wake up?

A = Amnesia: Has a friend or relative ever told you things you said or did while you were drinking that you could not remember?

K = Kut (cut): Do you sometimes feel the need to cut down on your drinking?

CAGE (Ewing, 1984)

C = Cut down: Has anyone ever recommended that you cut back or stop drinking?

A = Annoyed: Have you ever felt annoyed or angry if someone comments on your drinking?

G = Guilt: Have there been times when you felt guilty about or regretted things that have occurred because of drinking?

E = Eye-opener: Have you ever used alcohol to help you get started in the morning to steady your nerves?

According to Jacobson (1989), this questionnaire accurately determines the presence or absence of alcoholism 90% of the time. Two or more positive responses indicate alcohol dependence.

OTHER ASSESSMENT INSTRUMENTS

The following information is summarized from Foa et al. (2009), the National Center for PTSD (2008), US Department of Veterans Affairs (2008) and the International Society for Traumatic Stress Studies (2008). Assessment instruments are not to be administered by mental health professionals who have not received adequate and appropriate education and training regarding the specific instrument. While there is some advocacy for combining instruments, it can be difficult, and there is a lack of empirical guidelines from which to support the validity.

Response bias is another concern associated with assessment. It is not difficult to discern what questions are seeking to clarify, and, therefore, pathological responses are easy to detect by respondents. This is why the use of multiple instruments are recommended at times and can be beneficial, at least offering several sources from which to draw information and serve as a reference for response consistency. Therefore, if there is some secondary gain by being identified as having PTSD for the purpose of compensation associated with disability or civil litigation, malingering should be suspected and clear documentation should be prepared, detailing the methods used to gather information culminating in the decision to render a diagnosis of PTSD.

There are two categories of PTSD evaluation: (1) the structured interview and the self-report questionnaire. The diagnosis is generally based upon the clinical interview in association with:

• Presenting problem

• Patient history and responses

• Behavioral observations

- Mental status examination
- Responses given to short answer/symptom questionnaire or inventory.

There have been a number of assessment instruments developed that allow clinicians to choose which single instrument or combination of instruments work best in conjunction with their own style for gathering information in making a diagnosis of PTSD. Some of the more commonly used instruments for assessing PTSD are listed here.

Structured Clinical Interview for DSM-IV (SCID)	Comprehensive structured interview designed to diagnose all major DSM-IV disorders. There are three versions. Information can be found at www.scid4.org.
PTSD Symptom Scale-Interview (PSS-I)	Structured interview modified from its original DSM-III version for use with the DSM-IV. Depending on the dimension being measured, severity and frequency ratings are given. It is relatively brief and easy to administer (Foa and Tolin, 2000).
Structured Interview for PTSD (SIP)	A benefit to this instrument is that it is brief and relatively simple to administer. Contains rating scale descriptors to clarify symptom inquiry and rating (Davidson et al., 1997).
Clinical-Administered PTSD Scale (CAPS)	This comprehensive structured interview assesses symptom frequency and intensity, as well as, including Criterion A (screening for trauma exposure) (Blake et al., 1990, 1995).
PTSD Checklist (PCL)	This is a self-report measure whereby respondents rate how much they are distressed by each symptom. It screens for PTSD, detects clinical change, and is able to predict an interview-based diagnosis of PTSD (Weathers et al., 1993).
Posttraumatic Stress Diagnostic Scale (PDS)	Designed to assess all of the DSM-IV PTYSD diagnostic criteria (Foa, 1995; Foa et al., 1997).

Detailed Assessment of Posttraumatic Stress (DAPS)	Comprehensive, self-report measure of trauma and PTSD, evaluating all DSM-IV criteria for PTSD (Briere, 2001).
Minnesota Multiphasic Personality Inventory II	Assesses personality, psychopathology, and various forms of response bias. Used extensively with military and civilian populations. The original MMPI was developed in 1951, making it one of the most used and most useful assessment instruments (Butcher et al., 2001).
Personality Assessment Inventory (PAI)	Used in clinical, research, and forensic settings. Contains both clinical and validity scales (Morey, 2007).
Mississippi Scale for Combat-Related PTSD	Self-report measure of PTSD symptoms and associated features. It is identified as being the most widely used measure of combat-related PTSD (Keane et al., 1988).

Additional instruments that the reader may want to literature search and utilize based upon their process of assessment includes:

- Anxiety Disorders Interview Schedule-Revised (ADIS-R)
- Beck Depression Inventory (BDI)
- Beck Anxiety Inventory (BAI)
- Disorder of Extreme Stress Inventory (DESI)
- Dissociation Experience Scale (DES)
- Hamilton Anxiety Scale
- Los Angeles Symptom checklist
- The Penn Inventory for Post Traumatic Stress.

REFERENCES AND FURTHER READING

Adams RE, Boscarino JA (2006) Predictors of PTSD and delayed PTSD after disaster: The impact of exposure and psychosocial resources. *J Nerv Ment Dis* 194: 485–493.

American Psychiatric Association (1994) *Diagnostic and Statistical Manual of Mental Disorders*, 3rd edn. Washington, DC: American Psychiatric Association.

American Psychiatric Association (2000) *Diagnostic and Statistical Manual of Mental Disorders*, 4th edn., text revised. Washington, DC: American Psychiatric Association.

American Psychiatric Association (2004) *Practice Guideline For the Treatment of Patients With Acute Stress Disorder and Posttraumatic Stress Disorder: Formulation and Implementation of a Treatment Plan*. Washington, DC: American Psychiatric Association.

Andreski R, Childcoat KS, Breslau N (1998) Post-traumatic stress disorder and somatization symptoms: a prospective study. *Psychiatr Res* 79: 131–138.

Asmundson GJ, Hadjistavropolous HD (2006) Addressing shared vulnerability for comorbid PTSD and chronic pain. *Cogn Behav Pract* 13: 8–16.

Australian Survey (2002) Trauma and posttraumatic stress disorder in Australia: Findings in the population sample of the Australian National Survey of Mental Health and Wellbeing. *Austr NZ J Psychiatry* 36: 515–520.

Baker C, Alfonso C (2006) *National Center for PTSD fact sheet: PTSD and Criminal Behavior*. Accessed from: http://www.ncptsd.va.gov/ncmain/ncdocs/fact_sheet/fs_legal.html.

Bandura A (1997) *Self-efficacy in Changing Societies*. New York: Cambridge University Press.

Basoglu M, Mineka A, Parker M, Aker T, Livanou M, Gok S (1997) Psychological preparedness for trauma as a protective factor in survivors of torture. *Psychol Med* 27: 1421–1433.

Benedek DM, Fullerton C, Ursano RJ (2007) First responders: Mental health consequences of natural and human made disasters for public health and safety workers. *Annu Rev Public Health* 28: 55–68.

Blanchard EB, Hickling E (2004) *After the Crash: Psychological assessment and treatment of survivors of motor vehicle accidents*, 2nd edn. Washington, DC: American Psychological Association.

Bolton EE, Gray MJ, Litz BT (2006) A cross-lagged analysis of the relationship between symptoms of PTSD and retrospective reports of exposure. *J Anxiety Disord* 20: 877–895.

Boscarino JA (1997) Diseases among men 20 years after exposure to extreme stress. Implications for clinical research and medical care. *Psychosom Med* 59: 605–614.

Brady KT (2008) Gender differences in PTSD. Medscape CE. Accessed March 2008. 154th Annual Meeting of the American Psychiatric Association.

Brady KT, Sinha R (2005) Co-occurring mental and substance use disorders: The neurobiological effects of chronic stress. *Am J Psychiatry* 162: 1483–1493.

Brady KT, Killeen TK, Brewerton T, Lucerini S (2000) Comorbidity of psychiatric disorders and posttraumatic stress disorder. *J Clin Psychiatry* 61: 22–32.

Brandes D, Ben-Schachar G, Gilboa A, Bonne O, Friedman S, Shav AY (2002) PTSD symptoms and cognitive perormance in recent trauma performance. *Psychiatry Res* 110: 231–238.

Braun BG (1988) The BASK (behavior, affect, sensation, knowledge) model of dissociation. *Dissociation* 1(1): 4–24.

Breslau N, Davis GC, Andreski P, Peterson EL, Schultz LR (1997) Sex differences in posttraumatic stress disorder. *Arch Gen Psychiatry* 54: 1044–1048.

Breslau N, Davis GC, Peterson EL, Schultz L (1998a) Psychiatric sequelae of posttraumatic stress disorder in women. *Arch Gen Psychiatry* 54: 81–87.

Breslau N, Kessler RC, Chilcoat HD, Schultz LR, Davis GC, Andreski P (1998b) Trauma and posttraumatic stress disorder in the community: The 1996 Detroit Area Survey of Trauma. *Arch Gen Psychiatry* 55: 626–632.

Breslau N, Davis GC, Schultz LR (2003) Posttraumatic stress disorder and the incidence of nicotine, alcohol and other drug disorders in persons who have experienced trauma. *Arch Gen Psychiatry* 60: 289–294.

Brewin C, Andrew B, Valentine JD (2000) Meta-analysis of risk factors for post-traumatic stress disorder in trauma-exposed adults. *J Consult Clin Psychol* 68: 748–766.

Brom D, Kleber RJ, Witztum E (1992) The prevalence posttraumatic psychopathology in the general and clinical population. *Isr J Psychiatry Relat Sci* 28: 53–63.

Brown DP, Fromm E (1986) *Hypnotherapy and Hypnoanalysis*. Hillsdale, NJ: Lawrence Erlbaum Associates.

Bulik CM, Prescott CA, Kendler KS (2001) Features of childhood sexual abuse and the development of psychiatric and substance abuse disorders. *Br J Psychiatry* 179: 444–449.

Cannistraro PA, Rauch SL (2003) Neural circuitry of anxiety: Evidence from structural and functional neuroimaging studies. *Psychopharmacol Bull* 37: 8–25.

Chilcoat HD, Breslau N (1998) Post traumatic stress disorder and drug disorders. *Arch Gen Psychiatry* 55: 913–917.

Cohen JA, Deblinger D, Mannarino A (2004) Trauma-focused cognitive-behavioral therapy for sexually abused children. *Psychiatric Times* 21: 52–53.

Cook A, Spinazzola J, Ford J, Lanktree C et al. (2005) Complex trauma in children and adolescents. *Psychiatric Annals* 35: 390–398.

Cottler LB, Compton WM, Mager D, Spitznagel EL, Janca A (1992) Posttraumatic stress disorder among substance users from the general population. *Am J Psychiatry* 149: 662–670.

Creamer M, Burgess P, McFarlane AC (2001) Post-traumatic stress disorder: Findings from the Australian National Survey of Mental Health and Well-being. *Psychol Med* 31: 1237–1247.

Curro E (1997) Assessing the physiological and clinical characteristics of acute vs. chronic pain. *Dental Clin N Am* 31: xiii–xxiii.

Davidson JR, Hughes D, Blazer DG et al. (1991) Post-traumatic stress disorder in the community: An epidemiological study. *Psychol Med* 21: 713–721.

Davis GC, Breslau N (2000) Are women at greater risk for PTSD than men? HealthyPlace.com Anxiety Community

Delahanty DL, Herberman HB, Craig KJ, Hayward MC, Fullerton CS, Ursano RJ et al. (1997) Acute and chronic distress and posttraumatic stress disorder as a function of responsibility for serious motor vehicle accidents. *J Consult Clin Psychol* 65: 560–567.

Dragica KK, Andreja B (2008) *Malingering PTSD*. Nova Publications. Accessed January 6, 2008 from:

Dunmore E, Clark DM, Ehlers A (1999) Cognitive factors involved in the onset and maintenance of posttraumatic stress disorder after physical or sexual assault. *Behav Res Ther* 37: 809–829.

Dutton DG (2008) My back pages: Reflections on thirty years of domestic violence research. *Trauma, Violence Abuse* 9: 131–143.

Dutton DG, Painter SL (1981) Traumatic bonding: The development of emotional attachments in battered women and other relationships of intermittent abuse. *Victimology: An International Journal* 6: 139–155.

Dutton DG, Painter SL (1993) Emotional attachments in abusive relationships: A test of trauma bonding theory. *Violence Victims* 8: 105–120.

Eichoff C (2008) A review of mental health services for soldiers with a focus on cultural competency. Accessed from: http://filebox.vt.edu/users/renchu/independent%20study%20outline.doc

Emery OV, Emery PE, Shama DK, Quiana NA, Jassani AK (2006) Predisposing variables in PTSD patients. *J Trauma Stress* 4: 325–343.

Ewing JA (1984) Detecting alcoholism: The CAGE questionnaire. *JAMA* 252: 1905–1907.

Foa EB (2000) Psychosocial treatment of posttraumatic stress disorder. *J Clin Psychiatry* 61: 43–48.

Foa EB, Rothenbaum BO (1998) *Treating the Trauma of Rape: Cognitive-Behavior Therapy for PTSD*. New York: Guilford Press.

Foa EB, Keane TB, Friedman MJ (2004) Guidelines for the treatment of PTSD. *J Trauma Stress* 13: 539–588.

Foa EB, Keane TB, Friedman MJ, Cohen JA (2009) *Effective Treatments for PTSD*. New York: Guilford Press.

Follette VM, Ruzek JI, Abueg RF (1998) *Cognitive-Behavioral Therapies for Trauma*. New York: Guilford Press.

Ford JD (2008) Trauma, PTSD, and ethnoracial minorities: Toward diversity and cultural competence in prinicples and practice. *Clin Psychol* 15: 62–67.

Frazier P, Schauben L (1994) Causal attributions and recovery from rape and other stressful life events. *J Soc Clin Psychol* 13: 1–14.

Friedman M (2004) Acknowledging the psychiatric cost of war. *N Engl J Med* 351: 75–77.

Friedman M (2005a) Deployment Health Clinic Center, Institute of Medicine Annual Report.

Friedman M (2005b) Veterans mental health in the wake of war. *New Engl J Med* 352: 1287–1290.

Friedman M (2006) Posttraumatic stress disorder among military retirees from Afghanistan and Iraq. *Am J Psychiatry* 163: 586–593.

Friedman M (2007) *Diagnosis and Assessment of PTSD. A Report to the Institute of Medicine.* Accessed October 2008 from: http://www.iomedu/Fileasox?ID=32925.

Gersons BPR, Olff M (2005) Coping with the aftermath of trauma. *BMJ* 330: 1038–1039.

Gold J, Cardena E (1993) Sexual abuse and combat related trauma: Psychometric and pharmacological resemblance. Paper presented at the 101st Annual Convention of the American Psychological Association, Toronto, Canada.

Grant M (1997) *Pain Control with Eye Movement Desensitization and Reprocessing.* Wyong, New South Wales, Australia: Wyong Medical Centre.

Grohol JM (2008) *New Insights into the Course of PTSD.* Accessed from: http://psychcentral.com/new/2008/12/10/new-insights-into-the-course-of-ptsd/3434.html.

Hall RCW (2006) Malingering of PTSD: forensic and diagnostic considerations, characteristics of malingerers and clinical presentations. *Gen Hosp Psychiatry* 28: 525–535.

Hall RCW (2007) Detection of malingered PTSD: An overview of clinical, psychometric, and psychological assessment: Where do we stand? *J Forensic Sci* 52: 717–725.

Hall W, Teesson M, Lynskey M, Degenhardt L (2002) The 12-month prevalence of substance use and ICD-10 substance use disorders in Australian adults: Findings from the National Survey of Mental Health and Well-being. *Addiction* 94: 1541–1550.

Hedtke KA, Ruggiero KT, Fitzgerald MM, Zinson HM, Saunders BE, Resick HS, Kilpatrick DG (2008) A longitudinal investigation of interpersonal violence in relation to mental health and substance use. *J Consult Clin Psychol* 76: 633–647.

Heffenan K, Cloitre M (2000) A comparison of posttraumatic stress disorder with and without borderline personality disorder among women with a history of childhood sexual abuse: etiological and clinical characteristics. *J Nerv Ment Disord* 188: 589–595.

Heim C, Plotsky PM, Nemeroff CB (1997) The impact of early adverse experience on brain systems involved in the pathophysiology of anxiety and affective disorders. *Biol Psychiatry* 46: 1509–1522.

Hein D (2003) Trauma and addictions: Empirically supported treatment strategies. *Social Intervention Group.* New York: Columbia University School of Social Work.

Hein D (2006) Women Treatment for trauma and substance use disorders: A randomized clinical trial (NIDA-CTN-0015). *Social Intervention Group.* New York: Columbia University School of Social Work.

Henderson S, Andrews G, Hall W (2000) Australia's mental health: An overview of the general population survey. *Aust N Z J Psychiatry* 34: 197–205.

Herman JL (1992) *Trauma and Recovery.* New York: Basic Books.

Herman JL (1999) Complex PTSD: A syndrome in survivors of prolonged and repeated trauma. In: *Essential Papers on PTSD* (Horowitz MJ, ed.). New York: New York University Press.

Hetzer JE (1984) The impact of combat on later alcohol use by Vietnam Veterans. *J Psychoactive Drugs* 6: 181–183.

Hoeft F, Watson CL, Kesler SR, Bettinger KE, Reiss AL (2008) Gender differences in the mesocorticolimbic system during computer game play. *J Psychiatr Res* 42: 253–258.

Horevitz RP, Loewenstein RJ (1994) The rational treatment of multiple personality disorder. In: *Dissociation: Clinical and Theoretical Perspectives* (Lynn SJ, Rhue JW, eds). New York: Guilford Press.

Horowitz MJ (1993) Stress response syndromes: A review of posttraumatic stress and adjustment disorders. In: *International Handbook of Traumatic Stress Syndromes* (Wilson JP, Rafael B, eds). New York: Plenum Press.

Institute of Medicine (2006) *Posttraumatic Stress Disorder: Diagnosis and Assessment.* Accessed from:

International Society for Traumatic Stress Studies (2008) *Resources for Clinicians.* Accessed from: www.istss.org/resources/browse.cfm.

Jacobs J, Horne-Myer HL, Jones R (2004) The effectiveness of critical incident stress debriefing with primary and secondary trauma victims. *Int J Emerg Ment Health* 1: 5–14.

Jacobsen LK, Southwick SM, Kosten TR (2001) Substance use disorders in patients with posttraumatic stress disorder. *Am J Psychiatry* 158: 1184–1190.

Jacobson GR (1989) A comprehensive approach to pretreatment evaluation: Detection, assessment and diagnosis of alcoholism. In: *Handbook of Alcoholism Treatment Approaches. Effective Alternatives* (Hester RK, Miller WR, eds). Boston: Allyn & Bacon, pp. 17–43.

Janet P (1889) *L'automatisme psychologique.* Paris: F. Alcan. (Revised: Societe' Piere Janet, Paris, 1973).

Johnson SL (2003) *Therapist's Guide to Substance Abuse Intervention.* San Diego: Academic Press.

Johnson SL (2004) *Therapist's Guide to Clinical Intervention*, 2nd edn. San Diego: Academic Press.

Katon W (2001) Complex PTSD. *J Clin Psychiatry* 8: 12–16.

Katon W, Roy-Byme P (2007) Anxiety disorders: Efficient screening is the first step in improving outcomes. *Ann Intern Med* 146: 390–392.

Katon W, Von Korff M, Lin E, Lipscomb P, Russo J, Wagner E et al. (1990) Distressed high utilizers of medical care. DSM-III-R diagnoses and treatment needs. *Gen Hosp Psychiatry* 12: 355–362.

Katon W, Sullivan M, Walker E (2001) Medical symptoms without identified pathology: Relationship to psychiatreic disorders, childhood and adult trauma, and personality traits. *Ann Intern Med* 134: 917–925.

Keane TM (2006) Issues in the assessment of PTSD. Institute of Medicine Report on PTSD. February 13, 2006. Accessed from: www.ncptsd.va.gov.

Keane TM, Phelps R (2008) Treating post traumatic stress disorder (PTSF) related to military combat. A question and answer article published by the APApractice.org. Spring 2008, (3): 6–12. Accessed from:

Kellner M, Yassouridis A, Hubner R, Baker DG, Wiederman K (2003) Endocrine and cardiovascular responses to corticotropin releasing hormone in patients with posttraumatic stress disorder: A role for atrial natreuric peptide. *Int J Exp Clin Res Biol Psychiatry* 47: 102–108.

Kendler KS, Bulik CM, Silberg J, Hettema JM, Myers J, Prescott CA (2000) Features of childhood sexual abuse and the development of psychiatric and substance use disorders in women. *Arch Gen Psychiatry* 57: 953–959.

Kessler RC, Sonnega A, Bromet E, Hughes M, Nelson CB (1995) Posttraumatic stress disorder in the National Comorbidity Survey. *Arch Gen Psychiatry* 52: 1048–1060.

Kessler R, Berglund P, Demler O, Jin R, Walters E (2005a) Lifetime prevalence and age-of-onset distribution of DSM-IV disorders in the National Comorbidity Survey Replication. *Arch Gen Psychiatry* 62: 593–602.

Kessler R, Chiu W, Demler O, Walters E (2005b) Prevalence, severity, and comorbidity of 12-month DSM-IV disorders in the National Comorbidity Survey Replication. *Arch Gen Psychiatry* 62: 617–627.

Khantzian EJ (1985) The self-medication hypothesis of addictive disorders: Focus on heroin and cocaine dependence. *Am J Psychiatry* 142: 1259–1264.

Kilpatrick DG, Acierno R (2003) Mental health needs of crime victims: epidemiology and outcome. *J Trauma Stress* 16: 119–132.

Kilpatrick DG, Ruggiero KJ, Acierno R, Saunders BE, Resick H, Best CL (2003) Violence and risk of PTSD, major depression, substance use/dependence, and comorbidity: Results from the National Survey of Adolescents. *J Consult Clin Psychol* 71: 692–700.

Kimerling R, Ouimette P, Prins A et al. (2006) Brief report: Utility of a short screening scale for DSM-IV PTSD in primary care. *J Gen Intern Med* 21: 65–67.

King LA, King DW, Leskin G, Fey DW (1995) The Los Angeles Symptom Checklist: A self-report measure of posttraumatic stress disorder. *Assessment* 2: 1–17.

Kluft RP (1984) Treatment of multiple personality disorder. *Psychiatr Clin N Am* 7: 9–29.

Kluft RP (1988) On the treatment of the older patient with multiple personality disorder: "Race against time" or "make haste slowly?". *Am J Clin Hypnosis* 30: 257–266.

Kluft RP (1989) Playing for time: Temporizing techniques in the treatment of multiple personality disorder. *Am J Clin Hypnosis* 32: 90–98.

Kluft RP (1992) Hypnosis with multiple personality disorder. *Am J Prev Psychiatr Neurol* 3: 19–27.

Kluft RP (1993) The initial stages of psychotherapy in the treatment of multiple personality disorder patients. *Dissociation* 6: 63–76.

Kluft RP (1998) Reflections upon the traumatic memories of dissociative identity disorder patients. In: *Truth in Memory* (Lynn SJ, McConkey KM, eds). New York: Guilford Press.

Koch WJ, O'Niell MO, Douglas KS (2005) Empirical limits for the forensic assessment of PTSD litigants. *Law Hum Behav* 29: 121–149.

Koenen KC, Lyons MJ, Goldberg J et al. (2003) Co-twin control study of relationships among combat exposure, combat related PTSD, and other mental disorders. *J Trauma Stress* 16: 1573–1598.

Kofoed L, Friedman MJ, Peck R (1993) Alcoholism and drug abuse in patients with PTSD. *Psychiatr Q* 64: 151–171.

Kosten TR, Krystal J (1988) Biological mechanisms in posttraumatic stress disorder relevance for substance abuse. *Recent Dev Alcohol* 6: 49–68.

Krakow B, Hollifield M, Johnson L et al. (2001) Imagery rehearsal therapy for chronic nightmares in sexual assault survivors with PTSD. A randomized trial. *JAMA* 286: 537–545.

Krause ED, DeRosa RR, Roth S (2002) Gender, trauma themes, and PTSD: Narratives of male and female survivors. In: *Gender and PTSD* (Kimerling R, Ouimette P, Wolfe J, eds). New York: Guilford Press, pp. 76–97.

Lange JT, Lange CL, Cabaltica RB (2000) Primary care treatment of post-traumatic stress disorder. *Am Family Physician* 62: 1035–1040.

Lanius RA, Bluhm R, Lanius U, Pain C (2006) A review of neuroimagery studies in PTSD: Heterogeneity of response to symptom provocation. *J of Psychiatric Research* 40(8): 709–729.

Lawson DM (2003) Incidence explanations, and treatment of partner violence. *J Consult Dev* 81: 19–32.

LeDoux J (1997) Emotion, memory and pain. *Pain Forum* 6: 36–37.

Lehman AF, Myers P, Corty E (1989) Assessment and classification of patients with psychiatric and substance abuse syndromes. *Hosp Community Psychiatry* 40: 1019–1025.

Levine P (1992) *The Body as Healer: Transforming Trauma and Anxiety*. Lyons, CO: USA.

Levine P (1998) *Waking the Tiger*. Berkeley, CA: North Atlantic Books.

Lindauer RTL, Meijel EPM, Jalink M, Olff M, Carlier IVE, Gersons BPR (2006) Heart rate responsivity to script driven imagery in posttraumatic stress disorder: Specificity of response and effects in psychotherapy. *Psychosom Med* 68: 33–40.

Litz BT, Weathers F (1992) The diagnosis and assessment of post-traumatic stress disorder in adults. In: *The Handbook of Post-Traumatic Therapy* (Williams MB, Sommer JF, eds). Westport, CT: Greenwood Press.

Malik ML, Connor KM, Sutherland SM et al. (1999) Quality of life and posttraumatic stress disorder: A pilot study assessing changes in SF-36 scores before and after treatment in a placebo controlled trial of fluoxetine. *J Trauma Stress* 12: 387–393.

Marshall RD, Olfson M, Hellman F, Blanco C, Guardino M, Stuening EL (2001) Comorbidity, impairment, and suicidality in subthreshold PTSF. *Am J Psychiatry* 158: 1467–1473.

Matsakis A (1994) *Post Traumatic Stress Disorder: A Complete Treatment Guide*. Oakland, CA: New Harbinger Publications.

Matsakis A (1998) *Trust after Trauma: A Guide to Relationships for Survivors and those who Love Them*. Oakland, CA: New Harbinger Publications.

Matshall RD, Olfson M, Hellman F, Blanco C, Strevning EL (2001) Comorbidity, impairment and suicidality in subthreshold PTSD. *Am J Psychiatry* 158: 1467–1473.

McFall ME, Mackay PW, Donovan DM (1992) Combat posttraumatic stress disorder and severity of substance abuse in Vietnam veterans. *J Stud Alcohol* 53: 357–363.

McNally RJ (2003a) Psychological mechanisms in active responses to trauma. *Biol Psychiatry* 53: 779–788.

McNally RJ (2003b) *Remembering Trauma*. Cambridge, MA: Harvard University Press.

Minkoff K (1989) An integrated treatment model for dual diagnoses of psychosis and addiction. *Hosp Community Psychiatry* 40: 1031–1036.

Mitchel JT (2005) Crisis intervention and critical incident stress management: A defense of the field. Accessed December 29, 2008 from: http://www/cisf.org/articles/Acrobat%20 Documents/CISM_Defense_of_Field.pdf

Mitchell JT, Everly GS (1993) *Critical Incident Stress Debriefing (CISD): An operations manual for the prevention of traumatic stress among emergency services and disaster workers*. Chevron Publishing Corporation.

Mitchell JT, Everly GS (1995) *Critical Incident Stress Debriefing (CISD) and the Prevention of Work Related Traumatic Stress*. New York: Plenum Press.

Mitchell JT, Everly GS (1996) *The Scientific Evidence for Critical Incident Stress Management (CISM)*. Maryland: International Critical Incident Stress Foundation.

Montero RP (2000) *The Concise Encyclopedia of Fibromyalgia and Myofascial Pain*. Philadelphia, PA: Haworth Press.

Murdoch M, Hodges J, Hunt C, Cowper D, Kressin N, O'Brien N (2003) PTSD gender differences. *Med Care* 4: 1417–1418.

National Center for PTSD (2008) (a) *PTSD Assessment Instruments: Combat Exposure Scale*. (b) *Primary Care PTSD Screen (PC-PTSD)*. Accessed December 28, 2008 from: http://www.ncptsd.va.gov.ncmain/assessment/assessmt_request_form.html.

National Institute of Mental Health (2000) Brochure: Post-Traumatic Stress Disorder: A Real Illness. Accessed June 4, 2000 from: http://www.nimh.nih.gov/anxiety/ptsdri2.cfm.

National Institute of Mental Health (2001) Fact Sheet: Reliving Trauma. NIMH Publication No. 01-497. Accessed from: http://www.nimh.nih.gov/publicat/reliving.cfm.

National Institute of Mental Health (2007) Patient-centered collaborative care for preventing post-traumatic stress disorder after traumatic injury. *ClinicalTrials* NCT00270959, April 2008. Accessed November 9, 2008 from: http://clinicaltrials.gov/ct2/show/ NCT00 270959.

National Institute of Mental Health (2008) The numbers count: Mental disorders in America. See all publications on NIMH: Statistics, America Web Archive. Accessed June 26, 2008 from:

Nelson EC, Heath AC, Lynskey MT, Bucholz KK, Madden PA et al. (2006) Child sexual abuse and risks for illicit drug-related outcomes: A twin study. *Psychol Med* 36: 1473–1483.

Norman SB, Stein MB, Davidson JR (2007) Profiling posttraumatic functional impairment. *J Ment Disord* 195: 48–53.

Norman SB, Stein MB, Dimsdale JE, Hoyt DB (2008) Pain in the aftermath of trauma is a risk factor for post-traumatic stress disorder. *Psychol Med* 38: 533–542.

North C, Nixon S, Shariat S, Mallonee S, McMillian J, Spitznagel E (1999) Psychiatric disorders among survivors of the Oklahoma city bombing. *JAMA* 282: 755–762.

Ogden P, Minton K, Pain C (2006) Psychological trauma and the brain: Toward a neurobiological treatment model. In: *Trauma and the Body Sensorimotor Approach*. New York: WW Norton and Co., pp. 88–99.

Oquendo MA, Friend JM, Halberstam B et al. (2003) Association of comorbid posttraumatic stress disorder and major depression with greater risk of suicidal behavior. *Am J Psychiatry* 160: 580–582.

Oquendo M, Brent DA, Birmaha B et al. (2005) Posttraumatic stress disorder comorbid with major depression: Factors mediating the association with suicidal behavior. *Am J Psychiatry* 162: 560–566.

Ozer EJ, Best SR, Lipsey TL, Weiss DS (2003) Predictors of posttraumatic stress disorder and symptoms in adults: A meta analysis. *Psychol Bull* 129: 52–73.

Parson ER (1984) The reparation of the self: Clinical and theoretical dimensions in the treatment of Vietnam combat veterans. *J Contemp Psychother* 14: 4–56.

Parson ER (2004) Traumatic stress personality disorder (TrSPD): Intertheoretical therapy for PTSD/PD dissociogenic organization. *J Contemp Psychother* 27: 323–367.

Paykel E (1978) Contribution of life events to causation of psychiatric illness. *Psychol Med* 8: 245–254.

Prigerson HG, Maciejewski PL, Rosenheck RA (2002) Population attributable factors of psychiatric disorders and behavioral outcomes associated with combat exposure among US men. *Am J Public Health* 92: 59–63.

Regehr C, LeBlanc V, Jelky RB, Barath I, Dacuik J (2007) Previous trauma exposure and PTSD symptoms as predictors of subjective and biological response to stress. *Can J Psychiatry* 52: 675–683.

Regier DA (2007) An interview with Darrel A. Regier, M.D., MPH: The developmental process for the diagnostic and statistical manual of mental disorders, fifth edition. *CNS Spectrum* 13: 120–124.

Robbins LN, Helzer JE, Davis DH (1975) Narcotic use in Southeast Asia and afterwards. *Arch Gen Psychiatry* 32: 955–961.

Rose S, Brewin CR, Andrews B et al. (1999) A randomized controlled trial of individual psychological debriefing for victims of violent crime. *Psychol Med* 24: 793–799.

Rose S, Bison J, Wesley S (2003) A systematic review of single-session psychological intervention (Debriefing) following trauma. *Psychother Psychosom* 72: 176–184. DOI: 10.1159/0000700781.

Rosen GM (2006) PTSD and malingering. *J Anxiety Disord* 20: 530–535.

Rosenberg SD, Mueser KT, Friedman MJ et al. (2001) Developing effective treatments for posttraumatic disorder among people with severe mental illness. *Psychiatric Serv* 52: 1453–1461.

Rosenman S (2002) Australian Survey: Trauma and posttraumatic stress disorder in Australia: Findings in the population sample of the Australian National Survey of Mental Health and Wellbeing. *Aust N Z J Psychiatry* 36: 515–520.

Roth S, Newman E, Pelcovitz D, van der Kolk B, Mandel FS (1997) Complex PTSD in victims exposed to sexual and physical abuse; results from the DSM IV Field Trial for Posttraumatic Stress Disorder. *J Trauma Stress* 10: 539–555.

Rothchild B (2000) *The Body Remembers: The Psychophysiology of Trauma and Trauma Treatment*. New York: WW Norton.

Rubenzer S (2005) Malingering psychiatric disorders and cognitive impairment in personal injury settings. Published in *For the Defense* (publication for the Defense Research Institute), April issue, 2005.

Russel M, Martier SS, Sokol RJ, Jacobson S, Bottoms S (1991) Screening for pregnancy risk drinking. TWEAKING the tests (abstract). *Alcoholism: Clinical Exp Res* 15: 368.

Ruzak JI, Brymer MJ, Jacobs AK, Layne CM, Vernberg EM, Watson PJ (2007) Psychological first aid. *J Ment Health Counsel* 1. Accessed from: http://www.accessmylibrary.com/coms2/summary_0286-29540647_ITM.

Schnurr PP, Green BL (eds) (2004) *Trauma and Health: Physical health consequences of exposure to extreme stress*. Washington, DC: American Psychological Association.

Seasholtz A (2008) Regulation of adrenocorticotropic hormone secretion: lessons from mice deficient in corticotropin-releasing hormone. *J Clin Invest* 105: 1187.

Sher L (2004) Recognizing post-traumatic stress disorder. *QJM* 97: 1–5.

Simmons CA, Granvold DK (2005) A cognitive model to explain gender differences in the rate of PTSD diagnosis. *Brief Treat Crisis Interv* 5: 290–299.

Simon RI (2003) *Posttraumatic Stress Disorder in Litigation*, 2nd edn. American Psychiatric Publications.

Solomon SD, Davidson JRT (1997) Trauma: prevalence: impairment; service use; and cost. *J Clin Psychiatry* 58: 5–11.

Solomon Z, Bleich A (1998) Comorbidity in posttraumatic stress disorder and depression in Israeli veterans. *CNS Spectrums* 3(suppl 2): 16–21.

Spinazzola J, Blaustein M, van der Kolk BA (2005) Posttraumatic stress disorder treatment outcome research: The study of unrepresented samples?. *J Trauma Stress* 18: 425–436.

Sukel K. (2008) Sex differences offer new insight into psychiatric disorders. The Dana Foundation. Accessed October 20, 2008 from: danainfor@dana.org.

Sullivan KA, King JK (2008) Detecting faked psychopathology: A comparison of two tests to detect malingered psychopathology using a simulation design. *Psychiatric Research*. Accessed 2008 from: http://eprints.qut.edu.au/archive/0001413/01/14143.pdf.

Thorp SR, Stein MB (2005) Post-traumatic stress disorder and functioning. *PTSD Res Q* 16: 1–7.

Tolin DF, Foa EB (2002) Gender and PTSD: A cognitive model. In: *Gender and PTSD* (Kimerling R, Ouimette P, Wolfe J, eds). New York: Guilford Press, pp. 76–97.

Tolin DF, Foa EB (2006) Sex differences in trauma and posttraumatic stress disorder: A quantitative review of 25 years of research. *Psychol Bull* 132: 959–992.

Tull M (2008) *Ethnic and Racial Differences in PTSD*. Updated October 29, 2008. Accessed 2008 from: http://ptsd.about.com/od/prevalence/a/raceptsd.htm.

Turkus JA (1991) Psychotherapy and case management for multiple personality disorder: Synthesis for continuity of care. *Psychiatr Clin N Am* 14: 649–660.

Turner JB, Turse NA, Dohnrenwend BP (2007) Circumstances of service and gender differences in war related PTSD: Findings from National Vietnam Veteran Readjustment Study. *J Trauma Stress* 20: 643–649.

Ullman SE, Fillpas HH (2005) Gender differences in social reactions to abuse disclosures, post-abuse coping and PTSD of child sexual abuse survivors. *Child Abuse Neglect* 29: 767–782.

US Department of Veterans Affairs (2008) Health Services Research & Developmental Services. Comparison of PTSD Symptom Assessment Instrument. Accessed December 28, 2008 from: http://hsrd.research.va.gov/for_researchers/measurement/practice/ptsd_measures_4.cfm.

van der Hart O, Horst R (2005) *Special section: Pierre Janet's contributions to traumatic stress theory and research*. Netherlands: Springer. 397–412. ISSN, 1573-6598.

van der Hart O, van der Kolk B, Boon S (1998) Treatment of dissociative disorders. In: *Trauma, Memory and Dissociation* (Bremner JD, Marmar CR, eds). Washington DC: American Psychiatric Press.

van der Kolk B (1988) The biological response to psychic trauma. In: *Post Traumatic Therapy and Victims of Violence* (Ochberg F, ed.). New York: Brunner/Mazel.

van der Kolk B (1991) The biological mechanisms and treatment of intrusions and numbing. *Anxiety Res* 4: 199–212.

van der Kolk B (1994) The body keeps score. *Harvard Rev Psychiatr* 1.

van der Kolk BA (1996) The complexity of adaptation to trauma: Self-regulation, stimulus, descrimination, and characterological development. In: *Traumatic Stress: The effects of overwhelming experiences on mind, body and society* (van der Kolk BA, McFarlane AC, Weisaeth L, eds). New York: Guilford Press.

van der Kolk B (1997) The body keeps score: Memory and the evolving psychobiology of post traumatic stress. In: *Essential Papers on Post Traumatic Stress Disorder* (Horowitz M, ed.). New York: New York University Press.

van der Kolk BA (2005) Developmental trauma disorder. *Psychiatr Ann* 35: 401–408.

van der Kolk BA, Pelcovitz D, Roth S, Mandel FS, McFarlance A, Herman JL (1996) Dissociation, somatization and affect dysregulation: the complexity of adaptation to trauma. *Am J Psychiatry* 153: 83–93.

van der Kolk B, Roth S, Pelcovitz D, Sunday S, Spinazzola J (2005a) Disorders of extreme stress: the empirical foundation of a complex adaptation to trauma. *J Trauma Stress* 18: 389–399.

van der Kolk B, Brown P, van der Hart O (2005b) *Special section: Pierre Janet's contributions to traumatic stress theory and research*. Netherlands: Springer. 376–378. ISSN: 1573-6598.

Violanti JM, Paton D (2006) *Who Gets PTSD? Issues of posttraumatic stress vulnerability*. Springfield, IL: Charles C Thomas.

Volpicelli JR (1987) Uncontrollable events and alcohol drinking. *Br J Addiction* 82: 381–392.

Wald J, Taylor S (2005) Interoceptive exposure therapy combined with trauma related exposure therapy for post-traumatic stress disorder: a case report. *Cogn Behav Ther* 34: 34–40.

Weathers FW, Keane TM (2007) The criterion A problem revisited: Controversies and challenges in defining and measuring psychological trauma. *J Trauma Stress* 20: 107–121.

Weathers FW, Newman E, Blake DD, Nagy LM, Schnurr PP, Kaloupek DG et al. (2004) *Clinical-Administered PTSD scale (CAPS)—Interviewers guide*. Los Angeles: Western Psychological Services.

Weiss D, Marmar C (1997) The Impact of Event Scale—Revised. In: *Assessing Psychological Trauma and PTSD* (Wilson J, Keane T, eds). New York: Guilford Press.

Wilson JP, Keane TM (eds) (1997) *Assessing Psychological Trauma and PTSD*. New York: Guilford Press.

Yehuda R, McFarlane A (1995) Conflicts between current knowledge and posttraumatic stress disorder and its original conceptual basis. *Am J Psychiatry* 152: 1705–1713.

Yehuda R, Wong C (2001) Pathogenesis for posttraumatic stress disorder and acute stress. In: *Textbook of Anxiety Disorders* (Stein DJ, Hollander C, eds). Washington, DC: American Psychiatric Publishers, pp. 374–385.

Yehuda R, McFarlane AC, Shalev AY (1998) Predicting the development of posttraumatic stress disorder from the acute response to a traumatic event. *Biol Psychiatry* 155: 841–843.

Young JE, Klosko JS, Weishaar ME (2003) *Schema Therapy: A Practitioner's Guide*. New York: Guilford Press.

Zalin L (2004) Collaborative care may prevent PTSD, alcohol abuse among trauma survivors. *Health Med* May 5. University of Washington.

Zayfert C (date?) Culturally competent treatment of PTSD in clinical practice:P An ideographic, transcultural approach. *Clin Psych* 150: 68–73.

Zimmerman M, Mattia JI (1999) Is posttraumatic stress disorder under diagnosed in routine clinical settings. *J Nerv Ment Dis* 187: 420–428.

Zlotnick C, Zimmerman M, Wolfsdorf BA, Mattia J (2001) Gender differences in patients with post-traumatic stress disorder in a general psychiatric practice. *Am J Psychiatry* 158: 1923–1925.

Zlotnick C, Franklin CL, Zimmerman M (2002) Is comorbidity of posttraumatic stress disorder and borderline personality disorder related to greater pathology and impairment?. *Am J Psychiatry* 159: 1940–1943.

Chapter 2

The Neurobiology of Posttraumatic Stress

DEFINING THE STRESS SYSTEM

The National Center for PTSD (Friedman, 1997; Friedman et al., 2007) has been a leader in acknowledging that people with posttraumatic stress disorder (PTSD) experience alterations in certain structures in the brain. These alterations influence how the brain processes information, in particular information perceived to be dangerous, thus demonstrating an impact from traumatic experience to both brain and body in the form of psychological problems and physical and/or somatic manifestations. The somatic and psychological manifestations of trauma have long been acknowledged.

Numerous neurobiological systems play a role in the phenomenon of PTSD. When threat is identified, parallel activations of numerous neurobiological systems (brain regions and neurotransmitter systems) participate in the assessment and response to the threat. In some individuals there is a dysregulation of these systems that contributes to or results in the development of PTSD. Research continues to reveal the implications of function and dysfunction, thus offering an increased understanding of what happens when neurobiological systems interpret traumatic events, but much of the information about functional aspects with regard to PTSD remains speculative.

In order to offer optimal treatment to those suffering from posttraumatic stress (PTS) and PTSD a fundamental understanding of neuroanatomy and neurophysiology is required; this focuses on the autonomic nervous system (ANS) and mechanisms such as the hypothalamic–pituitary–adrenal axis (HPA axis) and associated neurotransmitters. The goal is to understand how the neurobiology of stress affects responses by the body and mind regarding memory processes and resolution or reliving of traumatic events. Exploring and understanding the biological processes of and interaction between the environment, underlying genetics and neurobiological processes are crucial to the modulation of the psychopathology associated with PTSD.

The main regions of the brain involved in the fear response are (Vasterling and Brewin, 2005):

- Prefrontal cortex (PFC)
- Amygdala
- Hippocampus
- Dorsal raphe nucleus
- Locus coeruleus.

The neurotransmitter/neurohormone systems involved include:

- HPA axis
- Noradrenergic system
- Serotonergic system
- Neurotransmitter alterations.

In addition, there are numerous neurotransmitter changes or alterations in PTSD. Some of the more notable ones are (Sunada et al., 2004; Devine, 2007; Lukey and Tepe, 2008):

- Serotonin
- Norepinephrine/epinephrine
- Gamma-aminobutyric acid (GABA)
- Corticotropin-releasing hormone (CRH) (formerly known as corticotropin-releasing factor, CRF)
- Acetylcholine
- Cholecystokinin.

These neurotransmitters do not act independently, but rather elicit changes in one another directly, indirectly, and via various feedback mechanisms. For example, epinephrine and norepinephrine are excitatory (activating), while serotonin and GABA are inhibitory neurotransmitters (calm the stress response). This information has become increasingly important to the understanding of experience, symptom presentation and treatment.

The intricacies of the neurobiological response to threat is vast. Aspects of it have been understood for quite some time, and to this knowledge new pieces of information are integrated as researchers attempt to clarify the matrix in a most perplexing and interesting puzzle.

A brief review of the nervous system as it relates the cascade of responses to external and internal stimuli known as the stress response is outlined below. The nervous system informs the body about itself and the external environment and enables the body to respond or react to this information. The nervous system actively identifies, integrates, and interprets incoming sensory stimuli and produces electrochemical impulses that are distributed by the peripheral nerves to generate responses to both the environment and internal conditions.

The subdivisions of the nervous system are shown in Figure 2.1. The central nervous system (CNS) acts as an information center, feeding sensory information from the somatic and autonomic nervous systems. The somatic nervous system obtains information from the external world and generates motor responses to the voluntary muscles allowing movement. The autonomic nervous system (ANS) receives input from and relays output to the internal organs, controlling involuntary functions such as breathing, blood flow, digestion, etc. via

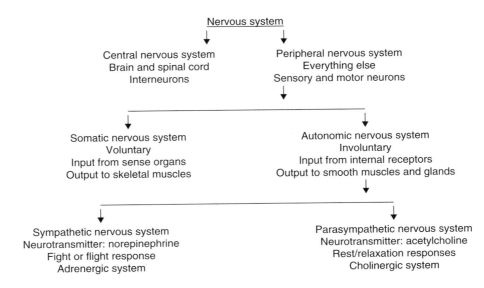

Figure 2.1   Divisions of the nervous system.

neurotransmitters. When the ANS interprets stimuli as a threat it releases chemical messengers, hormones that signal the body to prepare for defensive action of fight or flight. This is accomplished by the activation of the sympathetic branch of the ANS, leading to increased heart rate, decreased blood flow to the periphery of the body, and numerous other changes in physiology. Another ANS reaction releases hormones that heighten the parasympathetic branch of the nervous system, resulting in a freeze response or tonic immobility (Levine, 1997). As Levine points out, "Trauma is in the nervous system, not in the event".

The sympathetic nervous system effects are consistent with adaptive physiological changes necessary to cope with physical threat, whereas the parasympathetic nervous system effects are consistent with regulating processes when the body is not responding to high levels of stress or threats of harm. In general, the sympathetic and parasympathetic nervous system branches of the ANS work in balance with each other. Both branches are always engaged, but depending on the circumstances, one will be more activated than the other. This complementarity between the branches places the other branch in a suppressed mode. Nussbaum (2007) points out that the sympathetic and parasympathetic nervous systems are in constant complementarity. He further asserts that trance states are commonly established by use of yoga or meditation, but can also be the result of parasympathetic dominance when the sympathetic branch of the ANS is intensely aroused by sensory overload. In other words, when the sympathetic system experiences intense stimulation it results in a breakdown of the reciprocity between the two systems and a collapse of sorts into a state of parasympathetic dominance. This pattern of parasympathetic collapse or rebound can result in erasing previously conditioned responses, changes in beliefs, loss of memory, and enhanced suggestibility.

Ultimately, behavior is controlled by the nervous system.

INTERACTIONS BETWEEN THE NERVOUS AND IMMUNE SYSTEMS

The nervous system may affect immune function by directly innervating immune organs via secreted hormones from the pituitary gland and other endocrine organs. Likewise, the immune system cells may influence the nervous system by the secretion of numerous chemical messengers. Among these, cytokines are the best recognized. Traditionally, the brain has been considered "immunologically priviledged" (Byrne and Roberts, 2007). However, it has now been acknowledged that the cells of the immune system may indeed be active in the brain. Consequently, this may be an important factor in many central nervous system diseases.

Dunn (2000, 2005) outlines the evidence regarding the modulation of immune system function by the nervous system. Although alterations in immune response can be conditioned, the immunological specificity of these effects is not clear. "It is possible that at least some of the immunosuppressive effects are from a conditioning of hormone and neurotransmitter secretion (e.g. glucocorticoids or catecholamines)." Activation of the immune system is related to altered neurophysiological, neurochemical, and neuroendocrine activities in brain cells. Although it is accepted that there are immunosuppressive effects associated with glucocorticoids, they may not be the central mechanism of stress suppression upon immune function. According to Chatham et al. (2008), glucocorticoids have inhibitory and suppressive effects in a wide range of specific immune responses.

Tait et al. (2008) state that the communication between the CNS and the immune system are bidirectional. The ANS works in tandem with the HPA axis (via neurotransmitters and neuropeptides) to modulate inflammatory events. In turn, the immune system activates the CNS to coordinate negative feedback mechanisms that keep the immune system in check. Dysregulation of these actions are a likely contributor to psychiatric and somatic pathology.

The immune system protects against extrinsic pathogens and intrinsic cellular/tissue pathological changes resulting in alterations. It has inherent factors and components that act rapidly and non-specifically and adaptive components which act specifically but require time to respond. There has been considerable evidence indicative of immune system signaling and activation communicated to the nervous system (Oh et al., 2002; Webster et al., 2002; Steinman, 2004).

Glucocorticoids promote survival by mobilizing and directing bodily resources. According to Raison and Miller (2003) neuroendocrine studies offer evidence of insufficient glucocorticoid signaling in stress-related neuropsychiatric disorders. Impaired feedback of stress responses such as immune activation (inflammation) may contribute to stress-related immune pathology. This stress-related pathology includes behavior, insulin sensitivity, bone metabolism, and acquired immune responses.

Some researchers (McEwen et al., 1997; McEwen and Seeman, 1999; Sapolsky et al., 2000) take the evolutionary view that decreased glucocorticoid signaling may promote immune preparedness and increase arousal. Glucocorticoids bestow longer term stress-related benefits by shaping and ultimately restraining stress-related physiological processes. This would include early innate immune responses (inflammation), activation of the sympathetic nervous system, and stimulation of the CRH pathway, all of which are capable of producing negative health outcomes. Thus, the very processes to which they initially contribute, i.e. prolonged activation of the stress response, might cause illness under conditions in which glucocorticoid signaling is insufficient. Therefore, even when there is glucocorticoid hypersecretion, there can be glucocorticoid insufficiency when reduced glucocorticoid sensitivity in pertinent target tissues outweighs surplus circulating hormone.

Research suggests that alterations in neurotransmitter-linked signal transduction pathways that regulate glucocorticoid receptor function may play a part in the decreased glucocorticoid receptor signaling in the pathogenesis of psychiatric disorders such as major depression and PTSD. Cortisol, the most important glucocorticoid, supports and regulates a variety of homeostatic, cardiovascular, metabolic, and immunological functions, making it essential to life (Raison and Miller, 2003).

Many autoimmune diseases and disease states of chronic inflammation are associated with alterations in the complex interactions between the endocrine, nervous, and immune systems. Inflammatory disorders associated with glucocorticoid resistance may be a demonstration of the contributing factor related to the development of glucocorticoid/autoimmune diseases (Silverman et al., 2008).

There is a proliferation of literature on the impact of stress on depression, anxiety, insomnia, chronic pain, metabolic syndrome, essential hypertension, type 2 diabetes, atherosclerosis (cardiovascular consequences), osteoporosis, allergies, chronic fatigue syndrome, autoimmune inflammatory diseases, organ systems, reproduction, etc. (Chrousos and Kino, 2007). While the mechanisms are not fully understood, researchers continue to add to the body of knowledge on this topic.

THE HYPOTHALAMIC–PITUITARY–ADRENAL AXIS (HPA AXIS)

The HPA axis, also known as the limbic–hypothalamic–adrenal axis (LHPA axis), in conjunction with other systems, coordinates the response to environmental stress or threat. Studies suggest that the interactions between the HPA axis and other neurotransmitters, such as serotonin and norepinephrine, may provide the neurobiological substrate or circuit that affects the mediation of impact of stress (Lopez, 2004). The secretion of the end-product of the HPA axis, cortisol, is controlled within an optimal time-integrated narrow range by an elaborate negative feedback system.

The HPA axis is involved in the neurobiology of mood disorders and functional illnesses including anxiety disorders, bipolar disorder, insomnia, PTSD, attention deficit hyperactivity disorder (ADHD), major depressive disorder, burnout, chronic fatigue syndrome, fibromyalgia, irritable bowel syndrome, and alcoholism (Pariante, 2003). This is not only important to the clinical understanding of human experience but in developing an understanding of the mechanisms that underlie new medications and other potential treatments.

THE ANATOMY OF THE HPA AXIS

The HPA axis is a major part of the neuroendocrine system that controls reactions to stress and regulates body processes. The key elements of the HPA axis structure are as follows (LeDoux, 2003; Pariante, 2003; Englemann et al., 2004; Kabbaj, 2004; Douglas, 2005):

- Amygdala—involved in signaling the cortex about significant external motivational stimuli for responding to fear, reward, etc. Studies on fear conditioning concludes that the amygdala plays a critical role in linking external stimuli to defense responses.

- Hypothalamus—regulates the ANS by hormone production and release. As a result, it affects and regulates blood pressure, heart rate, hunger, thirst, sexual arousal, and the sleep/wake cycle.

- Thalamus—considered to be the "relay station" of the cerebral cortex.

- Cingulate gyrus—involved in autonomic functions associated with regulating heart rate, blood pressure, cognitive functions, and attentional functions.

- Fornix—carries signals from the hippocampus to the mammillary bodies (important for the formation of memory) and the septal nuclei (plays a role in reward and reinforcement and receives connections from the amygdala, hypothalamus, thalamus and hippocampus as well).

- Pituitary gland—"the master gland". It secretes hormones that regulate homeostasis. The pituitary provides a connection between the brain and the periphery.

- Hippocampus—plays a critical part in learning and memory (the formation of long-term memory and important to short-term memory as well). In addition, it records in memory the spatial and temporal dimensions of experience. It functions in the categorization and storage of incoming stimuli in memory. Therefore, a decrease in hippocampal function (i.e. dysfunction in cortisol/negative feedback loop) would lower or diminish these senses and an increase in cortisol would keep the person vigilant most of the time.

Central to the function of the HPA axis are two critical feedback loops:

- Cortisol, produced in the cortex region of the adrenal gland, negatively feeds back to inhibit both the hypothalamus and the pituitary gland. The result is a reduction in the secretion of corticotropin-releasing hormone (CRH) and vasopressin. It also directly decreases the cleavage of proopiomelanocortin into adrenocorticotropic hormone (ACTH) and β-endorphins.

- Epinephrine and norepinephrine are produced in the medulla region of the adrenal gland as the result of sympathetic stimulation and the local effects of cortisol (upregulation enzymes to make epinephrine/norepinephrine). Epinephrine and norepinephrine positively feed back to the pituitary and increase the breakdown of proopiomelanocortin into ACTH and β-endorphins.

ROUTE OF ACTION

CRH and vasopressin (a water conservation hormone/diuretic) are released and transported to the anterior pituitary. There, CRH and vasopressin work synergistically to stimulate the secretion of stored ACTH. ACTH is transported by blood to the adrenal cortex, thus stimulating the biosynthesis of corticosteroids such as cortisol from cholesterol. In the brain, cortisol (stress hormone) acts on two types of receptors: mineralcorticoid receptors and glucocorticoid receptors. A significant target of glucocorticoids is the hippocampus (a major controlling center of the HPA axis) (LeDoux, 2003; Englemann et al., 2004; Kabbaj, 2004; Douglas, 2005).

- The pituitary provides a connection between the brain and the periphery
- The brain and pituitary are linked by a direct pathway and an indirect pathway
- Hormone release is determined by a balance between stimulatory drive and inhibitory (glucocorticoid-mediated) negative feedback
- Differences in feedback efficacy explain individual differences in stress-related pathology.

HPA FUNCTION

The release of CRH from the hypothalamus is influenced by (1) stress/blood levels of cortisol and (2) the sleep–wake cycle. In a healthy individual, the level of cortisol rises quickly after wakening (reaching a peak in 30–45 minutes). It then gradually decreases during the course of the day. In the late afternoon cortisol levels rise again and then fall in the late evening, reaching a low point in the middle of the night.

Connections between the anatomical structures of the brain such as the amygdala, hypothalamus, and hippocampus facilitate the activation of the HPA axis. Sensory information arrives at the amygdala, is processed, and is projected to other areas of the brain which are involved in responses to fear. At the hypothalamus, fear-signaling impulses activate the sympathetic nervous system and the systems that modulate the HPA axis. The HPA axis together with the sympathetic nervous system connects the brain with the periphery of the body.

Any stress lasting longer than a few minutes results in increased levels of cortisol being released from the adrenal cortex. The release of cortisol is controlled by the paraventricular nucleus (PVN) of the hypothalamus, where CRH is released in response to stress. CRH then acts on the pituitary gland, stimulating the release of ACTH, which in turn causes approximately 15 minutes of sustained release of cortisol from the adrenal cortex. The prolonged release of ACTH causes the adrenal gland to increase in size (possibly in response to an increased demand for cortisol), whereas long-term ACTH deficiency results in a decrease in size. It is this combined hormonal system of CRH–ACTH–cortisol that is referred to as the HPA axis. Positive and negative feedback occurs at various neurological sites to ensure that cortisol production remains within certain limits, but it is also influenced by the demand presented by stress level. Glucocorticoid negative feedback serves to inhibit further activation of the HPA axis (LeDoux, 2003; Herman, 2007; Milkulincer et al., 2007; Sbarra et al., 2008).

It is the increased production of cortisol in the adrenal cortex that mediates the alarm reactions to stress. It facilitates an adaptive phase of a "general adaption syndrome" in which alarm reactions (including the immune response) are suppressed. This allows the body to attempt to act in defense against fear or threat of harm.

- Atrophy of the hippocampus resulting from exposure to extreme stress is believed to be caused by prolonged exposure to high concentrations of glucocorticoids.
- Deficiencies of the hippocampus may be associated with reducing the memory resources available to aid in the formulation of appropriate reactions to stress (associated with the hippocampus role in learning and memory).

As can be seen, the HPA axis is a complex set of interactions between the hypothalamus, pituitary gland and the adrenal glands. This complex communication system is responsible for effectively managing stress by regulating the production of cortisol, neurotransmitters, and key hormones. The HPA axis participates in the regulation of:

- Body temperature
- Immune function
- Digestion
- Mood
- Reproductive function
- Energy utilization.

It is also responsible for:

- Processing incoming sensory information about the external world and state of the body
- Comparing it with expectation about good, bad, punishment, reward, or neutrality
- Effective changes in both behavior and the internal environment via the ANS.

In relation to trauma, the HPA axis has three primary functions (van der Kolk and Saporta, 1991):

1. To guide the emotions that stimulate the behavior needed for self-preservation and survival of the species. A menu of complex behaviors includes:
   - Feeding
   - Fighting
   - Fleeing
   - Reproduction
   - Assigning meaning, truth, and free-floating feelings of significance to experiences.

2. To process memories (most likely explains the memory disturbances which follow trauma). The amygdala associates the quality of experience to memories (not the content, but the sensual/emotional experience of feelings). Was it a good, bad, or fear-provoking experience? In other words, motivation.

3. To control "kindling", associated with repeated traumatization (or when one traumatic experience is followed by intrusive re-experiencing). Kindling may lead to lasting neurological and behavioral (characterological) changes mediated by alterations in the temporal lobe. It may also be associated with the frequent identification of neurological soft signs in trauma victims.

The HPA axis receives and deseminates information from numerous sources. One way to conceptualize it is by the general neurocircuit pathway shown in Figure 2.2. The neurocircuits controlling the HPA responses (Dunn et al., 2004; Bremner, 2005; Herman, 2007; Medina, 2008) allow the convergence of information from multiple sources.

The amygdala mediates states of increased arousal, including negative emotions, the fear response and physical symptoms associated with autonomic arousal. From the sensory fibers to the thalamus, the information then relays the stimulus-related signal to the amygdala. The amygdala serves as the center of integration for the initiation of autonomic and behavioral

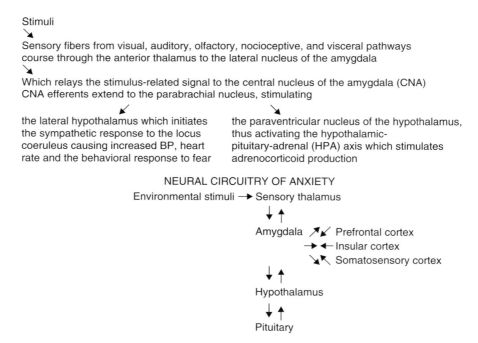

Figure 2.2 General HPA response pathway.

fear responses. As can be seen in Figure 2.2, once the stimuli is received by the sensory thalamus and various cortex areas there are reciprocal connections between the amygdala, sensory thalamus, prefrontal cortex, insular cortex and somatosensory cortex. These reciprocal connections allow for two paths of fear response and deficits:

1. The rapid, less fine-tuned path needed for response to immediate threat. This is activated via direct input from the sensory thalamus.

2. The slower, more finely tuned path which allows for valuable cortical assessments of threat-related information. This is made possible by the thalamo-cortico-amygdalo input.

Either or both of these pathways might be what underlies pathological anxiety.

Acute anxiety states occur when the circuits that are associated with emotion, mediated through the amygdala, override the prefrontal cortex behavioral controls. PTSD appears to be evidence of this, whereby protracted "extinction" after fear conditioning is seen. What starts as stress or anxiety and then escalates may in some way impair this mechanism, resulting in exaggerated responses. Chronic or acute/severe stress can result in structural and functional damage to certain brain regions or stress-induced brain damage (including the hippocampus). It is possible that if the hippocampus is damaged then the normal negative feedback loop of the HPA axis is disrupted, resulting in excessive exposure to cortisol. In addition, dysregulation in the processing of sensory input and memory are likely contributors to the physiological pathology of PTSD, such as dissociation and hypervigilance (Nutt and Malizia, 2004). With regard to the issue of extinction, Mueller et al. (2008) states that it is not known whether norepinephrine is necessary for extinction learning, but it is known that emotional arousal strengthens memory. The stress-related hormone norepinephrine enhances associations between sensory stimuli and fear-inducing events.

FACTORS REGULATING THE HPA AXIS

As illustrated in Figure 2.3, two factors regulate the HPA axis: (1) circadian rhythm and (2) stress. While the HPA axis has always been identified as the stress system of the body, ultimately controlling cortisol and other stress hormones, current research reveals a more global function. It is now thought to be more like the body's energy regulator because it is responsible for regulating all the hormones, the activity of the nervous system and the expenditure of energy. Hormone release is determined by a balance between stimulatory drive and inhibitory negative feedback. Hormones circulate in the blood and are relatively easy to

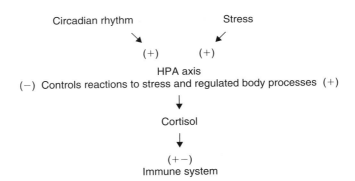

Figure 2.3   Factors regulating the HPA axis. *Adapted from Nutt and Malizia (2004), Cannistraro and Rauch (2003), Milkulincer et al. (2007), Etkin and Wager (2007), and Sbarra et al. (2008).*

measure. The release of hormones by the hypothalamus is regulated by neural stimuli. It often follows a periodic rhythm (the blood levels of these hormones fluctuate throughout the day) some of which appear to be intrinsic, independent of the environment, or linked to a 24-hour cycle (circadian). In addition, neuroimmune interactions, for example, some cytokines (immune system-derived hormones) potently activate the HPA axis. Modulation and termination of the HPA response to stress occurs through the process of glucocorticoid negative feedback. The end-products of the HPA activation—glucocorticoids— redirect physiological resources to meet the real or perceived challenge. They also modulate the immune system.

Various physical and mental symptoms are associated with burnout of the HPA axis systems or pathways (Herman, 2007).

Glucocorticoids have effects on various body systems, including the following:

- Carbohydrate metabolism—Overall, glucocorticoids increase blood glucose levels and glucogenesis (body production of new glucose for energy), and decrease glucose utilization

- Protein metabolism—Overall, glucocorticoids increase catabolism (protein breakdown, muscle wasting). They also decrease extrahepatic amino acid utilization and increase glucogenesis

- Fat metabolism—Glucocorticoids increase lipolysis (fat breakdown to be used as energy) and stimulate fat redistribution

- Circulatory—Glucocorticoids help to maintain extracellular fluid volume and vascular integrity. They also stimulate red blood cell production

- Central nervous system—Glucocorticoids modulate mood, appetite, sleep, and sensory perception. They also have a negative feedback effect on HPA axis activity

- Immune system—Glucocorticoids are anti-inflammatory and inhibit cytokine production. They also kill lymphocyte production (apoptosis is programmed cell death), cause a reduction in thymus size, and stimulate neutrophil migration from bone marrow to blood.

PATHOLOGY OF STRESS

The pathological consequences of chronic stress are associated with:

- The gastrointestinal system
- The cardiovascular system
- Energy metabolism
- The immune system
- The reproductive system
- Bone density
- Skeletal muscles
- General growth

- Physiological function
- Cognition.

NEUROACTIVE STEROIDS

Neuroactive steroids have been a particular focus of researchers trying to make sense of the puzzle of HPA functioning and its relationship to the development of and chronic course of PTSD. Most of the interest in neuroactive steroids has been on the impact of cortisol on frontal cortex functioning. Some researchers (Vasterling and Brewin, 2005; Cicchetti and Cohen, 2006) state that it appears that abnormal levels of cortisol in the CNS may be a contributor to deficits in cognitive functioning in those presenting with PTSD.

PTSD is marked by periods of symptom quiescence highlighted by acute episodes of symptom exacerbation. This requires that functional brain studies be conducted in both a resting and a symptomatic state. Researchers continue to piece together the intricacies of the complex HPA axis, neurochemical alterations/influences, and hippocampal size in association with PTSD and the premorbid physiological factors that could play a role in the predisposition to PTSD development. The following are some examples:

Kellner et al. (2002)
- Low plasma cortisol concentrations in spite of increased CRH levels.
- Atrial natriuretic peptide (ANP) may offer some insight into the neuroendocrine pathophysiology of PTSD. It is a neuromodulator with anti-anxiety effects which inhibits HPA activity at multiple levels.
- Patients with chronic PTSD and control subjects were given $100 \mu g$ of human CRH. The following results were found during basal conditions after CRH stimulation:
  - The CRH was indistinguishable
  - Basal ANP levels were significantly lower in PTSD patients in comparison to control subjects
  - No significant difference in basal CRH-stimulated ACTH or cortisol parameters could be observed
  - Systolic and diastolic blood pressure were baseline after CRH was significantly elevated in PTSD patients.
- All group differences remained significant after controlling for basal blood pressure and/or BMI (body mass index).
- Results did not support a role of ANP in abnormal HPA axis regulation in PTSD. However, the persistent low ANP plasma levels in PTSD patients despite elevated blood pressure may serve to facilitate anxiety behavior and have adverse long-term cardiovascular consequences.

Neylan et al. (2005)
- PTSD symptom severity significantly predicted pre-dexamethasone awakening cortisol levels (lower).
- These results replicate previous research indicating a relationship between greater PTSD symptoms and lower levels of basal cortisol on awakening.

Kozaric-Kovacic (2002)

- Thyroid function. Patients with Graves' disease have a higher rate of psychological trauma than the control subjects.
- Modest changes in thyroid hormone levels may have important clinical significance (even though they remain within normal limits) even though a third of the PTSD patients had hormone levels at the upper level of within normal limits. However, one study showed civilians with PTSD had marked reductions in triiodothyronine (T_3), thyroxine (T_4), and thyroid-stimulating hormone (TSH), while another showed no appreciable difference.

Haviland et al. (2006)

- There is a correlation between psychological symptoms and thyroid hormone levels in adolescent girls who have experienced the traumatic stress of sexual abuse.
- The strongest correlation was between free T_3 and PTSD—avoidance/numbing and general distress.
- The next significant correlation was between T_3 and depression, general distress, and PTSD arousal.

Baker et al. (2002)

- Using a serial cerebrospinal fluid (CSF) sampling technique, combat veterans with PTSD were found to have high basal CSF CRH concentrations and normal 24-hour urinary-free cortisol.

Gao (2004)

- Some studies have found that there is an association between poor physical health and PTSD.
- It has been found that PTSD patients maintain a high level of opiates (asset in pain relief) even after the danger has passed, which may be associated with dissociative disorder (that is also observed in patients with PTSD).
- It appears that levels of cortisol released from the adrenal cortex during stress, preparing the individual to deal with the stress factors and ensure that the brain receives adequate energy sources, are lower than normal.

Sapolsky et al. (1985)

- Cumulative exposure to corticosterone over the lifespan may be a cause of neuronal loss.
- Prolonged glucocorticoid exposure reduces hippocampal neuron number (thus accelerating neuronal loss as part of the aging process).

Pitman et al. (2006)

- Studied Vietnam veterans, including twin brothers (one who served in Vietnam and one who did not).

- Vietnam veterans who had PTSD had a smaller hippocampus than those who did not have PTSD.
- The identical twin who did not serve in Vietnam also had a smaller hippocampus (it was expected that identical twins share similar physiology).
- It was concluded that a smaller hippocampus may be a predisposing factor for the development of PTSD.

San Juan (2006)
- Veterans with combat esposure and PTSD are more likely to have an elevated heart rate when startled and possibly smaller hippocampal volumes.

Rasmusson et al. (2003)
- Reviewed a number of HPA axis studies on urine cortisol levels with the following inconsistent results which demonstrate how challenging and complex it is for researchers trying to clarify the consequences of abnormalities and dysfunction.
- In male veterans with PTSD there were mixed results with low to high levels of 24-hour urine cortisol levels in comparison to combat veterans and healthy male controls without PTSD.
- In premenopausal women with children who have PTSD there was increased 24-hour urinary cortisol output related to increased pituitary adrenocorticotropic hormone and adrenal cortisol activity.
- In postmenopausal female Holocaust survivors with PTSD there was decreased 24-hour urinary cortisol output (as in a study of male Holocaust survivors). Unfortunately, there was inadequate control for nicotine, psychotropic medications, and alcohol use by these subjects which could have confounded the results.

Other studies of note include that by Witchel et al. (1997) who found that genetic factors may contribute to variation in results. For example, functional mutations in the 21-hydroxylase gene (often present in some ethnic groups) is related to decreased cortisol synthesis. Baker et al. (2005) found that CSF cortisol levels in male veterans with chronic PTSD were high even when their urinary cortisol levels were not different than the healthy male controls. This implies that urinary cortisol levels may not always adequately reflect the level of glucocorticoid exposure experienced in the CNS. Yehuda (2002) reviewed the evidence of both hyperactive or sensitized cortisol activity in subjects with PTSD.

Some researchers have studied the release of DHEA (dehydropiandrosterone) by the adrenal gland. This steroid is secreted intermittently and in synchrony with cortisol in response to changes in ACTH levels (Compagnone and Mellon, 2000).

Rasmusson et al. (2004)
- Found that DHEA increased in response to stimulation of the adrenal gland during an ACTH stimulation in premenopausal women with PTSD.
- The magnitude of the DHEA response was inversely related to PTSD symptoms (measured by clinician-administered PTSD Scale (CAPS)). In other words, there was a negative relationship between DHEA reactivity and avoidance or hyperarousal symptoms of PTSD.

- This negative relationship between adrenal capacity for DHEA release and PTSD symptoms may be an indication that DHEA provides resistance to some of the disabling/decompensating effects of traumatic stress exposure.

Morgan et al. (2004)
- Demonstrated a negative relationship between the ratio of plasma DHEA/cortisol levels and dissociation. There was also a positive relationship between DHEA/cortisol ratio and behavioral performance during severe/acute stress in healthy military personnel undergoing survival training.
- Contrasting this, low levels of DHEA alone or in relation to cortisol have repeatedly been demonstrated to be associated with depression, while DHEA alone has been shown to be effective in the treatment of refractory major depression associated with deficiencies in frontal lobe processing.

Strous et al. (2003)
- DHEA was found to decrease negative symptoms of schizophrenia without demonstrating a decline in positive symptoms when administered as part of the routine medication regimen.

Sondergaard et al. (2002)
- Kosovo refugees demonstrated increased DHEA levels over several months in association with the development of PTSD.

Morfin and Starka (2001)
- Elevated DHEA release following trauma exposure with natural extinction or during exposure therapy may promote extinction as well as prevent future disruption of frontal lobe function by fluctuation in catecholamine by trauma-related cue exposure.
- Another possibility is that "antiglucocorticoid" effects asserted by DHEA in numerous tissue sites (including brain), may specifically target the frontal cortex.

Spivak et al. (2000)
- Israeli combat veterans with PTSD demonstrated higher levels of DHEA than their counterparts without PTSD.

Researchers have also looked at neuroactive steroids that deserve acknowledgment for their potential role in HPA axis impact upon the frontal cortex.

Compagnone and Mellon (2000)
- Some adrenally derived neuroactive steroids are able to modulate GABA receptors and enhance chloride movement into neurons. The most potent are allotetrahydro-deoxycorticosterone and allopregnanolone.

Rasmusson et al. (2005)

- Allopregnanolone levels in the CSF of premenopausal women with PTSD in the follicular phase of the menstrual cycle are about 50% lower than those in their healthy non-traumatized female counterparts.

Allopregnanolone is released by the adrenal gland in response to stress and is believed to provide delayed negative feedback inhibition of the HPA axis and promote anxiolytic and anesthetic effects. Therefore, a decrease in this neuroactive steroid may prolong activation of the HPA axis and promote enhancement of monoamine effects in the frontal lobe and amygdala by DHEA and cortisol.

Research conducted by provoking PTSD symptoms using trauma-related psychosocial cues is an important tool. However, to ensure validity of such studies requires that measurements include an accurate baseline prior to precipitating symptoms via exposure.

GENETIC VARIATIONS

Researchers have also studied the genetic variations associated with the neurobiological stress response.

Oswald et al. (2004)

- Gene polymorphism, whether genetic or stress-induced, produces variation in gene regulation and there is potential for it to impact adrenal neuroactive steroid synthesis or degradation.

Over 65 different functional mutations of the 21-hydroxylase gene that affect cortisol production have been identified.

Polymorphism is also known to affect other HPA axis-related genes, such as the catechol-O-methyltransferase gene, with the outcome being to enhance ACTH or cortisol responses to stress. Other genetic mutations that have been identified are:

- Angiotensin I-converting enzyme (Baghai et al., 2002)
- Glucocorticoid receptor gene (Wust et al., 2004)
- CRH or CRH receptor gene (Challis et al., 2004)
- ACTH gene (Slawik et al., 2004)

As research continues, more genes are being identified and their effects on neuroactive steroids assessed. It is hoped that this focus of research will render information that will lead to the development of clinical strategies for the treatment and prevention of PTSD.

As can be seen in Figure 2.4, stress increases the generation and release of CRH in the hypothalamus. CRH makes its way to the anterior pituitary with the resulting genesis and release of ACTH, which stimulates the production of glucocorticoids from the adrenal cortex. The consequence of glucocorticoid release is to signal a variety of metabolic changes associated with response to environmental stress/threat. In addition, they provide negative feedback at several levels of the HPA axis, acting to terminate the stress response and thus maintain homeostasis.

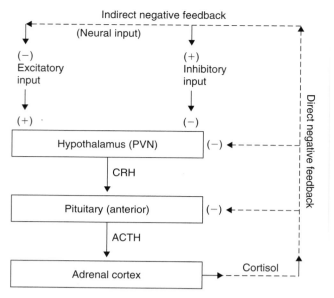

Figure 2.4 Positive and negative feedback in the HPA axis. *Adapted from Seasholtz* (2008).

NEUROIMAGING

There is growing evidence from neuroimaging (MRI, PET, SPECT, fMRI, VBM) studies to suggest that brain pathology and neurobiological changes may play an important role in the etiology of PTSD. Neuroimaging has advanced our understanding of the significant structural and functional changes that occur in patients with PTSD. Several studies demonstrate involvement of the hippocampus in chronic PTSD, particularly the structural deficits of the hippocampus (smaller volume).

The clinical features of anxiety disorders will continue to be a validating source of information when it comes to understanding psychological and emotional dysfunctions associated with anxiety management. The use of neuroimaging will likely be related to the identification of new targets for therapeutic intervention which correlate to the identified functional changes associated with structural changes. The converging pieces of evidence about the potential sites of pathology in anxiety disorders include the following (LeDoux et al., 1988; Davis, 1992; LeDoux, 1996; van der Kolk et al., 1996; Rauch et al., 1998; Hull, 2002; Cannistraro and Rauch, 2003; Nutt and Malizia, 2004; Mueller et al., 2008):

- The reciprocal connections between the amygdala and sensory thalamus/cortex.

- Hyperresponsive amygdala operating in the context of attenuated negative feedback from the medial prefrontal cortex and the anterior cingulate gyrus.

- Hippocampal processing of contextual information regarding safe versus dangerous contexts may have a temporizing influence on the fear response (pathological anxiety versus overgeneralization).

- Lesions in the medial prefrontal cortex significantly interfere with normal extinction, which may lead to pathological anxiety and therefore, an inability to efficiently modify previously experienced associations between threatening and non-threatening cues.

- Evidence from treatment and neuroimaging studies suggest that separate diagnostic categories may have overlapping pathology, and those within a category may have significantly different mechanisms.

- PTSD may be the result of amygdala hyperresponsivity to threat-related stimuli either being exacerbated or inadequately modulated by the ventral medial prefrontal cortex and hippocampus.

- Reduced gray matter volume in the the left hippocampus, left anterior cingulate cortex, and bilateral cingulars.

- Structural abnormalities in the insular cortex.

- Decreased activity at Broca's area.

Currently, anxiety disorders are identified in accordance with the presented constellation of symptoms. As research continues to reveal structural and functional deficits, exacerbations and potentiations of clear and distinct pathophysiology models of anxiety disorders will be developed.

Unlike other anxiety disorders, PTSD provides a clear model of the classical conditioning of fear which emphasizes the amygdala and its interactions with limbic and prelimbic structures. It is not known whether this pathophysiology is a direct path, a result of hyperresponsivity, inadequate modulation, or a deficiency in the extinction response (hippocampal dysfunction or influence of norepinephrine). Other factors may also play a role, such as substance abuse, years of education and gender. However, what is certain is that neuroimaging studies (Nutt and Malizia, 2004) demonstrate significant neurobiologic changes in three areas of the brain with PTSD: hippocampus, amygdala, and the medial frontal cortex. The central PTSD symptoms of exaggerated startle response and flashbacks appear to be related to a failure of higher brain regions (hippocampus and medial frontal cortex), and the amygdala appears to be hyperreactive to trauma-related environmental stimuli.

Whatever the causal biological influences, breaking the cycle of triggers is of primary importance. One way to think of PTSD is that the brain cannot tell the difference between the real traumatic event of the past and the reliving of it. The person becomes overly attentive to interoceptive reminders of the past threat and loses the connection to the exteroceptive cues (the five senses) that appraise the current environment. As a result, the body and brain continue to respond as if it were under threat of the traumatic event. Therefore, this response elicits the body preparedness for dealing with the trauma even though the traumatic event has ended.

People with PTSD suffer the experience of a vicious cycle of hyperarousal (autonomic nervous system activation). Hyperarousal can become chronic or can be triggered acutely. Physically the result is:

- Anxiety

- Stress

- Sleep disturbance

- Difficulty with concentration and attention

- Fatigue/exhaustion

- Weakness

- Muscle pain and stiffness.

According to van der Kolk et al. (1996) this means that objects, sounds, color, movement, etc. that would normally be considered insignificant become associated with the trauma and are translated into external triggers that are experienced internally as danger. This experience is associated with a feeling of confusion when the recognition of external safety is incongruent with the inner experience of threat.

The National Comorbidity Survey 1990–1992 (Kessler et al., 1995) asserts that traumatic events cause lasting changes in the nervous system. These changes include:

- Abnormal secretions of stress hormones
- Changes in the amygdala and hippocampus (parts of the limbic system linked to fear and memory)
- Impacts on parts of the brain that govern speech and language (as evidenced by PET scans of trauma survivors).

HPA AXIS DYSREGULATION

Herman (2007) states that chronic stress-induced activation of the HPA axis is associated with neuroplastic changes at multiple neural levels, and it is likely that these stress-induced alterations (like PTSD) serve as a major influence in HPA axis abnormalities.

PTSD involves dysregulation of the HPA axis, thyroid, and endogenous opioid systems. The intense stress in PTSD is accompanied by the release of endogenous, stress-responsive hormones, such as cortisol, epinephrine, norepinephrine, vasopressin, oxytocin, and endogenous opioids. Norepinephrine is critical in alerting a person to deal with threat and initiating fight or flight behaviors. Studies of people with PTSD have demonstrated a compensatory downregulation of adrenergic receptors in response to increased norepinephrine levels. The serotonin system also plays a role in modulating noradrenergic responsiveness to arousal. Low serotonin in animals is related to an inability to modulate arousal, exemplified by an exaggerated startle and increased arousal in response to novel stimuli, handling, or pain.

Chronic physiologic arousal leads to reduced regulation of autonomic reactions to internal and external stimuli and decreased capacity to respond normally to behavioral arousal or external stressors. To compensate for the chronic hyperarousal, the person shuts down behaviorally, avoiding stimuli reminiscent of the trauma, and has numbing and defensive emotional responses. People with chronic PTSD develop numbing of responsiveness to the environment and hyperarousal in response to both specific reminders of the trauma and neutral but intense stimuli such as loud noises (Pissiota et al., 2002; Yehuda et al., 2004; Devine, 2007; Herman, 2007; Cullinan et al., 2008; Mueller et al., 2008).

In summary, PTSD is associated with dysregulation of the following neurochemical systems:

- Norepinephrine
- HPA axis
- Thyroid
- Endogenous opioids
- Serotonin.

Upgraded catecholamine levels, which are typical of the fight or flight responses, are balanced by downregulated adrenergic receptors.

Chronic physiologic arousal leads to:

- Reduced regulation of autonomic reactions to internal and external stimuli
- Decreased capacity to respond normally to emotional arousal

- Decreased capacity to respond normally to external stressors
- Hyperarousal
- Hyperstartle
- Disturbance of the appraisal process, learning, and memory.

The consequences of PTSD are numerous. For example, distortion of the normal appraisal process causes people with PTSD to see the world differently. It also affects memory. Interestingly, while some people cannot forget their traumatic experiences, others cannot remember them.

Models of learning and memory can be used to understand the symptoms of PTSD, which form the basis of behavioral treatments. The body remembers stress. The brain structures that are central to memory storage are the amygdala and hippocampus:

• Amygdala	is activated by the external/environmental threat and makes an interpretation with regard to the quality of the threat
	does not store memory
	processes the memory so that it can be stored as implicit memory in the brain's cortex
• Hippocampus	does not store memory
	makes cognitive sense of memories as per their proper perspective and timeline in the course of a person's life
	processes information so that it can be recorded as explicit memory in the brain's cortex

The activity of the hippocampus may be suppressed by stress hormones. If this happens, the traumatic event is prevented from becoming an explicit memory and the unresolved memory of trauma may remain in the implicit memory system. This is the mechanism that underlies PTSD. These images, emotions, and somatic sensations can all be provoked, but without explicit memory they cannot be articulated or understood. This is the flashback experience, whereby the patient experiences episodes of reliving the traumatic event as if it were happening now. The body and brain are not differentiating the past from the present.

HIPPOCAMPAL CHANGES ASSOCIATED WITH PTSD

The hippocampus is the evaluation center involved in behavioral inhibition, obsessional thinking, scanning, and construction of a spatial map. Once the experience has been catalogued, the hippocampus disengages from active control of behavior. External stress increases corticosterone production which decreases the firing rate of the hippocampus.

The hippocampus deals with short-term memory, and the encoding and retrieval of long-term memory (LeDoux, 1996). Changes in the hippocampus could be the result of hormones flooding the brain during and after a stressful episode.

Two studies of brain changes associated with abuse, used magnetic resonance imaging (MRI) to measure hippocampal volumes. Stein et al. (1997) found that the most significant deficits were on the left side (5%) and that PTSD and dissociative symptoms were more pronounced in abuse survivors with a smaller hippocampus. Those born with a smaller hippocampus could be more vulnerable to acquiring PTSD or dissociation if subjected to extreme stress. Bremner (2001), on the other hand, found a 13% reduction in left hippocampal volume and impaired short-term verbal memory. The author concluded that this could be the time frame over which the hippocampus organizes experiences into how a person views and interprets their life experiences.

GENDER CONSIDERATIONS

In general, there are many more similarities than differences in biologic abnormalities among males and females with PTSD. In other words, males and females both qualitatively demonstrate functional and structural neural changes associated with PTSD, but these differ quantitatively. And even though there are some differences in the stress response, many differences are not changed or amplified in those with PTSD. Brady (2001) noted that hippocampal volume is decreased more in men than in women and that women with PTSD have less memory loss and impairment in cognitive function than men with PTSD.

In general, people with PTSD have lower levels of circulating cortisol. In a study using victims of motor accidents, low cortisol levels immediately after the accident were associated with the development of PTSD and high levels of cortisol were associated with depression. Studies using the dexamethasone suppression test (DST) demonstrated that this decrease in cortisol with the PTSD subjects is a result of enhanced sensitivity of the glucocorticoid receptors to negative feedback for circulating cortisol at the level of the pituitary.

Yehuda and co-workers (Yehuda, 1999; Yehuda and Wong, 2001) state that biologic systems altered in PTSD may be modulated by sex hormones. This could account for the increased severity of response of the HPA axis to stress in women in comparison with that in men. Ogilvie and Review (1997) cited research with animals demonstrating change in the stress response during different phases of the menstrual cycle. Specifically, the HPA axis stress response during the follicular phase of the cycle is lower than that during the luteal phase.

Other studies have noted that:

- In individuals with PTSD and depression there is an enhanced sensitivity of the glucocorticoid receptors at the hippocampal level.

- Women with and without PTSD had lower baseline cortisol levels than men with and without PTSD.

- There was some gender difference in DST response indicating greater dysregulation/DST suppression of the glucocorticoid receptors in women. Women with PTSD were twice as likely to have depression and anxiety disorders compared with men diagnosed with PTSD.

RELATIONSHIP BETWEEN PTSD AND BORDERLINE PERSONALITY DISORDER

The overlap in definition and presentation between PTSD and borderline personality disorder has raised questions about the relationship between these two disorders. Are they separate and distinct variants, or comorbid conditions? Heffenan and Cloitre (2000) conducted a study with an outcome which suggests that PTSD and borderline personality disorder are independent symptom constructs. An additional finding was that those with both PTSD and borderline personality disorder scored higher on several other clinical measures, including anger, anxiety, dissociation, and interpersonal problems. Driessen et al. (2000) hypothesize that patients with borderline personality disorder, who are often victims of early traumatization, have decreased hippocampal and amygdala volumes. It was assumed that the volumes of these brain regions are negatively correlated with both traumatic experiences and neuropsychological deficits. The results of this study on borderline personality disorder patients revealed:

- Hippocampal volumes were 16% smaller and amygdala volume was 8% smaller than in the control subjects.
- The volumes of the hippocampus were negatively correlated with the extent and the duration of self-reported early traumatization only when borderline personality disorder and control subjects were considered together.
- Neuropsychological levels of functioning were associated with the severity of depression.

Considering the information from this research, Becker (2000) states that increased use of the PTSD label for women formerly diagnosed with borderline personality disorder has been helpful from an intervention perspective.

PTSD AND MAJOR DEPRESSION

A distinct similarity between the neurobiology of PTSD and major depression has been noted. Both PTSD and depression are associated with hyperactivity of the HPA axis and the catecholamine/sympathetic nervous system. However, people with PTSD often have normal to low cortisol levels (hypocortisolemia) despite hypersecretion of CRH and a blunted ACTH response to CRH stimulation. An additional difference between PTSD and depression is seen in research indicating cortisol suppression in DST—a test of HPA axis negative feedback—and increased density of glucocorticoid receptors on peripheral lymphocytes. This suggests that hypocortisolemia associated with PTSD is possibly a consequence of an exaggerated HPA axis negative feedback. These findings are in contrast to the research outcome of similar studies on patients with major depression (Newport and Nemeroff, 2000; Yehuda et al., 2004).

NEUROBIOLOGICAL PATHWAYS IN RESPONSE TO STRESS

The neurobiological pathways known to process responses to stress are mapped out in Figure 2.5. When information regarding potential danger is received by the amygdala, the amygdala reacts dramatically, triggering the "fight or flight" mechanism. This reaction pumps epinephrine (adrenaline) and other hormones into the bloodstream so that physiologically the individual can act accordingly to the presented danger. A fraction of a second

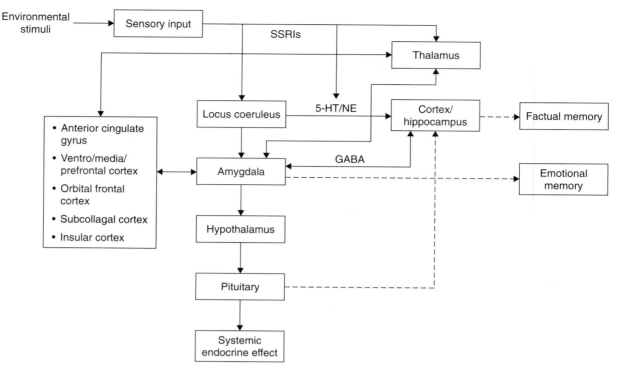

Figure 2.5 Neurobiological pathways that process responses to stress. GABA, gamma-aminobutyric acid; NE, norepinephrine; 5-HT, serotonin; SSRIs, selective serotonin reuptake inhibitors. *Adapted from Nutt and Malizia (2004) and Cannistraro and Rauch (2003).*

later the higher regions of the brain get the signal and begin to sort out whether the danger is real. What is most significant about that delay of a fraction of a second? It is that shard of time that causes a person to experience the associated fear far more potentiated than the coinciding rational response. In addition, because of the manner in which the brain is wired—the nerve signal travels more readily from the amygdala to the higher regions than from the higher regions to the amygdala—the internal alarm is hair triggered, but does not shut down as easily.

In addition to perception of risk, the neglect of probability plays a role in impulses and decision-making. Perception of risk is often functioning at a feelings level rather than a cognitive level. According to Slovic (2002) two systems for analyzing risk exist:

- An automatic, intuitive system

- A cognitive process.

He further states that more often than not people function in the automatic/intuitive system. The advantage is that in dangerous situations the chance of survival is increased by being responsive at the intuitive level due to decreased time associated with intuitive responsiveness versus the time required for thoughtful responsiveness. Fight or flight, engaging in danger or fleeing from it, are constantly in a state of crossed swords. This allows a person to review the cost and benefits of responding to any given situation in association with the short-term risks. When the risk and consequences of the response emerge slowly it is more likely that the analytical system will come into play.

Sunstein (2007) weighs in with a different perspective on the probability of neglect, a cognitive bias, where there is a tendency to disregard probability when making a decision (which is often associated with violating normative rules for decision-making). Under this bias, unfamiliar threats create more distress than familiar threats. This can result in habituation to an unpleasant stimulus. The risk is that the person responds in extremes with too little attentional focus or too much. The probability of neglect is best operationalized in circumstances of terrorism and predictable natural disaster outcomes. People refer to them as "wake up calls" but they are more like a "snooze alarm," where appropriate action is lost from focus and not followed through. It is also commonly seen in health behaviors (like smoking, substance abuse, and obesity).

THE NORADRENERGIC SYSTEM

LOCUS COERULEUS AND NOREPINEPHRINE

According to the National Institutes of Health (2001), a key aspect of acute responses to trauma events is that those with PTSD have a general tendency toward abnormal levels of specific hormones that are involved in the body's protective stress response. When the brain mechanisms associated with protection and survival identify there is danger, there is production of high levels of endogenous opiates. Unfortunately, after the danger has ended, those with PTSD continue to produce increased levels of some hormones, which may result in blunted emotions, and decreased levels of another. For example, cortisol levels are sometimes shown to be at lower levels.

The neurochemical mechanisms that alter the hippocampus under such conditions remain somewhat unclear. The brain response to intense stress is ultimately activated by epinephrine, norepinephrine, cortisol, opiates, and other hormones that are released into the bloodstream. These chemicals alter neuronal connections and mediate psychological reactions.

CRH- and norepinephrine-containing neurons in the brain are activated during stress, and both are associated with the resulting behavioral responses. Norepinephrine neurons in the brainstem can stimulate CRH neurons in the hypothalamic paraventricular nucleus (PVN) to activate the HPA axis, and this can perhaps affect other CRH neurons. CRH-containing neurons in the PVN, amygdala, and other brain areas project to the area of the locus coeruleus.

Anatomically, the locus coeruleus is the core of the physiological arousal mechanism in the CNS (van der Kolk and Saporta, 1991; Herman, 2007). It is the principal source in the CNS of norepinephrine (the neurotransmitter responsible for sending messages to the rest of the brain alerting the preparation for and response to emergencies) and the noradrenergic connection readies the hypothalamus defense mechanism reaction for action. The locus coeruleus is connected by another noradrenergic bundle to the septo-campal system (part of the limbic system involved in the evaluation of incoming stimuli with the general message of "this is important"). Endogenous opioids inhibit firing of the locus coeruleus.

Vasterling and Brewin (2005) state that "central noradrenergic nuclei play an important role in orientation to novel stimuli, alertness, vigilance, selective attention, and cardiovascular responses to life threatening stimuli."

- Drowsiness is associated with a lower rate of locus coeruleus firing.

- Alertness is associated with a higher rate of locus coeruleus firing.

- The locus coeruleus is activated by novel sensory stimuli, and thus orientation directed to novel stimuli. Norepinephrine is directed, selective attention to meaningful stimuli.

Gao (2004) states that:

- Epinephrine, secreted by the adrenal medulla, known as the fight or flight hormone, is responsible for increased metabolism

- Norepinephrine (neurotransmitter), which is released during stress to activate the hippocampus, is responsible for short-term memory and retrieval of long-term memory and is found at higher than normal levels in people with PTSD. This is believed to be why flashbacks are experienced by those with PTSD.

According to Dunn et al. (2004) chronoamperometric research indicates a significant delay in the increase in norepinephrine released, which indicates that the CRH input to locus coeruleus/norepinephrine neurons is an indirect rather than a direct mechanism. The reciprocal interactions that take place between the cerebral norepinephrine and CRH systems have been proposed to create a "feed-forward" loop. It is suggested that a sensitization of such a feed-forward loop may be the foundation, or part of a mechanism, of clinical depression. Twardowska and Rybakowski (1996) found an association between dysfunctions of the HPA axis, depression, and immune system abnormalities. As can be seen, the research is mixed on this hypothesis and studies focused on understanding these mechanisms and associated clinical outcomes continues. Despite increasingly detailed knowledge about each of the components of the HPA axis and the body's stress response, it remains difficult to predict from this information how this network of interactions will perform.

As previously mentioned, epinephrine and norepinephrine, the neurotransmitters released during stress, have numerous functions, such as activating the hippocampus, the brain structure that plays a role in organizing and storing information for long-term memory.

Norepinephrine has numerous modes of action and is thought to be associated with the phenomenon whereby those with PTSD can generally remember emotionally arousing events better than other situations or experiences. When a person is under the extreme stress of a traumatic event, norepinephrine may act longer and more intensely on the hippocampus. This results in the formation of abnormally strong memories that are then experienced as flashbacks or intrusions. Cortisol normally limits norepinephrine activation and when cortisol levels are low it may indicate a significant risk factor for developing PTSD.

The majority of noradrenergic neural cell bodies are found in the locus coeruleus. These neurons process sensory information, thus facilitating anxiety and somatosensory responses (Aston-Jones et al., 1994):

- Cardiovascular
- Neuroendocrine
- Skeletomotor
- Cognitive responses.

In a study on animals, Aston-Jones et al. (1994) reviewed the important role played by central noradrenergic nuclei regarding orientation to novel stimuli, selective attention, alertness, vigilance, and cardiovascular responses when an organism is confronted by life-threatening stimuli. The locus coeruleus response is associated with the rate of locus coeruleus firing. This view of physiological responding was reinforced by Zigmond et al. (1995) with the statement that thoughts and feelings are chemical and electrical. Thus, utilizing electrical or pharmacological stimulation of the locus coeruleus the following effects were noted:

- Fear-related behavior and increases in release of norepinephrine in multiple brain regions (for instance; amygdala, hippocampus, hypothalamus and prefrontal cortex)
- The brain regions responding to threatening stimuli are associated with perception, evaluation, memory, and response.

Abercrombie and Zigmond (1995) assert that catecholaminergic neurons have the ability to adjust the level of transmitter synthesis and release depending on both current demands and past history. This was demonstrated by exposing animals to repeated shock, which increased dopamine, beta-hydroxylase activity, tyrosine hydroxylase, synaptic levels of norepinephrine, and locus coeruleus responsivity to excitatory stimuli. Additional neurobiological factors such as CRH and neuropeptide Y have also been inferred in the exaggerated noradrenergic release with exposure to chronic uncontrollable stress (animal subjects) (Rasmusson et al., 2000). This "stress sensitization," or enhanced reactivity, is known to most likely result after repeated events of uncontrollable stress.

Aston-Jones and Cohen (2005) make reference to the locus coeruleus as the brain's analog of the adrenal gland, serving to regulate arousal and sensitization. The locus coeruleus is the principal site for norepinephrine production in the brain. The norepinephrine from the locus coeruleus has an excitatory effect on much of the brain, thus mediating arousal and preparing the brain's neurons for activation by stimuli. These neuromodulating effects of norepinephrine target cortical sites to gain responsivity associated with task performance. The locus coeruleus/norepinephrine is involved in integrating autonomic and environmental stimuli. Nieuwenhuis et al. (2005) have reviewed the response of the locus coeruleus/norepinephrine system to the outcome of the internal decision-making processes and the consequent effects of noradrenergic potentiation of information processing.

The locus coeruleus is activated by stress and is responsible for mediating numerous sympathetic effects during stress. It responds by increasing norepinephrine secretion, which increases cognitive function, motivation, the sympathetic nervous system, and activates the HPA axis. With regard to the HPA axis, norepinephrine stimulates CRH from the hypothalamus, which stimulates the release of ACTH and results in the release of epinephrine/norepinephrine from the adrenal glands (Berrige and Waterhouse, 2003).

Locus coeruleus neurons can modulate neuroendocrine activity focused on stress-induced alterations in locus coeruleus gene expression. The outcome has suggested that the locus coeruleus/norepinephrine system is stress responsive to an acute mild challenge, and that this activation of locus coeruleus/norepinephrine neurons may take part in modulating the neuroendocrine stress response during development (Dent et al., 2001).

The architecture of the neural network model of locus coeruleus function represents excitatory links on a response unit with three fundamental levels (Aston-Jones and Cohen, 2005):

1. Input layer
2. Decision layer
3. Reponse layer.

This leads to motor system activation.

PTSD, HORMONAL LEVELS AND BRAIN STRUCTURES

Van der Kolk and Saporta (1991) state that the stress response and the psychobiology of PTSD is best understood by looking at the following disturbances in personal experience:

- Arousal
- Numbing
- Memory disturbance
- Sleep disturbance
- Psychosomatic reactions.

AROUSAL

The mechanism of arousal is the body's response when increased physical and psychological demands result in the release of norepinephrine from the locus coeruleus and ACTH from the anterior pituitary. Peripherally, the body's stress response consists of norepinephrine secretion by the sympathetic nerves and epinephrine release by the adrenal medulla and the stimulation of ACTH, which leads to secretion of glucocorticoids by the adrenal cortex. These hormones assist in the mobilization of energy needed to deal with stressors (i.e. increased glucose, enhanced immune function, etc.).

The amygdala detects and interprets threat of harm. Therefore, it is involved in both the acquisition and expression of fear (Davis, 1992). Though the hypothalamus and brainstem mediate fear responses such as changes in heart rate and blood pressure, sweating, freezing behavior, and the release of stress hormones, the strong association with the amygdala is significant.

Dopamine and norepinephrine play a significant role in stress-induced prefrontal cortex dysfunction (Arnsten, 1998). In addition, there is the action of inhibiting irrelevant and distracting sensory processing, which allows for concentration on the contents of working memory. However, under stressful circumstances (such as uncontrollable stress) when norepinephrine is increased above basal levels in the prefrontal cortex there is a decline in prefrontal cortex functioning as a result of the activation of postsynaptic alpha-1 receptors. Therefore, when the amygdala facilitates the release of catecholamines and cortisol it optimizes its influence while impairing the function of mediating behavior, thought, and affect by the prefrontal cortex (Ghashghaei and Barbas, 2002; Hains, 2008). Norepinephrine can be thought of as a switch for directing regulation of behavior. With modest norepinephrine release the role of the amygdala is suppressed and the prefrontal cortex regulates behavior, but when high levels of norepinephrine are released regulation of behavior by the amygdala is promoted (O'Rourke et al., 1994).

NUMBING

Persistent stress blunts the effectiveness of the stress response, resulting in desensitization. PTSD demonstrates a change in receptor activity that is consistent with downregulation secondary to chronic exposure to increased levels of circulating catecholamine.

This numbing of responsiveness is a psychological mechanism as a defense against the reliving of the traumatic memory and a physiological analgesia mechanism (opioid-mediated) in response to stimulation resembling the traumatic stressor.

MEMORY

A central feature of PTSD is memory disturbance, also described as intrusive re-experiencing of trauma (via nightmares, flashbacks, or somatic reactions). Traumatic memories are triggered by autonomic arousal hyperpotentiated by memory pathways and noradrenergic pathways emanating from the locus coeruleus.

The amygdala also has a role played by catecholamines to encode and consolidate memory associated to events that provoke arousal, fear, and stress. As far back as the 1970s Gold et al. (1975) reported that these recently formed memories could be enhanced by post-training administration of epinephrine or norepinephrine. Later research (McGaugh, 2004; Roozedaal et al., 2008) found that this effect is both time- and dose-dependent, intermediate doses of norepinephrine enhancing retention, while low or high doses do not. Stone et al. (1990) reported that norepinephrine also plays a role in memory retrieval, and when norepinephrine, amphetamine, or glucose was administered 30 minutes prior to retention testing each significantly enhanced memory.

SLEEP

Sleep disturbance appears to be related to chronic hyperarousal. Posttrauma nightmares can occur during any stage of the sleep cycle, but most happen during stages II and III of the cycle. It is these nightmares that are described by patients as a "reliving of the traumatic experience." Rapid eye movement (REM) sleep is more likely during anxiety-related dreams.

PSYCHOSOMATIC

Psychopharmacologic impairment in the form of psychosomatic reactions affecting the respiratory, digestive, cardiovascular, and endocrine systems are believed to have a causal association to inhibited expression of traumatic experience.

SEROTONERGIC SYSTEM

Neurons that synthesize and release serotonin generally originate in the raphe nucleus of the brainstem and project to the limbic structures, cerebral cortex, and many other regions of the brain. The serotonergic system is both excitatory and inhibitory in its actions. Serotonin is a monamine that is synthesized from tryptophan in serotonergic neurons within the brain and the gastrointestinal tract. It plays a significant regulatory role in the amygdala, hippocampus, and prefrontal cortex, which are also three structures that have been identified as being intricately connected with the pathophysiology of PTSD (Nestler et al., 2001).

The complexity and effects associated with the large number of serotonin projections and receptors continues to be investigated. Williams et al. (2007) suggest that the role that serotonin plays in orbitofrontal cortical functioning and psychological impairment is a significant key to understanding the pathophysiology associated with PTSD. The orbitofrontal cortex filters, processes, and evaluates social and emotional information. In other words, it evaluates the social context of cues, interprets the emotional properties of stimuli, and plays a role in processing affective memories. All of these processes are central to social and emotional decision-making. Damage to this area of the brain results in deficits in social decision-making, inappropriate social response, inability to recognize emotional responses of others (which helps modulate behavioral responses), and aggressive impulses. Historically, tryptophan-depletion studies have been used to examine these functions and the impact of serotonin on these areas of function.

Studies on changes in serotonergic function and their effects on the performance of orbitofrontal cortex-mediated tasks have demonstrated various impairments, including the following:

Bremner et al. (2003)
- Decreased regional cerebral blood flow in areas of the prefrontal cortex during retrieval of emotionally balanced word pairs
- A number of symptoms commonly observed in patients with PTSD: misinterpretation of emotional cues, impulsivity, aggression, enhanced emotional memory consistent with orbitofrontal cortex lesions
- Deficits in object alteration and reversal learning of patients with PTSD may reflect altered serotonin modulation of the oribitofrontal cortex.

Koenen et al. (2001)

- Patients with PTSD demonstrate alterations in both serotonergic function and in orbitofrontal cortex-mediated tasks (impaired ability to perform object alteration and reversal tests)

- Reported impaired performance on object alteration and reversal learning in combat veterans with PTSD.

Other symptoms commonly seen in patients with PTSD such as emotionally laden cues, impulsivity, aggression, and enhanced emotionally memory have also been described by patients diagnosed with orbitofrontal cortex lesions.

Studies on the impact of serotonin on the amygdala and locus coeruleus include the following:

Morgan et al. (2003)

- Reduced levels of serotonin in the amygdala associated with decreased firing of the amygdala.

Stutzman et al. (1998)

- The ability of serotonin (5-HT) to modulate glutamatergic activity is dependent on the presence of corticocosterone

- Increased serotonin increases the threshold of amygdala firing with a resulting decrease in vigilance and fear-related behaviors.

It has also been noted that the effectiveness of selective serotonin reuptake inhibitors (SSRIs) may be related to an increased threshold of amygdala firing.

Blier (2001)

- In rats with serotonin (5-HT) lesions, the activity and firing rate of locus coeruleus/norepinephrine neurons is approximately 50% greater than that recorded in intact animals.

- In a related study, prolonged administration of citalopam (SSRI at 14 and 21 days) led to a progressive decrease in the firing activity of norepinephrine neurons.

Goddard et al. (1995)

- Serotonin (5-HT) has modulating effects on norepinephrine.

- Tryptophan depletion has been shown to cause mild decreases in mood and concentration among healthy subjects.

- Subjects who underwent tryptophan depletion and then received yohimbine experienced a synergistic increase in subjective nervousness compared with administration of either yohimbine alone or a placebo.

Aston-Jones et al. (1991)/Aston-Jones and Cohen (2005)

- Serotonin has important effects on the locus coeruleus.

- An inhibitory role of serotonin (5-HT) on the locus coeruleus and nitric oxide (NO) neurons has been demonstrated in lesion, electrophysiological, and biochemical studies.

Charney et al. (1992)

- Yohimbine administration produced modest or no increase in subjective nervousness among healthy subjects, but in patients with panic disorder it caused an increase in symptoms consistent with anxiety and panic as well as elevations in physiological and neuroendocrine measures associated with heightened arousal and anxiety.

- Additional evidence which directly supports the role or function of serotonin in the pathophysiology of PTSD can be derived from studies on subjects with aggression, impulsivity, and depression as well as pharmacological treatment studies.

Davidson et al. (2000)

- Reduced CSF 5-hydroxyindoleacetic acid (5-HIAA) was noted in aggressive psychiatric patients, impulsive violent males, and completed suicides who have killed themselves through violent means.

Manuck et al. (1999)

- Genetic evidence can be found in the relationship between polymorphism in the gene that codes for tryptophan hydroxylase and individual differences in aggressive behavior.

Caspi et al. (2003)

- Studies of the association between genetic predisposition for altered serotonergic function and traumatic experiences reveals that one or two copies of the short allele of the serotonin transporter promotor polymorphism, significantly increasing the risk of depression (which is frequently experienced with PTSD).

Pharmacologic studies include the following:

Foa et al. (2000)

- SSRI treatment (US Food and Drug Administration (FDA)-approved sertraline and paroxetine) for PTSD have demonstrated significant improvement in all three PTSD symptom clusters (re-experiencing, avoidance, arousal).

- Monoamine oxidase inhibitors (MAOIs) increase serotonin by inhibiting degradation. They have also been shown to offer improvement in PTSD symptoms.

IMMUNE FUNCTION

In numerous situations involving acute stress, the body prepares the immune system to meet the challenge. It is under these conditions that the immune system is potentiated to prepare for the consequences of stress. However, there is a significant range of various stressors on different immune system responses. According to some studies (Miller et al., 2007; Wrosch and Schulz, 2008) acute stressors that elicit a fight or flight response can offer potentially beneficial changes in the immune system, whereas chronic stressors or cumulative stress may have a detrimental impact. In addition, there is a unique mechanism through which psychological stress potentially influences the onset and/or progression of conditions that involve excessive inflammation, like allergic, autoimmune, cardiovascular, infectious and rheumatologic illnesses (Segerstrom and Miller, 2004).

An example of the immunological consequence of chronic stress is the potential prolonged secretion of cortisol. Cortisol causes white blood cells to initiate a counterregulatory response which takes place by downregulating their cortisol receptors. This downregulation results in a reduction of the white blood cell capacity to respond to anti-inflammatory signals, thus allowing cytokine-mediated inflammatory processes to thrive. It has also been found that social support lessens immunological consequences.

The hormonal response to stress alters immune system function and influences the susceptibility to mental illness and physical disease processes. The perception of stress activates the interface between the endocrine system and the immune system, resulting in a cascade of physiological events with the potential for longer lasting damage. If the stressful sensory input is persistent, the dysregulation of the immune system causes an inflammatory state, possibly leading to disease states. In contrast, short bursts of stress may enhance the immune system (American Psychological Association, 2002; Segerstrom and Miller, 2004).

PSYCHONEUROIMMUNOLOGY

Research investigating immunosuppression includes measures of cellular and humoral immunity (Newport and Nemeroff, 2000).

Cellular Immunity

- Refers to the infection-fighting capacity of immune cells (natural killer cells, macrophages, lymphocytes, and neutrophils).

- Measures include the number of cells, the ability of those cells to attack invading organisms, and their ability to proliferate in response to invading organisms.

- The relative hypocortisolemia may preserve or even exaggerate cellular immune activity.

Humoral Immunity

- Refers to the capacity of the immune system to produce substances that ward off invading organisms.

- Measures include antibody titres and concentrations of regulatory cytokines (such as interferons and interleukins).

Interestingly, there are conflicting results from cellular immunity studies focused on depression which indicate that although there is a pattern of associated immunosuppression there are also areas of humoral immune system activation. This mixed representation includes immunological activation, immunological suppression, and HPA hyperactivity. In depression, increased CRH secretion has been associated with humoral immunity activation as demonstrated by increased proinflammatory cytokine release. Inflammatory cytokines augment HPA axis function by increasing CRH release and induce glucocorticoid resistance. The result is impairment of the negative feedback within the HPA axis. On the other hand, HPA axis hyperactivity also produces immunosuppression, as reflected by the decreased activity of natural killer cells.

CRH hypersecretion and humoral immunoactivation are common to both depression and PTSD and possibly represent a shared pathophysiology. However, as noted above, the immune system responses do differ between PTSD and depression.

FUNCTIONAL TRAUMA RESPONSE

The functional trauma response is evidenced by the following sequence (LeDoux, 1996; Bremner, 2005):

1. Traumatic event
2. Alarm
   – Cease current activity, crouch, scan, vigilance, readiness

3. Orienting
   – Focus
   – Head and neck extend for optimal hearing and environmental scanning
   – Visual scanning (eyes move) to determine explanation, "what is it?" and pupils dilate

4. Defensive response: fight or flight
   – Arms express fight or flight
   – Legs express flight
   – Peripheral narrowing (field of vision narrows)
   – Auditory exclusion

5. If neither fight or flight will be a successful response, freeze
   – Freezing is inhibited fight or flight
   – This energy is "frozen"
   – Can the nervous system "unfreeze"?

6. Discharge
7. Rest.

A relatively low-level example of this experience is what happens to some people when they watch horror or action movies or intense and exciting sports. The difference is that this form of fight or flight activation is controlled.

Trauma could result from repeated experiences or a single event. When trauma is not chronic or associated with repeated episodes it is a time-limited experience. Failure to take this normally time-limited experience and not allowing it to run its natural course can result in PTSD. To avoid being traumatized requires that this chemical explosion of energy be used up/ discharged. When an individual is unable to respond effectively to danger and cannot discharge the activation of energy (arousal) as an ongoing event and continue to activate this defensive energy to prevent overloading the body and mind the result is a dysfunctional trauma response.

The development of trauma symptoms is a cascading process with primitive and intricate biological mechanisms. At the center of this process is the freezing (immobility) reaction which is shown by the reptilian brain when the nervous system mobilizes this excess of available energy for defense with active aggression for fight or flight but neither takes place. The degree or magnitude of inhibition in the nervous system that is necessary to shut down this energy and, therefore, preserve the body and mind is the most important single factor in the subsequent development of trauma symptoms. Freezing occurs when an individual is overwhelmed.

When this freezing response gets stuck, all of the instinctive responses that are linked to survival are affected. All components of the primitive or "reptilian" brain (see below) are interconnected. If one part gets stuck they are all affected. The common result is to reproduce the orienting response repeatedly in the form of hypervigilance.

While the primary response to orienting and defending is fight or flight (if neither can be done, freezing) the defensive actions that precedes freezing are the intense emotions of rage and terror. Rage is viewed as the frustrated fight response, terror as the frustrated flight response. It is during this phase that phenomenal, beyond normal, feats of physical strength have been reported, such as a person lifting a car to save someone they love. The body and mind can only tolerate a certain level of these intense emotions before freezing and/or collapse of the individual takes place. Unfortunately, the high level of energy that is frozen remains closely associated with these intolerably intense emotional states. When the body and mind begin to be released from the freezing or immobility the rage and terror will be re-experienced. The reptilian brain interprets this activation of intense emotions as a new threat and automatically repeats the response to the original trauma—thus the cycle of reliving the trauma response is born. An additional aspect of this repetition is the fear experienced by being overwhelmed. This repetition or cycle is both simple and self-perpetuating.

Statistically, once a person has experienced being traumatized, their risk of experiencing further trauma is much greater (Yehuda and Wong, 2001).

THE REPTILIAN BRAIN AND PSYCHOPATHOLOGY

The reptilian brain is primitive (Levine, 1997; Bradley, 2000), and its basic functions make it a fertile place for the development of psychopathology. Psychopathology marginally alleviates the energy associated with the freeze response via compulsions and repetitive behaviors such as eating disorders, promiscuity, gambling, and substance abuse. Other forms of psychopathology that develop include depression, anxiety, sleep disturbance, and hyperactivity. This is double-edged because although it allows the initial movement through freezing, it is also where the intolerable experience of rage and fear resides. The level of distress is so great that the individual will use any thought, feeling, or behavior to contain this undischarged energy. This cycle interferes with the development of effective coping, and as energy builds there is an escalation of dysfunctional symptoms and behaviors as an effort to keep this energy under control. Another way to view this is that compulsive behaviors are an attempt to resolve frozen energy.

PSYCHOBIOLOGICAL MECHANISMS OF VULNERABILITY AND RESILIENCE

The complex regulation of emotion by the brain and the consequences of change are the focus of the psychopathology of vulnerability and psychological resilience. Stress plays a role in mental disorders, both as a causal factor and as an outcome of disordered thought and disrupted interpersonal relationships. One of the ways this is described is by "allostasis." Allostasis refers to the process of an adaptive physiologic response to acute stress which includes a set point that changes as a result of the process of maintaining homeostasis. Allostatic load refers to the outcome when there is inadequate recovery to homeostasis from the acute event to terminate the acute adaptive response of stress mediation and the detrimental effects on physiological and psychological function, or cumulative wear and tear that resulted from repeated efforts to adapt to stressors over time.

In summary, allostatic load refers to the active process of wear and tear on the body resulting from excessive/chronic stress or inefficient management of stress. In other words it results from:

- Not shutting off the stress response once the demand is met or is no longer needed
- Inadequately responding to stress from the beginning
- Adapting to repetition of the same response.

All of this interferes with the body's ability to recover and indicates that the parasympathetic nervous system response is impaired (McEwen, 1998, 2000; Loucks et al., 2008).

As a result, allostatic load increases over time and emphasizes multisystem dysregulation. These factors are the foundation for understanding why some individuals are able to cope with extreme stress with minimal psychopathological consequences while others demonstrate numerous psychological and physiological consequences. What is understood is that individuals who demonstrate symptoms of PTSD are displaying the effects of a build-up of undischarged arousal.

There are four types of allostatic load (McEwen, 1998, 2000):

1. Repeated hits from multiple novel or unrelated stressors

2. Lack of adaptation

3. Prolonged response due to delayed shut down

4. Inadequate response that leads to compensatory hyperactivity of other mediators, such as inadequate secretion of glucocorticoids. The result is increased levels of cytokines that are inversely related to glucocorticoids.

Behavior and cognition also play a very important role in allostatic load in determining what an individual identifies as stressful, and the factors that contribute to how they ultimately respond to stressful situations (McEwen, 2000):

- Interpretation—If the situation is evaluated as threatening, then the brain may initiate behaviors that avoid the threat, or it may produce behaviors that can escalate the danger. This means that an event perceived as non-threatening may be associated with little psychophysiological cost if no danger is truly involved. However, perceiving a situation as threatening when there is no danger can result in a high cost in terms of psychophysiological overreaction and wasted behavior.

- Physical condition—Individuals who are in good physical condition manage strenuous exercise and demonstrate better recovery from stress than their counterparts who are not in good physical condition.

- It is under the control of the brain to interpret whether an event is threatening or non-threatening, as well as determining the behaviors and habits that result in life being more or less dangerous to the individual both in the short term and in the long term (lifetime).

In addition, bear in mind that genetics plays a significant role in the expression of genetic traits. According to McEwen (1998), an individual's experiences, genetics, and behavior influence their interpretation of stress. When the brain interprets an event as stressful there is an initiation of physiologic and behavioral responses that lead to allostasis and adaptation. "Over time, allostatic load can accumulate, and the overexposure to neural, endocrine, and immune stress mediators can have adverse effects on various organ systems, leading to disease."

Chronic stress and the associated consequences of overexposure to stress hormones resulting in pathophysiology is easily understood by looking at life experiences:

Lynch et al. (1997)

- Individuals who have excessive stress in their lives, measured by multiple periods of poverty-level socioeconomic status, show earlier aging, more depression, and greater potential decline in both physical and mental functioning than others.

Felitti et al. (1998)

- Individuals who have been abused as children experience an increased risk of depression, substance abuse, and premature mortality and morbidity, resulting in a wide range of disease states.

The complex regulation of emotion by the brain and the consequences of change are the focus of psychological resilience and the psychopathology of vulnerability. Thoughts and feelings are chemical and electrical. Therefore, the long-term psychological outcome to acute psychological stress has been associated with neurotransmitters, neuropeptides, and hormones, all of which possess relevant functional interactions that mediate the neural mechanisms and neural circuits important to the following (Charney, 2004):

- Regulation of reward and motivation
  - Hedonia
  - Optimism
  - Learned helpfulness

- Fear conditioning (learns, remembers, and responds to fear)
  - Effective behaviors despite fear
- Social behavior
  - Altruism
  - Bonding
  - Teamwork.

If a profile could be established to identify those with a predisposition for vulnerability versus those predisposed to resilience it would be of significant benefit for both prevention and treatment models. Regarding allostatic load and an increased risk for psychopathology following exposure to stress, Charney (2004) has proposed the following potential profile (non-exhaustive) of vulnerability factors designated by high or low quartiles. People with the highest index for psychobiological allostatic load would be those who have the following:

Highest quartile:	Lowest quartiles:
HPA axis	DHEA
CRH	Neuropeptide Y
Estrogen activity	Testosterone
Locus coeruleus/norepinephrine	Galanin
	Serotonin receptor
	Benzodiazepine receptor

In contrast to the aforementioned factors, a potential profile for the resilient individual would include the following:

Highest quartile:	Lowest quartile:
DHEA	HPA axis
Neuropeptide Y	CRH
Galanin	Locus coeruleus/norepinephrine
Testosterone	
Serotonin receptor	
Benzodiazepine receptor	

Another major focus of researchers has been to unravel the role that "neurological soft signs" (see below) play in the development of PTSD. The initial review of vulnerability to PTSD is the association with these structural abnormalities.

It seems as though it should be easy to clarify and decisively conclude the psysiological and psychological consequences of acute and chronic stress. It is understood that the stress mechanisms that impact the autonomic nervous system and adrenocortico system offer a benefit when it is a short-term response (protective), but can damage and accelerate the disease process when activated over a long period of time (vulnerability). In other words, the concern is that altered states of brain chemistry and function result in an increased susceptibility to the vulnerable impact of stress hormones. These considerations are important to a conceptual understanding of the connection between stress and health in terms of life experiences, health behaviors, choices of thought/interpretation of experience, genetics, and socio-economic factors.

In addition, the outcome has remained ambiguous because the chemical mediators of stress vary in their basal secretion according to diurnal rhythm that is coordinated by the light–dark cycle and sleep–wake cycle. Perturbances in the diurnal cycles are associated with pathophysiological outcomes and these issues make it difficult to discern with distinction aspects of temporal patterns and intensity that discriminate between vulnerability and resilience factors.

VULNERABILITY

There is increased recognition that acute stress in early life may result in hypervigilance and hyperresponsiveness to stress in later life. This intense response to stress is one demonstration of an increased vulnerability to develop clinical depression during chronic immune suppression. The physiological mechanisms of the body's response to stress alter immune system function and influence vulnerability (onset and exacerbation) of mental and physical disease.

The identification of "neurological soft signs," which include subtle language abnormalities, poor motor coordination, sensory perceptual difficulties, and difficulties in sequencing of complex motor tasks, result from specific or diffuse brain structural abnormalities. While research continues to contribute to the body of knowledge related to the implications of neurological soft signs, clarity on this topic is "confounded by the underlying pathogenic process and by the use of psychotropic medications" (Dazzan et al., 2005). The origins of neurological soft signs remain undetermined and research continues into their neuroanatomical status in healthy individuals in an attempt to reveal which brain areas are associated with them (Dazzan et al., 2006). Though not well understood, neurological soft signs have been associated with various mental disorders, including schizophrenia, obsessive compulsive disorder, ADHD, social phobia, bipolar disorder, and PTSD.

The subjective experience of stress does not always predict the elevation of the physiological stress mediators, particularly cortisol and catecholamines. These physiological mediators are associated with both adaptation and pathophysiology. In other words, both cortisol and catecholamines mediate the adaptation of many body/organ systems when challenged by acute stress, and also contribute to pathological changes over protracted periods of time. The range of pathological developments include risks of immunosuppression, hypertension, atherosclerosis, heart disease, obesity, etc.

Gurvits et al. (2000) used neurological and psychological tests to assess research subjects with PTSD and found the following, even accounting for concurrent alcoholism and head injury:

- Increased incidence of neurodevelopmental problems
- Increased incidence of childhood ADHD
- Lower IQs.

All these outcomes were significantly correlated with neurologic soft signs, demonstrating the presence of neurologic compromise. The authors also concluded that "neurologic compromise is evident from subject history and findings from physical examination in both men and women with chronic PTSD who had experienced different kinds of traumatic events in childhood and adulthood."

For some time researchers have questioned whether studies revealing smaller hippocampal volumes in individuals with PTSD is the result of traumatic stress or that a smaller hippocampal volume is a pre-existing condition that increases vulnerability to the development of pathological stress response. In an effort to clarify this question Gilbertson et al. (2002) studies monozygotic twins discordant for trauma exposure and made the following observations:

- A smaller hippocampus constitutes a risk factor for the development of stress-related psychopathology.
- Disorder severity in PTSD patients who were exposed to trauma was negatively correlated with the hippocampal volume of the exposed twin and unexposed identical twin.
- Severe PTSD twin pairs (both trauma exposed and non-exposed) had significantly smaller hippocampi than non-PTSD pairs.

In a similar study (Gurvits et al., 2006; Pitman et al., 2006), investigating neurological soft signs as a pre-existing vulnerability factor or an acquired PTSD sign, researchers studied monozygotic twins in which one twin had been combat-exposed. The following results were found:

- Combat veterans with PTSD had significantly higher neurological soft signs scores than combat veterans without PTSD.
- The "high-risk" unexposed co-twins of the veterans with PTSD had significantly higher neurological soft signs scores than the "low-risk" unexposed co-twins. Incidentally, there was no explanation for this outcome that could be associated with age, number of potentially traumatic lifetime experiences, alcoholism, or the presence of a comorbid affective or anxiety disorder.
- The average neurological soft signs score in unexposed co-twins was not significantly associated with combat severity in combat-exposed twins.
- Average heart rate responses (HRR) to a series of sudden, loud-tone presentations were larger in combat veteran twins with PTSD than in the

non-combat-exposed co-twins, whose responses were similar to those of the non-PTSD combat veterans and their non-combat exposed co-twins. This suggests that larger HRR to sudden, loud tones represent an acquired sign of PTSD.

The overall conclusions of clinical relevance in these studies is that results from the combat-unexposed identical twins suggest that subtle neurologic dysfunction in PTSD is not acquired along with the traumatic experience or diagnosis of PTSD, but instead represents an "antecedent familial vulnerability factor for developing chronic PTSD on exposure to a traumatic event." In addition, it could be viewed as evidence for an acquired PTSD sign.

Other factors that have been explored for their association with risk of PTSD include the following:

Mixed Lateral Preference—Boscarino and Hoffman (2007)

- All three handedness measures were associated with current PTSD.

- When handedness was classified by high combat exposure all three measures were associated with PTSD.

- Veterans with mixed laterality and high combat exposure also had significantly increased PTSD symptoms.

Maternal Drug Abuse—Luthar and Sexton (2007)

- Results showed that negative parenting behaviors were linked with multiple adverse child outcomes.

- Parenting stress was linked with children's lifetime diagnoses.

- Limit-setting and closeness was linked with children's externalizing problems and impact to everyday competence.

Long-term Impact of Terrorism (Israel)—Bleich et al. (2006)

- 29.5% of subjects felt depressed; 10.4% felt anxious; 47% felt life-threatening danger; 9.7% felt the need for professional help.

- Immigrant status, low education, low sense of safety, low social support, high societal distress, and injury following life-threatening experiences were associated with traumatic stress-related symptoms.

- Traumatic stress-related symptoms did not increase with exposure severity.

- Prior experience of highly stressful events increases vulnerability to adverse psychological effects of terror.

McEwen (2000) considers the fact that mental disorders (depression, anxiety, etc.) are related to chemical imbalances in the CNS alters interpretations of environmental stimuli and can influence behavioral responses to potentially stressful situations. Allostatic load is the result of these chemical imbalances. In addition, the vulnerability of an individual to allostatic load is probably a reflection of developmental influence and genetic risk factors.

RESILIENCE

The importance of protective psychological factors in the prevention of psychological and physical illness is well established. In addition, "resilience in the face of loss or potential trauma represents a distinct trajectory … resilience is more common than believed, and that there are multiple and sometimes unexpected pathways to resilience" (Bonanno, 2004). Resilience can be thought of as the ability to maintain relative stability as well as healthy psychological and physical function in the face of loss and trauma.

Most studies on resilience have been carried out on those who have served in combat, but the results can be extrapolated to first responder professions such as firefighters and law enforcement officers. The manner in which they are able to respond effectively in the face of crisis and trauma is impressive and the context of their fraternity reveals important aspects of their resiliency (Charney, 2004):

- As a fraternity, they are able to bond with their group.
- They serve on a common mission.
- Altruism is highly valued.
- They are trained and conditioned to tolerate high levels of stress and fear and still perform.
- They are willing and able to approach a fear-evoking situation despite their subjective experience (emotional fear and physiological disturbance). Neural mechanisms that underlie these factors and mediate these functions are important to how one can respond to extreme stress and in some way account for the character trait of courage in addition to resilience.

Resilience is the process of adapting well in the face of adversity and stress. Some of the factors that contribute to resilience include:

- Personality
- Good intellectual functioning
- Positive affectivity
- Optimism
- Cognitive flexibility
- Coping
- Social support
- Emotion regulation
- Healthy attachment behaviors
- Altruism
- Ego defenses
- Mastery.

Resilience is demonstrated by the ability to utilize and mobilize resources and protective factors to facilitate coping when confronted with a stressor with the capacity to alter traumatic helplessness into learned helpfulness.

Bonanno (2004) hypothesized that the degree of human resilience has been underestimated. Unfortunately, there is a tendency to pathologize and not adequately distinguish resilience from recovery. The consequence for the resilient individual could range from ineffective interventions to harm. Bonanno points out that resilience is different from recovery and that resilience is much more common than thought:

Resilience is Different from Recovery

- Recovery implies a trajectory of improvement from a state of subthreshold to threshold psychopathology.
- This recovery phase could take place from a relatively short period of time to a couple of years.
- Resilience, in contrast, reflects the ability to maintain relative equilibrium.
- Resilience is not merely an absence of psychopathology, but exhibits a stable trajectory of healthy functioning across time, and demonstrates a capacity for generative experiences and positive emotions.
- Pathologizing normal reactions thereby undermines natural resilience processes.
- Initial screening for intervention of individuals who show potential risk factors instead of assuming the need and benefit for everyone exposed to loss or trauma would reduce the undermining of resilience individuals.

Resilience is Common

- The majority of individuals exposed to loss and trauma demonstrate the type of healthy functioning indicative of the resilience trajectory (i.e. healthy adjustment).
- The absence of grief should not be assumed to be an attachment dysfunction.
- Experiences associated with loss or trauma (including intrusive thoughts) that do not interfere with ability to function in the other areas of life, including the capacity for positive affect, should not be pathologized.

Bonanno (2004) also points out that there are multiple and sometimes unexpected pathways to resilience. There is no single means of maintaining equilibrium following highly aversive events. Those resilient to loss and trauma often appear to cope effectively in ways that, under normal circumstances, may not always be advantageous.

There are also distinct dimensions to consider for different types or pathways of resilience to loss and trauma:

Hardiness

The personality trait of hardiness helps to buffer exposure to extreme stress, and consists of:

- Being committed to finding meaningful purpose in life
- The belief that one can influence one's surroundings and outcome of events
- The belief that one can learn and grow from both positive and negative life experiences.

As a result of these beliefs, hardy individuals tend to appraise stressful situations as less threatening, thereby minimizing the experience of distress. Hardy individuals are more confident and better able to use active coping mechanisms and social support (to deal with distress).

Self-Enhancement	• A sometimes unrealistic or overly positive bias in favor of the self (self-enhancement) can be adaptive and promote well-being.
	• The trait of self-enhancement has been associated with benefits (high self-esteem), but also costs such as narcissism (which evokes a negative impression from others). It can be associated with being better adjusted.
	• The self-enhancer's salivary cortisol levels exhibit a profile indicative of minimal stress responding.

Self-Enhancement

- A sometimes unrealistic or overly positive bias in favor of the self (self-enhancement) can be adaptive and promote well-being.
- The trait of self-enhancement has been associated with benefits (high self-esteem), but also costs such as narcissism (which evokes a negative impression from others). It can be associated with being better adjusted.
- The self-enhancer's salivary cortisol levels exhibit a profile indicative of minimal stress responding.

Repressive Coping

- Repressors tend to avoid unpleasant thoughts, emotions, and memories.
- Repressive coping appears to operate primarily through emotion-focused mechanisms (such as emotional dissociation). This is in contrast to hardiness and self-enhancement which operate primarily on the level of cognitive processes.
- Emotional dissociation is generally viewed as maladaptive and associated with long-term health costs. However, these tendencies do appear to foster adaptation to extreme adversity.
- Although repressors reported initial increased somatic complaints, over time they did not demonstrate greater somatic or health problems than other participants.

Positive Emotion and Laughter

- Positive emotion and laughter is a demonstration of resilience in coping with adversity.
- Positive emotions can help to reduce levels of distress following adverse events both by quieting and/or undoing negative emotion and by increasing utilization of social support.
- Resilience and adjustment are mediated by the experience of positive emotions such as gratitude, interest, and love. Although there is some concern that if there is a lack of social intelligence this factor could be associated with decreased social competence.

Just as therapists must be careful in their assessment of the complexities of PTSD, they must be equally careful to not be simplistic to minimize coping advantages of the resilient individuals in the face of and aftermath of loss and trauma.

BUILDING PSYCHOLOGICAL RESILIENCE

Building resilience means that in the face and recovery of adversity and trauma an individual is able to emerge from a position of strength and triumph—dedicating themselves to the task of surviving, coping, and learning. The types of thinking and skills that accomplish this are:

- The acknowledgment that it is a common course of life experience to be challenged by physically and emotionally distressing events.
- Realizing that hope is never lost and is a guiding force in shaping future-oriented decision-making.

- Thinking and behaving in ways that lead to recovery, for example:
  - Deal with pain and stress in manageable chunks
  - Decide early to move forward
  - Search for answers and create useful reframes
  - Utilize social support
  - Don't waste time and energy on old resentments (let go)
  - Engage in active learning
  - Take decisive decisions
  - Identify and deal with problems "one at a time"
  - Respond to available opportunities
  - Allow others to buffer stress when appropriate
  - Have a deep-rooted belief in the system of meaning.

- Seeing problems as opportunities for growth, for example:
  - Live the perspective "if there is the will there is a way"
  - See small windows of opportunity and making the most of them
  - View life as a journey of self-understanding.

- Using active coping mechanisms, for example:
  - Identify the problems and consider possible solutions
  - Take action
  - Take responsibility
  - Be confident in ability.

REGULATION OF REWARD AND MOTIVATION

In an environment of chronic stress and lack of reward, in order to maintain optimism, hopefulness, and a positive self-concept when exposed to extreme stress or trauma, the resilient individual is able to maintain effectively functioning reward pathways and a hedonic tone. The reward and motivation pathway of a resilient individual tends to be either "hypersensitive to reward or is resistant to change, despite chronic exposure to neglect or abuse" (Charney, 2004). This pathway has the ability to discriminate between different rewards based upon their motivational value, which may facilitate mechanisms of behavioral responding directed toward reward and profitable goals. The amygdala is one of the structures involved in modulating conditioned responses. In combination with other components of the reward network it establishes the emotional value of a reward memory along with its strength and persistence.

FEAR CONDITIONING

In the context of PTSD, fear conditioning refers to the vivid recollection of memories of traumatic experiences, autonomic hyperarousal, and flashback evoked by the sensory and cognitive stimuli associated with traumatic experience. As a result of the associated distress, patients with these symptoms avoid these everyday cues or engage in numbing of emotional responsiveness in an effort to diminish the degree of distress experienced.

Classical conditioning is a process of learning whereby the expressed fear response to a neutral conditioned stimulus (specific environmental features) is paired to an aversive unconditioned stimulus (traumatic experience). As a result, the conditioned stimulus is able to evoke the entire spectrum of responses (behavioral, autonomic, and endocrine) that generally only occur in the face of danger. The result for trauma survivors is that this conditioning leads to a generalizing of cues which in turn leads to a continuous perception of threat, thus becoming conditioned to context or cue-specific. It is the rule rather than the exception that memories are reactivated by cues associated with the original traumatic experience. Unfortunately, every time a traumatic memory is retrieved, it becomes integrated as part of a perpetual (ongoing) emotional experience and becomes part of a new memory (Collins and Pare, 2000; Maren, 2001).

Exposure-based therapy leads to a reduction in the conditioned fear response. Keep in mind that extinction is characterized by many of the same neural mechanisms as seen in fear acquisition. Individuals who demonstrate an ability to assuage or calm learned fear quickly via efficient extinction mechanisms are likely to function more effectively under dangerous circumstances. There may also be less susceptibility to the effects of intermittent exposure to fear stimuli. Individuals who are resistant to the effects of acute stress generally experience fear but have the ability to function well while in high states of fear. Add to this, individuals who are commonly in high stress/fear situations where they are confronting circumstances that are inherently dangerous need to be able to extinguish learned fears quickly.

SOCIAL BEHAVIOR

Altruism, bonding, and teamwork are all characteristics indicative of the adaptive, resilient individual. Being altruistic brings with it the ability to attract and utilize support. In animal studies, oxytocin and vasopressin have been clearly identified in the prosocial bonding process. Reciprocal altruism is a core behavioral principle of human social relationships and is related to resilience. Rillings et al. (2002) found that mutual cooperation was associated with consistent activation of brain areas linked to reward processing and that this pattern sustains cooperative social relationships, thus inhibiting the impulse to accept but not to reciprocate as altruistic behavior in action. Highly resilient individuals are able to form supportive social attachments.

DISTINGUISHING ANXIETY AND FEAR

If there is a perception of the possible experience of negative consequences the result is anxiety. When anxiety reaches a pathological level it causes stress and functional impairment. Contrary to an anxiety-provoking stimulus, a fear-provoking stimulus carries with it the presence of harm. In addition, anxiety differs from fear in that the fear-producing stimulus is either not present or not immediately threatening, but in anticipation of danger. Different types of internal and external factors (triggers) act to produce the symptoms of different anxiety disorders. Fear is established via a classical conditioning paradigm:

- Unconditioned stimulus (traumatic experience) → Generates fear and anxiety (unconditioned response)
- Conditioned stimulus (associated sensory stimuli) → Conditioned response (fear, anxiety, arousal manifested through intrusive symptoms, such as flashbacks, nightmares).

When the conditioned stimulus is repeatedly presented with the conditioned response in the absence of the unconditioned stimulus, the conditioned response eventually becomes extinct (the process of extinction). This demonstrates the origin of anxiety/fear in the development of anxiety disorders and highlights the consequence of learned associations (Cannistraro and Rauch, 2003). The problematic behaviors of PTSD such as addiction, avoidance, poor anger management and impulse control are aimed at decreasing the anxiety associated with the event. Once established, these behavioral responses are maintained by operant conditioning where anxiety and arousal are decreased by these problematic behaviors. As a result, these behaviors are negatively reinforced, which increases the probability of them occurring. In other words, the problematic behaviors are reinforced by removal of fear, anxiety, and arousal or operant conditioning paradigm:

- Conditioned response (fear, anxiety, arousal) → Problematic behavior to reduce fear, anxiety, arousal → Anxiety decreased (negative reinforcement of problematic behaviors).

Confronting the memories associated with the traumatic event is a challenging process requiring a skilled therapist and motivated patient capable of tolerating the distress of confrontation. Careful structuring of the exposure (confrontation) and preparing the patient with management tools allows for mastery over the response of fear, anxiety, and arousal. Wolpe (1958) developed the theory of "reciprocal inhibition" whereby exposure to an anxiety-provoking stimulus is paired with the relaxation response to extinguish the conditioned response (fear, anxiety, arousal).

Exposure (to traumatic memory and/or cues)

+

Relaxation (while confronted with traumatic memory and/or cues

↓ (results in)

Extinction of symptoms or resolution

Therefore, it is not merely the focus on extinction of problematic behaviors but the development and practice of positive behaviors, such as relaxation, that provide the fertile soil of learning a better way of living that truly leads to resolution.

REFERENCES AND FURTHER READING

Abercrombie ED, Zigmond MJ (1995) Modifications of central catecholaminergic systems by stress and injury. In: *Psychopharmacology: The fourth generation of progress* (Bloom FE, Kupfer DJ, eds). New York: Raven Press, pp. 355–361.

Agaibi CE (2005) Trauma, PTSD and resilience. *Trauma Violence Abuse* 3: 195–216.

Ahmed AS (2007) Post-traumatic stress disorder, resilience and vulnerability. *Adv Psychiatr Treat* 13: 369–375.

American Psychological Association (2002) Chronic stress can interfere with normal function of the immune system, suggest new research. Public Affairs Office, November 3, 2002.

Arnsten AF (1998) Catecholamine modulation of prefrontal cortical cognitive function. *Trends Cogn Sci* 2: 436–447.

Arnsten AF (2000a) Stress impairs prefrontal cortical function in rats and monkeys: Role of dopamine D1 and norepinephrine alpha, receptor mechanisms. *Progr Brain Res* 126: 183–192.

Arnsten AF (2000b) Through the looking glass: Differential noradrenergic modulation of prefrontal cortical function. *Neural Plasticity* 7: 133–146.

Aston-Jones G, Cohen JD (2005) an integrative theory of locus-coeruleus-norepinephrine function: Adaptive gain and optimal performance. *Annu Rev Neurosci* 28: 403–450.

Aston-Jones G, Chiang C, Alexinsky T (1991) Discharge of noradrenergic locus coeruleus neurons in behaving rats and monkeys suggest a role in vigilance. *Prog Brain Res* 88: 501–520.

Aston-Jones G, Rajkowski J, Kubiak P, Alexinsky T (1994) Locus coeruleus neurons in monkeys are selectively activated by attended cues in a vigilance task. *J Neurosci* 14: 4467–4480.

Baghai TC, Schule C, Zwanzger P et al. (2002) Hypothalamic-pituitary-adrenocortical axis dysregulation in patients with major depression is influenced by the insertion/deletion polymorphism in the angiostensen I-converting enzyme gene. *Neurosci Lett* 328: 299–303.

Baker DG, West SA, Nicholson WE et al. (2002) Serial CFS corticotropin-releasing hormone levels and adrenocortical activity in combat veterans with posttraumatic stress disorder. *Military Med* October.

Baker D, Ekhator NE, KascKow JW et al. (2005) Higher levels of basal serum CSF cortisol in combat veterans with posttraumatic stress disorder. *Am J Psychiatry* 162: 992–994.

Becker D (2000) When she was bad: Borderline personality disorder in and posttraumatic age. *Am J Orthopsychiatry* 70: 422–432.

Berrige CW, Waterhouse BD (2003) The locus coeruleus-noradrenergic system: modulation of behavioral state and state dependent cognitive processes. *Brain Res Rev* 42: 33–84.

Bleich A, Gelkopf M, Melamed Y, Solomon Z (2006) Mental health and resiliency following 44 months of terrorism: a survey of an Israeli national representative sample. *BMC Med* 4: 21.

Blier P (2001) Crosstalk between norepinephrine and serotonin systems and its role in the antidepressant response. *J Psychiatry Neurosci* 26: 3–10.

Bonanno GA (2004) Loss, trauma, and resilience. *Am Psychol* 59: 20–28.

Bonne O, Brandes D, Gilboa A et al. (2001) Longitudinal MRI study of hippocampal volume in trauma survivors with PTSD. *Am J Psychiatry* 58: 1248–1251.

Boscarino JA, Hoffman SN (2007) Consistent association between mixed lateral preference and PTSD: Confirmation among a national study of 2490 US Army Veterans. *Psychosom Med* 69: 365–369.

Bradley SJ (2000) *Affect Regulation and the Development of Psychopathology*. New York: Guilford Press.

Brady KT (2001) Pharmacotherapeutic treatment for women with PTSD. *Program and abstract of the 154th Annual Meeting of the American Psychiatric Association*. New Orleans, Louisiana. Symposium 12 C.

Bremner JD (2001) Hypotheses and controversies related to effects of stress on the hippocampus: An argument for stress induced damage to the hippocampus in patients with PTSD. *Hippocampus* 11: 75–81.

Bremner JD (2002a) Neuroimaging studies in post-traumatic stress disorder. *Curr Psychiatry Rep* 4: 254–263.

Bremner JD (2002b) *Does Stress Damage the Brain?* New York: WW Norton and Co.

Bremner JD (2005) Effects of traumatic stress on brain structure and function: Relevance to early response to trauma. *J Trauma Dissociation* 6: 51–68.

Bremner JD, Vythilingham M, Vermetten E et al. (2003) Neural correlates of declarative memory for emotionally valenced words in women with posttraumatic stress disorder related to early childhood sexual abuse. *Biol Psychiatry* 53: 879–889.

Byrne JA, Roberts JL (eds) (2007) *From Molecules to Networks: An introduction to cellular and molecular neuroscience*. London: Elsevier Science/Academic Press.

Cannistraro PA, Rauch SL (2003) Neural circuitry of anxiety: Evidence from structural and functional neuroimaging studies. *Psychopharmacol Bull* 37: 8–25.

Caspi A, Sugden K, Moffitt TE et al. (2003) Influence of life stress on depression: Moderation by a polymorphism in 5HTT gene. *Science* 301: 386–389.

Challis BG, Luan J, Keough J, Wareham NJ, Farooqi IS, O'Rahilly S (2004) Genetic variation in the corticotropin-releasing factor receptors: Identification of single-nucleotide polymorphisms and association studies with obesity in UK Caucasians. *Int J Obesity Relat Metab Disord* 28: 442–446.

Charney DS (2004) Psychobiological mechanisms of resilence and vulnerability: Implications for successful adaptation to extreme stress. *Am J Psychiatry* 161: 195–216.

Charney DS, Woods SW, Krystal JH, Nagy LM, Heninger GR (1992) Noradrenergic neuronal dysregulation in panic disorder: The effects of intravenous yohimbine and clinidine in panic disorder patients. *Acta Psychiatr Scand* 86: 273–282.

Chatham WW, Stiehm ER, Feldweg AM (2008) Glucocorticoid effects on innate and acquired (adaptive) immunity. Up to date (version 16(3)). Last literature review October 2008 and topic last updated on August 2008. Accessed November 2008 from: www.utdol.com/patients/content/topic.do?topkey=tiZjOjqweev5-84k.

Chrousos GR, Kino T (2007) Glucocorticoid action networks and complex psychiatric and or somatic disorders. *Stress* 10: 213–219.

Cicchetti D, Cohen DJ (2006) *Developmental Psychopathology*, 2nd edn. New York: Wiley.

Collins D, Pare D (2000) Differential fear conditioning induces reciprocal changes in the sensory responses of lateral amygdala neurons to the CS= and CS-. *Neuroscience* 7: 97–103.

Compagnone NA, Mellon SH (2000) Biosynthesis and function of these neuromodulators. *Neuroendocrinology* 21: 1–56.

Cullinan WE, Ziegler DR, Herman JP (2008) Functional role of local GABAergic influences on the HPA axis. *Brain Struct Funct* 213: 1863–2661.

Dalgleish T (2004) The emotional brain. *Nat Rev Neurosci* 5: 583–589.

Damasio AR, Grabowski TJ, Bechara A et al. (2000) Subcortical and cortical brain activity during the feeling of self-generated emotions. *Nat Neurosci* 3: 1049–1056.

Davidson RJ, Putnam KM, Larson CL (2000) Dysfunction in the neural circuitry of emotion regulation—A possible prelude to violence. *Science* 289: 591–594.

Davis M (1992) The role of the amygdala in fear and anxiety. *Annu Rev Neurosci* 15: 353–375.

Dazzan P, Morgan KD, Orr KG et al. (2005) Different effects of typical and atypical antipsychotics on grey matter in first episode psychosis: the/ESOP study. *Neuropsychopharmacology* 30: 765–774.

Dazzan P, Morgan KD, Chitnis X et al. (2006) The structural braincorrelates of neurological soft signs in healthy individuals. *Cerebral Cortex* 16: 1225–1231.

Dent GW, Smith MA, Levine S (2001) Stress induced alterations in locus coeruleus gene expression during ontogeny. *Brain Res Dev Brain Res* 127: 23–30.

Douglas A (2005) Central noradrenergic mechanisms underlying acute stress responses of the hypothalamic-pituitary-adrenal axis; Adaptations through pregnancy and lactation. *Stress* 8: 5–8.

Driessen M, Herrmann J, Stahl K et al. (2000) Magnetic resonance imaging volumes of the hippocampus and the amygdala in women with borderline personality disorder and early traumatization. *Arch Gen Psychiatry* 57: 1115–1122.

Dunn AJ (2000) Interactions between the nervous system and the immune system: implications for psychopharmacology. Accessed November 2008 from: www.acnp.org/publications/psycho4generation.aspx. In: *Psychopharmacology—the fourth generation of progress*: American College of Neuropsychopharmacology.

Dunn AJ (2005) *Nervous System and Immune Interactions*. Chichester: Wiley and Sons.

Dunn AJ, Swiergiel AH, Palamarchouk V (2004) Brain circuits involved in corticotropin-releasing factor-norepinephrine interactions during stress. *Ann N Y Acad Sci* 1018: 25–34.

Englemann M, Landgraf R, Wotjac C (2004) The hypothalamic-neurohypophysial system regulates the hypothalamic-pituitary-adrenal axis under stress: An old concept revisited. *Front Neuroendocrinol* 25: 132–149.

Etkin A, Wager TD (2007) Functional neuroimaging of anxiety: A meta-analysis of emotional processing in PTSD. Social anxiety disorder, and specific phobia. *Am J Psychiatry* 164: 1476–1488.

Felitti VJ, Anda RF, Nordenberg D et al. (1998) Relationship of childhood abuse and household dysfunction to many of the leading causes of death in adults. The adverse childhood experiences (ACE) study. *Am J Prev Med* 14: 245–258.

Flouri E (2005) Post traumatic stress disorder. *J Interpersonal Violence* 20: 373–379.

Foa EB, Keane TM, Friedman MJ (eds) (2000) *Effective Treatments for PTSD: Practice Guidelines from the International Society for Traumatic Stress Studies*. New York: Guilford Press.

Friedman MJ (1997) Posttraumatic stress disorder. *J Clin Psychiatry* 58(suppl 9): 33–36.

Friedman MJ, Heane TM, Resick PA (2007) *Handbook of PTSD: Science and practice*. New York: Guilford Press.

Gao A (2004) Fear and anxiety: post-traumatic stress disorder. *Paper at Bryn-Mawr College*. Accessed November 2008 from: http://serendip.brynmawr.edu/bb/neuro/neuro04/web1/agao.html.

Ghashghaei HT, Barbas H (2002) Pathways for emotion: Interactions of prefrontal and anterior temporal pathways in the amygdala of the rhesus monkey. *Neuroscience* 115: 1261–1279.

Gianoni G, Baker D (2004) Inflammatory disorders of the central nervous system. *Curr Opin Neurol* 16: 347–350.

Gilbertson MW, Shenton ME, Ciszewski A et al. (2002) Smaller hippocampal volume predicts pathologic vulnerability to psychological trauma. *Nat Neurosci* 5: 1242–1247.

Gill J, Szanton S, Page G (2005) Biological underpinnings of health alterations in women with PTSD: a sex disparity. *Biol Res Nurs* 7: 44–54.

Glover DA, Stuber M, Poland RE (2006) Allostatic load in women with and without PTSD symptoms. *Psychiatry* 69: 191–203.

Goddard AW, Charney DS, Germine M et al. (1995) Effects of tryptophan depletion on response to yohimbine in healthy human subjects. *Biol Psychiatry* 38: 74–85.

Gorman JM, Kent JM, Sullivan GM, Coplan JD (2000) Neuroanatomical hypothesis of panic disorder, revised. *Am J Psychiatry* 157: 493–505.

Gurvits TV, Gilbertson MW, Lasko NB et al. (2000) Neurological soft signs in in chronic posttraumatic stress disorder. *Arch Gen Psychiatry* 57: 181–186.

Gurvits TV, Gilbertson MW, Lasko NB et al. (2006) Subtle neurologic compromise as a vulnerability factor for combat-related posttraumatic stress disorder; Results of a twin study. *Arch Gen Psychiatry* 63: 571–576.

Hains AB (2008) Molecular mechanisms of stress-induced prefrontal cortical impairment. *Learn Mem* 15: 551–564.

Haviland MG, Sonne JL, Anderson DL et al. (2006) Thyroid hormone levels and psychological symptoms in sexually abused adolescent girls. *Child Abuse Negl* 30: 585–588.

Heffenan K, Cloitre M (2000) A comparison of posttraumatic stress disorder with and without borderline personality disorder with a history of childhood sexual abuse: Etiological and clinical characteristics. *J Nerv Ment Disord* 88: 589–595.

Herman J (2007) Limbic-hypothalamic neurocircuits controlling the HPA axis stress responses. *Proc Physiol Soc* 5: SA7.

Herman J, Ostrander M, Mueller N, Figueriedo H (2005) Limbic system mechanisms of stress regulation: Hypothalamo-pituitary-adrenocortical axis. *Progr Neuro-psychopharmacol Biol Psychiatry* 29: 1201–1213.

Honig RG, Grace MC, Lindy JD, Newman CJ, Titchener JL (1999) Assessing long term effects of trauma: Diagnosing symptoms of avoidance and numbing. *Am J Psychiatry* 156: 483–485.

Hull AM (2002) Neuroimaging findings in post-traumatic stress disorder. Systematic review. *Br J Psychiatry* 181: 102–110.

Kabbaj M (2004) Neurobiological bases of individual differences in emotional and stress responsiveness. *Arch Neurol* 61: 1009–1012.

Karl A, Schafer M, Malta LS et al. (2006) A meta-analysis of structural brain abnormalities in PTSD. *Neurosci Biobehav Rev* 30: 1004–1031.

Kellner M, Yassouredes A, Hubner R et al. (2000) Endocrine and cardiovascular response to corticotropin-releasing hormone in patients with posttraumatic stress disorder: A role for atrial natriuretic peptide. *Neuropsychobiology* 47: 102–108.

Kellner M, Baker DG, Yassouridis A et al. (2002) Mineralcorticoid receptor function in patients with posttraumatic stress disorder. *Am J Psychiatry* 159: 1938–1940.

Kessler RC, Sonnega A, Bromet E, Hughes M, Nelson CB (1995) Posttraumatic stress disorder in the National Comorbidity Survey. *Arch Gen Psychiatry* 52: 1048–1060.

Koenen KC, Driver KL, Oscar-Berman M et al. (2001) Measures of prefrontal system dysfunction in posttraumatic stress disorder. *Brain Cogn* 45: 64–78.

Kolassa IT, Elbert T (2007) Sensitized and functional neuroplasticity in relation to traumatic stress. *Curr Directions Psychol Sci* 16: 321–325.

Kozaric-Kovacic D (2002) Elevation of serum total triiodothyronine and free-triidothyronine in Croatian veterans with combat-related post-traumatic stress disorder. *Military Med* 167: 846–849.

Lanius RA, Williamson PC, Densmore M et al. (2001) Neural correlates of traumatic memories in posttraumatic stress disorder: A functional MRI investigation. *Am J Psychiatry* 158: 1920–1922.

LeDoux JE (1996) *The Emotional Brain*. New York: Simon and Schuster.

LeDoux JE (1998) Fear and the brain: where have we been and where are we going?. *Biol Psychiatry* 44: 1229–1238.

LeDoux JE (ed.) (2002) *Synaptic Self: How our brains become who we are*. New York: Penguin.

LeDoux JE (2003) The emotional brain, fear, and the amygdala. *Mol Neurobiol* 23: 4–5.

LeDoux JE, Iwata J, Cicchetti P, Reis DJ (1988) Different projections of the central amygdaloid nucleus mediate autonomic and behavioral correlates of conditioned fear. *J Neurosci* 8: 2517–2529.

Levine P (1997) *Waking the Tiger*. Berkeley, CA: North Atlantic Press.

Lopez J (2004) Neural circuits mediating tress. *Biol Psychiatry* 46: 1461–1471.

Loucks EB, Juster RP, Pruessner JC (2008) Neuroendocrine biomarkers, allostatic load, and the challenge of measurement: A commentary on Gersten. *Soc Sci Med* 66: 525–530.

Lukey BJ, Tepe V (eds) (2008) *Biobehavioral Resilience to Stress*. Boca Raton: CRC Press.

Luthar SS, Sexton CC (2007) Maternal drug abuse versus maternal depression: Vulnerability and resilience among school-age and adolescent offspring. *Dev Psychopathol* 19: 205–225.

Lynch JW, Kaplan JA, Shema SJ (1997) Cumulative impact of sustained economic hardship on physical, cognitive, psychological, and social functioning. *N Engl J Med* 337: 1889–1895.

Mann JJ (1998) The neurobiology of suicide. *Nature Med* 4: 25–30.

Manuck SB, Flory JD, Ferrell RE, Dent KM, Mann JJ, Muldoon MF (1999) Aggression and anger related traits associated with poly morphism of the tryptophan hydroxylase gene. *Biol Psychiatry* 45: 603–614.

Maren S (2001) Neurobiology of pavlovian fear conditioning. *Annu Rev Neurosci* 24: 897–931.

McEwen BS (1997) Possible mechanisms for atrophy of the human hippocampus. *Mol Psychiatry* 2: 255–262.

McEwen BS (1998) Protective and damaging effects of stress mediators. *N Engl J Med* 338: 171–179.

McEwen BS (1999) Stress and hippocampal plasticity. *Annu Rev Neurosci* 22: 105–122.

McEwen BS (2000) Allostasis and allostatic load: Implications for neuropsychopharmacology. *Neuropsychopharmacology* 22: 108–124.

McEwen BS (2001) Plasticity of the hippocampus: Adaptation to chronic stress and allostatic load. *Ann NY Acad Sci* 933: 265–277.

McEwen BS, Seeman T (1999) Protective and damaging effects of mediators of stress: Elaborating and testing the concepts of allostatic load. *Ann NY Acad Sci* 896: 30–47.

McEwen BS, Biron CA, Brunson KW et al. (1997) The role of adrenocorticoids as modulators of immune function in health and disease, neural, endocrine and immune interactions. *Brain Res Rev* 23: 70–133.

McFarlane AC (1992) Avoidance and intrusions in posttraumatic stress disorder. *J Nerv Ment Dis* 1: 439–445.

McGaugh JL (2004) The amygdala modulates the consolidation of memories of emotionally arousing experiences. *Annu Rev Neurosci* 27: 1–28.

Medina J (2008) Neurobiology of PTSD 2008. *Psychiatric Times*. Available from: www.brainrules.net/pdf/JohnMedina_PsychTimes_March08.pdf.

Milkulincer et al. 2007

Miller G, Cohen S, Ritchey AK (2000) Chronic psychological stress and the regulation of pro-inflammatory cytokine: A glucocorticoid resistance model. *Health Psychol* 21: 531–541.

Miller G, Chen E, Zhou ES (2007) If it goes up, must it come down? Chronic stress and the hypothalamic-pituitary-adrenocortico axis in humans. *Psychol Bull* 133: 25–45.

Morfin R, Starka I (2001) Neurosteroid 7-hydroxylation products in the brain. *Int Rev Neurobiol* 46: 79–95.

Morgan CA, Rasmusson AM, Winters B et al. (2003) Trauma exposure rather than post traumatic stress disorder is associated with reduced plasma neuropeptide Y levels. *Biol Psychiatry* 54: 1087–1091.

Morgan CA, Southwick S, Hazlett G et al. (2004) Relationships among plasma dehydropiandrosterone sulfate and cortisol levels, symptoms of dissociation, and objective performance in human exposed to acute stress. *Arch Gen Psychiatry* 61: 819–825.

Mueller D, Porter JT, Quirk GJ (2008) Noradrenergic signalling in infralimbic cortex increases cell excitability and strengthens memory for fear extinction. *J Neurosci* 28: 369–375.

Muller N, Schwartz MJ (2006) The immune mediated alteration of serotonin and glutamate: Toward an integrated view of depression. *Mol Psychiatry* 12: 988–1000.

Murali R, Chan E (2005) Exposure to violence and cardiovascular and neuroendocrine measures in adolescents. *Ann Behav Med* 30: 155–163.

Nadel L, Jacobs WJ (1996) The role of the hippocampus in PTSD, panic and phobia. In: *Hippocampus: Functions and clinical relevance* (Kato N, ed.). Amsterdam: Elsevier Science.

Newport DJ, Nemeroff CB (2000) Neurobiology of posttraumatic stress disorder. *Curr Opin Neurobiol* 10: 211–218.

Nestler EJ, Hyman SE, Malenka RC (2001) *Molecular Neuropharmacology: A foundation for clinical neuroscience*. New York: McGraw-Hill.

Neylan TC, Brunet A, Pole N et al. (2005) PTSD symptoms predict waking salivary cortisol levels in police officers. *Psychoneuroendocrinology* 30: 373–381.

Nieuwenhuis S, Aston-Jones G, Cohen JD (2005) Decision-making, the P3, and the locus coeruleus-norepinephrine system. *Psychol Bull* 131: 510–532.

Nieuwenhuis S, Nieuwpoort JC, Veltman DJ, Drent ML (2007) Effects of the noradrenergic agonist clonidine on temporal and spatial attention. *Psychopharmacology* 193: 261–269.

National Institutes of Health (NIH) (2001) *Reliving Trauma: Post-Traumatic Stress Disorder*. No. 01-4597. Bethesda, MD: National Institutes of Health.

Nussbaum CO (2007) *The Musical Representation*. Boston: MIT Press.

Nutt DJ, Malizia AL (2004) Structural and functional brain changes in posttraumatic stress disorder. *J Clin Psychiatry* 65: 11–17.

Ogilvie KM, Review C (1997) Gender difference in hypothalamic-pituitary-adrenal axis response to alcohol in the rat: Activational role of gonadal steroids. *Brain Res* 766: 19–28.

Oh SB, Endoh T, Simen AA, Ren D, Miller RJ (2002) Regulation of calcium currents by chemokines and their receptors. *J Neuroimmunol* 123: 66–75.

Oswald IM, McCaul M, Choi L, Yang X, Wand GS (2004) Catechol O-methyltransferase polymorphism alters hypothalamic-pituitary-adrenal axis responses to naloxone: A preliminary report. *Biol Psychiatry* 55: 102–105.

Pariante CM (2003) Depression, stress and the adrenal axis. The British Society for Neuroendocrinology. Available from: www.neuroendo.org.uk/content/view/31/11/.

Phan KL, Wager T, Taylor SF, Liberzon I (2002) Functional neuroanatomy of emotion: a meta-analysis of emotional activation studies in PET and fMRI. *Neuroimage* 16: 331–348.

Phillips ML, Drevets WC, Rauch SL, Lane R (2003) Neurobiology of emotion perception 1: The neural basis of normal emotion perception. *Biol Psychiatry* 54: 504–514.

Pissiota A, Frans O, Fernandez M et al. (2002) Neurofunctional correlates of posttraumatic stress disorder: a PET symptom provocation study. *Eur Arch Psychiatry Clin Neurosci* 252: 68–75.

Pitman RK, Shin LM, Rauch SL (2001) Investigating pathogenesis of posttraumatic stress disorder with neuroimaging. *J Clin Psychiatry* 62(suppl 17): 47–54.

Pitman RK, Gilbertson MW, Gurvits TV et al. (2006) Clarifying the origin of biological abnormalities in PTSD through the study of identical twins discordant for combat exposure. *Ann N Y Acad Sci* 1071: 242–254.

Porges S (2001) Understanding the mechanisms of traumatic stress: The poly vagal theory and its role in treating disorders of attention, affect regulation, social communication, and aggression. *Paper presented at the Conference on Traumatic Stress, Neuroscience and Treatment Innovations*. Three Views of Traumatic Stress: Applied Neuroscience and Clinical Practice. Westminster, CO, January 26–28.

Raison CL, Miller AH (2003) When not enough is too much: The role of insufficient glucocorticoid signalling in the pathophysiology of stress related disorders. *Am J Psychiatry* 160: 1554–1565.

Rasmusson AM, Hauger RL, Morgan CM, Bremner JD, Charney DS, Southwick SM (2000) Low baseline and yohimbine stimulated plasma neuropeptide Y (NPY) levels in combat related posttraumatic stress disorder. *Biol Psychiatry* 47: 526–539.

Rasmusson AM, Vyhilingham M, Morgan CA III (2003) The neuroendocrinology of posttraumatic stress disorder: new directions. *Clin Nurs Spec* 8: 651–667.

Rasmusson AM, Vasek J, Lipschitz DS et al. (2004) An increased capacity for adrenal DHEA release is associated with decreased avoidance and negative mood symptoms in women with PTSD. *Neuropsychopharmacology* 29: 1546–1557.

Rasmusson AM, Pinna G, Weisman D et al. (2005) Decreases in CSF allopregnalone levels in women with PTSD correlates negatively with reexperiencing symptoms. *Paper presented at the Society of Biological Psychiatry Annual Meeting*, Atlanta, GA, May.

Rauch SL, Shin LM, Whalen PJ, Pitman RK (1998) Neuroimaging and the neuroanatomy of PTSD. *Clin Nurs Spec*(suppl 2): 30–41.

Rauch SL, Whalen PJ, Shin LM et al. (2000) Exaggerated amygdala response to masked facial stimuli in posttraumatic stress disorder: A functional MRI study. *Biol Psychiatry* 47: 769–776.

Rillings JK, Gutman DA, Zeh TR, Pagnoni G, Berns GS, Kilts CD (2002) A neural basis for social cooperation. *Neuron* 35: 395–405.

Roozedaal B, Costello NA, Vedana G, Barsegyan A, McGaugh JL (2008) Noradrenergic activation of the basolateral amygdala modulates consolidation of object recognition memory. *Neurobiol Learning Memory* 90: 576–579.

San Juan (2006)

Santa Ana EJ, Saladin ME, Back SE et al. (2006) PTSD and the HPA axis: Differences in response to cold pressor task among individuals with child vs adult trauma. *Psychoneuroendocrinology* 31: 500–509.

Sapolsky R (1998) *Why Zebras Don't get Ulcers: An updated guide to stress, stress-related disease, and coping*. New York: Freeman.

Sapolsky R, Krey LC, McEwen BS (1985) Prolonged glucocorticoid exposure reduces hippocampal cell number: Implications for aging. *J Neurosci* 5: 1222–1227.

Sbarra et al. 2008

Schacter DL, Scarry E (eds) (2000) *Memory, Brain and Belief.* Cambridge, MA: Harvard University Press.

Schneider F, Weiss U, Kessler C et al. (2000) Subcortical correlates of differential classical conditioning of aversive emotional reactions in social phobias. *Biol Psychiatry* 45: 863–871.

Seasholtz A (2008) Regulation of adrenocorticotropic hormone secretion: lessons from mice deficient in corticotropin-releasing hormone. *J Clin Invest* 105: 1187.

Segerstrom SC, Miller GE (2004) Psychological stress and the human immune system: A meta-analytic study of 30 years of inquiry. *Psychol Bull* 130: 601–630.

Shin LM, Whalen PJ, Pitman RK et al. (2001) An fMRI study of anterior cingulated functioning in posttraumatic stress disorder. *Biol Psychiatry* 50: 932–942.

Silverman et al. 2008

Slawik M, Reisch N, Zwermann O et al. (2004) Characterization of an adrenocorticotropin (ACTH) receptor promoter polymorphism leading to decreased adrenal respnsiveness to ACTH. *J Clin Endocrinol Metab* 89: 3131–3137.

Slovic P (2002) Perception of risk proposed by extreme events. *Paper presented at a conference on Risk Management Strategies in an Uncertain World*, New York, April 12–13.

Smith TC, Wingard DL, Ryan Mak, Kritz-Silverstein D, Slymen DJ, Salles JF (2008) Prior assault and posttraumatic stress disorder after combat deployment. *Epidemiology* 19: 505–512.

Solomon EP, Heidi KM (2005) The biology of trauma: Implications for treatment. *J Interpers Violence* 20: 51–66.

Sondergaard HP, Hansson LO, Theorell T (2002) Elevated levels of dehydroepiandrosterone sulphate vary with symptom load in posttraumatic stress disorder: Findings from a longitudinal study of refugees in Sweden. *Psychother Psychosomat* 71: 298–303.

Spivak B, Maayan R, Kotler M et al. (2000) Elevated circulatory level of GABA A-antagonistic neurosteroids in patients with combat-related post-traumatic stress disorder. *Psychol Med* 30: 1227–1231.

Stein MB, Koverola C, Hanna C, Torchia MG, McClarty B (1997) Hippocampal volume in women victimized by childhood sexual abuse. *Psychol Med* 27: 951–959.

Stein MB, Goldin PR, Sareen J, Zorilla LT, Brown GG (2002) Increased amygdala activation of angry and contemptuous faces in generalized social phobia. *Arch Gen Psychiatry* 59: 1027–1034.

Steinman L (2004) elaborate interactions between the immune and nervous system. *Nat Immunol* 5: 575–581.

Stone et al. (1990)

Strous RD, Maayan R, Lapidus R et al. (2003) Dehydropiandrosterone augmentation in the management of negative, depressive, and anxiety symptoms in schizophrenia. *Arch Gen Psychiatry* 60: 133–141.

Stutzman GE, McEwen BS, LeDoux JE (1998) Serotonin modulation of sensory inputs to the lateral amygdala: dependency on corticosterone. *J Neurosci* 18: 9529–9538.

Sunada Shankaranarayana R, Raju TR (2004) Restraint stress-indirect alterations in the level of biogenic amines, amino acids, and AChE activity in the hippocampus. *Neurochem Res* 25: 1547–1552.

Sunstein CR (2007) The Catastrophic Harm Precautionary Principle. *Issues in Legal Scholarship*, Catastrophic Risks: Prevention, Compensation, and Recovery (2007): Article 3. Accessed November 2008 from: www.bepress.com/ils/iss10/art3.

Tait AS, Butts CL, Sternberg EM (2008) The role of glucocorticoids and progestin in inflammatory, autoimmune, and infectious disease. *J Leukoc Biol* 84: 924–931.

Takeuchi Y, McLean JH, Hopkins DA (1982) Reciprocal connections between the amygdala and parabrachial nuclei: ultra structural demonstration by degeneration and axonal transport of horseradish peroxidase in the cat. *Brain Res* 239: 583–588.

Tolin DF, Foa EB (2006) Women are diagnosed with PTSD more than men, even though they experience fewer traumatic events. *APA Press Release* 19 November.

Twardowska K, Rybakowski J (1996) Limbic-hypothalamic-pituitary-adrenal axis in depression: literature review. *Psychiatr Pol* 30: 741–755.

Ulrich-Lai Y, Xie Wenrui, Meij TA, Dolgas CM, Yu L, Herman JP (2006) Limbic and HPA axis function in an animal model of chronic neuropathic pain. *Physiol Behav* 88: 67–76.

van der Kolk BA (1997) The psychobiology of posttraumatic stress disorder. *J Clin Psychiatry* 58: 16–24.

van der Kolk BA, Fisler R (1995) Dissociation and the fragmentary nature of traumatic memories: Overview and exploratory study. *J Trauma Stress* 8: 505–525.

van der Kolk BA, Saporta J (1991) The biological response to psychic trauma: Mechanisms and treatment of intrusions and numbing. *Anxiety Res (UK)* 4: 199–212.

van der Kolk BA, McFarlance AC, Weisaeth L (eds) (1996) *Traumatic Stress.* New York: Guilford Press.

van der Kolk BA, Burbridge J, Suzuki J (1997) The psychobiology of trauma memory: Clinical implications of neuroimaging studies. *Ann N Y Acad Sci* 821: 99–113.

Vasterling JJ, Brewin CR (2005) *Neuropsychology of PTSD: Biological, Cognitive, and Clinical Perspectives.* New York: Guilford Press.

Villareal G, Hamilton DA, Petropoulus H et al. (2002a) Reduced hippocampal volume and total white matter volume in posttraumatic stress disorder. *Biol Psychiatry* 52: 119–125.

Villareal G, Petropolous H, Hamilton DA (2002b) Proton magnetic resonance spectroscopy of the hippocampus and occipital white matter in PTSD: preliminary results. *Can J Psychiatry* 47: 666–670.

Walker DL, Davis M (2002) The role of amygdala glutamate receptors in fear-learning, fear-potentiated startle, and extinction. *Pharmacol Biochem Behav* 71: 379–392.

Webster JI, Tonelli L, Sternberg EM (2002) Neuroendocrine regulation of immunity. *Annu Rev Immunol* 20: 125–126.

Williams JHG, Perreti DI, Waiter GD, Pechey S (2007) Differential effects of tryptophan depletion on emotion processing to face direction. *Social Cogn Affect Neurosci* 2: 264–273.

Winson J (1993) The biology and function of rapid eye movement sleep. *Curr Opin Neurobiol* 3: 243–248.

Witchel SF, Lee PA, Suda-Hartman M, Trucco M, Hoffman EP (1997) Evidence for a heterozygote advantage in congeneital adrenal hyperplasia due to 21-hydroxylase deficiency. *J Clin Endocrinol Metab* 82: 2097–2101.

Wolpe J (1958) *Psychotherapy by Reciprocal Inhibition.* Stanford, CA: Stanford University Press.

Wrosch C, Schulz R (2008) Health engagment cortisol strategies and 2 year changes in older adults' physical health. *Psychol Sci* 19: 537–541.

Wust S, Van Rossum EF, Federenko IS, Koper JW, Kumsta R, Hellhammer DH (2004) Common polymorphisms in the glucocorticoid receptor gene are associated with adrenocortical responses to psychosocial stress. *J Clin Endocrinol Metab* 89: 565–573.

Yamasue H, Abe O, Suga M et al. (2008) Gender-common and specific neuroanatomical basis of human anxiety-related personality traits. *Cereb Cortex* 18: 46–52.

Yehuda R (1999) Linking the neuroendocrinology of post-traumatic stress disorder with recent neuroanatomic findings. *Semin Clin Neuropsychiatry* 4: 256–265.

Yehuda R (2002) Current status of cortisol findings in post-traumatic stress disorder. *Psychiatr Clin N Am* 25: 341–368.

Yehuda R, Wong C (2001) Pathogenesis of posttraumatic stress disorder and acute stress. In: *Textbook of Anxiety Disorders.* Arlington, VA: American Psychiatric Publishing.

Yehuda R, Goller J, Halligan S, Meaney M, Bierer L (2004) The ACTH response to dexamethasone in PTSD. *Am J Psychiatry* 181: 1397–1403.

Yehuda R, Flory JD, Southwick S, Charney DS (2006) Developing an agenda for translational studies of resilience and vulnerability following trauma exposure. *Ann N Y Acad Sci* 1071: 379–396.

Yehuda R, Bell A, Bierer LM, Schmeidler J (2008) Maternal, not paternal PTSD is related to increased risk in offspring of Holocaust survivors. *J Psychiatr Res* 42: 1104–1111.

Ziegler DR, Herman JP (2002) Neurocircuitry of stress integration: Anatomic pathways regulating the hypothalamo-pituitary-adrenocortico axis of the rat. *Integr Comp Biol* 42: 541–551.

Zigmond MJ, Finlay JM, Sved AV (1995) Neurochemical studies in central noradrenergic responses to acute and chronic stress. In: *Neurobiological and Clinical Consequences of Stress: From normal adaptations to PTSD* (Friedman M, Charnwy D, Deutsch A, eds). Philadelphia: Lippincott Press.

PART **II**

Treatment

Chapter 3

Transtheoretical and Multimodal Interventions

The term transtheoretical was chosen because it best describes the consolidation of core information from different theories on posttraumatic stress disorder (PTSD). For example, even though the theoretical perspective on somatic memory and biological mechanisms is not the central theoretical framework from which diagnosis and treatment interventions are derived, Foa et al. (2009) acknowledge in their text *Effective Treatments for PTSD* the concepts of complex PTSD and subthreshold PTSD as part of the "informal" diagnostic continuum that others have richly underscored for the presence of these features (le Doux, 1997; Levene, 1998; Matsakis, 1994; Rothchild, 2000; van der Kolk, 1999). In addition, the American Psychiatric Association (Regehr et al., 2007) espouses the importance of broadening the biological scope of mental disorders, designating the importance of integrating the major theories in anticipation that this is the direction of the next *Diagnostic and Statistical Manual* (DSM). Multimodality simply refers to the integration of the numerous modalities documented to be effective with the range of patients diagnosed with PTSD which is utilized for developing the individualized treatment plan.

PTSD is a complex condition that can impair life functions. Traumatic events negatively impact the body as well as the mind. One of the major categories in the constellation of symptoms listed in the *Diagnostic and Statistical Manual* (DSM-IV) of the American Psychiatric Association (2000) is those of the autonomic nervous system (ANS). These symptoms are described as, "persistent symptoms of increased arousal." A comprehensive diagnostic evaluation with a comprehensive plan of intervention requires consideration for the integration of treating the traumatized body as well as the traumatized mind. A central factor in all of the *Therapist's Guide* books (Johnson, 1997, 2003, 2004) is the importance of meeting the patient where they are at in their level of functioning, using an individualized treatment plan. In trauma work this decreases the risk of moving

Therapist's Guide to Posttraumatic Stress Disorder Intervention

too quickly in therapy and retraumatizing the patient as well as making their experience in working through less emotionally volatile. The primary symptoms of focus for clinical intervention include:

- Mood and affect instability/lability
- Self-destructive impulsivity
- Dissociation
- Pathological changes in identity
- Somatization
- Interpersonal difficulties.

PTSD has a better prognosis if clinical intervention is implemented as early as possible (Foa et al., 2000b, 2009). Due to the circumstances of trauma, many patients with PTSD exhibit difficulty with interpersonal trust. This requires special clinical attention to safety, trust, consistency, and respecting personal boundaries. In addition, PTSD symptoms can surface and become exacerbated in association with trauma anniversaries or other trauma reminders. When a therapist is addressing a diagnosis of PTSD it is important to normalize symptoms as an effort to facilitate feelings of relief and decrease reluctance to engage in the treatment process. Early intervention with acute stress disorder may prevent the development of PTSD or keep it from becoming chronic.

A therapist chooses a treatment approach based upon the clinical information and hypotheses identified by utilizing a comprehensive diagnostic evaluation.

STAGES OF TREATMENT FOR PTSD

In treating a patient with PTSD the therapist should consider the following points:

- Ensure safety
- Aim for stabilization—symptom containment and reduction
- Emphasize grounding—being in the here and now
- Allow remembrance and mourning
- Encourage the person to talk about their trauma—be sensitive in inquiring about trauma, loss, or violence
- Be emotionally supportive—meet the person where they are (be careful to not push beyond what they can manage to process)
- Create choices for management and control. Do not focus on eliminating defenses, they are often an internal resource and coping strategy
- Reassure them that it is not uncommon to experience distressing symptoms, while reinforcing skills development, progress, and mastery for managing those symptoms
- Aim for deconditioning of trauma memories, emotional responses, and somatic responses
- Relieve irrational guilt

- Provide education about acute stress and posttraumatic stress based upon symptom presentation and the timeframe of the traumatic event(s)

- Normalize their experience as a biological reaction which causes changes in the brain (which they have found a way to survive)

- Aim to restructure traumatic/personal schemas

- Aim to re-establish secure social connections and interpersonal efficacy

- Repair emotional experiences

- Reintegrate rehabilitation (rebuild self-esteem, self-confidence, and self-efficacy in all major life areas).

The therapist must be prepared to put aside their structured belief system and, instead, be prepared (themselves) to be a tool in the moment, meeting the patient at their level of thought, feeling and functioning. This does not mean suspending the global case conceptualization and the treatment plan, it refers to a level of clinical flexibility regarding intervention that does not neglect rich moments in treatment nor unnecessarily create distress in meeting the therapist's needs instead of the patient's needs. Imposing structure and techniques without regard to individuality can potentially result in more damage to a patient. Clearly, treatment must be adapted and tailored to the specific needs, skill level and associated resources of the patient. If a patient is non-responsive to treatment, systematically reassess for the presence of undisclosed or undetected conditions that are at the root of the poor outcome.

CREATING A SAFE AND SECURE ENVIRONMENT

In the epic work of Davis (1990) on survivors of trauma, the importance of creating an environment by which someone who had survived trauma could feel safe and secure was the starting point or "core of the healing process" (see also Chapter 5).

Safety is the experience of being protected from danger and hurt. Within a safe environment, we can relax and be ourselves because we know that our well being is secure. We feel free to take manageable risks toward growth and change. When you begin to talk honestly about your life in a safe environment, healing naturally begins to happen.

No matter what challenges a person has, it is important that a baseline be created for feeling safe and secure. Ask a patient, "have you ever imagined what it would feel like to have the stress of the trauma lifted so that you could fill your life with your own choices?" Facilitate them to explore the possibilities of feeling safe and secure by asking questions such as:

- Describe a time when you felt safe.

- What makes you feel safe?

- How safe is your environment?

- How safe are you with the people in your life?

- If you don't feel safe with the people in your home or the people in your life what can you do about it?

- For me to feel safe, I would need …
  - How can you protect yourself?
  - When do you feel safest?
  - How do you manage stressful environments which don't feel safe?

- Am I safe with myself?
  - Are you struggling with thoughts or urges to harm yourself?
  - harm others?

- Make a list of your negative/unsafe thoughts and urges and then write three thoughts to counter each of them

- Do you think you can ever feel safe?

- Do you believe that you have a right to healing and recovery? (why/why not?)

- How hard is it for you to give up your shield of fear and distrust and trust yourself to be and feel safe?

DIFFICULTIES AND CHALLENGES WITH THIS POPULATION

Patients with PTSD may demonstrate:

- Treatment ambivalence/avoidance
- Premature termination
- Rapid and unpredictable shifts in moods
- Inability to identify or describe feelings
- Difficulty regulating affect
- Avoidant/phobic about experiencing emotions
- Higher risk of self-harm and suicidality
- Confusion regarding the past with present environment
- Severe attachment issues
- Enmeshment with abusers
- Little expectation of being understood and helped
- Re-enactment of trauma in a therapeutic environment
- Risk of regression
- Risk of dependency
- Attitude of entitlement.

It should be remembered that this population sometimes evokes notable counter-transference responses in the therapist.

It may be validating, comforting, and reassuring to a person to normalize their experience and to help them to understand that their symptom presentation represents a biological reaction to an overwhelming experience. Explain that extreme stress causes a biological change in the way the brain works. Such dialogue offers hope that with time and appropriate treatment symptoms can be modified, alleviated, and/or eliminated. With appropriate intervention they are able to understand that PTSD is not a demonstration of weakness or defect, but rather psychobiological responses to extreme stress and trauma.

As with all treatment interventions, it is helpful to teach the person about all the various aspects of integrative interventions as well as the spectrum of symptoms associated with PTSD. This educative component is necessary in preparing the patient to fully participate in treatment planning decisions.

During the initial phase of treatment the therapist should:

- Assess for safety
- Rule out any medical issues
- Assess for substance abuse.

PSYCHOTHERAPEUTIC INTERVENTIONS

Intervention begins with the therapist. One of the most important contributions made by the therapist is to provide external regulation. While the interruptions associated with therapeutic intervention may be challenging to a patient, the following elements provided by the therapist are crucial to external regulation and breaking through the self-enclosure. (Self-enclosure symbolically re-enacts the sense of profound isolation experienced with traumatization and embodies a narcissistic quality.) Stopping the patient has the following functions:

- To gather information
- To encourage and facilitate the patient to pay attention to his or her body
- To slow the patient down (a step toward self-awareness and self-modulation)
- To encourage and support grounding and containment.

General psycho-education, as recommended by the Expert Consensus Guidelines (Foa et al., 1999c, 2009), should be offered regardless of the type of therapeutic modality chosen. It includes (but is not limited to):

- Familiarizing the patient with the general symptoms, thoughts, and feelings associated with experiencing trauma
- Offering reassurance that trauma-related symptoms are normal and expected to surface shortly following a traumatic event and can be overcome with time and treatment.

The basic components of the highly rated treatments by the Expert Consensus Panel, Veterans Administration, National Institute of Mental Health, the International Society for Traumatic Stress Studies, the Academy of Family Physicians, and numerous noted researchers and authors have been the source of information for this section. The guidelines have been overlapped to present an overall review of the range of recognized treatment interventions for the symptoms of PTSD.

The question often arises as to what structure of intervention should be used when there is clear comorbidity (such as substance use disorders). Safety is initially assessed with a concomitant review of the treatment needs. The case of a diagnosis of PTSD and substance abuse offers an excellent illustration of why it is important to meet the patient where they are at and to intervene in a manner that offers adequate support and symptom relief. Davis (2005) outlined a treatment intervention for such a case comprising:

- Inpatient detox (as needed)
- Inpatient and outpatient group in the substance treatment component
- Exposure therapy
- A 12-week structured treatment for PTSD and panic disorder.

INDIVIDUAL THERAPIES

COGNITIVE BEHAVIORAL THERAPY

Cognitive behavioral therapy (CBT) and the use of a selective serotonin reuptake inhibitor (SSRI) have been shown to be effective treatments of PTSD (Foa et al., 2000a, 2009). While there is some evidence that psychodynamic psychotherapy, hypnotherapy, and eye movement desensitization and processing (EMDR), along with a range of other treatment techniques, are also to be considered, more research is required for them to be viewed on a par with CBT and pharmacotherapy as a combination. The continual monitoring of mental distress and what is useful for management and recovery for any particular patient during the course of treatment is the act of clarification regarding both appropriate treatment and the treatment setting.

The goal of CBT is to identify and address the biopsychosocial aspects of PTSD experienced by an individual. CBT provides knowledge and skills related to processing the experience of trauma, such as:

- Enhancing safety
- Increased awareness
- Managing distressing thoughts
- Managing distressing feelings
- Managing distressing behaviors
- Improving communication
- Improving relationship functioning.

The central treatment features of CBT are as follows:

- Establishing and maintaining a therapeutic relationship
- Psycho-education about trauma and PTSD
- Emotional regulation
- Stress management
- Identifying and connecting thoughts, feelings and behaviors related to trauma
- Developing a beneficial narrative of the self and the world associated with trauma
- Encouraging appropriate and gradual exposure to trauma memories and reminders/cues
- Cognitive and affective processing of the trauma

- Education and rehearsal of healthy interpersonal relationships
- Personal safety skills training
- Coping with future reminders (prediction and preparedness for potential future trauma reminders)
- Relapse prevention.

COGNITIVE THERAPY

Beck is noted for his development of cognitive therapy (CT) which has evolved and been adapted to numerous diagnoses, including PTSD. Cognitive therapy involves working with affected individuals to change their emotions, thoughts, and behaviors associated with the traumatic event.

Beck (1964) developed CT as a structured, short-term, present-oriented psychotherapy for depressed patients. It has been successfully adapted to PTSD (Shipherd and Salters-Pedneault, 2008). The therapy generally begins with a brief education about how thoughts affect behavior and emotion, and then proceeds through the following processes to:

- Identify and clarify patterns of association in thoughts, feelings and behaviors (using journaling, group process, individual therapy, homework, bibliotherapy)
- Identify distressing trauma-related thoughts and challenge the irrational aspect of thought patterns into more accurate thoughts
- Identify and modify distorted core beliefs, about self, others, the world
- Challenge and correct irrational thoughts and beliefs. Improved accuracy in belief systems leads to improved mood and functioning
- Promote rational behavioral changes. Cognitive therapy teaches skills for recognizing the upsetting/disturbing thoughts, applying rational thinking/problem-solving which promotes the adoption of more realistic thoughts and behaviors. In accordance with one of the basic presuppositions of Neuro-Linguistic Programming, reality is a construction, therefore, you get what you focus on
- Strengthen resilience.

Contraindications for CT have not been established, but may include severe brain damage, severe intellectual deficit, or psychosis.

DIALECTICAL BEHAVIORAL THERAPY

This therapeutic approach may offer the most utility when PTSD is complicated by destructive impulsivity, suidality, and a chaotic lifestyle. Dialectical behavioral therapy is based on the value of a strong therapeutic alliance, supportive therapy, and cognitive behavioral therapy. Therapy is structured in stages and at each stage is a clear hierarchy of defined targets. Patients are taught the necessary skills to understand and deal with their behaviors and any problem they may encounter in applying those skills. The clinician supports, encourages and reinforces the patient to take responsibility for managing their life challenges, as well as providing advice and support between sessions.

According to van der Bosch et al. (2002), Verheul et al. (2003), and Kerr et al. (2008), women in dialectical behavioral therapy with borderline personality disorder achieved improved rates of retention and significant decreases of self-destructive/self-mutilating behaviors in comparison with those receiving other treatments. Van der Bosch et al. (2002) also found that comorbid substance abuse did not decrease the effectiveness of this therapy. However, there was no identified impact to the substance problem.

When self-help booklets containing elements of dialectical behavioral therapy in combination with six sessions of cognitive therapy were made available, there was a reported decrease in the number of suicidal acts/month and improvement in depressive symptoms as per self-rating (Evans et al., 1999).

Dialectical behavioral therapy emphasizes the importance of self-acceptance and self-awareness. Self-acceptance starts with self-awareness, which can be one of the significant challenges for traumatized patients who have become disconnected from the body. This disconnection is a source of betrayal. Therefore, it is important that the patient finds a way to get back in touch with the internal and physical responses to stimuli and develop appropriate and effective ways of thinking and behaving in order to maintain awareness and improve functioning.

Various techniques are used in dialectical behavioral therapy, including the following:

Beanbag Tapping

This technique is similar in its goal to meditation, but whereas meditation requires self-control and high cognitive demand, which may not be available in the PTSD patient, beanbag tapping creates self-control, requires minimal cognitive demand, allows the patient to "feel in the present," initiates self-awareness, reinforces self-control through physiology, and invites integration. The technique was developed to provide strong, deep pressure touch input to the body.

Beanbag tapping can be done throughout the day or at designated times (morning, noon, night). The beanbag is 10 cm by 10 cm and is used to give firm taps to the body, beginning with the hands, then the arms, the shoulders, back of the neck, the lower back if comfortable, and the legs and feet (the stomach area is always avoided). The patient taps for two minutes, moving from one body area to the next.

Music with Movement

This is helpful for relaxation, self-awareness and self-acceptance. Choose music carefully: it is better to use sections with no words and a good beat. Music that is too soft or quiet may allow thoughts to drift to flashbacks or dissociations.

Repeat Breathing

This is a walking meditation with intermittent deep breathing. Work up from 3–8 breaths. Walking coupled with breathing avoids the tendency for thoughts to drift to flashbacks or dissociations.

Cue Cards

When a patient is overwhelmed or frightened, cues cards can be used to come back to self-awareness and being mindful/in the moment.

Journaling

Journals should be very simple, using a smiley face or sad face for a corresponding feeling. Feelings can also be rated using a Likert scale.

TRAUMA COUNSELING

Trauma counseling involves controlling or containing something that can easily go out of control. It emphasizes the establishment of rapport and offering a safe environment in which to express and explore feelings, with the goal of helping survivors:

• To manage their reactions
• To express and deal in a productive manner with their feelings

- To come to terms with the difficult experiences they have lived through
- To solve associated problems in daily living.

EXPOSURE THERAPY

Exposure to the traumatic event via imaging allows the survivor to re-experience the event in a safe, controlled environment while also carefully experiencing their reactions and beliefs in relation to that event. The central clinical issue is avoidance. This avoidance is an attempt to avert activation via stimuli elements. Exposure therapy seeks to correct the pathological elements of the fear structure by pairing an incompatible element with the existing pathological element. With exposure therapy the activation creates an opportunity to integrate corrective information, thus resulting in a modification or change to pathological trauma memory which no longer serves a purpose.

Exposure therapy is not recommended for those diagnosed with severe mental illness, self-injurious behaviors, or suicidal (i.e. those who demonstrate a higher level of vulnerability).

Two behavior therapy techniques used in exposure therapy are imaginal exposure and *in vivo* exposure. These help a person to:

- Confront situations, people, and emotions associated with the stressor/trauma
- Identify, reorganize, and neutralize environmental cues.

The purpose of exposure therapy is to correct underlying mechanisms of PTSD. It is designed to facilitate confrontation of the patient's fears (people, object, emotions, memories) for varying amounts of time in either imaginal or *in vivo* situations. The exposure can also be arranged in a hierarchical fashion. Richards et al. (1994) found that patients with PTSD who were given four sessions of imaginal exposure followed by four sessions of *in vivo* exposure (or vice versa) improved considerably. Tarrier et al. (1999) cited a significant improvement in all measures at post treatment and follow-up, with no significance difference between exposure therapy and cognitive therapy. The Expert Consensus Panel for PTSD (1999) recommends exposure therapy for the treatment of intrusive thoughts, flashbacks, trauma-related fears, panic attacks, avoidance (Foa et al., 2009), and generalized anxiety disorder (GAD). They listed exposure therapy as the fastest acting psychotherapy and one of the two most effective treatments for PTSD. The International Society for Traumatic Stress Studies described exposure therapy as quite effective in the treatment of a mixed variety of trauma symptoms, "In fact, no other treatment modality has evidence this strong indicating its effectiveness." However, there may also be increased risk of treatment dropout because treatment may cause increased distress and PTSD symptoms in the short term.

The goal is to activate the fear by introducing the feared stimuli so that a person has the opportunity to learn that:

- Being in a safe situation that reminds them of the trauma is not dangerous
- Remembering the trauma is not the same as reliving it
- Anxiety can decrease (without avoidance)
- Experiencing symptoms of PTSD does not necessarily lead to a loss of control.

Repeated and prolonged exposure promotes habituation. This allows patients to discover that anxiety diminishes even without avoidance or escape. Reliving the trauma in the presence of an empathic therapist facilitates patient realization that thinking about trauma is not dangerous.

Exposure therapy is contraindicated if the patient is not able to tolerate an increased level of distress or for those living in potentially dangerous environments (such as domestic violence).

SYSTEMATIC DESENSITIZATION

This is a variation of exposure therapy (development of an anxiety hierarchy) paired with relaxation. This treatment was developed by Wolpe (1958) and is referred to as "reciprocal inhibition." In general, the constructed stimuli is imaginal exposure, however, it can be *in vivo*. The ultimate challenge is established by pairing an anxiety response elicited by exposure and coupled with relaxation as anxiety is increased. This incompatible pairing of short periods of elicited anxiety interrupted by relaxation, over time, allows the patient to confront anxiety-provoking stimuli without the (conditioned) anxiety response.

SELF-REGULATION THERAPY

Self-regulation therapy is a non-touch mind/body desensitization technique whereby the patient deals with different aspects of the trauma in small and tolerable doses in the context of a safe and supportive environment.

ANXIETY MANAGEMENT

A major component of CBT, anxiety management teaches trauma survivors to cope with post-traumatic memories, reminders, and feelings without becoming overwhelmed or emotionally numb. It is not uncommon that trauma memories do not go away entirely with treatment, but become manageable with new coping skills. According to the Expert Consensus Guidelines (2000) anxiety management is among the most useful treatment for patients with PTSD (Foa et al., 2000a, 2009).

Anxiety management techniques offer incredible benefits for treatment and prevention of numerous stress-related health and mental health issues such as:

- Hypertension
- Headaches
- Heart disease
- Gastrointestinal disorders
- Obsessing
- Attention deficit
- Anger
- Depression.

Some of the techniques used are as follows:

- Progressive muscle relaxation—teaches patients to control fear and anxiety by relaxing major muscle groups
- Deep breathing—teaches slow abdominal breathing to prevent hyperventilation and its associated unpleasant physical sensations
- Positive thinking and self-talk—replacing negative self-talk
- Assertive training—appropriate, honest communication without alienating
- Thought stopping—a distraction technique to overcome distressing thoughts by inwardly shouting "stop!"

- Role playing/covert modeling (imagery rehearsal)/psychodrama. An example is provided by Forbes et al. (2001), who states that nightmares in the general population are at 4–8% and at about 60% for those with PTSD. Imagery rehearsal therapy induces a systematic increase in imagery control by changing the content of the patient's nightmares to promote mastery over the content threat. This alters the meaning, importance, and orientation of the nightmares.
- Biofeedback.

Education About Nervous System Responses

Re-experiencing trauma and arousal symptoms are thought of as conditioned emotional responses resulting from classical conditioning. Avoidance and other cognitive behavioral excesses or deficits are under operant control. Clinical problems arise from:

- Ineffective management attempts
- Lack of environmental reinforcers
- Inappropriate stimulus control.

Therefore, treatment is not focused on the trauma but on the ineffective or maladaptive thoughts and behaviors developed following the trauma. Effective management and mastery are more quickly developed when a patient understands what is happening to them physiologically. The goals are to:

- Memorize signs of sympathetic nervous system reactions
- Identify tools for braking
- Teach self-monitoring
- Maintain dual awareness.

Dual Awareness

Dual awareness (van der Kolk et al., 1996; Rothchild, 1999) is a technique used to slow down the process that utilizes language for reinforcing reference to the "here and now." Remaining in a flashback and hyperaroused state is additive to the experience of trauma. It is the ability to maintain a dual awareness of past and present which makes it possible for patients to work through the trauma. This ability is indicative of adequate ego development, which allows dual awareness to be used as a braking tool (Rothchild, 1999). There are three dualities:

1. Observing self versus experiencing self: van der Kolk et al. (1996), states that there may be a marked split between the "experiencing self" and the "observing self" in the traumatized individual and that learning to acknowledge both parts by stating the reality of both selves at the same time may be an important key to calm.
   - "I am feeling [emotion] right now, because I am remembering [trauma]"
   - "I am afraid, but I am not in any danger"
   - "This is just the way my body has learned to respond, I can slow it down by breathing slowly and deeply."

2. External reality vs. internal reality
   - "It is not abnormal to feel this way, I know it will pass"
   - "I understand what I am feeling (as a result of the trauma), and why. I am alright."

3. Present vs. past (effective for stopping a flashback)
   - "I am afraid because I am remembering … while at the same time I am looking around this room and can see that I am not in any danger"

- "It is not then, it is now"
- "I am looking around, and can see where I am and know I am safe."

Zayfer and Becker (2007) discuss the "mindful" mindset of engaging in therapy. They reinforce a mindset of viewing therapy tasks with the realistic perspective that anxiety may be uncomfortable but cultivating a mindset that accepts anxiety as a valuable life experience where an individual asserts control over how they choose to manage it is beneficial. They also offered the acronym "AWARE."

A = Accept and embrace anxiety and the associated fear that accompanies it.

W = Watch and acquaint yourself with the qualities of anxiety such as the fluctuations of fear.

A = Act in concert with the anxiety, focusing on what you have control over and how you choose to manage it which demonstrates acceptance of anxiety.

R = Repeat acceptance by utilizing positive self-talk and letting yourself be with anxiety, managing it which allows it to diminish over time.

E = Expect and accept anxiety and associated fear to reappear. Replace the apprehension and avoidance with trust in your ability to manage your anxiety.

STRESS INOCULATION THERAPY (SIT)

Stress inoculation therapy (Meichenbaum, 1996, 2007) is tailored to population and circumstance. It is a complex CBT which incorporates:

- An encouraging therapeutic alliance
- Psycho-education (discovery-oriented inquiry)
- Collaborative goal setting which enhances hopefulness
- Direct-action, problem-solving
- Acceptance-based coping skills
- Training in generalization guidelines
- Relapse prevention
- Self-attributional training programs.

A major treatment goal is that survivors of trauma be able to share their history of experience with full consideration of the impact to themselves, how they see themselves as a result of their experience, and conclusions they draw about the world and future. It is the process of constructing a more useful and adaptive narrative and to change their view of themselves to survive and thrive versus the constriction of identifying themselves as a victim of trauma. This promotes the concept of finding meaning and moving from emotional pain to a healing process as they reclaim their life. It is the acknowledgment that everything that happens to an individual becomes part of who they are and with that comes the challenge to strive in growth, skill, and resilience instead of being personally and inescapably diminished.

Conscious thoughts about negative experiences, situations, and people determine the intensity of emotional and behavioral responses. Therefore, the emotional and behavioral response is rarely incongruent but rather an overreaction. In order to resist the full potential of stress first requires learning to not catastrophize, and to identify and reinforce the resolution to life questions which resides within the individual. In other words, what has happened cannot be changed. Whatever the patient has experienced they have survived and it has become a part of their life history. Therefore, they need to be encouraged to (1) make an interpretation which is empowering versus diminishing, and (2) decide how they choose to respond and move forward from this moment. The mastery of relaxation techniques enables an individual to experience a decreased level of distress while they evoke a state of relaxation. This allows them to be emotionally available, in the moment to focus on management, and improve their coping.

Stress inoculation therapy uses the techniques outlined in anxiety management, but also is used to prepare an individual for inevitable stress or ongoing stress. It maximizes control over thoughts, feelings, and behavior. In addition, it is a technique that is not only useful for decreasing anxiety, but for chronic anger too. SIT involves self-talk to decrease stress and anxiety. The individual could be asked to develop a list of stressful situations arranged from least to most stressful. Additionally, they are to carefully choose the appropriate self-talk messages associated with each situation (i.e. positive/coping thoughts) which is first visualized and then practiced on in real situations.

Stress inoculation therapy is broken down into three phases consisting of 8–14 sessions and can be applied to individuals or a group.

Phase 1: Conceptualization

This first phase involves education regarding the treatment format, the nature and consequences of stress, and how the appraisal process inadvertently exacerbates the level of stress experienced. Development of a therapeutic alliance is necessary for the collaboration between the therapist and the patient to identify positive coping skills.

- Interview
- Identify stressors
- Identify automatic reactions, coping resources and utility of both
- Begin to identify achievable tasks and set goals
- Self-awareness for all reactions and implement self-monitoring
- Identify deficits in coping resources
- Reinforce strengths, normalize response, and begin to bring meaning to perception of trauma experience
- Reassure that an individual's unique responses to stress are normal and expected.

Phase 2: Skills Acquisition, Consolidation, and Rehearsal

The focus is on acquiring cognitive, behavioral, and physiological skills to manage negative emotions such as stress, anxiety, fear, guilt, and anger. The therapeutic alliance plays a significant role in encouraging and reinforcing change through:

- Perception and meaning (self-talk, develop new interpretations, reframe)
- Emotional reactions triggered by situations or memories of stressful or traumatic experiences
- Changing the stressful environment/situation when possible.

Techniques include:

- Skill training and rehearsal
- Reinforce what works

- Utilize solution-focused problem-solving to match desired goals and break it down into manageable steps

- Mentor emotion-focused coping skills to prepare for times of minimal/lack of control (grounding, relaxation techniques, self-talk, self-care, reframing, humor, removing self from situation and use of resources)

- Work toward a broad and expanded picture of coping resources and skills development

- Rehearse skills through:
  - engaging in imaginary and behavioral rehearsal
  - modeling coping in various identified stressful situations
  - challenging self-defeating self-talk and reinforcing positive adaptive self-talk

- Commit to continued resourcefulness and efforts which reinforce resiliency

- Identify impediments to adaptive coping.

Numerous coping skills are used to achieve these goals. From a response perspective, situational demands are identified as a problem focus or emotional focus. Active coping is associated with decreased emotional distress for both genders. Problem-focused coping is an attempt to deal with a problem situation with the possible result of changing the associated emotions. Emotion-focused coping emphasizes the attempt to manage the negative affect associated with the stressful experience.

Phase 3: Application Training

Training practice is initiated with imaginary rehearsal, role-playing, and *in vivo* graduated exposure. Relapse prevention is a core part of stress inoculation therapy. In addition, an optimistic disposition is associated with better adjustment and effective skills acquisition to a range of stressors. An optimistic disposition is associated with coping strategies focused on reducing, eliminating, and managing stressors and emotions, and negative association with avoidance coping strategies where the focus is to ignore, avoid, and withdraw from stressors and emotions. Overall, optimistic individuals are better at adjusting their coping strategies to match the demands of the current stressor (Meichenbaum, 2007).

The techniques used in this phase are:

- Apply adaptive coping skills

- Utilize self-awareness and self-monitoring skills for directing the use of new coping skills when responding to stressors

- Escalate level of stress in imagery exposure exercises

- Relapse prevention and rehearse coping responses

- Practice identifying the specifics of when to apply acquired skills

- Reinforce the fact that it is the efforts of the individual that has led to the desired change

- Maintenance and generalization of newly acquired skills

- Involve support system in reinforcement and practice of new skills

- Encourage a sense of self-control (choosing when to stay and utilize acquired skills and when to remove self from an unmanageable situation as a form of control)

- Reinforce a realistic and optimistic attitude. Every experience is an opportunity for learning.

PSYCHODYNAMIC THERAPY

According to psychodynamic philosophy, posttraumatic symptoms are an attempt to manage the traumatic stress. Consequently, it is viewed not as a defective but rather an adaptive response. For example, when the survivor of a traumatic event experiences intrusive and avoidant symptoms (core symptoms of PTSD) it is viewed as a biphasic attempt to cope with the trauma (Van der Hart et al., 1989; Foa et al., 2009). A fundamental point of distinction between psychodynamic therapy and other forms of therapy is the concept of symptoms as compromises whose meanings must be understood and resolved. In addition, the concept of transference, unique to this philosophy, plays a significant role in reflecting a realistic appraisal of the therapist's character and the ensuing therapeutic alliance. The psychodynamic therapist elicits meanings in order to make unconscious meaning and symbolism conscious. As the patient develops increased understanding of their experience, response, and underlying belief system which guides or reinforces how they operate it presents an opportunity for improved coping. Due to the focus of psychodynamic psychotherapy being on basic problems in interpersonal relationships it may be useful in working with patients diagnosed with complex PTSD. Psychodynamic therapy is a sophisticated, highly focused psychotherapeutic approach, beneficial when the patient and therapist have a strong therapeutic alliance (indicative of intelligence, ability to verbalize, high-level thinking process, trust, ability to tolerate negative feelings, etc.) and are in agreement regarding the identified clinical issues and the treatment plan. Brief psychodynamic therapy can be beneficial when there are identified distinct points of focus in therapy versus common general points of distress often presented by patients with PTSD who also demonstrate instability which would be contraindicative of this method of intervention (Foa et al., 2009).

Psychodynamic therapy benefits the patient by facilitating the recovery of a sense of self and helping the patient to learn new coping strategies to deal with intense emotions. It typically consists of three phases:

- Establish a sense of safety

- Explore the trauma experience in depth

- Help the patient re-establish connections with family, friends, societal interactions, and other sources of meaning.

While the general focus of psychodynamic therapy is on Sigmund Freud's theoretical point of view there are numerous theories which deviate from Freud in some beliefs or are additive to the understanding of fundamental beliefs. Combining beliefs and interventions in this theoretical orientation can be useful. Psychoanalytic techniques stem from the central concepts of conscious and unconscious levels of mental activity, defenses, conflicts, symptoms as meaningful representations, transference, and the therapeutic relationship. The analyst's (a neutral responder) single investment is in the patient's progress toward autonomy and health. This is primarily an expressive therapy that seeks to enhance and broaden a patient's understanding of unconscious issues within the safety of the therapeutic relationship. It is sometimes difficult to separate the boundaries between psychodynamic and cognitive behavioral therapies; both recognize the specific needs of the individual (Brierre and Scott, 2006).

The techniques used in psychodynamic therapy include the following:

- The therapist is a facilitator of the therapeutic process (ultimately, the patient analyzes themselves)

- The analyst must be trusted and considerate with a shared commitment to honesty and candor. The therapist employs observation, confrontations, and interpretations to test hypotheses with the patient

- Free association is the fundamental aspect of the patient saying whatever is on his or her mind

- Analysis follows associations, explore dreams, symptomatic acts, transference, and counter-transference (which allows for the understanding of the complex network of ideas, memories, wishes, fears, and fundamental individuality
- The use of observations, appropriate confrontations, and interpretations to test hypotheses with the patient
- Hypnotic and other abreaction techniques (to uncover repressed material)
- Methods to facilitate the re-establishment of a sense of coherence and meaning
- Processing and diminishing irrational guilt
- Finding meaning.

The use of "brief psychodynamic therapy" (Mann, 1973; Foa et al., 2009) emphasizes the factor of separation by keeping the number of sessions (12) at the forefront of their work, with the belief that impending closure results in a final burst of progress. This form of therapy works best when treatment focuses on a single theme such as a conflictual relationship.

The Veterans Health Administration, Department of Veterans Affairs (2007) states that brief psychodynamic psychotherapy helps survivors of trauma to learn new ways of dealing with emotional conflicts caused by traumatic experience. Psychodynamic psychotherapy helps patients to understand how their past affects how they feel now specifically by:

- Identifying cues/triggers of stressful memories and other symptoms
- Finding ways to cope with intense feelings about the past
- Becoming more aware of their thoughts and feelings, so that they can change their reactions to them
- Raising their self-esteem.

PROBLEM-FOCUSED PSYCHOSOCIAL ADJUNCTIVE SERVICE

This type of treatment as used by the Veterans Health Administration, Department of Veterans Affairs (2006) is designed to be helpful for those with PTSD who develop incapacitating mental illness with severe symptoms which cannot be tolerated, and are not able to generalize coping skills for PTSD from the treatment setting to personal environment (home/work/community). As a result of the most severe consequences of a traumatic event, they struggle at the most basic levels of functioning at home (marital/family), work/school, or in social environments. Their symptoms are persistent, severe, and intolerable. These patients are likely to benefit more from case management and psychosocial rehabilitation than from traditional therapy and psychotropic interventions.

Psychosocial rehabilitation seeks to target personal goals and adapt appropriate rehabilitation services for those debilitated by PTSD. The stages of recovery are individualized based upon the needs of the patient. According to the Veterans Administration Guidelines, rehabilitation services are carried out by a case manager for maximum benefit and reducing negative patterns/outcomes (such as hospitalization). Services are categorized in the following manner:

- Self-care and independent living skills techniques
- Supported housing
- Marital/family training
- Social skills training
- Vocational rehabilitation.

The way it works is illustrated by the example shown in Table 3.1.

Table 3.1 Example of problem-focused psychosocial adjunctive service in action

Problem	Service/treatment
Lacks full information on health needs and does not avoid high risk behavior	Provide education
Lacks sufficient self-care/independent living skills	Refer to appropriate social service agency for independent skills training
Lacks adequate, decent, safe, affordable, stable living arrangement consistent with goals	Refer to supportive housing services
Not socially active	Social skills training
Lacks a job that provides adequate income or fully utilizes skills	Refer for vocational/rehab training
Not able to locate and coordinate access to services (as previously listed)	Refer for case management services
Requests spiritual support	Provide appropriate referrals for religious/spiritual advising and associated services
Borderline personality disorder typified by para-suicidal behavior	Consider dialectical behavioral therapy
Has current substance abuse problem	Integrate PTSD and substance abuse treatment

DUAL REPRESENTATION THERAPY

Brewin et al. (1996) describes dual representation theory as acknowledging that sensory input influences both the conscious and the unconscious mind, therefore including information-processing and social-cognitive theories. This theory proposes two types of emotional reactions:

- Primary emotional conditioning that takes place during the traumatic experience (fear/anger) which is coupled with re-experienced sensory and physiological information
- Secondary emotions resulting from the consequences and implications of the traumatic event (fear/anger/guilt/shame/loss, etc.).

In other words, emotional processing has two parts: the activation of unconscious memories and a conscious effort to search for meaning (cause/blame, etc.) and to resolve conflicts between the prior belief system, associated expectations and the reality of the experience.

If negative emotions are decreased, the goal of restoring a feeling of safety and control to an individual's environment is achieved.

EYE MOVEMENT DESENSITIZATION AND REPROCESSING

According the Department of Veterans Affairs (2007) eye movement desensitization and reprocessing (EMDR), a fairly new treatment technique for PTSD, is believed to help patients change how they react to memories of their trauma. While talking about their memories, patients are directed to focus on distractions such as eye movements, hand taps, and sounds. The result could be fewer PTSD symptoms. Many seasoned therapists recognize the exposure therapy component of EMDR and believe that it is likely the effective aspect of EMDR that alleviates symptoms. Exposure therapy has been identified as one of the most effective treatments for PTSD. According to Foa et al. (2009) most, but not all, of the established clinical practice guidelines currently consider EMDR as an evidenced-based treatment for PTSD.

Shapiro (1995, 1999) developed techniques of certain eye movements that are supposedly able to decrease the intensity of disturbing thoughts that have not been discharged or released. It is a structured, multi-component treatment regimen that incorporates the following stages:

1. Prior to initiating therapy a patient must be able to identify the following associations with the traumatic experience
   - Images associated with the event
   - The affective and physiological response elements
   - Negative self-representations
   - Desired positive self-representations

2. Patient history. The clinical interview evaluates
   - Patient readiness
   - Barriers to treatment (rule out secondary gains)
   - Dysfunctional behaviors
   - Symptoms
   - Illness characteristics
   - Identifies remedial skills/behaviors which may be useful later

3. Treatment planning. The second part of the interview process where suitable trauma memories ("target") are identified as the focus of treatment
   - Trauma-specific memories (psychopathology)
   - Present reminders of the traumatic event

4. Preparation
   - Establishment of a treatment-appropriate therapeutic relationship
   - Educate the patient about the rationale of EMDR
   - Teach specific coping skills to facilitate the processing of emerging trauma-related material
   - Assist the patient in learning to maintain perspective when confronted with trauma reactivation

5. Assessment
   - The patient brings together the components of the trauma memory in the structured manner
   - Identifying a distressing image in memory
   - Identifying an associative negative cognition
   - Identifying an alternative positive cognition
   - Rating the validity of the positive cognition (VoC) using a 7-point scale
   - Identify the emotions associated with the traumatic memory
   - Rating the subjective level of disturbance (SUD) using an 11-point scale
   - Identifying trauma-related physical sensations and their anatomical location (racing heart, stomach flutter, etc.)

6. Desensitization and reprocessing
   - The patient is asked to hold in their mind the disturbing image, the negative cognition, and the bodily sensation associated with the traumatic memory
   - The therapist moves their finger back (or other alternative such as tone or tapping) and forth, approximately 30 cm in front of the patient's face, while the patient tracks the moving finger with their eyes

- After approximately 20 back and forth eye movements, the therapist stops and asks the patient to let go of the memory, take a deep breath, and give feedback about any changes (image, physical sensations, thoughts of the self, and emotions). It is not uncommon, at this time, for patients to offer the emergence of new memories, physical sensations, thoughts or feelings
- After each successive eye movement treatment (or alternative stimulation), based upon the patient response, the therapist instructs the patient on the next step (generally, minimum instruction)

7. Installation of positive cognition
   - When the SUD rate has been decreased to a point of no discomfort (as close to zero as possible) step 5 is reinitiated to assess the positive cognition.
   - The patient is instructed to think of the target image while at the same time covertly rehearsing the positive cognition
   - The eye movements are then used again, followed by another reassessment. This cycle is repeated until the VoC rating approximates 7 (completely valid) as closely as possible
   - Specific coping mechanisms designed to deal with past memories and present emotions, as well as optimal behavioral responses to potential future situations are given

8. Body scan
   - The patient is asked to check for any signs of residual physical tension/discomfort (indicators of incomplete trauma processing)
   - The patient is instructed to attend to physical sensations while additional eye movement treatments are given

9. Closure
   - Prepare the patient for leaving/transition each session utilizing relaxation/visualization etc.
   - The patient keeps a journal of feelings, thoughts, and dreams related to the trauma between sessions
   - Utilization of self-control techniques

10. Re-evaluation
    - Following each session a re-evaluation is incorporated to determine whether treatment goals have been reached and maintained
    - Trauma-related material that emerges following a session will be addressed
    - Additional sessions are scheduled as needed to assess trauma memories and current reminders, as well as reinforcing skills development.

A model of "accelerated information-processing" has been proposed to account for the resolution of using this method on traumatic memories. The main points of this model include:

- The acknowledgment that traumatization interferes with psychological and biological processes that under other circumstances promote adaptation to experiences and memories. The normal representative "state-dependent" format of the semantic-affective network contains traumatic memories which are partially dissociated
- A personal healthy core or intrinsic self-healing mechanism exists that when activated reintegrates traumatic, partially dissociated, memories into a normalized form. Conjugated eye movement, tone, or tapping performed as per the EMDR procedure activates this mechanism

- There is an encoding of cognitive, affective, and physiological response elements along with information about the attributes of self and others
- For patients who have experienced multiple traumatizations, the EMDR treatment regimen is determined by the number of trauma memories which need to be accessed and resolved. In some instances, where a theme of traumatic experiences is evident, they may be grouped for treatment.

When neural information is associated with trauma or chronic pain which gets frozen in time with associated emotions, EMDR is purported to change the way the information is processed. The five tasks of pain management using EMDR are:

1. Verify that pain is adequately managed
2. Verify that medical diagnosis is correct, acknowledged, and accepted
3. Identify and prioritize targets of EMDR
4. Use desensitization and relaxation exercises to change pain sensations
5. Develop resources for psychological pain management through EMDR.

SOMATIC TREATMENT

Those who do somatic work believe that the somatic nervous system can carry a blockage of undischarged arousal because much of what happened when a person was traumatized never made it to the cortical level (higher cognition with words, perception, and meaning) (Matsakis, 1994; van der Kolk et al., 1996; Levine, 1997; Rothchild, 1998, 1999, 2000). Instead trauma symptoms such as anxiety and obsessive compulsive behavior both contain and discharge the arousal. However, they do not resolve the underlying somatic freeze, requiring a return to the somatic sensory level where the information was first stored.

Distressing somatic symptoms demand a treatment which focuses on the body as a resource. Considering the traumatic impact on the body is crucial to understanding and treating PTSD. There must be a solid foundation for safe trauma therapy. This means safety (at both a feeling level and management level) for the patient inside and outside of therapy. Both the patient and the therapist must experience a feeling of confidence in being able to adequately manage negative affect and physiological responses to avoid becoming overwhelmed, retraumatized, and digging into the difficult trauma work. This requires building and reinforcing both internal and external resources, and identifying defenses that serve a protective purpose.

The clinician must meet the patient where they are and should be prepared to use their skills in an adaptive and flexible manner to meet the needs of the patient in order to promote a successful outcome. Sometimes this could mean simply providing a most important human quality: listening with sincere care and positive regard.

The patient needs to learn to identify and gain a greater sense of body self-awareness, self-knowledge, and self-control. It is also important to learn to recognize the indication (physical and cognitive) of chronic and acute hyperarousal (ANS over-activation) in order to break the cycle. This involves:

- Memorizing the signs of sympathetic and parasympathetic nervous system symptoms and combined activation as well as practicing by observing them in others

Indentifying the responses of the autonomic nervous system

Sympathetic branch of the ANS Activation during stress traumatic events	Parasympathetic branch of the ANS Activation during rest and relaxation
Indications: Rapid shallow respiration Increased heart rate (pulse) Increased blood pressure Pupils dilate Pale skin color Skin cold and increased sweating Digestion slows	*Indications:* Slow, deep respiration Slower heart rate Lower blood pressure Pupils constrict Flushed skin color Skin warm and dry Digestion increases

Figure 3.1   Autonomic nervous system responses.

- Self-monitoring (increased awareness of physical functioning). Periodically check heart rate, breathing, etc. in order to gauge the patient's arousal state (Figure 3.1).

For individuals with severe mental health problems, components of a trauma-based treatment include:

- Education on trauma issues
- Skill-building programs aimed at assisting the survivor in identifying symptom triggers and self-soothing strategies.

During an actual traumatic event or a flashback (visual, auditory, or somatic) there can be a concurrent activation of the two branches of the ANS. When high sympathetic activation becomes masked by high parasympathetic activation (both branches being aroused at the same time) the following signs may be observed:

- Pale skin with slow breathing
- Dilated pupils with flushed skin
- Slow heart rate with rapid breathing.

In this situation the therapist will immediately bring the patient to a neutral/braking stance in treatment to stabilize and bring the session to a close. The patient is likely experiencing a flashback in images, somatic sensations, emotions, or a combination of any two or all of them. As the session is being brought to a close, redirect with self-care, soothing behaviors and being in the now to prevent retraumating or further decompensation.

For example, there are marked indications of sympathetic and parasympathetic activation. A specific example is the masking of the sympathetic nervous system activation leading to a freeze response (tonic immobility).

SOMATIC TREATMENT TECHNIQUES

Somatic treatment techniques are highly valued for their contribution to management and recovery. Observation of the responses of the ANS in combination with basic somatic techniques can make trauma therapy safer and less traumatic as well as being a useful and effective adjunct treatment for containment and reducing symptoms of trauma.

Body Awareness and Boundary Exercises

Body awareness (Rothchild, 1999) is a skill that allows a person to accurately assess what they are experiencing somatically: "this what is happening to my body." When a patient is ready, and they have developed the body awareness set of skills, it can accelerate the therapy process. Body awareness encompasses skin, muscles, bones, organs, breathing, movement, spatial orientation/position in space, etc. However, it does not end there; body awareness includes how the body is actually being experienced in the here and now. Body awareness techniques are excellent braking tools that can be used to prevent escalation of unnecessary feelings/experiences of being out of control, decompensation and re-traumatization.

Sense of Skin Level Boundary
Sometimes a body that has been physically assaulted (e.g. rape, motor vehicle accident, beating, surgery, etc.) experiences a loss in the sense of body integrity. It is this loss that can escalate or accelerate a trauma process to the bounds of being out of control. The basic technique described below is very useful for increasing a sense of body integrity (except for those cases where for a person even to touch their own skin is provoking, therefore proceed with caution).

Gently touch or rub the surface of the skin with a variety of textures:

- Own hand
- Towel/terry cloth
- Wall
- Furniture.

The purpose is to reinforce the boundary between the self and objects. The integrity of the self, "this is where I begin and end." Boundaries can be further reinforced by the "safe" touch of someone trusted.

"Here and Now" Experience
Once patients develop a rhythm of somatic association with periodic somatic reviews it can become a secure intrapersonal resource. Self-knowledge is powerful and acts to decrease erroneous catastrophizing and panic responses to normal somatic sensations. Body sensations or somatic experiences in the here and now include:

- Temperature
- Humidity (sweating hands, etc.)
- Pain
- Pressure
- Tingling/prickles/vibration
- Tension/relaxation
- Hungry/growling/gurgling/acid stomach
- Bowel reactions
- Heart rate.

Sense of Solidarity of Bones

For those who do not manage feeling their skin very well, feeling the solidness of the bones can be a good braking technique (unless it frightens them because it reminds them of skeletons, death, etc.).

- Encourage awareness of the frame, how the body is held, postured, and pivots
- Sensing the spine can be a great aid to braking
- Emphasize awareness of the rigidity and strength of the spine
- Feel the spine against a wall, sitting and standing
- Bone against bone
- Tapping on the elbow, wrist, knee, ankle—or use a wooden spoon to gently tap on bone projections.

Muscular Tension

Some of the exercises that can be used to increase awareness of muscular tension include the following:

- Tensing muscles which feel weak, vulnerable, shaky
- Sitting upright in a wooden chair
- Muscular resistance, tensing and relaxing major muscles and the abdominal wall
- Body armoring. Reich (2003) refers to body armor as a protective layer which serves to protect a person from the outside world as well as their own desires and instincts. (The body remembers trauma and protects itself from potential assault(s) by creating a muscular armor which "holds on" in the form of muscular tension or armor. The therapeutic goal is to "melt" this muscular tension through body work described by Rothchild (2000))
- Comparing awareness of feeling for muscle tensing, relaxing and stretching
- Tensing peripheral muscles.

It can be calming and containing to tense the peripheral muscles of the arms and legs (Rothchild, 1999). Tensing is a good braking technique which can be effective for reducing hyperarousal. Muscle tensing is done until there is the feeling of muscle fatigue. The muscle is then slowly released. Once the muscle is released, take the time to evaluate body awareness and acknowledge any adverse reaction such as nausea, anxiety, or spaciness. If there are any adverse reactions they can generally be soothed and neutralized by stretching the muscle where the reaction originated in the opposite direction.

Here are some examples of exercises using peripheral muscles.

- **Legs:** Using good posture, stand with feet a little less than shoulder distance apart, knees relaxed (not locked or bent). Press the knees out directly to the sides so that you can feel the tension along the sides of the legs from the knee to the hip.
- **Left arm:** Sit or stand with arms crossed right over left. The right hand needs to cover the left elbow.
  1. Use the right hand as resistance as you lift the left arm directly away from your body. You should feel the tension in the forward-pointing part of the upper arm from shoulder to elbow.

2. Use the right hand as resistance to the back of the elbow as you push the left arm directly left. You should feel tension in the left-directed part of the upper arm from shoulder to elbow.

Use the same technique in mirror form for the right arm.

Organs, Breathing, and Movement

Autogenic breathing is an example of slowing down a body process which requires focus on all aspects of the body involved. For example, inhale through the nose to a count of 4, feel the diaphragm fill with oxygen, hold for 4 seconds, and exhale to a count of 4 through the mouth and at the same time feel tension leave the body.

Developing Language to Facilitate Focus on Body Sensations

Useful questions include:

- How does your body feel when you are feeling unsafe?
- Where in your body do you feel it?
- How do you soothe or calm it?
- What happens in your body when you acknowledge the traumatic event?
- What thoughts or feelings do you have when you physically feel that?
- What is that like?

Learning to Recognize Signs of Hyperarousal and Shock

- Educate yourself about the signs of nervous system stress and shock
- Observe and gauge your own signs and state of the ANS

Awareness of the Mechanisms of Dissociation States

Dissociation (Rothchild, 1999) is a disruption in the usually integrated functions of consciousness, memory, identity, or perception of the environment. It also refers to the faculties, feelings, functions, and memories that become split off from immediate consciousness (awareness) and compartmentalized in the mind as separate identities emerge.

The purpose served by dissociation is the escape (separation) of intolerable or psychologically incongruous situation. It provides:

- A barrier to painful or overwhelming events
- Analgesia to prevent or avoid feeling pain
- A way of avoiding or escaping from experiencing an event
- A survival mechanism (splitting) for children.

Dissociation is associated with the disordered states listed in Table 3.2.

Grounding Techniques

Grounding is a strategy used to detach from emotional pain (dealing with a trigger, flashback, dissociating, or a high level of emotional distress) by the process of distracting one's focus on the external environment (outside of oneself) versus inward focus on obsessing, negative thought/impulses/feelings (Rothchild, 2000; Najavits, 2002). This distraction or

Table 3.2   Disordered states associated with dissociation

Amnesia	Blocks of childhood years
	Recent blocks of time
	Loss of personal information
	"Spacing out" or "zoning"
	Time disorientation
Fugue	Sudden unexpected travel from home
	Inability to recall the past
	Confusion of personal identity
	Assumption of a new identity
Depersonalization	Feeling of detachment from the body
	Spectator (seeing the body from a distance)
	Unreality of self
	Anhedonia (loss of affective responses)
	Sense of physical fragmentation
	Proprioceptive (as if floating)
	Affective (as if numb/dead)
Derealization	Environmental surroundings seem unreal (foreign)
	Perceptual disturbances or distortions
Identity confusion	Feelings of confusion or turmoil
	Uncertainty regarding self (explained as feeling of another person inside)
	Identity confusion (sexual orientation)
	Sense of uncertainty, conflict
Identity alteration	Internal dialogue
	Different or inappropriate levels of functioning and/or behaviors
	Different names, ages, identities associated with split parts of the self
	Inability to recollect personal information incompatible with what would be considered normal forgetting
Somatization	Fainting spells, collapses, epileptic-like seizures
	Headaches
	Chronic pain symptoms
	Hysterical anesthesias
	Hysterical paralyses

centering serves to create feeling safe when overwhelmed by emotional pain by anchoring to the present and being reality based. It is a strategy that reinforces being in control, and it can be done anywhere and anytime without the knowledge of others. Grounding can be mental, physical, or soothing.

Some of the exercises to improve grounding include the following:

- Pay attention to body sensations: keep your feet on the floor, feel your body weight/presence, pay attention to posture

- Visual focus: purposefully look at the details of the environment

- Use senses to reconnect, including sight, sound, taste, smell, and touch/pressure/sensations

- Pay attention to posture while sitting: sit upright/tall

- Breathe deeply: take a deep breath and pay attention to its path in the body

- Wriggle toes and flex fingers: focus and feel the sensation

- Active touch: feel objects on you and in your environment such as jewelry and furniture

- Applying pressure: gently pinch the arm muscle
- Drink water: have a glass of water, paying careful attention and focusing on the associated sensations
- Walk around: get up and with conscious awareness walk around noting the sensation of movement and the environmental details
- Acknowledge trance state: talk to self to move out of it, note how it feels, note provocation, if any, which precipitated trance state
- Grounding in the present moment.

Traumatic Incident Reduction ("videotape")	This is a technique whereby a patient treats their traumatic event memory like a videotape and runs through it (repeated rewind and play) with their therapist until all negative emotions have been discharged.
Thought Stopping (use of distraction to overcome distressing thoughts)	This skill is paradoxical to exposure therapy and may be counterproductive. It is advisable to be careful in making this selection as part of skill development.
Stress Inoculation Training (SIT)	As described above.

PHARMACOLOGICAL TREATMENTS

In presenting the different theories of treatment a thread of commonality through them all is self-awareness and symptom management. For example, the premise of anxiety management skill sets is that the PTSD response stems from skill deficiencies that can be corrected by teaching the skills to manage anxiety when it occurs. In addition, pharmacotherapy is useful in reducing or eliminating primary (core) and secondary symptoms of PTSD. Usually, medication is used as treatment for patients who have severe PTSD to decrease the stress of intrusive symptoms, as well as anxiety and depression. Medication is generally dispensed as one aspect of a treatment plan that includes psychotherapy and/or group therapy. To date there is no single medication that is the answer to PTSD.

One benefit of pharmacologic intervention is that it may help to uncover pain and thereby facilitate behavioral and other forms of psychotherapy. According to Foa et al. (2009) the first-line pharmacotherapy treatment choice for PTSD are SSRIs. These should be tried at a low dose for at least eight weeks, evaluating every 1–2 weeks and increasing the dose as needed. If there is no response after eight weeks, initiate nefazodone or venlafaxine.

If there is only a partial response, a mood stabilizer such as divalproex may be added.

For severe insomnia, consider short-term treatment with trazodone. For severe anxiety, a short-term benzodiazepine or longer term buspirone may be considered. Note that if there is a substance abuse disorder, avoid treating with a benzodiazepine (aside from an initial/brief use during detox).

DUAL DIAGNOSIS

When there is comorbidity with other diagnoses, successful treatment requires a broad approach to target the salient diagnostic features with commonsense prioritization focused on stability, amelioration of symptoms, and skill building for the purpose of maintaining change, necessary internal management, and adequate external support. An example of this is the comorbidity of PTSD and substance abuse/dependency. Treatment in this case would use cognitive behavior therapy, group therapy, self-help groups, and possibly psychotropic medication.

When the theory of classical conditioning is applied to treatment with these comorbid diagnoses it would be expected that the stimulus that reliably precedes the administration of substances may elicit a variety of possible substance-related responses such as craving. This means that exposure to these triggers, along with the substance-related conditioned emotional and physical responses, will increase the likelihood of consuming substances. Pierce et al. (1996) and Roshenow et al. (1990) state that in substance-abusing individuals the presence of traumatic reminders, memories, or PTSD symptoms may elicit urges to use substances. While this makes sense, it has not resulted in an array of successful treatment strategies. Coffey et al. (2005) asserts that the most current developments in treatment combine some form of exposure therapy for PTSD with an empirically supported treatment for the substance abuse/dependence disorder.

INTEGRATIVE TREATMENT

In *Medical Research News* Zalin (2004) reports that research conducted by Harborview Injury Prevention and Research Center (HIPRC) suggests that integrative treatment, combining medication and psychotherapy, can decrease alcohol abuse by trauma survivors and prevent the development of PTSD. This study was basically initiated at bedside to patients admitted with traumatic injury.

Follette et al. (1998) states that a general treatment strategy for dual diagnosis is to use assessment to direct the treatment process and intermittently reassess to determine any trends, patterns, or events that create anxiety or trigger PTSD symptoms. Consider the following:

1. Acknowledge the importance of the therapeutic relationship. Focus on interpersonal difficulties associated with flat affect and other PTSD symptoms. This would include the difficulties which would be experienced in group, where the therapist can be instrumental in choosing the most appropriate groups (12-step groups are known to be useful)

2. Build motivation (based upon Miller and Rollnick's method 1991):
   - Express empathy
   - Develop discrepancy. Amplify in the patient's mind the discrepancy between current behavior and future goals
   - Avoid argumentation
   - Roll with resistance
   - Support self-efficacy

3. Set goals

4. Modify social environment

5. Implement a relapse prevention plan.

Pharmacologic treatment should acknowledge the addictive properties of some of the medications used to treat PTSD. This increases the risk of abuse. The following research offers some insight into this area:

Follette et al. (1998)
- Treating the substance problem first is more effective than treating the PTSD first followed by substance treatment or simultaneous treatment.

Asnis et al. (2004), Hubbard and Martin (2001)
- Preferred medications are SSRIs (fluoxetine and sertraline).

Taylor and Gorman (1992)
- There may actually be more of an issue of treatment compliance (keeping people on medication).

Mason (1996)
- Higher doses of these medications may be required for those with a history of alcohol abuse/dependency as a result of liver damage.

Hubbard and Martin (2001)
- Neuroleptics such as chlorpromazine and olanzepine are also used to treat anxiety associated with PTSD
- For opioid dependence, methadone and buprenorphine are used and may be helpful with PTSD patients with narcotics dependence.

Mithoefer (2006)
- Stringently recommends against the new 3,4-methylenedioxymethamphetamine (MDMA) experimental therapy due to addiction potential for PTSD patients with a history of substance abuse/dependence.

An additional complication regarding pharmacotherapy for comorbidity of PTSD and substance abuse/dependence is the difficulties that may be experienced entering 12-step programs (Alcoholics Anonymous and Narcotics Anonymous) where total sobriety is the goal. Some 12-step communities are accepting of dual diagnosis where prescribed and monitored medication is a part of treatment and some are not. Therefore, prepare patients for the possibility of exploring this issue with their sponsor to assure that they are in an accepting and supportive environment.

GROUP THERAPY

According to the Department of Veterans Affairs (2007), group therapy provides a safe environment for patients to talk about their trauma with others who have had similar experiences.

The process allows them to feel more comfortable in talking about what happened to them and potentially improves their ability to cope with symptoms, memories, and other related life issues. This enables them to focus on their present life, instead of being overwhelmed by the past.

Foy et al. (2000), Ouimette (2003), and Witkiewitz et al. (2005) all state that group therapy helps patients with PTSD deal with isolation, alienation, and diminished feelings. Lindy et al. (1983) refer to a "traumatic membrane" that envelops all of those in a community involved in a disaster. By nature, group therapy uses the therapeutic factors within the group via support and interaction, not only to heal but to modify maladaptive reactions.

Foy et al. (2000) organizes group therapy into three approaches (supportive, cognitive behavioral, psychodynamic) which offer the experience of homogeneous group composition, acknowledgment of the trauma, and normalization of the trauma response. Current research does not favor any specific form of group therapy over another.

CRITICAL INCIDENT STRESS DEBRIEFING/PSYCHOLOGICAL DEBRIEFING

Critical incident stress debriefing (CISD) and psychological debriefing are therapies offered to patients within 48 hours following a traumatic event. The intent is to weaken the acute symptoms of the trauma and to diminish the risk of developing PTSD. The effectiveness of debriefing significantly depends upon the system of leadership and the management of morale, which honors the dignity of the individual and the importance of all individuals to the system.

According to Mitchell (1983), CISD has seven phases:

1. Introduction—offers an explanation of the purpose of debriefing, guidelines, introductions, etc.

2. Fact phase—seeks a factual description of exactly what happened with the associated emotions/reactions

3. Thought phase—considers thoughts at the time of the critical incident

4. Reaction phase—a detailed focus on emotions associated with the event

5. Symptom phase—facilitates group members to move from their emotional reactions to a cognitive realm, allowing for the discussion of trauma-related symptoms/reactions

6. Teaching phase—The symptom phase blends into the teaching phase where coping strategies are coupled to symptoms of stress

7. Re-entry phase—a consolidation for group members to:
   - clarify issues
   - ask questions to get further details and useful information
   - summarize techniques and individual benefits of debriefing, culminating with closure.

Psychological debriefing (Dyregrov, 1989; Rose, 1997), as with CISD, is intended for a group format. It is reflective of CISD with the exception of focus on:
- Sensory information experienced at the time
- Increased attention to individual reactions
- Increased attention to normalization reactions.

The seven phases of psychological debriefing are:

1. Introduction. The debriefer clarifies the purpose
   - Review and discuss the reactions to trauma
   - Identify methods of dealing with trauma reactions to prevent further problems

- Introduce group rules (no obligation to participate, confidentiality, and the focus of discussion is on the impressions and reactions of group participants)

2. Expectations and facts
   - Details of what actually happened
   - Participants are encouraged to describe "did they expect what happened" in an effort to understand why they reacted as they did

3. Thoughts and impressions
   - What were your thoughts when you realized what had happened?
   - What did you do? (to facilitate): Picture/frame of what happened. Puts individual reactions into perspective. Aids in integration of traumatic experience
   - Sensory impressions are elicited (sight, sound, touch, taste, smell) to increase the realism of what was experienced

4. Emotional reactions
   - This is the longest phase
   - Much of the earlier discussion leads to increased understanding of emotion
   - A release of emotion is facilitated by the debriefer inquiring about common reactions, such as anger, helplessness, guilt, frustration, fear, self-reproach/self-criticism, anxiety, depression

5. Normalization
   - Facilitation of acceptance
   - Reinforces that reactions are normal
   - Normalizes that it is not expected to experience all of the potential emotions in an individualized experience, though it is not uncommon that many reactions are shared among group members
   - Debriefer describes common symptoms that may be experienced at a later time, such as intrusive thoughts and images, distress when reminded of what happened, attempts to avoid thoughts/feelings/reminders, detached from others, loss of interest in activities previously enjoyed, anxiety/depressed mood, irritability, guilt/shame, anger, hypervigilance/amplified startle response

6. Future planning/coping
   - Focus is on ways of managing symptoms, i.e. coping mechanisms, both internal and external support mechanisms (family, friends, physician, clergy, therapy, etc.)
   - Emphasizes importance of speaking openly with family and close friends to educate/alert them to the potential need for support

7. Disengagement
   - Information/summaries of normal reactions and coping mechanisms
   - How to access further professional help if needed, e.g. if symptoms do not decrease in 4–6 weeks, psychological symptoms increase, there is continuing inability to function normally at work or in the family, others give feedback about personality changes.

ADDITIONAL INFORMATION ABOUT GROUP THERAPY

Groups are generally formed for survivors of a specific trauma, such as combat, rape/incest, or natural disasters. They help survivors recognize that survivors of shared experiences have similar emotional reactions to trauma and that group work benefits patients in resolving guilt issues and other negative/difficult emotions associated with their behavioral reactions to the traumas. They also support and reinforce learning to cope.

Group candidacy may be determined by utilizing the indications and contraindications provided by Foy et al. (2000). General indications for the candidacy of group therapy include:

- Initial individual assessment and completion of brief course of individual therapy
- Ability to establish interpersonal trust
- Previous group experience
- Not actively suicidal/homicidal
- Ability to share traumatic experience in group setting
- Ability and willingness to follow group rules, especially confidentiality.

General contraindications for the candidacy of group therapy include:

- Actively psychotic
- Actively suicidal/homicidal
- Severe organicity
- Limited cognitive capacity
- Pending litigation/compensation-seeking.

Indications specific for psychodynamic or cognitive behavioral group therapy include:

- Ability to tolerate high anxiety arousal (or other strong negative emotions)
- Not actively suicidal/homicidal
- All dual diagnosis issues are under control (including substance abuse)
- The rationale for trauma uncovering work is accepted
- Ability and willingness to share personal trauma experience
- Not immersed in struggles of current life crisis.

Three different types of group are described in Table 3.3.

Table 3.3 Types of group

Supportive	Emphasis on addressing current life issues Explore affect such as frustration, lack of focus, general avoidance with the goal of diffusing more extreme PTSD core symptoms Less reliance on formal content Less demand on group members for homework/mastery of materials Offers a sense of interpersonal comfort (which also minimizes transference) Orientation toward coping
Cognitive behavioral	Uncovering as a means to address patient's specific trauma experiences and memory Primary goals are to alleviate symptoms, enhance self-control, improve quality of life Applies systematic, prolonged exposure and cognitive restructuring to the traumatic experience of each group member Relapse prevention emphasizes coping skills/resources
Psychodynamic	Uncovering specific traumatic experiences and memory Help patients find meaning in the trauma experience Encourage and facilitate patients to confront the issues that are a consequence of the trauma event Allows patients to retrace painful emotions back to how they view themselves and others (could be very irrational) Effort to provide appropriate affective involvement/response and is monitored to control overwhelming feelings and decrease the risk of perpetuating dissociative reactions

CONJOINT/FAMILY THERAPY (WHEN APPROPRIATE)

PTSD can negatively impact the entire family (Veterans Health Administration, Department of Veterans Affairs, 2007). A survivor's children and/or life partner may not understand all of the distress and internal conflicts that they experience. Family therapy involves the entire family, facilitated by a therapist skilled in family systems dynamics, to improve communication, maintain good relationships, and cope with difficult emotions. In family therapy the family can learn more about PTSD and how it is treated. In this setting each family member can express their fears and concerns.

There is a bidirectional relationship between trauma and familial relationships which suggests the importance of considering marital/family therapy as part of a comprehensive, individualized treatment plan for PTSD.

- Marital and family therapy play a potentially significant role in trauma recovery (Davidson et al., 1991)
- Traumatic events and the associated consequences can significantly impact marital and family relationships (Foa et al., 2009)
- Partners and family members sometimes demonstrate their own difficulties in dealing with the consequences of trauma which negative impacts the family system and recovery.

Figley's (1986, 1988, 1989) goal of systemic family therapy with trauma survivors highlights:

1. Empowering the family to:
   - Overcome issues of loss, stress and adjustment
   - Learn from the experience (no experience can be wasted. Everything that happens to a person becomes part of their life history that has the potential to keep taking or can be used for personal growth). The goal is to integrate the trauma into the family system

2. Increased preparedness to manage future difficulties by developing the skills of:
   - Effective communication
   - Problem-solving
   - Conflict resolution

3. Conceptualization of five phases of systems therapy to address the disruptions in the aftermath of trauma:
   - Commitment to therapeutic objectives
   - Framing the identified problem(s)
   - Reframing the problem(s)
   - Developing a healing theory
   - Closure and preparedness.

Erickson (1989) defined the tasks of systems intervention as being a strengthening or cohesive influence by developing

- More effective communication
- Mutual support
- Recognizing the trauma as a family crisis (shared experience and response)

- Recognizing and responding to the needs of each family member
- A safe environment and encouraging appropriate self-disclosure and affective response
- Increased understanding that the damage caused by trauma can be healed/repaired.

Johnson et al. (1995) developed a systems approach that focused on the general patterns of marital interactions (based on Vietnam veteran families). They defined a "critical interaction" as a "repetitive conflict that is covertly associated with the trauma memory." They further describe critical interactions as following a sequence of events. The series of interventions includes:

- Teaching the couple about their interactional process
- Pointing out the connection to (the veteran's) traumatic experience
- Allowing the couple to offer support instead of blaming one another
- Promoting/reinforcing better communication and problem-solving.

It is generally the consequences of distress associated with the traumatized individual which results in the initiation of therapy. However, there are times when it is the distress associated with the actions of the traumatized individual that serves as the impetus of engaging in therapy. For example, there has been a demonstrated escalation in domestic violence associated with military personnel who have been in active combat. The decision to engage in therapy when there is domestic violence is very complex and the consideration for both severity and frequency of violence plays a major role. However, it is the issues of safety, self-responsibility, and boundaries that serve as the initial premise of decision-making with such system dynamics, specifically the therapists recommendation regarding appropriate referrals and treatment modalities. Conjoint treatment is often contraindicated in cases of domestic violence.

PHARMACOLOGICAL TREATMENTS

There is no compelling evidence that a brief pharmacologic trial will prevent the development of PTSD. Rose et al. (2005) state that there is insufficient research to support a recommendation for use of a pharmacological agent to prevent the development of PTSD. The effectiveness of SSRIs has been demonstrated, however, for the core symptoms of PTSD. In addition, the evidence for the use of benzodiazepines is mixed (Mellman et al., 1998).

The Veterans Health Administration, Department of Veterans Affairs (2007) states that SSRIs can help a patient struggling with PTSD to feel less sad and worried. For some people they are helpful and for others very effective. The SSRIs highlighted are citalopram (Celexa), fluoxetine (such as Prozac), paroxetine (Paxil), and sertraline (Zoloft). SSRIs raise the serotonin level in the brain (when someone is depressed they may not have enough serotonin).

For acute chronic PTSD, psychotherapy is the first-line treatment choice (Foa et al., 2000a, 2000b, 2009; American Psychiatric Association, 2004). The psychotherapeutic techniques found to be most valuable included exposure therapy, cognitive therapy, and anxiety management. It is recommended that for severe cases which do not meet the desired threshold of benefit with these techniques alone, a combination of medication and psychotherapy be used. Foa et al. (2009) added additional treatment strategies such as EMDR, psychodynamic psychotherapy and hypnotherapy.

Table 3.4 Some short-term pharmacologic interventions

Symptoms	Medications
ASD symptoms	Imipramine to ameliorate symptoms
Sleep disturbance/insomnia	Benzodiazepines (up to 5 days) Temazepam within 1–3 weeks of the trauma for 5 nights, tapered to 2 nights, then discontinued improves sleep and reduces stress symptoms of hyperarousal/panic attacks Chloral hydrate (up to 5 days) (Robert et al., 2000)
Hyperarousal/panic anxiety	Propranolol or other antiadrenergic medications for post-event hyperarousal (up to 10 days). May reduce subsequent PTSD symptoms (Pitman et al., 2002). Within 6 hours of a traumatic event, 10-day course of 40 mg (four times a day). It is suggested that acute, post-trauma propranolol may have preventive effect on subsequent PTSD Imipramine (up to 7 days) Benzodiazepines (up to 5 days) (avoid short-acting agents like Xanax)

According to the Veterans Health Administration, Department of Veterans Affairs (2006) Treatment Guidelines it is recommended to initiate treatment by meeting physical needs, to normalize reactions, and to offer psycho-education unless acuity of symptoms is not manageable. Wait 24–48 hours following a traumatic event before beginning medication. There may be a benefit in the slight delay in determining if the patient suffers from excessive adrenergic arousal, symptoms of psychomotor withdrawal, or if cognitive behavioral treatment interventions fail to improve symptomology.

Possible short-term pharmacologic interventions are listed in Table 3.4.

PHARMACOLOGIC RECOMMENDATION

The symptoms resulting from psychobiological dysfunctions associated with PTSD make it a diagnosis with considerable potential for pharmacological treatment. Foa et al. (2009) outline the most current pharmacotherapy treatment choices. Treatment guidelines recommend first-line choices of SSRIs and SNRIs being the best, evidenced-based, choice. Monoamine oxidase inhibitors (MAOIs) (moderately effective) and tricyclic antidepressants (TCAs) (mildly effective) along with numerous other medications may be considered if SSRIs and SNRIs have not been effective or their side-effects have not been well tolerated. However, the moderately and mildly effective rating for MAOIs and TCAs suggests a negative side-effect profile. Medication compliance assessments should be conducted at each session given the level of distress associated with PTSD. Since PTSD is at times a chronic disorder, pharmacologic intervention may need to be continued indefinitely. Intermittent reassessments should be viewed as a reasonable practice standard. For the most current information available for pharmacotherapy see http://www.ncptsd.va.gov/ncmain/information/.

Medications listed by Foa et al. (2009) include:

- SSRIs (sertraline, paroxetine, fluoxetine)
- SSNI (venlafaxine)
- Other second-generation antidepressants considered for managing PTSD (mirtazapine, bupropion, nefazodone, trazodone)
- MAOI (phenylzine)
- TCAs (imipramine, amitriptyline, desipramine).

Table 3.5 Symptom response by drug class

Drug class	Individual drug	Global improvement	Re-experiencing	Avoidance/numbing	Hyperarousal
SSRIs					
	Fluoxetine	√	√	√	√
	Sertraline	√		√	√
	Paroxetine	√	√	√	√
SNRI	Venlafaxine	√	√	√	√
TCAs		√	√		
MAOIs		√	√	√	
Sympatholytics			√		√
	Prazosin	√			
	Propranolol				
Novel antidepressants					
	Trazodone		√	√	√
	Nefazodone		√	√	√
Anticonvulsants					
	Carbamazepine		√		
	Valproate				√
Benzodiazepines				√	√
Atypical antipsychotics			√		√

Veterans Health Administration, Department of Veterans Affairs (2006)

Prazosin can be prescribed to help the management of nightmares and other symptoms of PTSD. Antiadrenergic agents (prazosin, propranolol, clonidine) demonstrate benefit in reducing arousal, re-experiencing, and (possibly) dissociative symptoms. Additionally, research does not find benzodiazepines to be useful in treating PTSD symptoms, citing the exacerbation of depression and psychomotor slowing as complicating factors.

As per the Department of Veterans Affairs Guidelines, areas of insufficient evidence for recommending pharmacological intervention for the treatment of PTSD include the following:

- Mood stabilizer (e.g. lamotrigine)
- Atypical antipsychotics

- Any pharmacological agent to prevent the development of PTSD
- Long-term use of benzodiazepines to manage core symptoms of PTSD.

The symptom responses of various drugs are listed in Table 3.5.

INTEGRATIVE INTERVENTIONS

The Expert Consensus study contributed to the following list.

HYPNOSIS

Hypnosis is actually an adjunctive technique to therapy and has been shown to enhance the positive outcome for a variety of clinical conditions including the treatment of shell shock, battle fatigue, traumatic neurosis, PTSD, and dissociative symptomology (Kiersch, 1994; Kiersch et al., 1998). In other words, hypnosis can be used to facilitate therapy. Hypnotic phenomena are behavioral, cognitive, and experiential alterations that either emerge or are enhanced by hypnotic induction. There is no guarantee that a hypnotic procedure will result in hypnotic phenomena in any individual. In addition, hypnotic responsiveness varies over the course of lifespan (the peak of suggestability being around age 12). The use of hypnosis should only be done by a therapist is working within their area of professional expertise. Sherman (1998) and Kiersch et al. (1998) found that a major benefit of hypnosis is at follow-up rather than at the end of treatment.

According to Foa et al. (2000a, 2000b, 2009; Kaplan et al., 2007) there are a variety of indications for the use of hypnosis as a treatment for PTSD symptoms such as:

- Pain
- Anxiety
- Dissociation and nightmares.

It can also be used to modulate emotion (distance from traumatic event memories) or to modulate cognitive distance from traumatic event memories.
Contraindications to hypnotherapy include:

- Patients who are refractory or minimally responsive to suggestion
- Patients who are reluctant based upon a belief system.

Cardena (1996) states that patients with PTSD, or experiencing symptoms of PTSD, tend to be notably susceptible to hypnotism, even more so than patients in other clinical or non-clinical groups. The use of hypnosis may be considered as an addition to treatment for the following reasons:

1. To capitalize on the hypnotizability of PTSD patients.
2. Since hypnosis may induce dissociation within a structured and controlled setting it allows patients to learn management and coping techniques.

3. While under hypnotic suggestion, dissociation may be reframed and utilized for therapeutic benefit (i.e. identifying the positive/negative aspects of dissociation).

4. Hypnosis can be an adjunctive addition to diverse treatment approaches (cognitive behavioral, psychodynamic, pharmacotherapy).

5. Two prevalent theoretical orientations of PTSD treatment, cognitive behavioral and psychodynamic, both espouse the importance of recollection of the traumatic event to achieve emotional and cognitive integration (such as with implosion).

6. Hypnosis can be useful for working through traumatic memories and developing more adaptive responses.

7. Hypnosis provides the patient with the ability to pace and control the intensity, and associated distress, of the traumatic memory.

8. According to the theory of state-dependent memory, hypnosis may facilitate the retrieval of memories associated with a similar state of mind (time of the trauma). Careful attention should be utilized to assure that hypnosis does not unduly enhance a patient's confidence on reported versus accurate recall of traumatic memories (warn patients regarding overconfidence mitigated by memory recall which may be inaccurate or confabulated).

Kluft (1994) and Brown and Fromm (1986) describe techniques that are employed for intervention with dissociative patients which are also relevant to those with PTSD. These include:

- Fractional or gradual abreactions
- Time sense alterations
- Relaxation
- Projective techniques
- Restructuring
- Age regression
- Affect bridge
- Imaginal memory containment.

SPIRITUAL/RELIGIOUS COUNSELING

Traumatic events can affect a patient's spiritual views or beliefs. Counseling with a trusted spiritual/religious advisor may be helpful. There is a growing number of pastoral counselors seeking advanced training/credentials in trauma intervention. The goal is to decrease PTSD symptoms and improve patient functioning utilizing social and spiritual support. Hunter (1996) states that the successful treatment of PTSD addresses emotional, psychological, cognitive and interpersonal processes, and existential meaning.

BODY WORK

Yoga (and other forms) can be useful as a means of releasing physical tension/muscle soreness resulting from anxiety or hypervigilance.

MARTIAL ARTS TRAINING

Martial arts can be used as a method to restore a patient's sense of personal effectiveness and safety. There are some martial arts programs developed specifically for survivors of rape and other violent crimes (for example, Model Mugging, which role-plays defensive action).

ART THERAPY, DANCE THERAPY, OR CREATIVE WRITING

These all offer a safe outlet for strong emotions.

JOURNALING

This allows for venting, clarifying, monitoring, and problem-solving.

ACUPUNCTURE

Acupuncture is considered both medical and holistic. Noted benefits include decreased cravings, decreased anxiety, mental and physical stability, less hostility, a greater sense of confidence, a decrease/elimination of medication. Chinese medicine considers and articulates how the elements of emotion and the spirit of day-to-day life combine to influence physical health which, of course, influence, emotional health.

MASSAGE THERAPY

Massage therapy increases body awareness, promotes relaxation, and decreases muscle fatigue and strain, which is viewed as complimenting the therapeutic process.

QI GONG

This is a relaxing form of tai chi with an emphasis on conscious control of the breath and remaining totally relaxed, while moving through a series of postures. It combines elements of movement, controlled breathing, and relaxation.

REIKI

Reiki is a Japanese method of healing used to promote well-being and relaxation.

SHIATSU

Shiatsu is a Japanese form of acupressure. This therapeutic bodywork technique uses pressure to stimulate points on acupressure meridians.

SOMATIC EXPERIENCING (PETER LEVINE)

Somatic experiencing is a treatment approach that addresses how the human triune brain (made up of the neocortex, limbic system, and primitive brain) functions in a complex and highly interconnected network to handle the experience of traumatic events.

YOGA

There are a number of techniques which share working with breath and posture to facilitate inner quietness and realization.

REFERENCES AND FURTHER READING

American Psychiatric Association (2000) *Diagnostic and Statistical Manual of Mental Disorders*, 4th edn, text revised. Washington, DC: American Psychiatric Association.

American Psychiatric Association (2004) *Practice Guideline For the Treatment of Patients With Acute Stress Disorder and Posttraumatic Stress Disorder: Formulation and Implementation of a Treatment Plan*. Washington, DC: American Psychiatric Association.

Andreski R, Childcoat KS, Breslau N (1998) Post-traumatic stress disorder and somatization symptoms: a prospective study. *Psychiatry Res* 79: 131–138.

Asnis GM, Kohn SR, Henderson M, Brown N (2004) SSRI's versus non-SSRI's in post traumatic stress disorder: an update with recommendations. *Drugs* 64: 383–404.

Astin MC, Rothbaum B (2000) Exposure therapy for the treatment of post-traumatic stress disorder. *Clin Q* 9(50): 52–55.

Beck A (1964) Thinking and depression: II theory and therapy. *Arch Gen Psychiatry* 10: 561–571.

Beers MH, Berkow R (eds)(1999) Posttraumatic stress disorder. In: *Merck Manual of Diagnoses and Therapy*, 17th edn. New Jersey: Merck Research Laboratories.

Bisson J, Deahl M (1994) Psychological debriefing and prevention of post-traumatic stress: More research is needed. *Br J Psychiatry* 165: 717–720.

Bisson J, Jenkins P, Bannister C (1997) A randomized controlled trial of psychological debriefing for victims of acute burn trauma. *Br J Psychiatry* 171: 78–81.

Boscarino JA (1997) Diseases among men 20 years after exposure to severe stress: implications for clinical research and medical care. *Psychosom Med* 59: 605–614.

Bourne E (2001) *Beyond Anxiety and Phobia: A step by step guide to lifetime recovery*. Oakland, CA: New Harbinger Publications.

Brady K, Pearlstein T, Asnis GM et al. (2000) Double-blind placebo controlled study of the efficacy and safety of sertraline treatment of posttraumatic stress disorder. *JAMA* 283: 1837–1844.

Breslau N, Kessler RC, Chilcoat HD, Schultz LR, Davis GC, Andreski P (1998) Trauma and posttraumatic stress disorder in the community: The 1996 Detroit Area Survey of Trauma. *Arch Gen Psychiatry* 55: 626–632.

Brewin CR, Dalgleish T, Joseph H (1996) A dual representation theory of post-traumatic stress disorder. *Psychol Rev* 103: 670–686.

Brierre J, Scott C (2006) *Principles of Trauma Therapy: A guide to symptoms, evaluation, and treatment*. Washington DC: American Psychiatric Association.

Brown DP, Fromm E (1986) *Hypnotherapy and Hypnoanalysis*. Hillsdale, NJ: Erlbaum.

Brown PJ, Crosby Ouimette P (1999) Substance use disorders and PTSD. *Psychol Addict Behav* 13: 75–77.

Busuttil W (2002) The development of a 90-day residential program for the treatment of complex PTSD. In: *Simple and Complex PTSD: Strategies for Comprehensive Treatment in Clinical Practice* (Williams MB, Sommers JF, eds). Binghampton, NY: Haworth Press.

Cardena E (1996) Dissociativity in Gulf War PTSD patients. *Int J Clin Exp Hypnosis* 44: 394.

Carroll EM, Rueger DB, Foy DW, Donohoe CP (1985) Vietnam combat veterans with PTSD: Analysis of marital and cohabitating adjustment. *J Abnorm Psychol* 94: 329–337.

Chemtob C, Tomas S, Law W, Creminiter D (1997) Post disaster psychosocial interventions: A field study of the impact of debriefing on psychological distress. *Am J Psychiatry* 154: 415–417.

Coffey SF, Schumacher JA, Brimo ML, Brady KT (2005) Exposure therapy for substance abusers with PTSD. *Behav Modif* 29: 10–38.

Covey S (1999) *The 7 Habits of Highly Successful People.* New York: Simon and Schuster.

Davidson JRT, Hughes D, Blazer DG, George LK (1991) Post-traumatic stress disorder in the community: An epidemiological study. *Psychol Med* 21: 713–721.

Davidson JRT, Weisler RH, Malik ML, Connor MK (1998) Treatment of posttraumatic stress disorder with nefazodone. *Int Clin Psychopharmacol* 13: 111–113.

Davis L (1990) *The Courage to Heal Workbook: For Adult Survivors of Childhood Sexual Abuse.* New York: Harper and Row.

Davis JL (2005) Simultaneous treatment of substance abuse and post-traumatic stress disorder. *Clin Case Studies* 4: 347–362.

Department of Veterans Affairs (2007) National Center for PTSD. Fact Sheet. Accessed from: http://www.ncptsd.va.gov/ncmain/information/.

Dyregrov A (1989) Caring for helpers in disaster situations: psychological debriefing. *Disaster Manag* 2: 25–30.

Dyregrov A (1998) Psychological debriefing—an effective method. *Traumatology* 4(2). Accessed from: http://www.fsu.edu/-trauma/art3v4i2.htm.

Erickson CA (1989) Rape in the family. In: *Treating Stress in Families* (Figley CR, ed.). New York: Brunner/Mazel.

Evans K, Tyrer P, Catalan J et al. (1999) Manual-assisted cognitive-behaviour therapy (MACT): A randomized controlled trial and intervention with bibliotherapy in the treatment of recurrent deliberate self-harm. *Psychol Med* 29: 19–25.

Everly GS, Mitchell JT (1999) *Critical Incident Stress Management (CISM), A new era and standard of care in crisis intervention.* Ellicot City, MD: Chevron.

Figley CR (1986) Traumatic stress: the role of the family and social support system. In: *Trauma and its Wake: Volume II. The study and treatment of post-traumatic disorder* (Figley CR, ed.). New York: Brunner/Mazel.

Figley CR (1988) A five-phase treatment of post-traumatic stress disorder in families. *J Trauma Stress* 1: 127–141.

Figley CR (1989) *Helping Traumatized Families.* San Francisco: Jossey-Bass.

Figley CR (1995) *Compassion Fatigue: Coping with secondary traumatic stress disorder in those who treat the traumatized.* New York: Brunner/Mazel.

Foa EB, Kozak MJ (1986) Emotional processing of fear. Exposure to corrective information. *Psychol Bull* 99: 20–35.

Foa EB, Steketee G, Rothbaum BO (1989) Behavior/cognitive conceptualization of post traumatic stress disorder. *Behav Ther* 20: 155–176.

Foa EB, Davidson JRT, Frances A, Ross MA (1999a) Expert consensus treatment guidelines for posttraumatic stress disorder. A guide for patients and families. *J Clin Psychiatry* 60(suppl 16): 69–74.

Foa EB, Dancu CV, Hembree CA, Jaycox LH, Meadows EA, Street GP (1999b) A comparison of exposure therapy, stress inoculation training and their combination in ameliorating posttraumatic stress disorder in female assault victims. *J Consult Clin Psychol* 67: 194–200.

Foa EB, Davidson JRT, Frances A (eds) (1999c) Treatment of posttraumatic stress disorder. The Expert Guideline Series. *J Clin Psychiatry* 60(suppl 16): 1–34.

Foa EB, Keane TM, Friedman MJ (eds) (2000a) *Effective Treatments for PTSD: Practice Guidelines from the International Society for Traumatic Stress Studies.* New York: Guilford Press.

Foa EB, Keane TM, Friedman MJ (2000b) Guidelines for the treatment of PTSD. *J Trauma Stress* 3: 539–588.

Foa EB, Keane TM, Friedman MJ, Cohen JA (2009) *Effective Treatments for PTSD*, 2nd edn. New York: Guilford Press.

Follette VM, Ruzek JI, Abueg RF (1998) *Cognitive Behavior Therapies for Trauma*. New York: Guilford Press.

Forbes D, Phelps A, McHugh T (2001) Treatment of combat related nightmares using imagery rehearsal: A pilot study. *J Trauma Stress* 14: 433–442.

Foy DW, Glynn SM, Schnurr PP et al. (2000) Group therapy. In: *Effective Treatments for PTSD: Practice Guidelines from the International Society for Traumatic Stress Studies* (Foa EB, Keane TM, Friedman MJ, eds). New York: Guilford Press, pp. 155–175.

Freeman A, Datillo F (eds) (1996) *Comprehensive Casebook of Cognitive Therapy*. New York: Plenum Press.

Friedman MJ (1997) Drug treatment for PTSD: Answers and questions. *Ann N Y Acad Sci* 821: 359–371.

Friedman, MJ (guest ed.) (1999) Progress in psychobiological research in PTSD. *Semin Clin Neuropsychiatry* 4: 229–316.

Friedman MJ (2000) *Post-Traumatic Stress Disorder: The latest assessment and treatment strategies*. Kansas City, MO: Compact Clinicals.

Friedman MJ, Charney DS, Deutsch AY (1995) *Neurobiological and Clinical Consequences of Stress: From normal adaptation to PTSD*. Philadelphia: Lippincott-Raven.

Hamner MB (1996) Clonazpine treatment for a veteran with comorbid psychosis and PTSD. *Am J Psychiatry* 153: 841.

Herman JL (1997) *Trauma and Recovery: The aftermath of violence from domestic abuse to political terror*. New York: Basic Books.

Hobbs M, Mayou R, Harrison B, Warlock P (1996) A randomized trial of psychological debriefing for victims of road traffic accidents. *BMJ* 313: 1438–1439.

Hubbard JR, Martin PR (eds) (2001) *Substance Abuse in the Mentally and Physically Disabled*. New York: Marcel Dekker.

Hunter R (ed.) (1996) *Dictionary of Pastoral Care and Counseling*. Nashville: Abington Press.

Johnson SL (1997) *Therapist's Guide to Clinical Intervention*. San Diego, CA: Academic Press.

Johnson SL (2003) *Therapist's Guide to Substance Abuse Intervention*. San Diego, CA: Academic Press.

Johnson SL (2004) *Therapist's Guide to Clinical Intervention*, 2nd edn. San Diego, CA: Academic Press.

Johnson DR, Feldman SC, Lubin H (1995) Critical interaction therapy: Couples therapy in combat-related post-traumatic stress disorder. *Family Process* 34: 401–412.

Kaplan HJ, Saddock BJ, Saddock VA (2007) *Synopsis of Psychiatry*. Wolters Kluwer Health.

Kerr PL, Muehlenkamp JJ, Larson MA (2008) Implementation of DBT-informed therapy at rural university training clinic: A case study. *Cogn Behav Pract*. Article in press. DOI: 10.1016/j.cbpra.2008.09.003.

Kessler RC, Sonnega A, Bromet E, Hughes M, Nelson CB (1995) Post traumatic stress disorder in the National Comorbidity Survey. *Arch Gen Psychiatry* 52: 1048–1060.

Khantzian EJ (1985) The self-medication hypothesis of addictive disorders; focus on heroin and cocaine dependence. *Am J Psychiatry* 142: 1259–1264.

Kiersch I (1994) APA definition and description of hypnosis: Defining hypnosis for the public. *Contemporary Hypnosis* 11: 142–143.

Kiersch I, Capafons A, Cardena E et al. (1999) Clinical hypnosis and self-regulation therapy: An introduction. In: *Clinical Hypnosis and Self-regulation Therapy: A cognitive-behavioral perspective* (Kirsch I, Capafns E, Cardena E et al., eds). Washington, DC: American Psychiatric Association.

Kofoed L, Friedman MJ, Peck R (1993) Alcoholism and drug abuse in patients with PTSD. *Psychiatr Q* 64: 151–171.

Kosten TR, Krystal J (1988) Biological mechanisms of post traumatic stress disorder relevance for substance abuse. *Recent Dev Alcohol* 6: 49–68.

LeDoux J (1997) Emotion, memory and pain. *Pain Forum* 6: 36–37.

Lee C, Slade P, Lygo V (1996) The influence of psychological debriefing on emotional adaption in women following early miscarriage: A preliminary study. *Br J Med Psychol* 69: 47–58.

Lehman AF, Myers P, Corty E (1989) Assessment and classification of patients with psychiatric and substance abuse syndromes. *Hosp Community Psychiatry* 40: 1019–1025.

Levine P (1998) *Waking the Tiger*. Berkeley, CA: North Atlantic Books.

Lindy JD, Green BL, Grace M, Titchener J (1983) Psychotherapy with survivors of the Beverly Hills fire. *Am J Psychother* 37: 593–610.

Mann J (1973) *Time Limited Psychotherapy*. Cambridge, MA: Harvard University Press.

Mason BJ (1996) Dosing issues in the pharmacotherapy of alcoholism. *Alcohol Clin Exp Res* 20: 10A–16A.

Matsakis A (1994) *Post-Traumatic Stress Disorder: A complete treatment guide guide*. Oakland, CA: New Harbinger Publications.

McCann IL, Pearlman LA (1990) *Psychological Trauma and the Adult Survivor: Theory, therapy and transformation*. New York: Bruner/Mazel.

McFall ME, McKay PW, Donovan DM (1992) Combat-related posttraumatic stress disorder and severity of substance abuse in Vietnam veterans. *J Stud Alcohol* 53: 357–363.

Medical Research News (2006) Care that combines medication and psychotherapy can reduce alcohol abuse by trauma survivors. *Med Res News* May 5.

Meichenbaum D (1993) Stress inoculation training: A twenty year update. In: *Principles and Practices of Stress Management* (Woolfolk RL, Lehrer PM, eds). New York: Guilford Press.

Meichenbaum D (1996) Stress inoculation training for coping with stressors. *Clin Psychol* 49: 4–7.

Meichenbaum D (2007) *Practice of Stress Management*, 3rd edn. New York: Guilford Press.

Mellman TA, Byers PM, Augenstein JS (1998) Pilot evaluation of hypnotic medication during acute traumatic stress disorder. *J Trauma Stress* 11: 563–569.

Mellman TA, David D, Bustamante V et al. (2001) Predictors of post-traumatic stress disorder following severe injury. *Depression Anxiety* 14: 226–231.

Miller WR, Rollnick S (1991) *Motivational Interviewing: Preparing People to Change Addictive Behavior*. New York: Guilford Press.

Minkoff K (1989) An integrated treatment model for dual diagnosis of psychosis and addiction. *Hosp Community Psychiatry* 40: 1031–1036.

Mitchell JY (1983) When disaster strikes. *J Emerg Med Serv* 8: 36–39.

Mitchell JT, Everly GS (1995) *Critical Incident Stress Debriefing: An operations manual for the prevention of traumatic stress among emergency services and disaster workers*. Ellicot City, MD: Chevron.

Mithoefer MC (2006) Phase II clinical trial testing the safety and efficacy of 3,4 methylenedioxymethamphetamine (MDMA)-assisted psychotherapy in subjects with chronic post traumatic stress disorder. FDA Study no. 63–384. Multidisciplinary Association for Psychedelic Studies. Accessed April 17, 2007. http://www.maps.org/mdma/protocol/index.html.

Nagel AE, Follette WC (1998) A functional analysis of trauma symptoms. In: *Cognitive-Behavioral Therapies for Trauma* (Follette VM, Ruzak JI, Abueg FB, eds). New York: Guilford.

Najavits LM (2002) *Seeking Safety: A Treatment Manual for PTSD and Substance Abuse*. New York: Guilford Press.

Neal LA, Shapland W, Fox C (1997) An open trial of moclobemide in the treatment of post-traumatic stress disorder. *Int Clin Psychopharmacol* 12: 231–237.

National Institutes of Health (1996) Integration of behavioral and relaxation approaches into the treatment of chronic pain and insomnia. *JAMA* 276: 313–318.

National Institute of Mental Health (2000) Post-Traumatic Stress Disorder: A Real Illness. Brochure. Available at http://www.nih.gov/govanxiety/ptsddri2.cfm.

National Institute of Mental Health (2001) Reliving Trauma. Fact Sheet: NIH Publication No. 01-4597. Available at http://www.nimh.nih.gov/publcat/reliving.cfm.

National Institute of Mental Health (2008) Mental Health and Mass Violence: Evidence-Based Early Psychological Intervention for Victims/Survivors of Mass Violence. US Government Printing Office, NIH Publication No. 02-5138. Available at http://www.nimh.nih.gpv/research/massviolence.pdf.

Ouimette P (2003) Self-help group participation among substance use disorder patients with posttraumatic stress disorder. *J Subst Abuse Treat* 20: 25–32.

Pennebaker JW, Campbell RS (2000) The effects of writing about traumatic experience. *Clin Q* 9(17): 19–21.

Pierce JM, Brown JM, Long PJ, Nixon SJ, Borrell GK, Holloway FA (1996) Comorbidity and subjective reactivity to meaningful cues in female methadone maintenance patients. Reported in Follette VM, Ruzek JI, Aburg RF (1998) *Cognitive Behavioral Therapies*. New York: Guilford Press.

Pitman RK, Sanders KM, Zusman RM et al. (2002) Pilot study of secondary prevention of posttraumatic stress disorder with propranolol. *Biol Psychiatry* 51: 189–192.

Prins A, Kaloupek DG, Keane TM (1995) Psychophysiological evidence for autonomic arousal and startle in traumatized adult populations. In: *Neurobiology and Clinical Consequences of Stress: From normal adaptation to post-traumatic stress disorder* (Friedman MJ, Charney DS, Deutch AY, eds). Philadelphia: Lippincott-Raven.

Regehr C, LeBlanc V, Jelky RB, Barath I, Dacuik J (2007) Previous trauma exposure and PTSD symptoms as predictors of subjective and biological response to stress. *Can J Psychiatry* 52: 675–683.

Regier D (2007) An interview with Darrel A. Regier, MD, MPH: The developmental process for the diagnostic statistical manual of mental disorders. Fifth edition. *CNS Spectrum* 13: 120–124.

Reich W (2003) Body Armour. Accessed from: http://www.catalase.com/bodyamour.htm.

Richards DA (2001) A field study of critical incident stress debriefing versus critical incident stress management. *J Mental Health* 10: 351–362.

Richards DA, Lovell K, Marks IM (1994) Post-traumatic stress disorder: Evaluation of a behavioral treatment program. *J Trauma Stress* 7: 669–680.

Robert R, Blakeney PE, Villareal C et al. (2000) Imipramine treatment in pediatric burn patients with symptoms of scute stress disorder: A pilot study. *J Acad Child Adol Psychiatry* 38: 873–882. Also found in the VA/DoD Guidelines for Management of PTSD contact no. V101(93)P-1633. Accessed from: www.ncptsd.va.gov/ncmain/ncdocs/nc_prod/VAPracticeGuidelines1_2004pdf.

Rose S (1997) Psychological debriefing: History and methods counseling. *J Br Assoc Counselling* 8: 367–382.

Rose S, Bisson J, Wessely S (2005) Psychological debriefing for preventing post traumatic stress disorder (PTSD). *Cochrane Database Syst Rev*(2). CD000560. DOI: 10.1002/14651858.

Roshenow DJ, Childress AR, Monti PM, Niaura RS, Abrams DB (1990) Cue reactivity in addictive behaviors: theoretical and treatment implications. *Int J Addict* 25: 957–993.

Roshenow DJ, Childress AR, Monti PM, Niaura RS, Abrams DB (1990) Cue reactivity in addictive behaviors: theoretical and treatment implications.

Rothbaum BO, Hodges L, Alarcon R et al. (2000) Virtual reality exposure therapy for PTSD Vietnam Veterans. *Behav Ther* 31: 583–595.

Rothchild B (2000) *The Body Remembers: The psychophysiology of trauma and trauma treatment*. New York: WW Norton.

Rothchild B (1998) *Introduction to Somatic Trauma Therapy*. Accessed from: http://www.riverscentre.org.uk/Main/ComplexTrauma.

Rothchild B (1999) Making trauma therapy safe. *Self and Society* 27.

Samson AY, Benson S, Beck A, Nimmer C (1999) Posttraumatic stress disorder in primary care. *J Family Pract* 48: 222–227.

Shapiro F (1995) *Eye Movement Desensitization Reprocessing*. New York: Guilford Press.

Shapiro F (1999) Eye movement desensitization and processing (EMDR) and the anxiety disorders-effectiveness and autonomic correlates. *J Anxiety Disorders* 13: 35–67.

Shapiro F (2001) *Eye Movement Desensitization and Reprocessing: Basic Principles, protocols and procedures*, 2nd edn. New York: Guilford Press.

Sherman JJ (1998) Effects of psychotherapeutic treatments for PTSD: A meta-analysis of controlled clinical trials. *J Trauma Stress* 11: 413–435.

Shipherd JC, Salters-Pedneault K (2008) Attention, memory, intrusive thoughts, and acceptance in PTSD: An update on the empirical literature for clinicians. *Cogn Behav Pract* 15: 349–363.

Society Medical Decision Making Committee (SMDMC) (1992) Protocol for Clinical Algorithm Standards. SMDMC on Standardization of Clinical Algorithms. *Medical Decision Making* 12: 149–154.

Solomon SD, Davidson JRD (1997) Trauma: Prevalence, impairment, service, use, and cost. *J Clin Psychiatry* 58(suppl 9): 5–11.

Stein DJ, Bandelow B, Hollander E et al. (2003) WCA Recommendations for the long-term treatment of posttraumatic stress disorder. *CNS Spectr* (suppl. 8): 31–39.

Tarrier N, Pilgrim H, Sommerfield C, Reynolds M, Graham E, Barrowclough C (1999) A randomized trial of cognitive therapy and imaginal exposure in the treatment of chronic post traumatic stress disorder. *J Consult Clin Psychol* 67: 13–18.

Taubman-Ben Ari O, Rabinowitz J, Friedman D et al. (2001) Post-traumatic stress disorder in primary care settings: prevalence and physicians' detection. *Psychol Med* 31: 555–560.

Taylor L, Gorman J (1992) Theoretical and therapeutic considerations for the anxiety disorders. *Psychiatr Q* 63: 319–342.

Taylor F, Cahill L (2002) Propranolol for reemergent posttraumatic stress disorder following an event of retraumatization: A case study. *J Trauma Stress* 1: 433–437.

Tedeschi RG, Park CL, Calhoun LG (eds) (1998) *Post-traumatic Growth: Positive changes in the aftermath of crisis*. Mahweh, NJ: Lawrence Erlbaum Associates.

The Expert Consensus Panel for PTSD (1999) Treatments of posttraumatic stress disorder. *J Clin Psychiatry* 60: 3–76.

US Preventive Service Task Force (2003) *Guide to Clinical Prevention Services 2000–2003*, 3rd edn. Periodic Updates. Agency for Healthcare Research and Quality Publication No. 03-0007, March 2003. Rockville, MD. Available at http://www.ahrq.gov/clinical/periodorder.htm.

van der Bosch LM, Verhuel R, Schippers GM et al. (2002) Dialectical behavior therapy of borderline patients with and without substance abuse problems. Implementation and long-term effects. *Addict Behav* 27: 911–923.

Van der Hart O, Brown P, van der Kolk BA (1989) Pierre Janet's treatment of post-traumatic stress. *J Trauma Stress* 2: 397–412.

van der Hout M, Muris P, Salemink E et al. (2001) Autobiographical memories become less vivid and emotional after eye movements. *Br J Clin Psychol* 40: 121–130.

van der Kolk BA (1994) The body keeps the score: memory and the evolving psychobiology of posttraumatic stress. *Harv Rev Psychiatry* 1: 253–265.

van der Kolk BA (1997) The psychology of posttraumatic stress disorder. *J Clin Psychiatry* 58: 16–24.

van der Kolk B, McFarlane A, Weeisaeth L (eds) (1996) *Traumatic Stress: The effects of overwhelming experience on the mind, body and society*. New York: Guilford Press.

Verheul R, Van Den Bosch LM, Koeter MW, DeRidder MA et al. (2003) Dialectical behavior therapy for women with borderline personality disorder: 12 month, randomized clinical trial in the Netherlands. *Br J Psychiatry* 182: 135–140.

Veterans Health Administration, Department of Veterans Affairs and Health Affairs, Department of Defense (2003) Management of post-traumatic stress. VA/DoD Clinical Practice Guideline Working Group, December 2003. Office Quality and Performance publication 10Q-CPG/PTSD-04.

Veterans Health Administration, Department of Veterans Affairs (2006) *The Post Traumatic Stress Treatment Guidelines*. Accessed from: http://www.vaonline.org/doc_trauma.html.

Veterans Health Administration, Department of Veterans Affairs (2007) *The Post Traumatic Stress Treatment Guidelines*. Accessed from: http://www.vaonline.org/doc_trauma.html.

Volpicelli JR (1987) Uncontrollable events and alcohol drinking. *Br J Addict* 82: 381–392.

Wilson JP, Keane TM (eds) (1997) *Assessing Psychological Trauma and PTSD*. New York: Guilford Press.

Witkiewitz K, Marlatt GA, Walker D (2005) Mindfulness-based relapse prevention for alcohol and substance use disorders. *J Cogn Psychother* 19: 211–228.

Wolpe J (1958) *Psychotherapy by Reciprocal Inhibition*. Stanford, CA: Stanford University.

Wolpe J (1969) *The Practice of Behavior Therapy*. Oxford: Pergamon Press.

World Health Organization (2009) F43.0 Acute stress reaction. In: *The ICD-10 Classification of Mental and Behavioural Disorders*. Geneva: World Health Organization. Accessed January 1, 2009 from: http://who.Int/classifications/icd/en/bluebook.pdf.

Yehuda R (1997) Sensitization of the hypothalamic-pituitary-adrenal axis in PTSD. In: *Psychobiology of Posttraumatic Stress Disorder* (Yehuda R, McFarlane A, eds). New York: Annals of New York Academy of Sciences, pp. 57–75.

Yehuda RE, McFarlane AC (1997) Psychobiology of posttraumatic stress disorder. *Ann N Y Acad Sci* 821.

Yehuda R, McFarlane AC, Shalev AY (1998) Predicting the development of post-traumatic stress disorder from the acute response to a traumatic event. *Biol Psychiatry* 44: 1305–1313.

Zalin L (2004) Collaborative care may prevent PTSD, alcohol abuse among trauma survivors. *Health Med* May 5. University of Washington.

Zampelli SO (2000) *From Sabotage to Success: Ways to overcome self-defeating behavior and reach your true potential*. Oakland, CA: New Harbinger Publications.

Zayfer C, Becker CB (2007) *Cognitive-Behavioral Therapy for PTSD: A case formulation approach*. New York: Guilford Press.

Zimmerman M, Mattia JI (1999) Is posttraumatic stress disorder underdiagnosed in routine clinical settings? *J Nerv Ment Dis* 187: 420–428.

Chapter 4

Treatment Planning

Posttraumatic stress disorder (PTSD) has a better prognosis if clinical intervention is implemented as early as possible (Foa et al., 2000). According to the Veterans Health Administration, Department of Veterans Affairs (2008) treatment choices are based upon unique qualities of the patient (unique life challenges, relative strengths and weaknesses, comorbidity of other psychiatric symptoms/diagnoses, the fluctuating course of PTSD, motivation, social support), therapist resources and skill level, and other factors such as treatment side-effects and potential negative effects, cost, length of treatment, cultural appropriateness, the need to foster resilience, and the legal, administrative, and forensic concerns.

The therapist must be prepared to meet the patient "where they are" regarding symptoms, strengths, weaknesses, social support, etc. This clearly means that the therapist does not impose a limited or narrow frame upon the patient, but instead utilizes the vast richness of information provided by the patient to offer interventions that match his or her needs in developing a treatment plan to (1) ameliorate/eliminate symptoms, (2) improve coping, (3) improve functioning, and, therefore, (4) improve quality of life. While cognitive behavioral therapy reduces the symptoms of PTSD and other trauma-related problems by helping patients to process their traumatic experience emotionally there is also a strong somatic presentation by some patients which should be incorporated into the understanding of their unique emotional and physiological response to trauma.

Motivated patients do not want to be pathologized, they want to increase self-understanding and master skills for management and recovery. In treatment they are seeking recovery and resolution. If the reader has taken the time to thoroughly review the transtheoretical treatment options available they will recognize that some aspect of all the major theories of trauma treatment can be integrated into cognitive and behavioral interventions, albeit at lower or higher levels of functional ability. In addition, psychodynamic interventions offer personal insight and

Therapist's Guide to Posttraumatic Stress Disorder Intervention

development of interpersonal safety that change thought and behavior, although they may not be a useful treatment choice of benefit to everyone. Furthermore, with a rudimentary knowledge of the nervous system and the hypothalamic–pituitary–adrenal axis (HPA axis) (see Chapter 2) a therapist can acknowledge how the body remembers trauma and learns from it and there are a variety of treatment theories which can be used to validate this experience (cognitive behavioral therapy, psychodynamic therapy, somatic/body work) which offer equal utility or benefit, again based upon the unique qualities, resources, and functional abilities of the individual patient.

Two major clinical errors therapists tend to make are to:

- Offer the same treatment plan to all patients as a consequence of the therapist's limitations

- Offer treatment because it "feels good" but does not lead to progress in terms of symptom alleviation and resolution. Such a treatment strategy reinforces dependency on the therapist versus development of personal skill and mastery.

Some of the recommendations for comprehensive and integrated treatment are as follows:

Christopher et al. (2004)
- Proposes a model for a comprehensive, multi-component cognitive behavioral therapy (CBT) treatment program which includes "elements of consumer education, anti-anxiety training, social skills training, exposure therapy," etc. Meeting the wide-ranging needs of the those seeking treatment.

Ford et al. (2005)
- Treatment recommendations for complex posttraumatic self-dysregulation address a comprehensive treatment planning perspective for a three-phase integrative therapy comprising alliance formation and stabilization; trauma processing; and functional reintegration
- Acknowledges the importance of merging treatment models that address PTSD, dysregulation of consciousness, bodily functions, emotion, and interpersonal attachments.

Back et al. (2006)
- Highlights evidenced-based time-limited treatment with co-occurring substance use disorders and PTSD.

Foa et al. (2009)
- Recommends a first-line treatment composed of CBT and pharmacotherapy.

FIRST-LINE INTERVENTIONS

The two treatments consistently identified as first-line interventions for the PTSD spectrum are cognitive behavioral therapy and pharmacological treatment.

COGNITIVE BEHAVIORAL THERAPY

Exposure therapy, in which patients are asked to describe their traumatic experiences in detail, on a repetitive basis, with the goal of decreasing the distress and hyperarousal associated with their memories. It has two components:

- Cognitive therapy focuses on helping patients identify their trauma-related negative beliefs such as guilt, anger, fear, and distrust, and change them to decrease distress and alleviate anxiety and depression
- Behavior therapy develops skills such as anger management, assertiveness training, impulse control, etc.
- Combination cognitive behavioral therapy is useful for mood management and overall skill development.
- Anxiety management for improved coping and alleviating anxiety and depression
- Stress inoculation training (SIT) whereby patients are taught skills for managing and decreasing anxiety (relaxation, breathing, self-talk, etc.).

PHARMACOLOGIC TREATMENT

The predominant medications used are:

- Serotonin reuptake inhibitors (SSRIs)
- Tricyclics
- Monoamine oxidase inhibitors (MAOIs)
- Benzodiazepines.

INDIVIDUAL INTERNAL AND EXTERNAL RESOURCES

In accordance with the patient factors set forth by the Veterans Health Administration, Department of Veterans Affairs, a therapist working with trauma survivors must be well trained, sensitive to the human condition, a good listener, intuitive, and possess a high level of self and environmental awareness to promote recovery in an individualized manner. In other words, meeting a patient where they are at in their ability to understand and cope with what they have experienced.

The individualized treatment plan requires careful assessment, specific goals, and intervention strategies directly related to an individual's internal and external resources taking into consideration:

- Object relations
- Ego strength and self-capacity

- Pre- and post-trauma risk
- Resiliency factors
- Severity of symptoms
- Degree of social connection
- Level of functioning
- External resources
- Environmental circumstances
- Level of disability
- Motivation and desire for change
- History of experience and demonstrated coping.

Consideration of these factors encompasses the acknowledgment of the traumatic origin and associated pathology of the patient's difficulties as being in context to their entire life experience, or focus on the entire person not just current pathology. According to Shalev's (1997) "healing forward," the focus on the past trauma is only in the interest of the future and a life less encumbered by the trauma the individual has experienced.

Another treatment issue is associated with consistency. Some patients will remain consistent with their appointments in working through to their treatment goals while others demonstrate treatment initiation and pauses as their personal way of being able to engage the therapeutic process changes. Dealing with avoidance of fear and distress are a significant treatment challenge. In addition, one of the key factors in treatment is the development and maintenance of the "self-of-the-therapist" (Friedman, 1996). While in the presence of survivors of traumatic events and trauma material, the therapist should be able to develop and maintain a non-anxious environment and promoting resilience.

BASIC TREATMENT PLANNING

Symptoms associated with chronic PTSD are quite complicated. This clinical picture is further complicated by comorbid diagnoses. Therefore, the development of a treatment plan must be comprehensive. Many patients with a history of prolonged traumatization and chronic PTSD require psychiatric and rehabilitative services of long duration, which takes into consideration the cyclical patterns of relapse, decompensation, and improvement. Treatment could be in an individual or group modality. Group therapy is important and recognizes the critical role of the group environment (Foa and Meadows, 1997; Foa et al., 2009) or therapeutic community of peers in offering support to counteract the effects of interpersonal victimization and traumatization.

Treatment planning must always consider multimodal treatment and a multidisciplinary treatment team to address the following treatment planning issues:

- Comprehensive assessment
- Inability to function
- Stabilization or resolution of suicidal, self-destructive, or homicidal impulses
- Safety: stabilization and resolution of crisis issues other than danger to self/others

- Reduction of core PTSD symptoms. Address and resolve psychiatric dysfunctional and irrational cognitions and beliefs associated with traumatization in an effort to decrease core PTSD symptoms, such as intrusion, avoidance, and hyperarousal
- Reduction of other PTSD symptoms
- Identification and stabilization of comorbid conditions/symptoms, including depression disorders, anxiety disorders, anger, impulse control, dissociative disorders (present-centered focus versus past-oriented cathartic trauma recollection strategy), and compulsions. Compulsions are often viewed as a means to not think or feel, self-medication, and/or experience a sense of control. While compulsions can take numerous forms, substance abuse will be focused on in the treatment planning section because of its high rate of comorbidity with survivors of traumatic experience
- Improved coping and management
- Improvement of personality and interpersonal difficulties/deficits demonstrated in the family setting, social setting, and work setting
- Improvement of functional status and reduction of key symptoms creating or reinforcing difficulties
- Improvement of specific areas of disability
- Comprehensive and extensive treatment planning
- Skill rehearsal, reinforcement, and refinement of goal to change
- Relapse prevention
- A new narrative of the self and the self in the world regarding the impact of surviving a traumatic experience.

These treatment planning issues are distilled down into the following key areas:

- Personal safety and symptom stabilization
- Crisis management and resolution
- Patient and family education regarding trauma and the range of potential responses
- Assessing current level of functioning and coping
- Self-management of symptoms via education, appropriate skill development and relapse prevention
- Pharmacologic intervention
- Healthy reconnection with others and associated boundaries (object relations, attachment, and capacity to cope)
- Rehabilitation
- Reintegration of the individual into everyday family, work, and social life.

Multidisciplinary input is particularly important in PTSD because some symptoms and disorders have been found to mimic, overlap, or obscure others, which interferes with accurate psychiatric and medical diagnoses. This treatment format also positively contributes to the identification of primary diagnoses that are not trauma-related but are comorbid or possibly even malingering (Foa et al., 2000, 2009). The transtheoretical and multimodal intervention process is best suited to the treatment of PTSD. In this process techniques and strategies drawn from various treatment models have been shown to be beneficial, even though CBT remains the first-line psychological intervention. Pharmacologic intervention is also an important component of treatment, but alone has not been demonstrated to be effective.

Social support has repeatedly been identified as a critical component of recovery following a trauma. For example:

Perry et al. (1992)

- Less psychological support post trauma was predictive of PTSD whereas more severe injury did not predict PTSD.

Andersson et al. (1997)

- The high rate of psychosocial complications is associated with poor social support.

Buckley et al. (1996)

- Delayed onset versus those who met criteria for acute onset had poorer social support.

Landsman et al. (1990)

- The level of psychological distress 3–39 months after a traumatic event was predicted less by injury severity than by subjective impact of the event, injury-related financial and employment problems, and family and social environment.

Additional issues that can complicate PTSD are referred to as "second injury" and "sanctuary trauma" (Knafo, 2004).

SECOND INJURY

This term is used to describe the experience when rejection, abandonment, and/or blaming on the part of the support system further compounds the trauma. It includes negative post-trauma experiences with first responders/rescue workers, or hospital personnel.

SANCTUARY TRAUMA

This occurs when an individual who has suffered a traumatic experience next encounters what they anticipated or expected would be a protective and supportive environment but instead were offered more vulnerability and trauma.

Traumatic experiences at the hands of others invalidates the basic human assumption that the sense of reality and safety are based upon. In other words, a feeling of safety is created (people can be trusted) when the past is known and the future seems reasonably predictable.

INITIAL ASSESSMENT

See Chapter 1.

TREATMENT SETTING

The disposition of the treatment setting should be assessed for and determined during the initial clinical interview and diagnostic evaluation. Continual monitoring of mental status throughout the course of treatment is important for the identification of needed (warranted) and appropriate changes in the treatment setting.

Hospitalization as Indicated

While there may be inpatient programs specific for the treatment of PTSD the level of functioning may be a contraindication for admission into such a program. When an individual is in imminent danger of harm to self or others, or gravely disabled in their ability to function, all of which require a safe and secure environment, then psychiatric hospitalization is considered. When a patient enters an inpatient program there is a collaborative effort with their outpatient providers so that the necessary continuum of services can be accessed in anticipation of the need for episodic intensive treatment in the case of chronic PTSD and/or level of risk.

Long-term inpatient treatment for chronic PTSD should not be viewed as the exclusive efficacious treatment approach, and that many of these patients would be better served by ongoing outpatient treatment with residential or community-based care. In other words, hospitalization should be reserved for the most serious and intensive treatment efforts when there has been no demonstrated benefit from other forms of treatment, or when considerable pathology remains explicitly evident and where safety is an issue which cannot be achieved in a less intensive setting. Whatever the treatment setting, it is important that the recovery from PTSD be facilitated in a non-traumatizing environment.

Hospitalization Contraindicated

When a patient is unwilling or unable to participate in milieu-based treatment, hospitalization is considered to be contraindicated. When considering a specialized PTSD inpatient program, this would include those whose characters are impaired to the degree that they are unable/unwilling to maintain safety in such a milieu setting, or have a life-threatening diagnosis such as an eating disorder or substance abuse disorder (unless it is an integrated treatment component of the program) which requires stabilization before the consideration of integrating other treatment needs. Inpatient PTSD treatment is contraindicated when:

- Malingering is suspected
- The patient experiences psychotic symptoms or other pathology requiring immediate intervention
- Character/social impairment is at a level which would not allow therapeutic work to take place in the hospital milieu.

A central factor in developing an individualized treatment plan is the consideration of structure and support needed by the patient to prevent further decompensation and begin to develop improved coping. It also considers the importance of reinforcing the appropriate use of management skills such as adaptive defenses of repression, suppression, and displacement.

If a patient is self-medicating (for example, abusing alcohol) a psychiatrist might prescribe a medication to reduce anxiety and need for alcohol with an additional introduction of a longer acting pharmacologic agent for the management of symptoms associated with acute anxiety or panic disorder as well as medication to ameliorate craving while they are engaged in an intensive outpatient program.

It is important that every individual entering treatment be assessed for substance abuse, acknowledging the prevalence of self-medication and the spectrum of substance use disorders.

PSYCHOSOCIAL REHABILITATION

The goal of therapeutic interventions are to ameliorate or eliminate negative emotions and other negative consequences associated with experiencing trauma. Stage-dependent treatment is used to conceptualize program format and is individualized to meet the specific needs of a patient. In stage-dependent treatment, stages are not mutually exclusive and may be best utilized in later phases of treatment in which a patient is focusing treatment on the re-establishment of emotionally healthy and effective social interactions. The development of positive emotional experiences challenges trauma responses in a corrective manner to offset the trauma and its effects.

In order to develop a better way of being, as a survivor of trauma, the development of positive coping mechanisms requires (Marmar et al., 1994; van der Kolk et al., 1996; Foa et al., 2009):

- Stabilization

- Deconditioning results of trauma to offset pain and helplessness. Exposure therapy is one way to decondition habituation to traumatic memories. Alternatively it may be possible to develop positive daily structures and resume approximations of normalcy to work toward mastery of daily productive life tasks. This may involve:
  - testing new ways of coping which can be learned and generalized
  - providing interactions where new, positive and pleasurable experiences are learned
  - targeting and problem-solving specific symptoms of PTSD which negatively influence daily coping.

The skills developed are generalized to functioning associated with comorbid disorders such as depression, anxiety, etc. This generalizability is intrinsically considered in the individualized treatment plan.

- Restructuring of personal trauma schemes (changing organization, arrangement, or perspective)

- Restoration of secure social connections and interpersonal efficacy, including relapse prevention

- Consolidation and accrual of restitutive emotional experiences, including self-monitoring.

Foa et al. (2000, 2009) offer a psychosocial rehabilitation checklist, which assesses the need for specified services. This identifies a potential psychosocial deficit with an associated

Table 4.1 Psychosocial rehabilitation checklist

1. Education	Emotional and physical health needs
	Treatment expectations (including treatment compliance) and self-responsibility: Education about the benefits of medication for PTSD and the various forms of psychosocial and behavioral interventions
	Harm-avoidance and wellness: High-risk behaviors (substance abuse and other compulsive or self-defeating behaviors)
	Education/training associated with dual-diagnosis issues
2. Self-care/independent living skills	Refer to appropriate community services as needed
3. Supported housing services	Safe, secure, stable housing
4. Supported family skills services	Education of family members in an effort to improve understanding of PTSD and appropriate supportive behaviors
5. Social skills training	Increase appropriate and satisfying social skills which effectively meet needs of social affiliation and appropriate collaboration
6. Supported employment	Vocational rehabilitation
	Refer to Americans with Disabilities Guidelines for reasonable accommodations in the workplace
7. Case management	Coordinate access to services

Based on Foa et al. (2000).

psychosocial resolution/solution. Psychosocial rehabilitation requires that the therapist and patient work together, just as in all aspects of treatment planning, to determine the course of psychosocial rehabilitation. Additional psychosocial rehabilitation interventions do not exclude other levels of treatment. All interventions, at every stage of treatment are to match the patient's level of functioning and their needs of intervention. An adapted form of this checklist is given in Table 4.1.

Rehabilitation is initiated when the therapist and patient are in consensus that a sufficient degree of stability has been achieved and the patient is prepared to learn more about PTSD and the various treatment choices associated with the array of PTSD symptoms and potential comorbid diagnoses. The comprehensive treatment planning and/or referral for rehabilitation includes consideration of psychosocial functioning, physical health, self-care, and independent living.

Psychosocial Functioning

- Education
  - Diagnosis
  - Nature of PTSD

- Treatment expectations
  - Role of patient and therapist
  - Outcome

- Family support
  - Educate about PTSD and expected course of treatment and recovery
  - Identification of family systems difficulties
  - Reinforce healthy lifestyle
  - Education associated with importance of family involvement
  - Guidance for family involvement
  - Interventions and skill development
  - Networking to minimize social isolation and reinforce desired changes

- Importance of treatment compliance
  - Maintaining stabilization
  - Facilitating continued positive therapeutic change
  - Consequence associated with a lack of compliance

- Rehabilitation schedule
  - Information about pharmacotherapy for PTSD, including symptoms targets, benefits/risks, dosage information
  - Information about the numerous forms of psychosocial and behavioral therapies
  - Socialization programs, including social skills training, supportive group environment. Types of intervention include token economy, symptom cues and helpful responses for management, medication and symptom management, problem-solving, community social skills, management of leisure and recreation
  - Dual diagnosis treatment
  - Vocational rehabilitation programs/option/resources.

Physical Health Rehabilitation

- Education about:
  - Health
  - Diet and exercise
  - Drug use/abuse/dependence
  - Relapse
  - Sexually transmitted diseases
  - Smoking cessation/smokeless tobacco cessation

- Promoting wellness:
  - Identify goals
  - Choices and associated influences/outcomes
  - Beneficial resources (including bibliotherapy)

- Harm reduction:
  - Identify goal(s)
  - Positive impact of any reduction in self-defeating/self-destructive behaviors
  - Goal(s)
  - Relapse prevention
  - Management resources
  - Self-monitoring.

Self-Care Plan

- Daily routine
- Use of recovery supportive resources.

Independent Living Environment

- Safe and adequate housing
  - Family style
  - Community environment (Veterans Health Administration programs, housing with clinical services)
- Personal care

- Hygiene
- Financial management
- Shopping
- Cooking
- Transportation
- Medication compliance
- Leisure/recreation resources/skills.

As can be seen, skills development can be tailored to specific needs of an individual and numerous points of intervention take place in a parallel manner to promote improved skills, education and use of resources.

THERAPEUTIC GROUPS

The use of a therapeutic group recognizes the critical role that a therapeutic community of peers offers as support to counteract the effects of interpersonal victimization and traumatization (Foa and Meadows, 1997; Foa et al., 2000, 2009). It offers the opportunity to be with others who have had similar traumatic experiences and posttraumatic after-effects in a context that provides for new learning, the development of new coping skills, relationship skills, and reworking some of the problematic interpersonal issues. It also offers a context that is normalizing, instructive and supportive.

Patients are supported to take personal responsibility for their thoughts and behaviors and to attempt to substitute healthier coping skills in response to compulsive, self-destructive, and/or violent urges where others or themselves may be at risk of harm.

Patients are taught about dysfunctional interpersonal behaviors that have been found to be associated with traumatization (and poor interpersonal relating in general). The education and skill development goals of the group provide specialized treatment which includes:

- Boundaries and interpersonal difficulties
- The roles of victim, perpetrator, rescuer and bystander
- Reenactment dynamics
- How to communicate assertively
- Functional and empowered ways of interacting with others.

CASE MANAGEMENT

Case management follows a continuum of goals and objectives associated with specific interventions/services and treatment reviews of progress. This process and continuum is initiated with safety issues and follows through to intensive teaching of patient psychosocial rehabilitation efforts. Not surprisingly, there is a tendency for a more favorable outcome for those who receive more intensive case management.

Once a thorough evaluation has been completed, the next step is to develop an individualized treatment plan based upon the identified and presented symptoms and level of functioning. In addition, the therapist must remain highly vigilant about changes in the patient, who may be easily overwhelmed or over-activated in therapy.

Healing and recovery take place at the pace afforded by management and mastery.

Following assessment and disposition of treatment setting the treatment plan is developed, agreed upon between therapist and patient, and initiated.

TREATMENT PLAN: SYMPTOM REVIEW

A review of the targeted symptoms includes:

1. Issues of safety and stabilization

2. Persistent re-experiencing of the traumatic event
   - Recurrent, intrusive, distressing recollections
   - Acting as if the event was recurring
   - Recurrent nightmare/dreams of the event (Imagery rehearsal therapy is associated with improvement in sleep quality and in decreasing PTSD severity)
   - Intense psychological distress when exposed to triggers
   - Exaggerated emotional and physical reactions to triggers
   - Flashbacks

3. Emotional numbing
   - Feeling detached, estranged, or alienated
   - Lack of emotion, restricted range of emotional experience
   - Loss of interest in formerly enjoyable activities

4. Avoidance of stimuli associated with the trauma
   - Avoidance of thoughts, feelings or conversation about the traumatic event
   - Avoidance of activities, places or people who trigger recollections of the event
   - Inability to recall an important aspect of the event
   - A sense of foreshortened future

5. Increased arousal
   - Difficulty sleeping
   - Irritability or outbursts of anger
   - Difficulty concentrating
   - Hypervigilance
   - Exaggerated and distressing startle response
   - Increased sensitivity to environmental stimuli
   - Increased heart rate/blood pressure
   - Agitated movement/tremors when relaxed or resting
   - Gastric distress
   - Immediate responsiveness to situations without taking the time to think it through
   - Lack of self-control leaving a feeling of defectiveness resulting in shame
   - Difficulty focusing on the big picture (tendency to focus on a single aspect of the situation)
   - Difficulty problem-solving (unable to maintain attention to non-trauma factors)
   - Difficulty soothing and calming self
   - Feeling crazy and that life is out of control
   - Increased use of substances
   - Increased compulsivity and emotionality

In addition to these symptoms, complex facets of "intra" and "inter" relationship dynamics associated with PTSD include the following:

1. Alterations in self regulation
   - Persistent dysphoria
   - Chronic suicidal preoccupation
   - Self-injury
   - Explosive or extremely inhibited anger
   - Compulsive or extremely inhibited sexuality

2. Alterations in consciousness
   - Amnesia or hyperamnesia
   - Transient dissociative episodes
   - Depersonalization/derealization
   - Reliving experiences with intrusive PTSD symptoms or ruminative preoccupation

3. Alteration in self-perception
   - Sense of helplessness or paralysis of initiative
   - Shame, guilt, and self-blame
   - Sense of defilement or stigma
   - Sense of difference from others (specialness, utter aloneness, inhuman, no-one else could understand)

4. Alterations in perception of perpetrator
   - Preoccupation with relationship with perpetrator
   - Unrealistic attribution of total power to perpetrator
   - Idealization or paradoxical gratitude
   - Sense of special or supernatural relationship
   - Acceptance of belief system or rationalization of perpetrator

5. Alteration in relation to others
   - Isolation and withdrawal
   - Disruption in intimate relationships
   - Repeated search for rescuer
   - Persistent distrust
   - Repeated failures of self-perception

6. Alterations in systems of healing
   - Loss of sustaining faith
   - Sense of hopelessness and despair

7. Somatization
   - Cardiopulmonary symptoms (most often symptoms of panic anxiety)
   - Gastrointestinal problems (irritable bowel syndrome, diarrhea, constipation)
   - Autoimmune disorder (fibromyalgia, chronic fatigue)
   - Chronic pain (no discrete source)
   - Sexual problems (pelvic pain, recurring infections, discomfort, lack of sexual desire, erectile dysfunction)
   - Adrenal fatigue.

The effects of adrenal dysfuntion include fatigue and weakness, muscle and bone loss, moodiness or depression, hormonal imbalance, skin problems, autoimmune disorders, etc. It may also be a factor in such related conditions as fibromyalgia, hypothyroidism, chronic fatigue syndrome, arthritis, premature menopause. Thorough work-up by an endocrinologist known for their knowledge in this area is needed, as well as:

1. Tests of the diurnal rhythm of cortisol (elevated in the morning to help activate for the day, with a lower but steady level throughout the day to sustain energy, then fall in the evening to support restful sleep)

2. Dietary changes to enrich nutrition and reduce carbohydrates and stimulants (the physician may also recommend the addition of high-quality supplements)

3. Stress reduction, including moderate exercise and taking more time for oneself. Make a list of stressors, classified according to whether constant or intermittent

4. More rest (the body requires rest to heal).

TREATMENT: SAFETY FACTORS

SAFETY AND STABILIZATION

In ensuring that safety and stabilization are optimized, it is important to:

- Build rapport and a therapeutic alliance
- Address practical problems
- Mobilize social support
- Encourage self-management and calming strategies
- Address suicidal ideation and problem solve management/elimination of risk
- Involve multidisciplinary treatment team as appropriate
- Set secure therapeutic boundaries
- Assign an appropriate treatment setting.

Safety is an encompassing treatment issue of the self (van der Kolk, 2005). Aside from suicidal ideation and homicidal ideation, other issues to consider are:

- Dangerous behaviors
- Dysfunctional/destructive relationships
- Self-harm
- Substance abuse
- Impulse dysregulation.

All of these issues are explored and problem-solved in accordance with the tolerance of the patient while identifying core goals associated with:

- Dissociation
- (Re)-establishing secure attachments

- Developing self-management skills
- Developing a coherent self-narrative.

The initial stage of treatment and support focuses on developing a therapeutic alliance so that work can be initiated on physical and psychological safety issues and the management of PTSD symptoms. This serves as a foundation for trauma memory work if appropriate. Some aspects of the issues of safety can be identified and interventions be made during the initial session (danger to self or others). However, a patient's ambivalence to seek treatment or remain in treatment is a cornerstone of treatment and takes time and patience to mediate. Remember, the trusted therapeutic relationship offers an opportunity to heal.

A patient may be reluctant to participate for varied reasons that will need to be worked through. They may believe that:

- Instead of helping them, therapy will create more distress and make them feel worse about themselves
- If they could just forget about what happened their feelings and other symptoms would go away
- Nothing will help and that nothing will work to resolve what they have experienced
- They should be able to handle it themselves, without any help.

Therapeutic skills to accomplish this include:

- Listen when a patient talks about their feelings (don't judge)
- Offer support, be resourceful (don't pity)
- Acknowledge that the experience of a traumatic experience(s) was the cause (they are not to blame)
- Validate their experience
- Be reality-based and honest about realistic expectations, limitations and boundaries.

This includes identifying the patient role of commitment and participation in treatment. Initiating treatment includes the following:

1. Developing positive therapeutic alliance/developing safe attachments (trust):
   - Alter the internalized early childhood attachment dynamic. Identify what the model of a secure attachment would look like that results in the patient seeing themselves as lovable, valued and socially effective. Identify parenting that was inconsistent, unreliable
   - Identify the effects of early posttraumatic stress on subsequent development
   - Identify the distortions of the cognitive understanding of self, others and future
2. Normalizing reactions to abuse experiences/trauma as adaptations to trauma
3. Developing self-awareness and self-acceptance (working on identity issues)
4. Developing awareness of internal strengths
5. Enhancing self-care skills
6. Developing interpersonal skills (i.e. setting boundaries and assertiveness skills)
7. Identifying pacing treatment to tolerance level and grading emotions

8. Developing distress tolerance skills
9. Developing social supports
10. Self-monitoring (staying on tasks, what works?, what has improved?).

ASSESSING RISK (JOHNSON, 2004)

SUICIDE

Assess Suicidal
Ideation

- Ask directly if they have thoughts of suicide
- Are the thoughts pervasive or intermittent with a definite relationship to a given situation?
- Do they have a plan? If so, how extensive is their plan?
- What is the lethality of the means/method defined?
- Is there access to the identified means?

Suicide Gestures/
Attempts

- Immediate referral for a medical evaluation for medical stability if method and current level of impulse control warrant it (always intervene with the least intrusive means of intervention warranted to maintain safety)
- Assess:
  - Means, location, collaborator, rescuer, number of attempts
  - Thoroughness of plan and its implementation
  - Signs of impairment and physical harm
  - Level of treatment required. Engage patient in this decision-making. Often when patients do not feel safe they are willing to agree to hospitalization. The therapist should feel assured about the efficacy of the decision of means for safety collaborated with the patient.

Risk Factors to
Consider During
Assessment

1. Intention and history
   - Recent/prior attempts or gestures
   - Direct or indirect communication of intent
   - Extensiveness of plan
   - Lethality of means
   - Access to means
   - Family history of suicidal behaviors

2. Demographics
   - Age (teens, middle age, and elderly are at highest risk)
   - Gender (males more often complete suicide because of lethality of means, but females make more attempts)

- Homosexual (additional stressors/lack of social supports)
- Race/ethnic background influences on interpretation/coping/resources
- Marital status (separated, widowed, divorced)
- Social support (lack of support system, living alone)
- Employment status (unemployed, change in status or performance)

3. Emotional functioning
   - Diagnosis (major depression, bipolar disorder, recovery from recent depression, schizophrenia, borderline personality disorder, significant losses)
   - Auditory hallucinations commanding death (bizarre methods may also indicate psychosis)
   - Recent loss or anniversary of loss
   - Fantasy to reunite with a deceased loved one
   - Stresses (chronic or associated with recent changes)
   - Poor coping ability
   - Degree of hopelessness or despair

4. Behavioral patterns
   - Isolation
   - Impulsivity
   - Rigid

5. Physical condition
   - Chronic insomnia
   - Chronic pain
   - Progressive illness
   - Recent childbirth.

Although many of these factors appear to be more general in nature, it is the clustering of factors, state of mind/current mood, ability to cope, belief system, and support that contribute to increased risk.

Suicidal impulse and gestures constitute a response by a patient whose coping mechanisms have failed. They often feel despair, desperate, and ashamed. Be calm and caring in approach, establishing a setting conducive to eliciting the necessary information for sound decision-making regarding intervention. Be reassuring in letting the patient know that their participation is integral to proceeding with further evaluation, treatment planning, and appropriate treatment setting.

For some, what appears to be a suicidal impulse is a "death wish." Over time, when overwhelmed, they stepped over the threshold of thinking about not being alive as means of avoidance in their effort to cope to distress. The consequence becomes that when overwhelmed, thoughts of not being alive immediately come to mind and interfere with more effective and manageable choices for coping with difficult circumstances. For these patients, challenging the thoughts and using substitute rational statements for coping is the first step towards change and becoming free of the "death wish," and the beginning of using their emotional energy to learn effective problem-solving and management skills.

Treatment Focus and Objectives

Outpatient Therapy and Management
Utilized when risk of suicide is low and/or manageable with appropriate support, the precipitating crisis is no longer present, and the patient has developed an adequate plan of coping with the therapist. The least restrictive and appropriate means of intervention are always utilized.

Hospitalization

Utilized when there is high risk of suicide, lack of adequate supports, lack of adequate impulse control, patient is intoxicated or psychotic. Initially pursue voluntary admission. If they are unwilling and the criteria warrant hospitalization, involuntary admission is initiated with an evaluation by designated person/facility.

Techniques/Interventions

- Alleviate the patient's isolation by recommending that they stay with family or friends (safe and supportive environment)
- Facilitate the removal of weapons, medication or other means of suicide attempt from their environment. Deal with issues of substances (abuse) if necessary
- Support the development and utilization of a support system, or the re-establishment of their support system (family, friends, community/meetings, church, etc.)
- Facilitate the appropriate expression of anger or other feelings which are contributing to self-destructive impulses
- Validate the patient's experience of the crisis, but also identify their ambivalence and the fact that suicide is a permanent solution to a temporary problem. May be especially beneficial when the outcome of finality is contrary to their desired goals/accomplishments
- Refer for medication evaluation making sure that the physician is aware of their suicidal ideation/impulses
- Educate them regarding the impact that a lack of sleep has on coping effectively, and reassure them that the depression can be managed or eliminated
- Identify irrational, negative beliefs. Help the person recognize that the associated negative self-talk contributes to keeping them in a state of hopelessness. Facilitate the identification of alternatives to the difficulties that they are currently experiencing
- Do not verbally or non-verbally express shock or horror
- Do not emphasize how much they have upset or concerned other people
- Do not offer psychological or moral edicts of suicide
- Explore with them what they hoped to accomplish with suicide
- Identify life issues that have contributed to their emotional state
- Discuss the fact that suicide is a permanent solution, especially useful if contrary to desire to see other outcomes or accomplishments
- Review resources and relationships (family, friends, family physician, clergy, employer, police, emergency response team, therapist, community support groups, 12-step groups, emergency room, psychiatric hospital)
- Be reassuring and supportive
- Facilitate improved problem-solving and coping
- Facilitate development of a self-care program, including:
  - Daily structure
  - Pleasurable activities
  - Self-soothing activities

- Resources/support system (including therapy and medication compliance)
- Identification of crisis/potential crisis situations and plausible choices for coping
- Identification of warning signs (self-monitoring) that indicate that the person is not utilizing their self-care plan, noting medication side-effects, etc.
- Regular aerobic activity
- Adequate sleep and nutrition
- Relaxation skills
- Reinforcement of efforts, behavior shaping and accomplishments.

DANGEROUSNESS

Assessing Thoughts of Violence

- Ask directly if they have thoughts of harming another person
- Are the thoughts pervasive or transient (venting without intent) in relationship to a response to a given situation?
- Do they have a plan? If so, how extensive is their plan?
- What are the means to be used in harming someone?
- Do they have access to the planned means/method?
- Do they have a history of violent behavior (have they ever seriously harmed another person, or carried out any actions of harm/property destruction against another person?
- Do they wish to be helped to manage the aggressive impulses?
- If the clinical interview is in progress with someone who has a history of violent behavior be alert to signs of agitation and losing control.

If it is determined that the person is at risk to harm another person, immediate steps need to be taken. If they demonstrate some semblance of being reasonable aside from their aggressive impulse toward another person, focus on their ambivalence and talk with them about voluntary admission to a hospital to gain control over their impulses and to learn appropriate means of dealing with their feelings. If there is concern that such a discussion would only escalate a patient who is already demonstrating significant agitation, then contact the police for transport to a hospital and fulfill the obligation of duty to warn.

Remember that there is a distinction between having thoughts of wanting to harm someone and having the intention to act on those thoughts. Act accordingly when venting is taking place. However, if threats with intent to harm are present there is a duty to contact the police and the intended victim so that necessary precautions for safety can be taken.

Risk Factors to Consider During Assessment

1. Intention and history
   - Specific plan for injuring or killing someone
   - Access or possession of the intended method of harm
   - History of previous acts of violence
   - History of homicidal threats
   - Recent incident of provocation
   - Conduct disorder behavior in minors/antisocial personality disorder adult behaviors
   - Victims of childhood abuse

2. Demographics

- Gender (males are at higher risk to act out aggression)
- Low socioeconomic status (increased frustration, general feelings of lack of control in life, aggressive environment or survival issues)
- Social support (lack of social supports/resources)
- Overt stressors (marital conflict, unemployment, legal issues, etc.)

3. Emotional functioning

- Diagnosis (depression with agitation, drug/alcohol intoxication or withdrawal, delirium, mania, paranoid or catatonic schizophrenia, temporal lobe epilepsy, antisocial personality disorder, paranoid personality disorder)

4. Behavioral patterns

- Poor impulse control
- Extreme lability of affect
- Excessive aggressiveness
- Loud or abusive speech
- Bizarre behavior or verbalizations.

PSYCHOLOGICAL DEBRIEFING AS AN INDIVIDUAL INTERVENTION

Psychological debriefing (see also Chapter 3), initially designated as part of a group intervention (one component of a critical incident stress management program) following trauma, has also been used as an intervention for individuals. The purpose of psychological debriefing is to review the impressions and reactions of individuals following a traumatic event, focusing on the reactions.

Psychological debriefing is a routine intervention following major traumatic events. There are several methods, generally consisting of a single session (lasting up to a few hours) of semi-structured crisis intervention techniques designed to decrease and prevent psychologically distressing symptoms following a traumatic experience. This is accomplished by promoting emotional processing through the expression and normalization of reactions, as well as preparation for possible future experiences. Even though it may not prevent the development of post-traumatic stress symptoms or PTSD it still offers utility for screening, education and support.

Psychological debriefing is contraindicated when intense re-exposure could result in retraumatizing individuals who have not had adequate time for habituation.

If psychological debriefing is used it must be part of an objective evaluation procedure where additional resources are provided.

TREATMENT PLANNING: GOALS, OBJECTIVES, AND INTERVENTIONS

- Processing trauma memory:
  - Intrusions/re-experiencing
  - Avoidance

        – Hyperarousal
        – Dissociation

- Capacity to modulate emotion and improve coping
  - Depression
  - Anxiety
  - Grief
  - Stress management inoculation
  - Anger
  - Impulse control
  - Assertive communication
  - Substance abuse
  - Personality disorder
  - Eating disorder.

The worksheets in the skill-building section (Chapter 5) are an adjunct resource that can be integrated into the following treatment planning outlines for individualized treatment plans.

INTRUSIONS

People with PTSD often find that memories of the trauma reoccur unexpectedly, and that flashbacks intrude into everyday life, accompanied by painful emotions, or that they have powerful nightmares. Such intrusions are associated with:

- Feeling unsafe
- Confusing memories
- Grieving
- Guilt
- Shame
- Flashbacks
- Nightmares
- Negative self-beliefs
- Disrupted lifestyle
- Triggers
- Family dysfunction.

The goals associated with therapy for intrusions include the following:

1. *Safety*   • The therapist provides a safe and trusting environment in which the patient can safely process the impact of events:
        – Deep breathing
        – Grounding
        – Peaceful meditation
        – Being in the moment

- The patient creates their own safe place:
  - A room or other physical place
  - A detailed visual image

- Identify all of the people/places that offer a feeling of calm and safety.

2. *Central Details Remembered About the Traumatic Event(s)*

- Talk through/process memory (experience) fragments:
  - What are the emotions experienced as they talk?
  - Are they surprised by any emotion experienced (unexpected)?

- Journal about experience:
  - Journaling allows the person to go back and fill in spaces as information is revealed
  - What has been helpful about the fragments of memory that they have?
  - Identify how their life has been impacted by the exposure to trauma

- Understand the fragments of memory that do exist:
  - Identify the emotions that are attached to memories
  - Reframe challenging/distressing memories so that they are useful.

3. *Grieving the Losses Associated With the Trauma*

- Help patient to accept the original trauma without being so overwhelmed by memories:
  - Be in the moment
  - Encourage acceptance that they have already survived the experience
  - Facilitate embracing what is now a part of who they are (i.e. what they have survived is now a part of their personal history)
  - Challenge them to identify what they have gained as a result of the experience, instead of focusing on what has been lost

- Identify a loss in sense of safety and security

- Identify potential shock and denial as part of unresolved grief

- Identify numerous hidden questions of confusion, loss and self-doubt:
  - Why me?
  - How can I go on?
  - Why did this happen to me?
  - How has it affected me?
  - What is the meaning of what has happened?

- Identify compounded losses and be thorough in resolution of losses

- What did they learn from their family about grieving losses?
  - How do they feel their grief?
  - How do they show their grief?
  - How does family and friends respond to their grief/loss?

4. *Challenging Guilt*

- How have they dealt with other situations where they felt guilt:
  - What helped, what made it more difficult?
  - How is guilt dealt with in their family (what did they learn from family)? Do they think it was rational or useful? How is guilt defined in their family? Does their family reinforce feelings of guilt or do they see things differently?

- Identify feelings of guilt about the trauma:
  - List what happened and why they feel they deserve to feel the guilt
  - Identify whether they feel responsible for the traumatic event(s) because of their immaturity/impulsivity, innocence/carelessness, morality/lack of skill, etc. Was there a role played by others in the event? (Describe in detail)
  - Challenge inaccurate beliefs of guilt
  - If there is survivor guilt it may be a way to honor the dead and not forget them without grieving or putting the issue to rest
  - Separate survivor guilt from other emotions
  - What would they do differently if the event happened again. Would they be able to do things differently? Are there amends for them to make or anyone that they need to talk to/confront in association to what they have experienced?
  - What have they learned or how have they grown as a person as a result of the traumatic event?
  - What opportunities can be created from the traumatic event?

5. *Challenging Feelings of Shame*

- The patient used in an unacceptable or degrading manner (such as sexual abuse/assault)
  - Identify the source of shame

- Were they told messages during or after the traumatic event which made them feel ashamed (introjects)?

- Challenge that they were in a situation where they did not have the power to choose
  - Challenge perfectionism or unrealistic expectations
  - Challenge associated feelings of inadequacy
  - How do they avoid disapproval or ways to prove they are to blame?
  - Do they feel invisible?
  - Facilitate development of affirmations to combat feelings/thoughts of shame

- Clarify that the source of shame lies in the abuse, violation, assault, or betrayal by another

- Were they shamed in their family when growing up?
  - How was shame used?
  - How did it make them feel?
  - How did it affect how they feel about themselves?

6. *Flashbacks*

- What is the flashback trying to tell them?
  - Are they afraid to understand it, process it, be in control of it?
  - What happens when they think about the flashbacks (emotional/somatic experience)?
  - Do they understand that they are in control of choosing to think and talk about their flashbacks?
- Is there more to learn or accept about what has happened?
  - Talk about it with those they feel safe with
  - Journal about it

- Talk to others that have had similar experiences
- Read about flashbacks

- Have them describe the flashback and what they experienced:
  - How did the flashback sound, smell, feel (is this the same or different from the original event)?
  - When they experienced the flashback what did they do to attempt to feel better?
  - How can they ground themselves and stay in the present when experiencing flashbacks?
  - Facilitate development of a sense of control by helping them to create a VCR tape in their mind of a repeating flashback but in a shortened form that they can "choose" to fast forward or rewind. When would they choose to use this technique? Facilitate it being framed with positive images and discuss how that would change the experience
  - Desensitize self by using systematic desensitization

- Containment of traumatic memories:
  - Use grounding to stay in touch with reality

- Developing dual awareness (reconciliation between the experiencing self and the observing self; Rothchild, 2000)
  - While in a secure "present" environment, look at the traumatic event from a past and current perspective
  - Begin with a mildly distressing memory/flashback. As the patient allows themselves to remember the event encourage them to also pay careful attention to their current experience of physical sensations as well as details of the past environment

- Learning systematic desensitization.

7. *Nightmares*
- Dual awareness used before sleep as a ritual to manage flashbacks/intrusions in the form of nightmares

- Containment in the form of grounding: prior to sleep make statements out loud affirming being the present

- Cognitive behavioral preparation of nightmares:
  - Be prepared to write down the details of nightmares (pad/pen by the bed)
  - Develop alternative endings to the nightmare.

8. *Resolving Unfinished Business*
- Use grounding to reconcile the past from the present
- What are their current choices of management?

- Containment of unresolved issues by imagining them being held in a container where by choice and control the patient takes out an issue to review, problem-solve and resolve

- Learn systematic desensitization

- Accept that they have survived their experience and can now choose how they will think about it and manage it.

9. *Identifying and Challenging Negative Self-Beliefs Formed at the Time of the Trauma/Abuse*	• Make a list of these thoughts:
	  – Identify thoughts which influence quality of life.
	  – How do they influence how the patient lives their life?
	• Clarify rational from irrational
	• Where did those thoughts of the self come from (the patient or someone else)?
	  – What did they have control over?
	  – What do they think is their most harmful belief about the self? Is it true (why or why not)?

10. *Normal Life Activities Disrupted*	• Change the memory of the abuse experience from one of helplessness to one of empowerment of being a survivor
	• Reassure self that an intrusion is an old memory and "it will pass" or "I am safe"
	• Bring up an image of a safe place that promotes feeling safe and calm
	• Identify desired lifestyle structure:
	  – Write down the desired structure
	  – Practice the daily and weekly aspects of lifestyle structure
	  – Modify as needed, based upon increased understanding, available resources and goals.

11. *Identify Triggers*	• Identify specific triggers (people, places, situations, time frames, etc.) • Identify how their family system has been impacted • Identify emotional and physical/somatic responses to triggers • Problem-solve different choices for dealing with triggers • Develop a list of activities to control intrusive thoughts • Identify resources for dealing with triggers, such as people, places, or situations/activities that bring relief, feelings of safety/security and prevent the intrusion from altered reality.
12. *Family Education (When Appropriate)*	• Educate family members/social support system about the quality of intrusions and what they are • Educate regarding how they may be supportive • Remove the survivor from the identified patient role • Identify how the family has been impacted • Develop appropriate support and communication skills • Improve communication associated with this topic • Identify and break patterns of trauma repetition • Problem-solve and resolve disruptive emotions such as rage, shame, and guilt

- Identify the needs of family members and appropriately refer
- Educate regarding appropriate boundaries and how to reinforce self-care of the person experiencing intrusions.

There are numerous variations of containment. There is no way to know what will be most effective for an individual. Be persistent and creative in trying different techniques.

Self-soothing is achieved by developing a mental image of a safe place. The patient can practice pairing a distressing thought with the image of a safe place. Grounding refers to technique repeatedly used in the treatment section. It is used to bring a patient's awareness back to the present.

AVOIDANCE

Efforts to avoid emotional distress interferes with significant relationships (marriage, family, close friends) and other responsibilities (work, school). Capacity to engage in meaningful relationships is an important aspect to quality of life. Avoidance is not always associated with fear of bad things or intolerable emotion. It could be fear of how others will perceive them and lack of trust. Common issues associated with avoidance include:

- Avoidance of going to certain places, going out at night, being alone, thoughts, feelings, or conversation associated with the trauma
- Isolation (difficult to feel trust, safe and secure anywhere)
- Ineffective coping
- Lack of goals
- Anxiety
- Low self-esteem
- Improve poor peer relationships
- Emotionally numb (unable to experience usual to normal feelings acting impersonally to those they are closest to)
- Family dysfunction.

The goals associated with therapy for avoidance include the following:

1. Decrease
Avoidance

- Help patient accept the original trauma without being so overwhelmed by memories or planning their lives around avoiding situations that remind them of the trauma
- Identify fear:
  - Understand fear
  - Normalize fear
  - Manage fear
- Correct irrational thinking
  - Challenge irrational thoughts with reality
  - Substitute irrational thoughts with rational thoughts
  - Encourage appropriate risk-taking (plug-in guaranteed successes)

- Identify safe behaviors (people, places, situations) that have not been engaged in, but could be as part of recovery
- Identify desired, reasonable incremental steps of behavioral change to be engaged in and practiced
  - Desire to share with others (trust in self, boundaries, demonstration of mutual respect and confidentiality)
- Teach assertive communication
- Teach appropriate social skills
- Role-play responses to variety of social situation
- Challenge the fear of being emotionally overwhelmed by using systematic desensitization:
  - Develop hierarchy of increasing anxiety-provoking situations to facilitate feelings of being in control
  - *In vivo* desensitization may work faster for some individuals than imaginal exposure (carefully explore all factors for this treatment decision).

2. *Decrease Isolation*

- Develop and utilize support system:
  - Identify safe individuals (practice spending time with them and identify what makes them safe)
  - Identify the characteristics of a supportive relationship
  - Identify what is needed and wanted from a supportive relationship
  - Identify what stands in the way of developing a support relationship. How are they going to challenge and change that?
  - Identify reasonable characteristics expected or desired from a friend
  - Clarify boundaries along with realistic expectations and limitations

Note there is a grieving associated with isolation. The patient may have lost the comfortable and carefree decision-making and social participating *or* grieve that they have never been able to do that and are thus not "normal"

- Identify what stands in the way of utilizing their social supports:
  - What can they do to challenge and change it?
  - How are they going to begin practicing utilizing their support system?
  - Do they not use their support system because they don't want to owe anyone anything?
- Identify the reasons why isolation have been used for coping:
  - Do they believe isolation has been helpful (why)?
  - How has isolation been harmful to them?
- Problem-solve how to intervene and change isolation behavior in identified situations which have historically resulted in isolation.

3. *Improve Coping*

- Facilitate identification of thoughts/feelings:
  - Journal writing about the thoughts and feelings associated with past experiences
  - Write for themselves, uncensored, honest, with the realistic expectation that it will be an emotional experience (practice expressing emotion makes it easier to not avoid)
  - What are their choices? Choices of thought (useful/not useful). Choices of behavior (useful/not useful) associated with thoughts

- Encourage appropriate expression of emotion:
  - Are they afraid to express their emotion?
  - Are they afraid to hear it out loud? Will it make it real? Will it make them responsible to do something about how they feel?
  - Is it difficult to hear the emotion of others?
  - Is it not safe to have certain emotions?

- Identify effective solutions to anxiety/distress-provoking situations:
  - Journal writing
  - Use of social support
  - Containment
  - Use of systematic desensitization

- Practice positive, rational, realistic thinking, and effective behaviors in a variety of safe situations (graduated levels of stress):
  - Educate regarding the impact of self-talk and its importance of being rational, positive and useful
  - Identify negative and irrational self-talk
  - Replace it with useful and rational self-talk

- Focus on efforts and accomplishments:
  - Strive to be honest and objective about choices, efforts and outcome
  - Be honest about strengths, assets, and skills
  - If something is difficult to achieve, discuss how to break it down into manageable steps

- Positive feedback and reinforcement.

4. *Develop Goals*

- Identify strengths and interests
- Break down objectives into manageable steps
- Focus on efforts and accomplishments:
  - What facilitates accomplishments?
  - What are the resources that would help?
  - What are the impediments and how can they be challenged or changed?

- Positive feedback and reinforcement.

5. *Managing Anxiety*

- Identify relationship between anxiety and thoughts/behavior
- Teach effective utilization of relaxation techniques:
  - Practice management techniques

- Challenge irrational beliefs and behaviors
- Facilitate development of appropriate substitute self-statements and behaviors for irrational ones (useful and beneficial narration)
- Create mastery experiences, breaking each one down into successive approximations:
  - Teach the skill of breaking down tasks into manageable steps

- Utilize positive self-talk
- Exercise to decrease body tension
- Accept that stress is a normal part of life.

6. *Improve Self-Esteem*	Self-esteem is improved by doing and attaching appropriate and reinforcing self-talk.
	• Support and encourage appropriate risk-taking behavior
	  – Identify a step-wise progression of reasonable risks
	
	• Encourage participation in problem-solving
	  – Practice being rational versus emotional or influenced by distorted beliefs
	
	• Reframe mistakes and less than desired outcomes as opportunities to learn
	• Identify desired areas of change
	• Identify strengths and develop daily affirmations for reinforcing positive self-image
	• Facilitate development of assertive communication
	  – Practice communication that is honest, respectful with consideration to boundaries
	  – Improve social intelligence by increasing awareness of a match between desired outcome and actual/real outcome
	
	• Create opportunities for a person to demonstrate strengths/desired change
	• Positive feedback and reinforcement for effort and changes.

7. *Improve Peer Relationships*	• Encourage participation in activity where additional benefit is time-shared with peers who share similar interests • Encourage participation in engaging situations or activities that offer distraction, thereby increasing mastery over associated anxiety while in the company of peers • Reinforce internal locus regarding boundaries in peer relationships • Be interested in others and a good listener • Get involved in activities of interest so that relationships are developed with those who share similar interests.

8. *Emotionally Reconnecting*	• Identify what is experienced, what is expected or desired (within normal range of emotional experience)
	• Utilize feeling list and chart of congruent facial expressions to identify normal range of emotion
	• Explore the fear associated with allowing themselves to feel the identified emotion:
	  – Journal
	  – Practice containment and desensitization
	  – Reinforce efforts

- What are the identified risks for no longer being emotionally numb?
  - What are they giving up?
  - How does it make them vulnerable?
  - What are the potential benefits?

- What is the safest way to initiate the allowing of normal emotions?
  - Identify safe people and situations for easing control over emotions
  - What stands in the way of allowing the expression of normal emotions?

- Create a hierarchy of emotional experiencing and how they will use resources to buffer against becoming overwhelmed

- Memory containment versus numbing:
  - Plan ahead for distress times/events when there is advanced warning/cues
  - Allow crying to vent emotions
  - Journal thoughts/feelings
  - Engage in positive and productive distractions, such as doing a puzzle, playing solitaire, baking cookies, drawing, etc.
  - Utilize grounding to stay in the present.

9. *Improve Family Interaction*

- Evaluate role of family interactions
- Explore how family may help sustain or reinforce dysfunctional behavior
- Teach communication skills
- Educate regarding appropriate boundaries.

HYPERAROUSAL (PHYSIOLOGICAL REACTIVITY)

Body awareness and self-care are important factors in controlling trauma-based reactions. It can facilitate the discharge of stored-up emotion and serve as a conduit of reconnection where numbing and emotional blunting exist. States of hyperarousal are associated with:

- Insomnia
- Physical sensations
- Memory disturbance (may not remember the entire event)
- Difficulty concentrating/distractibility
- Emotional disturbance (jumping with fear, irritability or explosiveness without apparent reason). All reactions are out of proportion with the current experience
- Symptoms of acute anxiety/panic (physical symptoms: headaches, abdominal distress, dizziness, nausea, sweating diarrhea, chest pains, rapid heart beat, hypertension). All lead to deterioration in functioning (work/school/relationships)
- Family dysfunction.

The goals of therapy associated with hyperarousal include the following:

1. Decrease or Eliminate Sleep Disturbance (Difficulty Falling or Staying Asleep)

- Preparing for sleep:
  - Remove triggers from the environment (avoid seeing, hearing, or thinking about traumatic things prior to going to bed)
  - Create an environment conducive to sleep. Make the bedroom sleep friendly (cool, dark, quiet, uncluttered). The bedroom is for sleep and/or sex, no TV, no computer, no reading in bed
  - At the close of the day take an inventory of positive things in life
  - Listen to soothing music, sounds of the surf, gentle rain, mountain waterfall, etc.
  - Try to avoid substances to induce sleep because of the effort to recondition the body to restful sleep (Discuss with physician possibilities such as warm milk, turkey (L-tryptophan), melatonin, valerian root, camomile, etc.). A physician can increase understanding of the benefits and risks of the use of medications to treat insomnia
  - Make sure that currently prescribed medications are not interfering with sleep, and indulge in caffeine only in the morning

- Behaviors that help condition the body for restful sleep:
  - Daily aerobic exercise (not prior to bed)
  - Relaxing music, nature sounds, white noise machine
  - Progressive muscle relaxation
  - Deep breathing
  - Meditation (including prayer)
  - Reading a boring book
  - Warm bath/shower
  - No naps during the day (or during what are normally the waking hours)
  - Regular bed time in the same place (no matter what time they awake)

- Factors that do not help:
  - Alcohol use. A drink before bed may initially sedate, but it can disrupt sleep later in the night
  - Over the counter medications. While antihistamines may help with sleep, they can also lead to daytime drowsiness and dry mouth

- Reset the biological clock:
  - Light therapy is a promising treatment for correcting a confused body clock. Bright light early in the day may help bring on sleep earlier in the night. Likewise, bright light later in the day may defer sleepiness by helping to suppress the production of melatonin (sleep-inducing hormone)

- Deal with snoring:
  - Snoring can be the consequence of weight gain (it only takes a few grams of fat in the neck to cause snoring). Improved health behaviors with appropriate weight loss
  - If a bed partner snores try noise-blocking ear plugs, a fan, or other white noise to buffer snoring

- Improve daytime energy:
  - Power nap. A nap 10–30 minutes in duration is a good recharger (longer naps may result in drowsiness)

- Make a list of 10 things to do if not able to sleep

- Managing nightmares:
  - Process the dream material with someone trusted (to neutralize emotion). Relax and describe the dream material in detail
  - Keep a dream journal to record details
  - Confront and modify the nightmare
  - With journaling and verbal processing of dream material there is a lot of detail, including the ending of the dream. Practice talking about it while being in the moment and feeling calm. Use containment and the reminder that "this is just a dream." Create a new ending. Create a dream that reflects the positive new changes and growth taking place.

2. *Increased Awareness of Physical Sensations*

Developing awareness of physical sensation is an important step in controlling trauma-based reactions.

- Increase awareness of projecting emotions onto other people, events, or circumstances:
  - Listen to the body, keep a journal for interpretations and choices of management associated with physical sensations. What do the symptoms mean? What is the body trying to communicate? Identifying physical sensations allows for the development of specific self-soothing. Identify whether or not increased physical arousals are the foundation of irritability and angry outbursts
  - Reinforce current body awareness (i.e. basic mechanisms). Does the body communicate when it is thirsty, hungry, happy, sad, rested, fatigued? (if so how, and what are appropriate self-care and healing responses?)
  - Journal about the following thoughts/emotions (emotions are related and translated into physical sensation): Cognitive understanding and working definition of what is "safe." How is "not being safe" personally experienced (challenges to trust and feel safe); anger, fear, calm, overwhelmed, sad, happy?
  - Identify "over" focus on physical sensations which impedes being in the moment and impedes moving forward in treatment

- Identify where emotion and stress is carried in the body
  - Replace pain with acceptance
  - Create visual images of their strength and resilience
  - Reinforce the goal of finding meaning and strength following a crisis
  - Utilize coping imagery: seeing themselves safe and in control, easily separating the past pain from being safely in the present
  - Focus awareness and energy on areas where control/choices can be asserted (i.e. areas of control).

3. *Decreased Distractibility*

- Improved memory
  - Educate regarding the role of energy and memory and distress/fear and memory

- Improved concentration
  - Practice being in the moment, focused, and able to report environmental detail, conversation content, personal interpretation/experience, etc.
  - Practice reading comprehension. Brief reading assignments with a verbal or written summary of content and understanding/interpretation of material
  - Relaxation exercises, for example: progressive muscle relaxation, deep breathing, visualization/positive mental imagery, meditation
  - Make a list of what needs to be dealt with to decrease/eliminate avoidance
  - Make a list of what needs to be remembered to remove the stress and energy associated with keeping it in the forefront of memory as something to avoid

       – Practice thought stopping

       – Engage in rational self-talk (internal dialogue)

- Explore the source of distraction
  - Is it the struggle to continuously deal with all the information in their head, their heart, and/or physical sensations?
  - Is it an effort to keep certain information out of consciousness?
- Have they ever been identified as having attention deficit hyperactivity disorder (ADHD) in association with the excessive energy that is really associated with the avoidance of thinking about or dealing with the experience of trauma?

4. *Improved Mood Management (Especially Anger and Rage)*	• Increased awareness of projecting emotions onto other people • Explore if anger is a safe emotional choice masking fear, grief, shame, or guilt • Explore the possibility of negative emotion (anger/rage) being the foundation of motivation to change themselves or to work for a cause • Identify the pattern or cycle of expression of negative emotion: – Has it been helpful, hurtful, or both? • Explore what needs to be done to resolve negative emotion • Explore how much fear is associated with learning to relax and letting go of anger • Make a list of the signs of anger (or other negative mood states) and how they can be challenged in a positive manner (alternative interpretations, reframes, and choices of management) • Make a list of situations where anger was expressed inappropriately (and why it happened: To feel safe? To distance other? To feel in control?).

5. *Improved Anxiety Management*	• Make a list of anxiety symptoms experienced (if necessary provide a comprehensive symptom list) such as short fuse, ready to snap, bomb ready to explode, on the edge, on the verge of a melt-down, ready to fight, ready to run, etc.
	
	• Make a list of what needs to be done to change or modify environment/relationships in order to feel safe
	
	• Encourage them to do whatever they need to do to feel safe
	
	• Grounding, i.e. the reality of being in the moment/present to challenge the lack of control and feelings of being overwhelmed by past fear/danger
	
	• Explore the self-defeating aspect of anxiety/panic symptoms (which reinforce negative emotion and hypervigilance), for example:
	  – Avoidance of goal-directed behaviors
	  – Becoming physically ill as a legitimate reason to avoid
	  – Changing the topic when becoming uncomfortable
	  – Avoiding emotional intimacy to feel safe and in control
	  – Engaging in compulsive behaviors to avoid thinking/feeling (eating, spending, substances, gambling, sex, etc.)
	  – Late to appointment/disorganized

– Remaining in a harmful situation/relationship
– Not focusing on beneficial self-change
– Covering up to impress others and avoiding living honestly/authentically.

6. *Challenging Hypersensitivity/ Hypervigilance*

- Keep a journal to maintain awareness about:
  – Identifying what is experienced as or identified as personally dangerous
  – Identifying inaccurate perceptions of danger
  – Clarifying what needs to be done to manage thoughts of danger and to decrease painful feelings/experiences

- Engage in steps to control/manage/eliminate fear of arousal (Meichenbaum, 1994):
  – Recognition of physical symptoms that indicate an imminent panic attack
  – Engage in self-care behaviors to manage acute anxiety, such as relaxation, deep breathing, exercise, balance in rest and demands
  – Identify symptoms of panic anxiety as an opportunity to review self-care plan
  – Clarify whether panic attacks create a "legitimate" excuse for avoidance
  – Identify misinterpretation of body signs that something is wrong. Facilitate understanding that misinterpretation fuels negative self-talk which influences hypersensitivity
  – Facilitate learning how to control breathing to pre-empt the beginning of hyperventilation
  – Interpret the panic attack and identify the trigger that began it and the feelings that accompany it (fear, sadness, hopelessness, helplessness, loss)
  – Develop a list of various coping skills to learn that panic attacks generally subside in 5–10 minutes and that they do not involve dying or going crazy. For example, grounding (being in the present), changing behaviors (do something distracting such as make a phone call to a friend, etc.), doing something fun, finding a way to engage in laughter
  – Reinforce taking charge of their behavioral responses to interrupt a panic attack and taking credit for their accomplishment
  – Allow the body to readjust chemically from the acute anxiety (identify as a natural consequence/process). Engage in relaxation and gentle exercise such as yoga or stretching
  – Adequate sleep and good nutrition
  – Aerobic exercise. Walking is excellent. It facilitates being in the moment, offers positive distraction by taking in environmental details, feels good and facilitates positive brain chemistry
  – Identify different sources of soothing using all the senses. The use of odor for relaxation (vanilla and the fragrance of bread baking are two examples). Massage for touch. Relaxing or meditative music. Serene imagery (mental or *in vivo*). Camomile tea etc.
  – Make a list of personal strengths, sources of resilience and resources.

7. *Improve Family Functioning*

- Educate family regarding hyperarousal and how they can help (not personalize)
- Explore any role family has in contributing to hyperarousal
- Improve family communication
- Support, reinforce, and encourage efforts.

DISSOCIATION

Dissociation is an inability to recall important aspects of the trauma. It is associated with:

- Altered thought processes
- Lack of consistent sense of reality (not able to remain in the present)
- Ineffective coping skills
- Ineffective stress management
- Lack of personality integration
- Family dysfunction.

The goals associated with therapy for dissociation include the following:

1. Thought Processes Intact

- In addition to assessing the patient directly, gather information from family and significant others for broader and more accurate information (life, experiences, pleasurable activities, likes/dislikes, responses/reactions, favorite music, places the patient finds relaxing)
- Expose patient to positive past experiences and pleasurable activities
- Slowly elicit personal information from the patient to prevent flooding, which could result in regression
- As the person allows memories to surface, engage them in activities to stimulate the forthcoming memories such as photographs, talking about a significant person from the past, and the role that various other people have played in their life
- Encourage the person to talk about situations that have posed significant stress
- Facilitate the patient to verbalize stressful situations and to explore the feelings associated with those situations
- Facilitate increased awareness and understanding of all of the factors that have contributed to the dissociative process
- Facilitate identification of specific conflicts that are unresolved
- Develop possible solution to the unresolved conflicts
- Be supportive and offer positive feedback and reinforcement for the courage to work through these issues
- Identify five situations/circumstances where they currently dissociate (or space out):
  - When do they dissociate?
  - What are the indications that they are going to dissociate? It may be helpful to create sentence stems that they complete such as "When I dissociate, I ..."
  - Educate them about the adaptive origin of dissociation and the maladaptive or harmful effects of dissociation since the time of the traumatic experience
  - Have them identify what they have learned about their use of dissociation.

2. Decrease or Eliminate Sensory/Perceptual Distortions

- Identify the nature, extent, and possible participants of the dissociative state
- Obtain a collaborative history of the nature and extent of the dissociative states from family/friends
- Educate the person regarding the depersonalization experience, behaviors, and the purpose they generally serve for the patient (or did serve originally)

- Validate feelings of fear and anxiety related to the depersonalization experience
- Educate the person regarding the relationship between severe anxiety and stress and the depersonalization experience
- Explore past experiences such as trauma and abuse
- Encourage the identification and working through of feelings associated with these situations
- Identify effective and adaptive responses to severe anxiety and stress
- Encourage practice of these new adaptive behaviors. This may be initiated through modeling and role-play
- Facilitate the patient's ability to separate past from present to more effectively cope with the traumatic memories and feelings.

3. *Improved Coping*

- Educate regarding the origin of some coping mechanisms having served a useful purpose at an earlier time that have become dysfunctional and possibly detrimental. Be supportive and reassuring
- Identify situations that precipitate severe anxiety
- Facilitate appropriate problem-solving in order to intervene and prevent escalation of anxiety and to develop more adaptive coping in response to anxiety
- Explore feelings that the patient experiences in response to stressful situations
- Consider using environmental manipulation to improve coping
- Whenever possible, encourage maintenance of some form of employment as long as possible
- Facilitate understanding that the emotion experienced is acceptable and often predictable in times of stress
- As the patient develops improved coping abilities, encourage them to identify the underlying source(s) of chronic anxiety
- Encourage identification of past coping strategies and determine if the response was adaptive or maladaptive
- Develop a plan of action for effective, adaptive coping to predictable future stressors
- Explore with the patient the benefits and consequences of alternative adaptive coping strategies
- Identify community resources that can be utilized to increase the patient's support system as they make efforts to manage effectively
- Facilitate identification of how the patient's life has been affected by trauma
- Offer positive feedback and reinforcement for efforts and accomplishments.

4. *Improved Stress Management*

- Relaxation techniques
- Time management
- Self-care (exercise, nutrition, utilization of resources, etc.)
- Educate regarding role of negative self-talk.

5. *Personality (Re)Integration*	• Develop a trusting therapeutic relationship. With a multiple personality, this means a trusting relationship with the original personality as well as subpersonalities.
	• Educate patient about multiple personality disorder in order to increase their understanding of subpersonalities
	• Facilitate identification of the needs of each subpersonality, the role they have played in psychic survival
	• Facilitate identification of the need that each subpersonality serves in the personal identity of the person
	• Facilitate identification of the relationship between stress and personality change
	• Facilitate identification of the stressful situations that precipitate a transition from one personality to another
	• Decrease fear and defensiveness by facilitating subpersonalities to understand that integration will not lead to their destruction, but to a unified personality within the individual
	• Facilitate understanding that therapy will be a long-term process, which is often arduous and difficult
	• Be supportive and reassuring.
6. *Improve Family Coping*	• Explore family knowledge on the issue
	• Explore how they respond and what is/is not useful
	• Offer education and choices in responding that are helpful.

DEPRESSION (JOHNSON, 2004)

The issues to be addressed with regard to depression include:

- Assessment of danger to self and others
- Providing a safe environment
- Assessing the need for medication evaluation referral.

Depression may be associated with:

- Ineffective problem-solving skills
- Ineffective coping skills
- Lack of appropriate support system
- Issues of loss
- Low self-esteem
- Cognitive distortions
- Poor eating patterns
- Sleep disturbance
- Ineffective depression management
- Poor medication compliance.

The goals associated with therapy for depression include the following:

1. Suicide Risk Assessment (Danger to Others Ruled Out)

The level of emotional distress may be alleviated by validating the patient's experience and encouraging them to vent their feelings and their intentions associated with danger to self. Talking about the issues that have resulted in despair and hopelessness creates the opportunity for intervention. It is during the course of their ventilation of feelings and thoughts that they can be facilitated to think about the consequences of and impact that their suicide would have upon those who care about them. It is also possible to then gain an understanding of the reasons behind not taking action on their thoughts/plan of suicide. Offering validation and reassurance may increase their ambivalence. If there is evidence of adequate social support and a desire to resolve this level of emotional distress in a more positive manner, a short-term verbal contract with a coinciding written contract can offer some structure for dealing with self-destructive impulses. An urgent care approach with therapy and increased frequency of meeting for a briefer period of time may also be helpful through this crisis time. Likewise, increasing the frequency of outpatient contacts may be appropriate if the patient denies intent but lacks adequate resources or demonstrates vulnerability which indicates increased support.

If the patient is not able to adequately assure that they do not intend to commit suicide or to utilize a collaborative plan of management, then hospitalization may be necessary. If this is the case, initiate discussion about safety and voluntary admission to a psychiatric facility. If they are unwilling to voluntarily admit themselves, then an involuntary admission is likely to ensue following assessment by designated personnel.

While danger to self is often the critical clinical dilemma requiring immediate attention and intervention, it is equally important to assess and rule out any homicidal thoughts and intentions that place others in a position of potential harm. If there is intention to harm another person, the appropriate clinical interventions and legal issue of duty to warn must be dealt with immediately.

2. Provide Safe Environment

- Evaluate whether patient is demonstrating adequate cooperation (removal of firearms, medications, etc. that may be used in actions of danger to self or others)

- Evaluate adequacy of social support

- Adjust level of care if necessary:
  - Urgent care. Flexible time for meeting, along with extended meeting time to allow the patient to ventilate their emotions and initiate problem-solving
  - Partial hospitalization
  - Inpatient hospitalization.

3. Referral Assessment for Medication Evaluation

- If this is an initial assessment and a history of depression is determined that has clearly affected quality of life and functioning, refer for a medication evaluation

- If this has been an ongoing case and acute depressive symptoms are present that are interfering with level of functioning, refer for medication evaluation

- Assess for mood congruent psychotic features. They can be present and not identified. If positive, convey information to prescribing physician.

4. *Improved Problem-Solving*	• Define the problem(s)
	• Brainstorm all plausible solutions
	• Identify the outcomes in relation to the various solutions
	• Make a decision that appears to best fit the demands of the problem situation
	• Prepare the patient for the possibility that the solution may not work out as planned; therefore, have a contingency plan.

5. *Improved Coping*	• Help the patient to recognize that they can only do one thing at a time
	• Teach relaxation skills to combat feeling overwhelmed
	• Facilitate prioritizing issues that must be dealt with
	• Facilitate classification of boundaries, especially related to issues of pleasing others versus self-care
	• Rule out secondary gains
	• Helplessness: – Encourage taking responsibility and making decisions – Offer support and critical thinking to decision-making – Provide positive feedback for decision-making – Facilitate development of realistic goals – Identify areas of life and self-care in which the person has control, as well as those areas where the person lacks control – Encourage expression of feelings related to areas of life outside their control and explore how to let go of it.

6. *Development or Utilization of Resources and Social Supports*	• Encourage patient to resist the desire to withdraw and isolate
	• Identify positive social/emotional supports that the person has been avoiding
	• Make commitment to utilize resources and supports in some way every day
	• Educate regarding role of isolation in maintaining depression
	• Evaluate impaired social interaction: – Convey acceptance and positive regard in creating a safe, non-judgmental environment – Identify people in the person's life and activities that were previously found pleasurable – Encourage utilization of support system – Encourage appropriate risk-taking – Teach assertive communication – Give direct, non-judgmental feedback regarding interaction with others – Offer alternative responses for dealing effectively with stress-provoking situations – Use social skills training in how to approach others and participate in conversation – Role-play and practice social skills for reinforcement and to increase insight for how the person is perceived by others – Daily structure to include social interaction.

7. *Appropriate Grieving*	• Evaluate stage/symptoms of grief that person is experiencing
	• Demonstrate care and empathy
	• Determine if the person has numerous unresolved losses:

- – Validate
- – Identify specific losses and time line
- – Identify their interpretation of the loss
- – Identify choices in working toward integration and/or resolution by facilitating the understanding that whatever has happened is a part of their life experience. How can they interpret and integrate that in a manner that is beneficial and strengthening?
- – Challenge irrational thinking and negative self-talk
- – Be sensitive to cultural diversity associated with grieving

- • Encourage identification and expression of feelings
- • Use the empty chair technique or have the person write a letter to someone they have lost, which may provoke the resolution process
- • Educate person on stages/symptoms of grief and normalize appropriate feelings such as anger and guilt
- • Support them in letting go of their idealized perception so that they can accept the positive and negative aspects of their object of loss
- • Positively reinforce adaptive coping with experiences of loss (taking into consideration ethnic, cultural and social differences)
- • Refer to a grief group
- • Explore the issue of spirituality and spiritual support.

8. *Improved Self-Esteem*

- • Focus on strengths and accomplishments (self-esteem development is an active process)
- • Avoid focus on past failures
- • Reframe failures or negative experiences as a normal part of the learning process
- • Identify all areas of desired change and objectives to meet these goals
- • Encourage independent effort and accepting responsibility
- • Teach assertive communication and appropriate setting of limits and boundaries
- • Teach effective communication techniques by using "I" statement, not making assumptions, asking for clarification, etc.
- • Offer positive reinforcement for tasks performed independently.

9. *Cognitive Restructuring*

- • Identify the influence of negativism on depression and educate regarding positive self-talk
- • Seek classification when the information communicated appears distorted
- • Reinforce reality-based thinking

	• Facilitate development of intervention techniques such as increased awareness with conscious choice of what to focus on (positive thoughts), thought stopping, and compartmentalizing
	• Facilitate person's clarification of rational versus irrational thinking.
10. *Appropriate Diet and Eating Patterns*	• Evaluate eating pattern and fluid intake • Educate regarding importance of good nutrition for energy and clear thinking.
11. *Adequate Sleep*	• Evaluate sleep pattern and overall amount of sleep • Encourage appropriate and adequate sleep/wake cycle • Discourage daytime napping • Recommend avoidance of caffeine and other stimulants • Suggest relaxation exercises or listen to relaxing music before sleep • Suggest daily aerobic exercising such as walking • Administer sedative medications in the evening instead of other times during the day • Suggest activities such as a relaxing reading, warm bath, massage, herbal tea, light snack, and so on, to promote sleep.
12. *Facilitate Managing Depression*	This requires a thorough review of lifestyle. Managing depression requires a commitment by the person to take responsibility for improving his or her quality of life. • The components of a self-care plan to manage depression include the following: – Structured daily activities – Development and utilization of social supports – Positive attitude and identification of the positive things in one's life – Awareness – Regular aerobic exercise – Eating nutritionally balanced diet – Living in accordance with one's own value system.
13. *Educate Patient (and Family if Appropriate) on Medication Issues*	• Emphasize the importance of compliance. Encourage patient to clarify potential side-effects including those that require immediate attention • Recommend that they familiarize themselves with any restrictions related to medication use • Refer person to clarify medication issues with his or her physician and pharmacist

- Educate regarding chemical imbalance related to depression
- Educate regarding role of decompensation related to lack of medication compliance
- Possible side-effects of antidepressant medications (general):
  - Sedation
  - Anticholinergic effects
  - Orthostatic hypotension
  - Tachycardia/arrhythmia
  - Photosensitivity
  - Decrease in seizure threshold
  - Hypertensive crisis (monitor for symptoms such as palpitations, nausea, vomiting, sweating, chest pain, severe occipital headache, fever, increased blood pressure, coma)
  - Weight loss or gain
  - Sexual dysfunction; decreased libido, protracted orgasm, priapism
- If the patient reports the experience of medication side-effects, consult with the prescribing physician and encourage the patient to do the same
- If the patient experiences seasonal affective disorder, be sensitive to the issue of light treatment as a depression management tool
- Since a therapist is likely to have significantly more contact with an individual in treatment who is being prescribed psychotropic medication than the prescribing physician, it is imperative to monitor the patient's response to medication and to communicate salient information to the prescribing physician:
  - At least moderate improvement should be achieved in 4–8 weeks
  - Monitor for presence of side-effects (especially those that require immediate attention)
- Risk factors for recurrence of major depressive symptoms:
  - History of multiple episodes of major depression
  - Evidence of dysthymic symptoms following recovery from an episode of major depression
  - Comorbid non-affective psychiatric diagnosis
  - Presence of chronic medical disorder
- Clinical features that influence treatment planning:
  - Crisis issues
  - Psychotic features
  - Substance abuse
  - Comorbid axis I or axis II disorders
  - Major depression related to cognitive dysfunction (pseudodementia)
  - Severe, complicated grief reaction
  - Seasonal major depressive disorder
- Educate regarding atypical major depressive disorder features (defined by reversal of vegetative symptoms):
  - Increased sleep versus decreased sleep
  - Increased appetite versus decreased appetite
  - Weight gain versus weight loss
  - Marked mood reactivity
  - Sensitivity to emotional rejection

- Phobic symptoms
- Extreme fatigue with heaviness of extremities

- If there is little or no symptomatic response by 4–6 weeks:
  - Assess treatment compliance
  - Reassess diagnosis
  - Reassess adequacy of treatment.

Co-occurrence of depression with other medical, psychiatric, and substance abuse disorders should always be considered and assessed for during the evaluation process. Awareness and treatment can improve overall health and decrease suffering. A thorough assessment and accurate diagnosis are imperative.

ANXIETY (JOHNSON, 2004)

For the patient with anxiety symptoms, it is important to assess whether they need a medication evaluation referral. Issues associated with anxiety include:

- Unmanageable anxiety and fears
- Ineffective coping skills
- Ineffective problem-solving skills
- Inadequate self-care skills
- Inadequate feelings of control
- Ineffective communication skills
- Cognitive distortions
- Low self-esteem
- Ineffective stress management skills
- Inadequate family education
- Inadequate information regarding compliance and side-effects of medication.

The goals associated with therapy for anxiety include the following:

1. Assess for Referral for Medication Evaluation

Patients with heightened anxiety, withdrawal, lack of sleep, obsessive thoughts, and compulsive behaviors etc. may benefit from the treatment of psychotropic medication. If there is comorbidity of depression or other diagnostic concerns, convey this information to the prescribing physician.

2. Increased Awareness of Feelings of Anxiety and Fear

- Validate person's emotional experience
- Identify factors contributing to anxiety
- Problem-solve factors contributing to anxiety:
  - What is the problem?
  - Brainstorm various choices for dealing with the problem if it is within the patient's control

– Make a decision and follow through. Have a contingency plan
– If it is out of the patient's control, encourage them to let go of it

- Explore methods of managing anxiety:
  – Relaxation techniques, including deep breathing
  – Distracting, pleasurable activities
  – Exercise
  – Meditation
  – Positive self-talk

- Assess medication for effectiveness and for adverse side-effects

- Educate regarding signs of escalating anxiety and various techniques for interrupting the progression of these symptoms. Also explore possible physical etiology of exacerbation of anxiety.

- Identify source and consequences of fear:
  – Explore the source of the fear
  – Clarify the reality and rationality of the fear base. Encourage venting of feelings of fear. If the fear is irrational, the patient must accept the reality of the situation before any changes can occur and be sustained
  – Develop alternative coping strategies with the active participation of the patient
  – Encourage the patient to make their own choices and to be prepared with a contingency plan
  – Use systematic desensitization to eliminate fear with gradual exposure to the feared object or situation (exposure can be real or through visual imagery)
  – Use exposure therapy
  – Educate patient regarding role of internal, self-talk associated with feelings of fear (and other negative emotions), and develop appropriate counter statements

- Manage obsessive thoughts and compulsive behaviors:
  – Patients with obsessive thoughts should be encouraged to engage in reality testing and to redirect themselves into productive and distracting activity
  – Patients with compulsive behavior should develop a stepwise reduction in the repetition of ritual behaviors (medication can be very helpful for managing obsessive compulsive disorder features)

- Positive feedback and reinforcement for efforts and accomplishments.

3. *Improve Coping*
- Identify factors that escalate anxiety and contribute to difficulty coping

- Identify ritualistic behavioral patterns

- Educate regarding the relationship between emotions and dysfunctional/compulsive behavior

- Develop daily structure of activities

- Gradually decrease time allotted for compulsive ritualistic behaviors, utilizing daily structure of activities that acts to substitute more adaptive behaviors

- Positive feedback and reinforcement for efforts/changes to shape behavior

- Teach techniques that interrupt dysfunctional thoughts and behaviors, such as relaxation techniques, meditation, thought stopping, exercise, positive self-talk, visual imagery, and so on

- Facilitate shaping of social interaction to decrease avoidant behavior.

4. *Improve Problem-Solving*	• Teach problem-solving skills
	• Develop some realistic sample problems and give homework to practice new skills
	• Identify secondary gains that inhibit progress toward change (for example, if they make progress and functioning improves will higher expectations be placed on them, thus creating negative emotions associated with change?).

5. *Improved Self-Care*	• Support person to independently fulfill daily grooming and hygiene tasks
	• Adequate nutrition
	• Engaging in activities and being with people, all of which contribute to feelings of well-being
	• Use of positive self-talk and affirmations
	• Positive feedback and reinforce efforts and accomplishments
	• Time management
	• Prioritize demands/tasks
	• Develop and utilize support system.

6. *Improve Feelings of Control Over Life*	• Break down simple behaviors and necessary tasks into manageable steps
	• Provide choices that are within their control
	• Support development of realistic goals and objectives
	• Encourage participation in activities in which the person will experience success/achievement
	• Facilitate development of problem-solving skills
	• Facilitate shaping of social interaction to decrease avoidant behavior.

7. *Improved Communication*	• Assertive communication
	• Anger management
	• Role-play, rehearse, and problem-solve appropriate response choices in various situations
	• Positive feedback and reinforcement for efforts and accomplishments
	• Learn to say "no," avoid manipulation, set limits and boundaries.

8. *Cognitive Restructuring*	• Identify negative statements (the person makes to themselves)
	• Focus on thoughts and beliefs generated by the traumatic event rather than on the conditioned emotional response addressed by prolonged exposure

- Identify the connection between anxiety and self-talk
- Examine interpretations of the traumatic event and self/world appraisals (common themes include guilt, shame, vulnerability, disgust, anger, and sadness)
- Develop appropriate, reality-based counterstatements and substitute them for the negative ones
- Encourage patient to keep a daily record of dysfunctional thoughts to increase awareness of frequency and impact on emotional state
- Disrupt dysfunctional thoughts by increasing awareness for internal self-talk, distracting oneself through relaxation, exercise, or other positive activity, and using thought stopping
- Irrational beliefs
  - Identify false beliefs (brought from childhood, integrated parental statements, or based in experience)
  - Challenge mistaken beliefs with rational counterstatements
  - Identify effects that irrational beliefs have on emotions, relationships with self and others, and choices the person makes
- Challenge self-defeating beliefs/behaviors that perpetuate anxiety by identifying needs or tendencies that predispose the patient to anxiety, such as:
  - Need to control
  - Perfectionist tendencies
  - People pleaser with strong need for approval
  - Ignoring signs of stress
  - Self-critical
  - Perpetual victim role
  - Pessimistic, catastrophizes
  - Chronic worrier.

9. *Improve Self-Esteem*

- Self-care:
  - Identifying needs
  - Setting appropriate limits and boundaries
  - Seeking a safe, stable environment
- Identify realistic goals
- Identify external factors that negatively affect self-esteem
- Overcome negative attitudes toward self
- Address issues of physical well-being (exercise and nutrition) and positive body image
- Assertive communication
- Identify feelings that have been ignored or denied (i.e. identify thoughts about the self or the world that create fear and stress)
- Positive self-talk, affirmations
- Focus on efforts and accomplishments
- Positive feedback and reinforcement.

10. *Effective Stress Management*	• Challenge irrational self-talk
	• Ineffective use of defense mechanisms
	• Facilitate development of stress management techniques:
	– Deep breathing
	– Progressive muscle relaxation
	– Visual imagery/meditation
	– Time management
	– Self-care
	– Grounding strategies.

11. *Exposure Therapy*	• Prolonged exposure preparation:
	– Psycho-education
	– Rationale for treatment (and the importance of their use of prescribed relaxation training in conjunction with exposure therapy)
	– Breathing retraining
	– Explanation of substance use rating and how to use in combination with exposure therapy
	• Imaginal exposure
	• *In vivo* exposure
	– Exposure to trauma-related current cues
	– Progress through hierarchy
	– Use of substance use disorder ratings
	– Improves outcome rather than imaginal exposure alone
	• Reinforce efforts and accomplishments.

12. *Educate Patient/Family*	• Facilitate increased understanding of etiology, course of treatment, and the family role in treatment. Medical exam to rule out any physical etiology or complications
	• Encourage patient's participation in treatment planning
	• Educate regarding the nervous system and explain that it is impossible to feel relaxed and anxious at the same time. Therefore, mastery of stress management techniques such as progressive muscle relaxation works to slowly intervene and diminish the symptoms of anxiety
	• Educate regarding the use of medication, how it works, the side-effects, and the need to make the prescribing physician aware of the person's reaction/responses to the medication for monitoring (the anxious person may need reassurance from the physician about the medication and how to use it on more than one occasion). Some antianxiety medications exacerbate depressed mood.

13. *General Side-Effects of Medication*	• Physical and psychological dependence
	• May escalate symptoms of depression
	• Drowsiness

- Nausea/vomiting (identify other potential somatic symptoms)
- Orthostatic hypotension
- Dry mouth
- Blood dyscraias—if there is easy bruising, sore throat, fever, malaise, or unusual bleeding, report these symptoms immediately to the prescribing physician or go to the nearest emergency room.

GRIEF

Grief is a natural and normal reaction to loss. It can be worse when the loss is traumatic, sudden, or unexpected. It can be worse when there are losses in daily living/lifestyle associated with experiencing a traumatic experience. Traumatic grief may be complicated and protracted. Everyone grieves differently. There is no normal or expected time for grieving. Six areas to assess and intervene in are:

- Emotional reactions
- Physical reactions
- Social reactions
- Spiritual reactions
- Coping with triggers
- Self-care.

The goals associated with therapy for grief include the following:

1. Emotional Reactions

- Identify emotional reactions to traumatic event (shock, anger, fear, guilt, anxiety, depression)
- Identify the impact of the emotional response on daily life experience:
  – What/how have things changed?
  – Identify the compounded negative association with these changes
  – Outline a progression of beneficial changes to facilitate healthy daily functioning

- Identify the impact of the emotional response on relationships:
  – Identify what relationships have been affected
  – Identify ways to heal, or resolve their emotional response
  – What have they learned about themselves which can be useful?
  – What are realistic expectation/limitations in relation to others?
  – Is it possible that realistic needs be met in their current relationships?
  – Do they need to develop new resources?

- Identify the impact of the emotional response on utilizing resources:
  – Self-monitoring for patterns of avoidance and isolation
  – Plan for social activities that are positive and distracting
  – Don't force self to participate in social activities that create distress
  – Identify small manageable steps of a plan to recovery a normal and beneficial level of utilizing social resources

- Identify the impact of the emotional response on the choice to avoid and isolate:
  - What do they identify as the benefit to avoid and isolate
  - Do a cost benefit analysis of the choice to avoid and isolate (pros/cons)
  - Problem-solve what will help them to decrease isolation and avoidance
  - Problem-solve their options for emotional management should they find themselves in a distressing situation. What are their choices? Prepare ahead of time to give themselves permission to leave. Creates several other appropriate options for excusing themselves without feeling the need to explain their decision to others
- Identify any issues of survival guilt
- Identify and utilize grounding strategies for states of overwhelming emotions.

2. *Physical Reactions*

- Identify the physical reactions to the traumatic event (fatigue, restless, short of breath, headaches, abdominal distress, gastrointestinal tract problems, sleep disturbance, etc.):
  - How do they interpret the symptoms they experience? (Why did those specific symptoms develop—associated with coping style?)
  - How does the body generally cope with stress?
  - How do they manage in a positive manner which decreases the amount of physical reactions?
  - If there are reactions that require or benefit from medical intervention make the referral to their physician and offer helpful information to the physician. Also, prepare the patient to meet with the physician (make a list)
  - Review their health behaviors and work with them to refine a positive pattern of daily health behaviors
- Identify the impact of the physical reactions on relationships:
  - List the relationships that have been affected
  - Clarify how each relationship is affected (is there a pattern or are there unique variations of change in relationships)
  - How do they believe that these changes have affected how others see them or experience them? How does this affect them (such as increasing avoidance/isolation)? Has it altered what their normal social supports have been?
  - What have they learned about their body and themselves from this response? What have they learned about their coping mechanisms? How does their body deal with stress? How do they heal their physical stress reactions?
- Identify the impact of the physical responses on daily functioning/lifestyle:
  - What limitations in daily functioning/lifestyle have resulted from physical reactions?
  - What changes have they felt they had to make as a consequence of physical reactions?
  - What fears do they have associated with their physical reactions?
  - Do they understand the connection between their physical reactions and grieving?
- Identify the role of the physical reaction in avoidance and isolation (legitimate excuses):
  - How have they used their physical reactions to avoid/isolate socially
  - How have they used their physical reactions to avoid responsibility
  - What are the consequences of using their physical reactions to avoid/isolate (result of more losses/reinforcing ineffective coping)
  - Clarify the difference between isolation and avoidance versus a positive choice of self-care.

3. *Social Reactions*

- Identify the social reactions associated with the traumatic event:
  - What changes have benefited them or created more negative consequences?
  - What changes bother them the most?
  - What changes do they feel are most important or most helpful to resolve/alter?
  - What old social behaviors do they want to recapture? What stands in the way? What will be helpful in resuming old social behaviors (how/what will they do)?

- Identify the impact of the social reactions on relationships:
  - Identify experiences or patterns overreacting
  - Have there been any changes they needed to make anyway (reframe benefit)?
  - Have things been said to them that they need/want to address?
  - Have relationship changes resulted in more grieving? Are they experiencing feelings of aloneness and being overwhelmed?

- Identify the impact of the social reactions on daily functioning/lifestyle:
  - What are the most detrimental changes?
  - What would they need to do to resume the lost aspect of daily functioning/lifestyle?
  - Is there anything reinforcing changes in daily functioning/lifestyle (secondary gain)?

- Identify the role that social reactions play in avoidance and isolation or overdependence.

4. *Spiritual Reaction*

- Wondering why pain and suffering exist, why this has happened to them, feeling angry with God, feelings of being punished

- As a result of questioning have they avoided worship, church, talking with their minister/priest?
  - Would it be helpful to speak with their minister/priest regarding their spiritual feelings?
  - It may be helpful to explore through the use of written works?
  - Explore the possibility of finding a different way of fulfilling spiritual needs
  - Problem-solve a reasonable progression of working through such a difficult issue to reach their identified goal on this topic

- Encourage the use of their spirituality to work toward acceptance versus questions that cannot be answered.

5. *Coping With Triggers*

- Identify triggers (holidays, anniversaries, milestones, special days, pieces of music, etc.):
  - Make a list of triggers
  - Identify how to deal with each trigger

- Predict the reality that some triggers will be inevitable (signifying the importance of identifying them and deciding how to deal with them). For example:
  - There are a lot of "firsts" following a loss
  - Anniversary reactions generally bring strong emotional reactions (prediction)
  - Predict the potential for vivid details with recollection
  - Predict that they may experience difficulty with eating or sleeping, may develop headaches, stomach pain, or intestinal upset
  - Predict that a return of grief feelings does not indicate a set-back in the grieving process

- Triggers can be anywhere (sights, sounds, smells, in the news/TV). They can catch a person off guard:
    - Prepare for episodes of grief. Encourage the view of understanding the return of emotions as opportunities for healing
    - Even years after a loss there may be feelings of sadness when confronted with a reminder. Learn the difference between normal sadness and sadness which becomes depression

- Identify ways to cope with reminders of loss and to continue to heal:
    - Be reassured that anniversary reactions are normal and that their intensity diminishes over time (we learn to live better with losses)
    - Try to focus on the positive aspects rather than the negative
    - Start new traditions
    - Plan a distraction when a difficult time/anniversary is coming
    - Prepare to utilize resources versus avoiding them
    - Allow normal feelings of sadness, AND allow feelings of joy and celebration.

6. *Self-Care*

- Identify that experiences of grief are an opportunity for increased self-understanding and personal growth
- Develop a personalized self-care plan for optimal emotional health and a positive sense of well-being. Encourage patient to:
    - Use relaxation techniques to decrease body tension and to manage stress
    - Review available social supports. If necessary work at developing an adequate and appropriate support system
    - Initiate a journal. Instead of keeping thoughts and feelings inside, where they can build up and cause confusion and emotional/physical distress, get them down on paper. It can also be helpful in determining patterns, relationships, health, and emotional functioning. Keeping a journal will help monitor progress in life goals
    - Get adequate sleep and rest
    - Smile and have laughter often. Be spontaneous at times and playful
    - Feed the body, mind, and spirit. Eat nutritional meals regularly. Practice good hygiene and grooming. Participate in life for personal and spiritual growth
    - Approach each day with purpose. Be productive by outlining daily structure. No task is too small to feel good about. Each step can be important to reach identified goals
    - Avoid being self-critical. Support patients in being kind and understanding of themselves as they would be to another person. Encourage the use of positive self-talk for reassurance, coping effectively, and allowing them to see that there are always choices
    - Be sure to build into the daily schedule time for relationships and pleasurable activities
    - Take responsibility for their own life. Promote self-understanding, including their behaviors, beliefs, thoughts, and motivations.

STRESS MANAGEMENT/STRESS INOCULATION (JOHNSON, 2004)

When a patient enters treatment in an overwhelmed state or in crisis it presents an opportunity for cognitive behavioral changes that are beneficial to their overall ability to cope effectively. During a period of crisis their defenses are down and emotional distress is high. The patient feels an urgency to decrease the level of emotional distress. Because they are motivated toward alleviating emotional distress they are open to new ways of thinking and behaving.

Change is stressful, even when it is beneficial. Change requires effort and conscious awareness. In preparing to engage someone in the process of change, it is important to understand how they normally interact with their environment. The responses to stress are numerous and individualized, just as the variable approaches for intervening. Therefore, it is imperative to be prepared with a number of strategies for handling stress.

Because cognitions and mental processes have a strong influence, negative or positive, on the physical and emotional reactions to stress, cognitive restructuring is an important intervention. Five aspects of mental processing that play a role in stress include:

1. Expectations/self-fulfilling prophecy: What a person believes will happen or expects to happen sometimes influences their behavior in a manner which increases the likelihood of the feared outcome. Negative expectations increase anxiety and stress. Identifying goals for change and facing such challenges with optimism and a positive attitude will facilitate optimal coping and management.

2. Mental imagery/visual imagery: Coinciding with expectations for a given situation a person will develop an associated mental picture and internal dialogue. This mental imagery increases anxiety and stress reactions. Positive expectation, in contrast, minimize the effects of life stressors and increase effective coping.

3. Self-talk: Internal dialogue takes place 24/7. Self-talk is the conversation or messages that a person has with themselves. It is common that a person is not aware of this internal dialogue or the consequences upon anxiety, stress, and self-esteem. Self-talk also influences mental imagery. Negative mental images and negative self-talk can result in anxiety and psychosomatic symptoms, whereas positive self-talk encourages self-confidence, effective coping, and a general feeling of well-being. Once there is awareness for negative self-talk the task is to create rational substitute statements to replace the negative thoughts for cognitive restructuring. Keep a journal to identify the damaging self-statements so that a rational substitute state can be developed to replace them.

4. Controlling and perfectionistic behavior: Perfectionism and unrealistic expectations often go hand in hand. Responses of controlling and perfectionistic behaviors are frequently an effort to avoid abuse, conflict, the unknown, or a feeling of being on-edge and inadequacy. Placing unrealistic expectations on others is a form of controlling behavior. Self-management consumes enough energy without expanding into the realm to control other. Additional consequences to the effort of controlling others are stress, anxiety, frustration, and anger.

5. Anger: Anger is a normal, healthy emotion when expressed appropriately. It can be damaging to self and others when expressed inappropriately because of the internal tension, or build-up, that predisposes alienation and explosiveness with others. This behavior results in low self-esteem and poor interpersonal relating. Chronic anger and hostility are related to the development or exacerbation of a number of physical symptoms, illnesses, and diseases. Anger can be a self-defense or unfinished business.

Goals Used in the Development of Stress Management Skills

- Deal with stress when it strikes. Breathe slowly and deeply. Exercise to diminish adrenaline

- Think positively. A person does not necessarily have control over what happens to them but they do have choices in how they interpret it and deal with it

- Practice improved management of stress by visualizing stressful situations and how they can be managed effectively. That way when the stressful event occurs it feels like it has already been successfully dealt with before

- Set limits. Create a work frame of time and when the time is up, shift gears and stop thinking about work. Consider the unfairness to those close to an individual who is not respectful of what it is like for them to be with someone who is preoccupied with something else instead of being in the moment and emotionally available
- Be honest about what areas are and are not under your control. If it is an area of control make a choice and follow through. If it belongs to someone else, let go of it
- Self-control is to be reframed as taking responsibility for one's self, one's thoughts, and one's choices
- Situational control is the practice or implementation of problem-solving, assertiveness, conflict resolution, and time management
- Relaxation skills for emotional and physical well-being include:
  - Progressive muscle relaxation
  - Meditation/visual imagery/prayer
  - Deep breathing
  - Aerobic walking
  - Soothing music/artistic endeavors
- To decrease stress associated with these issues utilize basic stress inoculation techniques of:
  - Education
  - Rehearsal of skills
  - Implementation or carrying out the plan.

ANGER (DAHLEN AND DEFFENBACHER, 2001)

The expression of anger can take many forms. The first step in anger management is to identify the three aspects of anger. All three interact to create a state of being angry:

1. The anger-eliciting stimulus, either the generally easy to identify external source (somebody did something to them) or an internal source (emotional wound)
2. The pre-anger state (which includes cognitive, emotional, and physical state at the time of provocation, the person's enduring psychological characteristics, and their cultural messages about expressing anger)
3. The person's appraisal of the anger-eliciting stimulus and their ability to cope with the stimulus.

Next, it is necessary to identify the four related domains in which anger exists:

1. The emotional and experiential domain: anger is a feeling state ranging in intensity from mild annoyance to rage and fury
2. The physiological domain: anger is associated with adrenaline release, increased muscle tension, and activation of the sympathetic nervous system
3. The cognitive domain: anger is associated with biased information processing
4. The behavior domain: anger can be either functional (e.g. being assertive, setting limits) or dysfunctional (e.g. being aggressive, withdrawing, using alcohol and drugs, etc.).

There are numerous qualitative indicators that can be used to help patients understand whether their anger makes a beneficial contribution to function or dysfunction. Even though some of the following symptoms may be suggestive of other issues, they are often related to unresolved anger. The following are questions that may help them make this determination so that effective intervention can be initiated:

- Is the anger chronic, long-lasting, too intense, or too frequent?
- Does the anger disrupt the patient's thinking, affect their relationships, or affect their school or work performance?
- Does the patient exhibit frequent loss of temper at slight provocations, passive–aggressive behavior, a cynical or hostile personality, chronic irritability, and grumpiness?
- Has the patient begun to display low self-esteem, sulking, or brooding?
- Is the patient withdrawing socially from family and friends?
- Is the patient getting physically sick or doing damage to his or her own or others' bodies or property?
- Is the patient experiencing physical symptoms such as increased heart rate, increased blood pressure, or increased adrenaline flow?

Managing Anger

There are three main methods for managing anger (Wellness Reproductions, 1991):

1. **"Stuffing" Anger**

This is the process in which a person may or may not admit their anger to self or others and avoids direct confrontations. They may stuff their anger out of fear of hurting another, fear of rejection, fear of damaging relationships, or fear of losing control. Often, the person who stuffs anger is unable to cope with strong and intense emotions. They may also think that anger is inappropriate or unacceptable. Stuffing anger typically results in impaired relationships and compromised physical and mental health.

2. **Escalating Anger**

This is the process whereby an individual provokes blame and shame. The purpose is to demonstrate power and strength while avoiding the expression of underlying emotions. The individual who escalates their anger is often afraid of getting close to others and lacks effective communication skills. The escalation of anger often results in a short-term outcome, impaired relationships, and compromised physical and mental health. Additional results can be physical destruction to the property of others or physical abuse. Consequently, there can be legal implications.

3. **Anger Management**

The process in which an individual is open, honest and direct. They are mobilized in a positive direction. The focus is on the specific behavior that triggered the anger and on the present (past issues are not integrated into the current issue). An individual who manages anger does not employ black and white thinking, but uses effective communication skills to share thoughts/feelings/needs, checks for possible compromises, and is thoughtful in assessing the consequences of choosing to stay angry versus dealing with the anger. The positive outcomes of managing anger are increased energy level, effective communication skills, strengthened relationships, improved physical and mental health, and boosted self-esteem.

Goals Used in the Development of Anger Management Skills

- Decrease emotional and physiological arousal (Dahlen and Deffenbacher, 2001):
  – Relaxation skills. Relaxing to control anger
  – Choose to think cognitively versus emotionally
  – Self-care
- Appropriate expression of anger (Dahlen and Deffenbacher, 2001):
  – Behavioral coping
  – Social skills training (interpersonal communication, negotiation, feedback). And related coping skills (parenting, budgeting/finance, assertive communication)
  – Inductive social skills training (patient to identify and explore effective behaviors for coping with anger
- Improved general problem-solving to assess desired outcome (Skiba and McKelvey, 2000):
  – Improve general problem-solving skill for a variety of situations
  – Generate alternative solutions
  – Consider the consequences of each solution
  – Select an effective and appropriate response
  – Evaluate the outcomes of implementing the specific responses
- Identify situations where anger has been expressed inappropriately:
  – Was there a specific reason (such as distancing or avoidance)?
  – If you re-experienced such a situation what would be an appropriate response?
- Avoid provoking situations
- Improved communication
- Humor
- Modulation and self-responsibility (Johnson, 2004):
  – Appropriate expression of anger can be healthy when it is used to let go of stress and frustration.

Steps to taking responsibility include:

- Demonstration of a commitment to change in order to improve quality of life, and how self-responsibility will take place by avoiding substance use/abuse, taking time out, exercising or doing relaxation techniques to decrease body tension, and using a journal to express feelings, problem-solve, and self-monitor
- Increased awareness for how inappropriate expressions of anger affect themselves (consequences) and others
- Increased understanding for the role of self-care in management of anger
- Identifying and encouraging use of supports that emphasize appropriate expression of anger
- Setting clear boundaries and limits, which reinforces everyone being responsible for themselves

- Breaking down each goal associated with anger management into manageable steps for behavior shaping
- Identifying any unresolved issues that must be dealt with, unless any issues are unresolveable and require coming to terms with, making internal peace and letting go
- Clarifying thoughts, feelings, needs and wants. Learning to compromise with others when needs and wants put them in conflict with the boundaries of others
- Developing effective skills for improved management of daily lifestyle
- Assertive expression of emotion. Increased awareness of the consequences of un-expressing feelings, i.e. denial of anger results in stress, fatigue, and vulnerability. Depression is experienced as self-disappointment and feeling incompetent. Anxiety is often experienced as fear. Guilt is a socialized belief that it is wrong to feel angry. Self-destructive activities may include: substance abuse, eating to mask feelings, psychosomatic illness (headache, gastrointestinal problems, hypertension), aggression/violence, disguised anger (hostile humor (sarcasm), nagging, silence and withdrawal, withholding intimacy, displacement).

Forgiving

- Forgiving does not mean forgetting, minimizing the offense, condoning what has taken place, or minimizing the outcome of the offense
- Forgiving is a reconciliation for the self to find peace, "letting go", by:
  - Increasing understanding of the amount of energy required to hang onto negative thoughts and feelings
  - Identifying what the cost of anger has been to health and emotional well-being
  - Make a list of symptoms caused by anger
- Develop imagery of practicing forgiveness
- What stands in the way of forgiveness?

Additional Considerations

- Cultural impact of patient's natural environment: Will the culture support the changes in thinking and behaving? It should also be considered whether daily survival is an issue and how this may affect potential success in learning to manage anger more effectively
- Generalizing skills to school/work/home: According to Beasley (1999), change begins at a "teachable" moment, and four conditions are required for change:
  - The individual is in an environment where they feel safe
  - They are supported and encouraged during the change process
  - The environment is relevant to them
  - They are involved and have some degree of control in the change process
- Readiness for anger management interventions: An individual's perspective about their anger issues can impact their readiness. Some may believe that expressing anger is better than controlling or that being/acting angry gets the desired results. Anger may be adaptive (result in status, strength, competence). Attitudes of self-righteousness, low personal responsibility, and blaming others

decreases readiness to change. There must be adequate cognitive ability which allows for thinking about associated consequences. Impulsiveness can also interfere with the application of cognitive processes. All in all, the patient must identify treatment as useful/helpful to their desired goals.

Other variables that influence effective treatment include (Skiba and McKelvey, 2000):

- Length of treatment: Typically longer treatment yields better initial results and annual booster sessions improve long-term outcomes. It may be beneficial to make a follow-up appointment for review and reinforcement
- Proper framing: The more the training is made relevant to their environment, the stronger the initial outcomes
- Supplemental interventions: Utilizing aggression replacement training helps improve initial outcomes.

IMPULSE CONTROL

Impulse control is appropriate when there is:

- Risk of violence toward other(s)
- Risk of self-destructive behavior
- Ineffective coping
- Ineffective stress management
- Low self-esteem which negatively influences decision-making
- Need for relapse prevention.

The goals of therapy using impulse control are as follows:

1. Eliminate Danger to Others

- Reduce environmental stimuli
- Clarify positive regard toward the person, but stress that aggressive behaviors are unacceptable
- Remove all potentially dangerous objects
- Facilitate identification of the underlying source(s) of anger
- Remain calm when there is inappropriate behavior to support person in containing impulses
- Encourage use of physical exercise to relieve physical tension
- Facilitate recognition of warning signs of increasing tension
- Facilitate identification of choices
- Clarify the connection between behavior and consequences
- Positive feedback and reinforcement.

2. *Eliminate Danger to Self*

- Assess:
  - Mental status
  - History of self-destructive behaviors
  - Recent crisis, loss
  - Substance abuse
  - Plan
  - Means
  - Quality of support system

- Provide safe environment, and intervene to stop self-destructive behaviors (remove dangerous objects, monitor, etc.; the patient may require hospitalization)
- Facilitate identification of environmental or emotional triggers associated with self-destructive impulse
- Facilitate patient to identify areas of desired change
- Develop a plan for behavior modification to reach goals of desired behavior change
- Encourage appropriate venting of thoughts and feelings
- Avoid focus and reinforcement of negative behaviors
- Focus on efforts and accomplishments
- Positive feedback and reinforcement.

3. *Improve Coping Skills*

- Increase awareness and insight associated with behaviors
- Facilitate clarification of rules, values—right and wrong
- Encourage the patient to take responsibility
- Confront denial to take responsibility
- Facilitate development of understanding the relationship of behaviors to consequences
- Explore and clarify the patient's desire and motivation to become a productive member of society
- Clarify for/with patient socially acceptable behaviors versus non-socially acceptable behaviors (and associated consequences)
- Facilitate increased sensitivity to others (increased awareness and social intelligence)
- Facilitate increased awareness for how others experience the patient and how they interpret the behavior/responses of others
- Clarify that it is not the patient, but rather their behavior which is not acceptable
- Facilitate increasing ability to delay gratification
- Role-model and practice acceptable behaviors with the patient over a range of situations
- Use positive feedback and reinforcement for efforts and accomplishments.

4. *Improve Stress Management Skills*	• Teach relaxation techniques: – Progressive muscle relaxation – Visual imagery/meditation • Self-care (exercise, nutrition, use of resources) • Appropriate use of grounding strategies.
5. *Improve Self-Esteem*	• Focus on strengths and accomplishments • Avoid focus on past failures other than as a source of information helpful to learning new behaviors • Identify areas of desired change and objectives to meet those goals • Encourage independent effort and accepting responsibility • Teach assertive communication and appropriate setting of limits and boundaries • Positive feedback and reinforcement for efforts and accomplishments.
6. *Relapse Prevention*	• Self-monitoring • Reframe regression issues as an opportunity for taking responsibility to follow the patient's program for behavioral change • Journal writing to monitor progress and any other changes in behavior • Participation in community groups or utilization of other supportive resources which reinforce goals.

ASSERTIVENESS IN COMMUNICATION

The issues to be addressed in therapy to encourage assertiveness in communication include:

• Ineffective communication style
• Lack of awareness of verbal and non-verbal aspects of effective communication
• Lack of assertiveness
• Avoidance of communicating difficult feelings
• Ineffective listening skills.

The goals associated with therapy for assertiveness in communication include the following:

1. *Identify Communication Style (Johnson, 2004)*	There are four types of communications styles: 1. Passive: Always giving into what others want, do not honestly express their own thoughts and feelings for fear of how others will respond, afraid to say no, and discounting own wants and needs.

2. Passive–aggressive: Tell people what they want to hear in an effort to avoid conflict, however, lack of follow through results in the other person becoming frustrated

3. Manipulative: Attempt to get wants/needs met by making others feel guilty, tends to take on the victim or martyr role to get others to take responsibility for their wants and needs.

4. Assertive: Honest, direct and appropriate expression of thoughts and feelings, self-responsibility, respect for others, effective listener and problem solver.

- Identify why the particular style of communication has been used:
  - How have they benefited from their communication style?
  - How has it negatively impacted their life/relationships?
  - Role-modeled/learned/reinforced by family system (what is normal to them may not be the norm in effectively communicating to others)?

- Identify the benefits of changing the style of communication.

2. *Increased Awareness of Verbal and Non-Verbal Communication*	• Educate regarding the influence of non-verbal communication factors • Educate regarding non-verbal assertive behavior (eye contact, posture, personal space, remaining focused on the issue and avoiding emotionality) • Educate regarding social and emotional intelligence, i.e. what observations are validation of a message interpreted as intended.
3. *Facilitate Development of Assertive Communication*	• Increased recognition and appropriate expression of personal rights/boundaries • Encourage an honest look at themselves and their responses: – Do they have difficulty accepting constructive criticism? – Do they find themselves saying "yes" to requests that they should say "no" to just to avoid disappointing others? – Do they have difficulty voicing a difference of opinion with others? – Do they feel attacked when someone has a different opinion from theirs? • Increase awareness of own thoughts, feelings, wants and needs • Facilitate clarification of expectations, limits, and boundaries • Role-play and practice assertive communication and behaviors.
4. *Communication of Difficult Feelings*	• Educate how to talk to someone about difficult feelings (reporting facts, using "I" statements, and compromise • Educate regarding conflict resolution, compromise and the importance of not making assumptions about what the other person is thinking or feeling • Managing the physical tension associated with emotional stress • Educate regarding the consequences of ignoring or neglecting difficult emotions, or dealing with them in a non-productive manner (things that pile up over time show up as headaches, fatigue, depression, anxiety, panic attacks, anger, etc.).

5. *Improved Listening Skills*	• Assertive listening (desire to understand the point of view of another, to accurately understand what they are saying and to let another know that they have been heard)
	• Listening for accuracy (be relaxed, ask appropriate questions and reflect in summary their understanding of what has been heard).

PTSD AND SUBSTANCE USE

Substance abuse intervention is addressed because of the significant prevalence of comorbidity with PTSD. Traditional substance use programs often defer treatment of trauma-related issues and PTSD programs often do not accept patients with active substance use disorders. As a result, the needs of patients with comorbid PTSD and substance use disorders may not be met. Trauma, PTSD, and substance use disorders commonly occur. This relationship is a complex one, but researchers continue to strive toward new and promising treatments.

Integrated PTSD treatment and substance use treatment have been found to be the most useful:

Back et al. (2006) state that while consensus is lacking regarding the best treatment practice for the comorbidity of substance use disorders and PTSD, "integrated psychosocial treatments have shown empirically supported evidence in reducing symptoms for this dual diagnosis."

Issues to be addressed when treating substance abuse and/or dependence with PTSD include:

- Thorough assessment and appropriate referrals
- Encourage abstinence
- Denial
- Cognitive distortions
- Lack of behavioral self-control
- Lack of refusal skills
- Ineffective social skills
- Ineffective communication skills
- Ineffective coping skills
- Ineffective problem-solving skills
- Low self-esteem
- Support and educate family.

The goals associated with therapy for substance abuse include the following:

1. *Thorough Assessment for Referral and Treatment*	• Evaluate substance use (how much, how often, substances of choice, family history, patterns of use, prior treatment, level of impairment in major life areas, inability to control use, etc.). As substance abuse history is presented it is extremely important to understand
	• Refer for general physical examination and consultation with primary care physician. Refer for specific assessment of physiological impairment if warranted by history

- Referrals (assuming detox is not an issue or is completed):
  - If unable to remain in recovery, refer to residential program
  - Outpatient chemical dependency program
  - 12-step meetings or other supportive groups and programs
- Evaluate cognitive effects:
  - Establish baseline assessment of fund of knowledge, take into consideration level of education and level of development
  - Identify strengths and weaknesses
- Adequate nutrition:
  - Educate regarding balanced nutrition
  - Facilitate identification of prior eating patterns
  - Develop and establish eating three balanced meals a day.

2. *Abstinence*

- Individual has made a commitment to abstain from substance use
- Individual is participating in an outpatient program
- Individual has worked with therapist to develop own program for abstinence and recovery.

3. *Break Through Denial (Motivate)*

- Convey an attitude that is not rejecting or judgmental
- Confront denial with reality of use and education to correct misconceptions
- Identify the relationship between substance use and personal problems
- Do not accept or ignore the use of other defense mechanisms to avoid reality
- Encourage person to take responsibility for choices and associated consequences
- Provide positive feedback and reinforcement for insight and taking responsibility.

4. *Rational Thinking*

- Educate regarding positive self-talk to challenge negative self-statement and negative self-fulfilling prophecy
- Identify differences in statements prefaced as "can," "can't," "will," "won't"
- Seek clarification "Does my style of thinking help me or hinder me?"
- Challenge beliefs with factual information
- Accurately reflect reality to the patient.

5. *Improved Self-Control*

- Facilitate individual's analysis of substance use patterns and monitoring:
  - Identify situations, people, emotions, and beliefs associated with substance use
  - Monitor currently or through recollection of past behaviors
  - Facilitate preparation for anticipated difficult situations and planning strategies either to avoid or cope with these situations (strategies should be both cognitive and behavioral)
  - Encourage active participation in group affiliation and other self-care behaviors
- Facilitate development of assertive communication

- Offer relaxation training with positive self-statements attached to reinforce realistic positive internal dialogue
- Increase repertoire of coping skills through modeling, rehearsal, and homework assignments.

6. *Develop Refusal Skills*

- Goal is to develop the skills needed to refuse substances, refuse invitations to participate in activities, or be in the company of others associated with substance abuse
- Specific tasks to develop to strengthen refusal skills:
  - Asking for help
  - Honestly expressing thoughts and feelings
  - Confronting and dealing with fear(s)
  - Standing up for their rights/assertiveness
  - How to deal with being left out
  - How to deal with group pressure and persuasion.

7. *Improved Social Skills*

- Teach social skills through role-modeling, rehearsal, and role-playing
- Teach effective communication:
  - Non-verbal communication such as positioning, eye contact, and personal space
  - Verbal communication, including initiating conversation, reflecting, giving and accepting compliments, using "I" statements, dealing with criticism and teasing, and assertive communication
- Develop and utilize social supports
- Forming close and intimate relationships:
  - Steps of getting to know someone
  - Disclosure (how much/what/how soon)
  - Setting limits and boundaries
  - How to be close to someone and not lose focus on their goals
  - Establish trusting relationship reciprocating respect by keeping appointments, being honest, etc. Help person to clarify the impact substance abuse/dependence has had on their significant relationships, financial implications, work, physical health, and social supports/interactions or peer reference group. Once these issues are identified, facilitate insight, understanding, and the development of choices in dealing with these various situations.

8. *Improved Communication*

- Assertive communication. Educate using comparisons of assertive communication to passive and aggressive. Use vignettes and role-play
- Facilitate awareness for inappropriate behaviors and verbal expressions as ineffective attempts to communicate
- Identify feelings behind inappropriate behavioral and emotional expressions and facilitate problem-solving
- Use "I" statements to avoid blaming and manipulation
- Use vignettes, role-modeling, rehearsal, and role-playing for developing communication skills.

9. *Improved Coping*	• Facilitate identification of feelings
	• Encourage appropriate ventilation of feelings
	• Set limits on manipulative behavior (be consistent)
	• Facilitate development of appropriate and acceptable social behaviors
	• Educate person regarding the effects of substance use on social, psychological, and physiological functioning
	• Explore alternatives for dealing with stressful situations. Problem-solve appropriate responses instead of substance use
	• Facilitate the development of a self-care plan that outlines resources, skills to use in various situations, daily structure, red flags to regression, and so on
	• Encourage person to take responsibility for choices and associated consequences
	• Positive feedback for independent and effective problem-solving.
10. *Improved Problem-Solving*	• Teach problem-solving skills
	• Develop some sample problems and give homework to practice new skills on
	• Identify secondary gains that inhibit progress toward change.
11. *Improved Self-Esteem*	• Be accepting and respectful of person
	• Identify strengths
	• Encourage a focus on strengths and accomplishments
	• Facilitate identification of past failures and reframe with a perspective on how the person can benefit and learn from previous experiences
	• Identify desired areas of change and facilitate problem-solving the necessary objectives to meet the defined goals
	• Facilitate self-monitoring of efforts toward desired goals
	• Encourage and positively reinforce appropriate independent functioning
	• Facilitate development of assertive communication
	• Facilitate clarification of boundaries and appropriate limit-setting in relationships.
12. *Improved Family Interaction*	• Evaluate how family has been affected by their behavior (fear, isolation, shame, economic consequences, guilt, feeling responsible for the behavior of others)
	• Explore how family may help sustain or reinforce this dysfunctional behavior
	• Teach communication skills
	• Refer family members to appropriate 12-step groups, other community resources or therapy. Decrease isolation
	• Educate regarding appropriate boundaries.

PERSONALITY DISORDER

Because there is extensive information available elsewhere, a full breakdown of goals and objectives for personality disorders has not been outlined (the specific focus being border-line personality disorder) in this section. The recommended resources are Dialectical Behavior Therapy (Linehan, 1993) and *The Therapist's Guide to Clinical Intervention* (Johnson, 2004). There are numerous books on object relations and psychodynamic formulation of personality disorders which constitute a clinical understanding of the interpersonal and intrapersonal underpinnings of associated internal experience. Motivational interviewing (Rollnick et al., 1992) offers an opportunity for validation and engagement in the therapeutic process.

The treatment of motivated personality disordered patients needs to be consistent, respectful, supportive with clear boundaries, and facilitating of the development of improved management skills, including development of trust in the therapeutic relationship; awareness of excessive emotional and behavioral reactivity; appropriate expression of intense emotional experience; improved coping and management of self-defeating and self-destructive behaviors; rational self-talk; development of appropriate social support; and self-monitoring. An additional treatment intervention that is beneficial with this population is stress inoculation, through which they are prepared to deal with difficult circumstances and experience feelings of safety and security.

EATING DISORDERS

Because there is extensive information available elsewhere a full breakdown for the goals and objectives for the treatment of eating disorders has not been broken down in this section. Useful sources on cognitive behavioral therapy for eating disorders are provided by Fairburn et al. (1993, 2003). Nevertheless, eating disorders need to be a diagnostic consideration in every assessment. Sometimes they develop following the experience of a traumatic event. A central premise of eating disorders is the element of striving to feel in control. However, an eating disorder may predate the trauma event or develop years later.

Just as with other compulsions, eating disorders present a challenge to trauma treatment. When there is comorbidity of PTSD and eating disorders there are numerous issues for the therapist to consider:

- Health issues requiring assessment by their physician. Discuss the specific concerns with their physician (Johnson, 2004)
- Develop a knowledgeable treatment team for individual, group and family therapy components in addition to the physician
- Avoid colluding with the patient in manipulative efforts to avoid trauma work
- Utilize CBT techniques in eating disorders management (Fairburn et al., 1993, 2003)
- Education regarding trading compulsions. It is not uncommon to find that when highly compulsive behavioral patterns are altered, the individual begins to practice another compulsion. For example, the patient may demonstrate significant improvement in eating disorder behaviors but begins to abuse substances.

RECONNECTION

This is the last stage of treatment, focusing on redefining "self" in the context of the trauma/abuse experience. Another way of conceptualizing reconnection is that it is a consolidation of skills that have been learned and generalized to daily living. A central aspect of functioning is relational interaction, connection, and bonding or intimacy. It can be visualized as a concentric experience initiated with oneself in time and place leading to a continued life journey of personal growth. The concentric rings of reconnection are as follows:

1. *Body*
   - Centering
   - Positive body image
     – Able to identify positive characteristics of the self
     – Pro-health behaviors.

2. *Cognition*
   - Victim thinking
     – Has been challenged
     – Internal dialogue is objective and positive
   - Rewritten narrative:
     – Integration of the trauma/abuse experience into a new narrative of the self and the self in the world which includes commensurate self-talk (matching internal dialogue)
     – Developing an understanding of the trauma experience which integrates with hopeful life plans
     – Connection with others with a new understanding of the trauma experience
     – Lack of control has evolved into empowerment.

3. *Behavior*
   - Self-help and self-development
     – Embraces personal growth and recognizes that seeking of self-knowledge is a life journey to be appreciated.

4. *Emotion*
   - Memorial. Closure of the past as the information from the experience empowers the individual to a level of "letting go" and clearly separating the past and choosing to be in the present
     – No longer feels diminished by trauma
     – The consequences of traumatic exposure becomes defined as a chapter in their life. In other words, it is a part of them, it does not define them.

5. *Relationships*
   - Memorial to experiences of pain and loss associated with the trauma/abuse experience that is not a part of the present experience of new relationships embodied by self-esteem, assertiveness, and appropriate boundaries
   - Take responsibility for honest and effective communication
   - Develop a sense of humor:
     – Know what makes them laugh and how they can make others laugh
     – Learn to be lighthearted and laugh at themselves. Laugh and smile often—it is healthy and healing
     – Schedule fun time/play time
     – Celebrate successes.

| 6. Consolidation | Consolidation of all that has been learned and the growth that has resulted from integration of all the survived life experiences. |

7. *Finding Meaning*

- What are ways in which the experience(s) has changed the patient?
- What have they learned about their strengths?
- What have others possibly learned from them?
- How have they learned to take care of themselves as a result of experiencing trauma?
- What is their personal vision?
  - What do they want to do? "Do it!"
  - Seek solutions that benefit all of those involved
  - Use creative cooperation
  - Commit to a lifetime of self-improvement, self-responsibility, self-knowledge, and striving for balance
- How will they continue to heal:
  - Encourage becoming increasingly aware of the choices they make and identifying the outcome, being guided by their moral compass
  - Choose to find meaning in all endeavors, appreciating the order of all living things on earth
  - Seek to understand and to be understood, using patience, persistence, and courage
- Carefully prioritize what is important and must be taken care of
- Manage pain in constructive ways:
  - Take the time to see the beauty all around
  - Connect with nature
  - Be artistic/creative
- Contribute to a better outcome with wholesome work and giving
- Help the patient to develop an understanding of what causes resistance and how to change it. What stands in the way of change?
- Remind the patient that they have survived all that they have experienced and that they are responsible to do something positive with it
- Encourage the patient to remain aware and responsible for their own thoughts and feelings
- If they do not like the outcome of a situation choose to be creative and resourceful in dealing with it
- Commit to a lifetime of personal growth.

PHARMACOLOGICAL INTERVENTIONS

The American Psychiatric Association (2004) offers a quick reference guide for the pharmacologic treatment of acute stress disorder (ASD) and PTSD.

SPECIFIC TREATMENT STRATEGIES DECISION TREE

- No specific pharmacologic interventions can be recommended as efficacious in preventing the development of ASD or PTSD in at-risk individuals
- For ASD, selective serotonin reuptake inhibitors (SSRIs)/serotonin–norepinephrine reuptake inhibitors (SNRIs) and other antidepressants represent reasonable clinical interventions
- SSRIs/SNRIs are recommended as first-line medication treatment for PTSD because they:
  - Ameliorate all three PTSD clusters (i.e. re-experiencing, avoidance/numbing, and hyperarousal)
  - Are effective treatments for psychiatric disorders that are frequently comorbid with PTSD (e.g. depression, panic disorder, social phobia, and obsessive compulsive disorder).
  - May reduce clinical symptoms (such as suicidal, impulsive, and aggressive behaviors) that often complicate management of PTSD
  - Have relatively few side-effects
- Tricyclic antidepressants and monoamine oxidase inhibitors may also be beneficial. Minimal evidence is available to recommend the use of other antidepressants (e.g. venlafaxine, mirtazapine, bupropion)
- Benzodiazepine may be useful in reducing anxiety, but may increase depression:
  - Its efficacy in preventing PTSD or treating the core symptoms of PTSD has been neither established nor adequately evaluated
  - Concerns about their addictive potential in individuals with comorbid substance use disorders may prompt additional caution regarding the use of benzodiazepines
  - Worsening of symptoms with benzodiazepine discontinuation has been reported
- Anticonvulsant medications (e.g. divalproex, carbamazepine, topiramate, lamotrigine) may have benefit for treating symptoms related to re-experiencing the trauma
- Second-generation antipsychotic medications (e.g. olanzapine, quetiapine, risperidone) may be helpful in individual patients as well as for patients with comorbid psychotic disorders or when first-line approaches have been ineffective in controlling symptoms
- Alpha$_2$-adrenergic agonists and beta-adrenergic blockers may also be helpful in treating specific symptom clusters in individual patients.

Compliance

Improve medication compliance to treatment by emphasizing to the patient:

- When and how often to take medication
- The expected time interval before beneficial effects of treatment may be noticed
- The necessity to take medication even after feeling better
- The need to consult with the physician before tapering or discontinuing medication, to avoid the possibility of symptom rebound or relapse

- Steps to take if problems or questions arise
- Consult with prescribing physician
- Reinforce directions and monitor side-effects/compliance.

ADDITIONAL TREATMENT ISSUES ASSOCIATED WITH COMPLEX PTSD

According to Brierre (1997) many trauma survivors experience impairment in attachment, affect regulation, cognition, memory, self-reference, and meaning. The standard of treatment for complex PTSD is a three-phase process (Janet, 1973; Herman, 1992; Brierre, 1997; Brown et al., 1998; Ford and Kidd, 1998). Throughout the course of treatment, as with PTSD, therapy is carefully paced to the tolerance of the patient. The core goals that have been identified are (re)integration of dissociated personality, re-establishing safe and secure attachments, developing self-management skills, and the development of a coherent self-narrative. In addition, with a comprehensive individualized treatment plan there is careful multiaxial diagnostic consideration. Friedman (2000) highlights that pharmacotherapy is an important treatment to facilitate management of severe symptoms such as depression, anxiety, anger, impulsivity, and insomnia. While there are three stages outlined, some interventions initiated in stage one continue throughout all stages.

STAGE 1: STABILIZATION AND SAFETY

- Development of a therapeutic alliance
- Management or elimination of:
  - Self-destructive behaviors
  - Substance abuse
  - Impulse dysregulation

- Psycho-education/skill building:
  - To achieve internal safety, translating to a decrease in fearful thoughts, feelings, dissociative episodes, and general distress
  - Enhancing relationships
  - Improving affect regulation
  - Improving distress tolerance
  - Improving daily living skills

- Resolution of traumatic memory (a paced and modulated treatment approach is critical):
  - Resolution of intense and insecure attachments to neglectful/abusive relationships
  - Development of a coherent narrative of the trauma that does not retraumatize or exacerbate the experience

- Personality (re)integration and rehabilitation:
  - Functionality is reinforced to facilitate adaptation and integration of complex experiences

- Close monitoring for capacity to tolerate change and establish or resume normal daily challenges
- Enhancement capacity for emotional, physical, interpersonal autonomy, intimacy and sexual functioning and experience.

SPECIAL CONSIDERATIONS

MILITARY PERSONNEL

The wars in Afghanistan and Iraq have been the most sustained combat operations since the Vietnam War and with this frequency and intensity of exposure to combat comes an increased risk of PTSD (King et al., 1999; Schnurr et al., 2003; Bryant, 2004; Friedman, 2004; Hoge et al., 2004; Foa et al., 2009; National Association of Social Workers, 2009). However, combat as such is not the only source of danger, conflict, and severe stress in militarized zones. There is also:

- Guerilla warfare and terrorist actions such as roadside bombings
- Consequences associated with the lack of clarity regarding the ambiguity of civilians (friend/foe)
- Concerns about causing collateral damage to civilians in urban environments
- Threatening situations in which soldiers are not able/allowed to respond aggressively because of constrained rules of engagement.

The combined factors result in excess stress hormones which are known to have significant negative consequences on health maintenance, restoration/recovery, and coping capacity. There is a lot of research on this topic and below is a brief cross-section of articles which will, it is hoped, encourage the reader to further their knowledge regarding PTSD and military personnel.

Dohrenwend et al.
(2008)

- Elevated prevalence of chronic PTSD reported for Black and Hispanic Vietnam veterans. There is no comprehensive explanation for this information. However, part of the cultural experience for service during that time frame may be related.

Turner et al. (2007)
- Data from the National Vietnam Veteran Readjustment Study (NVVRS) shows that the prevalence of current PTSD in female Vietnam Theater veterans is half that of their male counterparts
- The findings suggest that high male levels of PTSD are associated with men who served under conditions giving a high probability of severity in war-zone exposure
- When pre-war demographic differences are controlled, male veterans who experienced low-exposure circumstances reveal a rate of PTSD much lower than that of female veterans.

Dohrenwend et al. (2004)

- When Vietnam veterans were sampled nationwide, it was revealed that 70.9% reported that the impact of the war on their current lives was mainly positive

- The results support the hypothesis that mainly positive appraisals are affirmations of successful wartime and post-war adaptations

- Public opinion, material support, and emotional support have been shown to have an impact on deployment sacrifices and exposure to trauma.

Bryant (2004)

- Approximately 70% of those who survive exposure to trauma who develop ASD go on to develop chronic PTSD.

The National Association of Social Workers (NASW, 2009) reported research which found that 16% of those returning from Iraq suffered from mental health problems, most notably PTSD. Lt. General Kevin Kiley (Army Surgeon General) reported that in 2007, of 1000 army soldiers surveyed 3–4 months following their return from Iraq, 30% had developed stress-related problems (Army Wellbeing, 2007). The concern for delayed onset of PTSD complicates the potential for accurate diagnosis at the time of discharge. In addition, factors such as embarrassment and distrust likely play a role in the disclosure (or lack of disclosure) of symptoms that would result in diagnosis and treatment.

When working with military personnel there are complicating diverse aspects of PTSD. For example, there are various comorbidities such as physical disfigurement, alcoholism/drug abuse, brain injury, and family stress. The last factor highlights the importance of promoting protective factors and minimizing negative family impact.

COMBAT-RELATED PTSD FACTSHEET

Prevalence

- Because the Department of Defense and the Veterans Health Administration, Department of Veterans Affairs do not adequately diagnose or effectively track PTSD in veterans, there is a lack of accurate statistics on the prevalence of PTSD in veterans. However, current studies estimate that the prevalence of PTSD among returning veterans ranges from 15 to 50%

- Because it can take months or even years for PTSD to manifest, many troops are subject to multiple deployments to Afghanistan and Iraq. Rates of PTSD continue to rise.

Consequences

- PTSD varies significantly in its severity. It sometimes can lead to addiction, antisocial behavior, and suicide. Troops who have served in Afghanistan and Iraq have killed themselves at much higher percentages than their counterparts who have served in any other war

- Numerous factors impact the degree of reaction to a traumatic experience: for example, the death and devastation witnessed, the extent to which responsibility is felt for not preventing the event, age, gender, and race.

- Early treatment is likely to be most effective. It may also deter a decline into addiction and other destructive behavior

- Types of treatment include individual psychotherapy, CBT, EMDR, group therapy, and medication.

FIRST RESPONDERS (LAW ENFORCEMENT, FIREFIGHTERS, ETC.)

First responders, in particular law enforcement officers (LEOs), can be an insular group, reluctant to be interpreted as being weak if they seek professional help. Again, LEOs tend to work alone, with a partner, or as part of a tactical team (who depend on their strength and resilience). This in comparison to firefighters who are trained as a team. Another major factor for LEOs is the fear that any demonstration of having a problem may result in a loss of their gun and badge or be used against them later should their fitness for duty be questioned.

The work and work environment of LEOs is unique. Officers work under the intense scrutiny of the community and their agencies, which are often punitive oriented, authoritarian environments. LEOs, because of their unusual rights (to carry weapons and use them), are held to a higher standard of community comportment. These issues add to their stress when they experience a critical incident and need support. What an officer needs most following an incident is a supportive response from command staff, but what they are likely to experience is the barrage of necessary questions about what has happened and why. This immediately puts such individuals in a defensive posture. Part of this scenario includes being referred to and assessed by a psychologist or psychiatrist for a fitness for duty evaluation, followed by a report forwarded to their agency regarding their current disposition (i.e. leave of absence/workers comp or release to return to work).

Under these circumstances officers feel increasingly vulnerable, with the most significant decisions about their well-being and work status being out of their hands. With this experience of acute stress and lack of control they are in need of genuine concern, advocacy, honesty, and confidentiality, along with a therapist's willingness to listen and understand their experience. If the therapist is not known to the officer, he or she needs to articulate their understanding of the structure of law enforcement agencies (paramilitary) and the toll that shift work and administrative challenges present for officers. Overall, in this circumstance, they are not seeking the confidence of another LEO, they are looking for a safe environment which offers validation and the development of a trusted relationship to problem-solve and alleviate stress.

Feedback that has been beneficial in my work with officers is echoed by the work experience reported by Blau (1994), and applies to all of those considered to be part of the first responder family:

- The first meeting between a LEO and therapist needs to result in establishing a safe and comfortable atmosphere by the therapist:
  - Expressing a positive endorsement of the officer's choice to seek help and develop a resource
  - Outlining a clear definition of the therapist's responsibilities, including the limits of confidentialty/privilege
  - Encouraging the officer to express any concerns they may have.

- The approach should be goal-directed and solution-focused, concentrating on:
  - Creating a safe environment (sanctuary)
  - Focusing on areas/issues of concern to the officer
  - Specifying desired outcomes

- Reviewing assets/strengths
- Reviewing self-efficacy
- Setting appointments for review, reassurance, and further implementation, which also facilitates positive self-monitoring efforts.

- Blau (1994) outlines effective individual strategies:
  - Active listening (good eye contact, appropriate body language, genuine interest (without inappropriate comments or interruptions)
  - Being there with empathy (an attitude that conveys availability, concern, and awareness of the emotional turmoil experienced by an officer during times of stress and trauma. It is beneficial to predict, when possible, the normal course of their experience when focusing on such issues
  - Reassurance (in acutely stressful circumstances "realistic reassurance" regarding resolution/course of routine matters, deferring responsibility to others when warranted, and that the officer has administrative/command support)
  - Supportive counseling (effective listening, restatement of content, clarification of feelings, reassurance, useful community referral, and networking with liaison agencies when necessary)
  - Interpretive counseling (to be used when the officer's emotional reaction is much greater that seemingly warranted by the critical incident. In some cases, this strategy can facilitate the exploration of underlying emotional issues and ongoing psychotherapy).

In addition, the appropriate use of humor may be of particular value with this population, and actually facilitate a letting down of their guardedness toward seeking help and developing a therapeutic relationship. "Gallows humor" is actually a method of venting in difficult circumstances—allowing for compartmentalization or a measure of emotional distance which aids in coping and resilience. The positive consequence may be resulting venting of anger, resentment, sadness, loss frustration, etc.

SEVERE MOTOR VEHICLE ACCIDENT

Regardless of the resource examined, the following information is consistent: PTSD among car-accident survivors is underdiagnosed across the United States. This is possibly associated with minimizing the emotional and psychological consequences as a result of cultural desensitization (communities are exposed to bad things happening on a regular basis). Risk factors for PTSD following a motor vehicle accident have been analyzed by Butler et al. (1999). They include:

- Severe accident
- Fatalities or severe injury among those involved
- Intrusive memory immediately following the event (flashback)
- Subsequent difficulty driving or traveling in vehicles
- History of prior traumatic experiences
- History of underlying psychiatric disorder
- Ongoing litigation.

J Gayle Beck at the University of Buffalo was funded by the National Institute for Mental Health to research the development of a group therapy program for survivors of car accidents. She states that survivors of severe motor vehicle accidents generally demonstrate three common symptoms:

1. Re-experiencing of their trauma via replay of thoughts throughout the day and recurring dreams
2. Avoidance behaviors, such as refusing to drive or refusing to acknowledge distressful feelings caused by the accident
3. Constant state of hyperarousal, continuously vigilant for potential trauma.

Beck's group therapy meets once a week for 2 hours. Her research trial groups lasted for a period of 14 weeks. Coping skills to manage PTSD symptoms include avoidance, anger, depression, and anxiety. While the benefit of group therapy is recognized by therapists, it is not available for many issues, currently including survivors of severe motor vehicle accidents. However, the identified issues remain the core symptoms to be targeted for improved coping:

- Re-experiencing
- Avoidance
- Hyperarousal
- Negative mood states, such as:
  - Anxiety
  - Depression
  - Anger.

According to Butler et al. (1999) screening for PTSD following a motor vehicle accident should be standard practice so that appropriate treatment can be initiated in an effort to prevent the occurrence of symptoms. The initial severity of PTSD symptoms is generally a central predictor of both short-term and long-term remission. However, there are also instances where the onset of a full PTSD syndrome can be delayed for some period of time. Additional complicating factors which need to be considered are litigation and pain due to accident-associated injuries and ongoing medical treatment.

Symptom persistence associated with litigation is particularly problematic because severely injured patients may be difficult to separate (from a symptom severity perspective) from "those inclined to portray themselves as symptomatic." However, it is not difficult to understand the exacerbating impact to symptoms associated with chronic physical impairment/pain and financial distress.

Most commonly, survivors present with physical symptoms in an appointment with their primary care physician following a motor vehicle accident. This means that the focus of treatment is medical, and quite often assessment of the patient for emotional symptoms of trauma is not even considered. Butler et al. (1999) suggest that any indication of head trauma requires thorough evaluation because symptoms of head injury may be exactly the same as or can be similar to PTSD symptoms and may potentially mask symptoms of PTSD. They also recommend that primary care physicians ask the following questions, given that a positive response to these questions indicates the possibility that acute stress disorder or PTSD is present:

- When you realized the accident was going to happen, what did you think was going to happen to you? (variation: At any time did you think you were going to die?)
- Do you have flashbacks or nightmares about the accident?
- Have you had any difficulty with driving or traveling in vehicles since the accident?

An additional question which potentially complicates the case with the need for extensive and detailed documentation and possible intrusions of confidentiality is:

- Do you anticipate contacting an attorney or do you intend to pursue litigation?

Butler et al. (1999) also recommended that physicians should maintain increased awareness of patients who are suggestible, have a history of somatization, or are pursuing litigation when it comes to symptom review because it can exacerbate or reinforce a specific constellation of symptoms.

Suitable medications were also discussed by Butler et al. (1999) with the following array of benefits:

- To help prevent later chronicity
- To improve symptoms of anxiety and avoidance
- To break the cycle of memories and reactions.

REFERENCES AND FURTHER READING

American Psychiatric Association (2004) *Treating Patients with ASD and PTSD: A quick reference guide for pharmacologic treatment.* Accessed from: http://www.trauma-pages.com/s/tx_guides.php

Andersson AL, Bunketorp O, Allebeck P (1997) High rates of psychosocial complications after road traffic injuries. *Injury* 28: 539–543.

Army Wellbeing (2007) Walter Reed Chief Relieved of Command. Accessed February 1, 2009 from [URL].

Back SE, Waldrop AE, Brady KT, Hein D (2006) Evidenced based time-limited treatment of co-occurring substance use disorders and civilian related post-traumatic stress disorder. *Brief Treatment and Crisis Intervention* 6: 283–294.

Bandura A (1982) Self-efficacy mechanism in human agency. *Am Psychol* 37: 122–147.

Baranowsky AB, Gentry JE (2002) *Resiliency and Recovery: Trauma Survivor Group*, 2nd edn. Toronto, Canada: Traumatology Institute.

Baranowsky AB, Gentry JE, Schultz FF (2004) *Trauma Practice: Tools for Stabilization and Recovery*, 2nd edn. Toronto Canada: Traumatology Institute.

Beasley KR (1999) Anger management: Immediate intervention by counselor coach. *Professional School Counseling* 3: 81–90.

Becker MA, Noether CD, Larson MJ et al. (2004) Characteristics of women engaged in treatment for trauma and co-occurring disorders: Findings from a national multisite study. *J Community Psychol* 33: 429–433.

Blanchard EB, Hickling EJ (eds) (1997) *After the Crash: Assessment and Treatment of Motor Vehicle Accident Survivors.* Washington, DC: American Psychological Association, 1997.

Blau TH (1994) *Psychological Services for Law Enforcement.* New York: Wiley.

Bolton E, Litz BT, Britt T, Adler A, Roemer L (2001) Reports of exposure to potentially traumatic events and PTSD in troops poised for deployment. *J Trauma Stress* 14: 249–256.

Bremner JD, Brett E (1997) Trauma related dissociative states and long term psychopathology in posttraumatic stress disorder. *J Trauma Stress* 10: 37–49.

Brierre J (1997) Treating adults severely abused as children: the self-trauma model. In: *Child Abuse: New Directions in Prevention and Treatment Across the Lifespan* (Wolfe D, McMahon R, Peters R, eds). Thousand Oaks, CA: Sage, pp. 177–204.

Brown D, Scheflin A, Hammond D (1998) *Memory, Trauma Treatment, and the Law.* New York: Norton.

Bryant RA (2000) Cognitive-behavior therapy of violence-related posttraumatic stress disorder. *Aggression Violent Behav* 5: 79–97.

Bryant RA (2004) Acute stress disorder: Course, epidemiology, assessment, and treatment. In: *Early Intervention for Traumatic Loss* (Litz B, ed.). New York: Guilford Press, pp. 15–25.

Bryant RA, Moulds ML, Guthrie RM et al. (2005) The additive benefit of hypnosis and cognitive-behavioral therapy in treating acute stress disorder. *J Consult Clin Psychol* 73: 334–340.

Buckley TC, Blanchard EB, Hickling EJ (1996) A prospective examination of delayed onset PTSD secondary to motor vehicle accidents. *J Abnorm Psychol* 105: 617–625.

Butler DJ, Moffic S, Turkal NW (1999) Post-traumatic stress reactions following motor vehicle accidents. *Am Fam Physician* 60: 524–531.

Chard KM (2005) An evaluation of cognitive processing therapy for the treatment of post-traumatic stress disorder related to childhood sexual abuse. *J Consult Clin Psychol* 73: 965–971.

Christopher FB, Buckley TC, Cusack KJ et al. (2004) Cognitive–behavioral treatment for PTSD among people with severe mental illness. A proposed treatment model. *J Psychiatr Pract* 10: 26–38.

Chu JA (1998) *Rebuilding Shattered Lives: the responsible treatment of complex post-traumatic and dissociative disorders*. New York: Wiley.

Creamer M, Morris P, Biddle D, Elliot P (1999) Treatment outcome in Australian veterans with combat-related posttraumatic stress disorder: A cause for cautious optimism?. *J Trauma Stress* 12: 545–558.

Dahlen ER, Deffenbacher JL (2001) Anger management. In: *Empirically Supported Cognitive Therapies. Current and future applications* (Lyddon WJ, Jone JV, eds). New York: Springer Publishing Company, pp. 163–181.

Dohrenwend BP, Neria Y, Tirner JB et al. (2004) Positive tertiary appraisal of posttraumatic stress disorder in the U.S. male veterans of the war in Vietnam: The roles of positive affirmation, positive reformulation, and defensive denial. *J Consult Clin Psychol* 72: 417–433.

Dohrenwend BP, Turner JB, Turse NA, Lewis-Fernandez R, Yager TJ (2008) War-related stress disorder in black, Hispanic, and majority white veterans: The roles of exposure and vulnerability. *J Trauma Stress* 21: 133–141.

Fairburn CG, Marcus MD, Wilson GT (1993) *Cognitive-Behavioral Therapy for Binge Eating and Bulimia Nervosa: A comprehensive treatment manual*. New York: Guilford Press.

Fairburn CG, Cooper Z, Shafran R (2003) Cognitive behaviour therapy for eating disorder: A "transdiagnostic" theory and treatment. *Behav Res Ther* 41: 509–528.

Falsetti SA, Resnick HS (1997) Frequency and severity of panic attack symptoms in a treatment seeking sample of trauma victims. *J Trauma Stress* 10: 683–689.

Figley CR (ed.) (2002) *Treating Compassion Fatigue*. New York: Brunner-Routledge.

Figley CR, Kleber RJ (1995) Beyond the "victim": Secondary traumatic stress. In: *Beyond Trauma: Cultural and Societal Dynamics* (Kleber RJ, Figley CR, eds). New York: Plenum, pp. 75–98.

Figley CR, Bride BE, Mazza N (eds) (1997) *Death and Trauma: The traumatology of grieving*. Washington, DC: Taylor & Francis.

Foa EB, Meadows EA (1997) Psychosocial treatments for posttraumatic stress disorder: A critical review. *Annu Rev Psychol* 48: 449–480.

Foa EB, Davidson JRT, Frances A (1999) The Expert Consensus Guideline Series: treatment of posttraumatic stress disorder. *J Clin Psychiatry* 60: 1–76.

Foa EB, Keane TM, Friedman MJ (2000a) *Effective Treatments for PTSD*. New York: Guilford Press.

Foa EB, Keane TM, Friedman MJ (2000b) *Guidelines for the Treatment of PTSD*. New York: Guilford Press.

Foa EB, Hembree EA, Cahill SP et al. (2005) Randomized trial of prolonged exposure for post-traumatic stress disorder with and without cognitive restructuring: outcomes at academic and community clinics. *J Consult Clin Psychol* 73: 953–964.

Foa EB, Keane TM, Friedman MJ, Cohen JA (2009) *Effective Treatments for PTSD*. New York: Guilford Press.

Fontana A, Rosenheck R (1997) Effectiveness and cost of the inpatient treatment of post-traumatic stress disorder: Comparison of three models of treatment. *Am J Psychiatry* 154: 758–776.

Ford J (1999) PTSD and disorders of extreme stress following warzone military trauma: Comorbid but distinct syndromes?. *J Consult Clin Psychol* 67: 3–12.

Ford J, Kidd P (1998) Early childhood trauma and disorders of extreme stress as predictors of treatment outcome with chronic PTSD. *J Trauma Stress* 11: 743–761.

Ford JD, Fisher P, Larson L (1997) Object relations as a predictor of treatment outcome with chronic posttraumatic stress. *J Consult Clin Psychol* 65: 547–559.

Ford JD, Courtois CA, Steele K, van der Hart O, Nijenhuis ERS (2005) Treatment of complex posttraumatic self-dysregulation. *J Trauma Stress* 18: 437–447.

Foy DW, Ruzek JI, Glynn SM, Riney SA, Gusman FD (1997) Trauma focused group therapy for combat-related PTSD. *J Clin Psych* 3: 59–73.

Friedman MJ (1996) PTSD diagnosis and treatment for mental health clinicians. *Community Ment Health J* 32: 37–61.

Friedman MJ (2000) A guide to the literature on pharmacotherapy for PTSD. *PTSD Res Q* 11: 1–7.

Friedman MJ (2004) Acknowledging the psychiatric cost of war. *N Engl J Med* 351: 75–77.

Friedman MJ, Schnurr P (1995) The relationship between trauma, post-traumatic stress disorder, and physical health. In: *Neurobiological and Clinical Consequences of Stress: From normal adaptation to PTSD* (Friedman MJ, Charney DS, Deutch AY, eds). Philadelphia, PA: Lippincott-Raven.

Gentry JE, Baranowsky AB (2002) *Early Intervention Field Traumaology—Full Program*, 8th edn. Toronto, Canada: Traumatology Institute.

Gentry JE, Baranowsky AB, Dunning K (2002) The accelerated recovery program (ARP) for compassion fatigue. In: *Treating Compassion Fatigue* (Figley CR, ed.). New York: Brunner-Routledge.

Herman J (1992) *Trauma and Recovery*. New York: Basic Books.

Hoge CW, Castro CA, Messer SC, McGurk D, Cotting DI, Koffman RL (2004) Combat duty in Iraq and Afghanistan, mental ealth problems, and barriers to care. *N Engl J Med* 351: 13–22.

Hollifield M, Sinclair-Lian N, Warner TD, Hammerschlag R (2007) Accupuncture for post-traumatic stress disorder: A randomized controlled pilot trial. *J Nerv Ment Disord* 195: 504–513.

International Society for Traumatic Stress Studies (ISTSS) (2000) Guidelines published in: *Effective Treatment for PTSD* (Foa E, Keane TM, Friedman MJ, eds). New York: Guilford Press. http://www.istss.org/resources.htm

Janet P (1973) *L'automatisme psychologique*. Paris: F. Alcan. (originally published 1889) (Revise Societé Piere Janet, Paris).

Johnson DR, Rosenheck R, Fontana A (1997) Assessing the structure, content and perceived social climate of residential PTSD treatment programs. *J Trauma Stress* 10: 361–376.

Johnson SL (2003) *The Therapist's Guide to Substance Abuse Intervention*. San Diego: Academic Press.

Johnson SL (2004) *The Therapist's Guide to Clinical Intervention*. San Diego: Academic Press.

Kessler R, Sonnega A, Broment E, Hughes M, Nelson CB (1995) Posttraumatic stress disorder in the National Comorbidity Survey. *Arch Gen Psychiatry* 52: 1048–1060.

King DW, King LA, Foy DW, Keane TM, Fairbank JA (1999) Posttraumatic stress disorder in a national sample of female and male Vietnam veterans: Risk factors, war-zone stressors, and resilience-recovery variables. *J Abnorm Psychol* 108: L164–L170.

Kluft RP (1996) Hospital treatment. In: *Treating Dissociative Identity Disorder* (Spira JL, ed.). San Francisco: Jossey-Bass.

Knafo D (2004) *Living with Terror, Working with Trauma*. Lanham, MD: Rowman and Littlefield.

Koenen KN, Stellman JM, Stellman S, Sommers JF (2003) Risk factors for course of post-traumatic stress disorder among Vietnam veterans: A 14 year follow-up of American Legionnaires. *J Consult Clin Psychiatry* 71: 980–986.

Landsman IS, Baum CG, Arnkoff DB et al. (1990) The psychosocial consequences of traumatic injury. *J Behav Med* 13: 561–581.

Linehan MM (1993) *Skills Training Manual for Borderline Personality Disorder.* New York: Guilford Press.

Litz BT, Gray MJ, Bryant R, Adler AB (2002) Early intervention for trauma: Current status and future directions. *Clin Psych: Sci Pract* 9: 112–134.

Marmar CR, Foy D, Kagan B, Pynoos RS (1994) An integrated approach for treating posttraumatic stress. In: *Posttraumatic Stress Disorder: A clinical review* (Pynoos R, ed.). Litherville, MD: Sidran Press.

McRae AL, Brady KT, Mellman TA et al. (2004) Comparison of nefazodone and sertraline for the treatment of posttraumatic stress disorder. *Depress Anxiety* 19: 190–196.

Meichenbaum D (1994) *A Clinical Handbook/Practical Therapist Manual for Assessing and Treating Adults with Post-traumatic Stress Disorder.* Waterloo, Ontario: Institute Press.

Mellman TA, Clark RE, Peacock WJ (2003) Prescribing patterns for patients with posttraumatic stress disorder. *Am Psychiatr Assoc* 54: 1618–1621.

Mitchell JT (1983) When disaster strikes…. *J Emerg Med Serv* 8: 36–39.

Najavits LM (2007) Seeking safety: a treatment manual for PTSD and substance abuse. *Psychiatr Serv* 58: 1012–1013.

National Association of Social Workers (NASW) (2009) Military Service-Related PTSD. Accessed January 2, 2009 from http://www.socialworker.org/research/naswResearch/org-military/default.asp.

Ouimette PC, Brown PJ (2002) *Trauma and Substance Abuse: Causes, consequences, and treatment of comorbid disorders.* Washington, DC: American Psychological Association Press.

Paykel E (1978) Contribution of life events to causation of psychiatric illness. *Psychol Med* 8: 245–254.

Pearlman LA (1995) Self-care for trauma therapists: Ameliorating vicarious traumatization. In: *Secondary Traumatic Stress: Self-care issues for clinicians, researchers and educators* (Stamm BH, ed.). Lutherville, MD: Sidran, pp. 51–64.

Perry JC, Herman JL, van der Kolk BA, Hoke LA (1990) Psychotherapy and psychological trauma in borderline personality disorder. *Psychiatric Ann* 20: 33–43.

Perry SM, Difede MA, Musngi GF, Jacobsberg L (1992) Predictors of posttraumatic stress disorder after burn injury. *Am J Psychiatry* 149: 931–935.

Resick PA, Schnicke MK (1993) *Cognitive Processing Therapy for Rape Victims: A treatment manual.* Newbury Park, CA: Sage.

Rhoades GF (2003) Anger management online conference transcript. Accessed September 2, 2004 from: www.healthyplace.com/Communities/Abuse/Site/transcripts/angermanagement.html.

Rollnick S, Heather N, Bell A (1992) Negotiating behavior change in medical settings: The development of brief motivational interviewing. *J Ment Health (UK)* 1: 25–37.

Ronis DL, Bates EW, Garfein AJ et al. (1996) Longitudinal patterns of care with patterns of care for patients with posttraumatic stress disorder. *J Trauma Stress* 9: 763–781.

Ross CA (1996) Short-term problem oriented inpatient treatment. In: *Treating Dissociative Identity Disorder* (Spira JL, ed.). San Francisco: Jossey-Bass.

Rothchild B (2000) *The Body Remembers: The psychophysiology of trauma and trauma treatment.* New York: Norton.

Scaer RC (2001) *The Body Bears the Burden: Trauma, dissociation and disease.* New York: Hawthorne.

Schnurr PP, Friedman MJ, Foy DW et al. (2003) Randomized trial of trauma-focused group therapy for post-traumatic stress disorder: Results from a department of veterans affairs cooperative study. *Arch Gen Psychiatry* 60: 481–489.

Seidel RW, Gusman FD, Abeurg FR (1994) Theoretical and practical foundations of an inpatient post-traumatic stress disorder and alcoholism treatment program. *Psychotherapy* 31: 67–78.

Shalev AY (1997) Discussion: Treatment of prolonged posttraumatic stress disorder. Learning from experience. *J Trauma Stress* 10: 415–423.

Shapiro F (1995) *Eye Movement Desensitization and Reprocessing: Basic priniciples, protocols and procedures.* New York: Guilford Press.

Shapiro F, Kaslow F, Maxfield C (2007) *Handbook of EMDR and Family Therapy Process.* New Jersey: Wiley & Sons Inc.

Skiba R, McKelvey J (2000) What works in preventing school violence? The safe and responsive fact sheet series—Anger Management. Accessed September 4, 2004 from: http://www.indiana. edu/-safeschl/Angermanagment.pdf.

Solomon EP, Heidi KM (2005) The biology of trauma: Implications for treatment. *J Interpers Violence* 20: 51–66.

Tinnen L (1994) *Time-limited Trauma Therapy for Dissociation Disorders.* Bruceton Mills, West Virginia: Gargoyle Press.

Turner JB, Turse NA, Dohrenwend BP (2007) Circumstances of service and gender differences in war-related PTSD: Findings from the National Vietnam Veteran Readjustment Study. *J Trauma Stress* 20: 643–649.

van der Hart O, Steele K, Boon S, Wittchen H (2000) Traumatic events and post-traumatic stress disorder in the community: Prevalence, risk factors and comorbidity. *Acta Psychiatr Scand* 101: 46–59.

van der Kolk B (1996) The complexity of adaptation to trauma: self-regulation, stimulus discrimination, and characterological development. In: *Traumatic Stress: The effects of overwhelming experience on mind, body, and society* (van der Kolk BA, McFarlane A, Weisaeth L, eds). New York: Guilford Press, pp. 182–213.

van der Kolk BA (2005) Child abuse and victimization. *Psychiatr Ann* 3: 374–378.

van der Kolk BA, McFarlane AC, van der Hart O (1996) A general approach to treatment of posttraumatic stress disorder. In: *Traumatic Stress: The effects of overwhelming experience on mind, body, and society* (van der Kolk BA, McFarlane A, Weisaeth L, eds). New York: Guilford Press.

van der Kolk BA, Burbridge J, Suzuki J (1997) The psychobiology of trauma memory: Clinical implications for neuroimaging studies. *Ann N Y Acad Sci* 821: 99–113.

Veterans Health Administration, Department of Veterans Affairs (2008) Combat-related PTSD fact sheet. Accessed August, 2008 from http://www.dralegal.org/downloads/cases/ Veterans/PTSD.

Wellness Reproductions (1991) Anger management. Accessed September 4, 2004 from: http://www.mun.ca/student/answers/wellness/angermangement.php

Witkiewitz KA, Marlatt GA (2007) *Therapist's Guide to Evidence-Based Relapse Prevention.* San Diego: Academic Press.

Wolpe J (1969) *The Practice of Behavior Therapy.* New York: Pergamon.

Wright DC, Woo WL, Ross S (1996) Inpatient treatment for chronic post traumatic stress disorder: Outcome of treatment for adult survivors of childhood trauma. *Int J Psychol* 31: 278.

PART III

Skill Building

Chapter 5

Resources for Improved Coping

FEELING SAFE AND SECURE

For many survivors of a traumatic experience the importance of creating a safe and secure environment is the starting point or "core of the healing process."

> Safety is the experience of being protected from danger and hurt. Within a safe environment, we can relax and be ourselves because we know that our well being is secure. We feel free to take manageable risks toward growth and change. When you begin to talk about your life in a safe environment, healing naturally begins to happen.
>
> (Davis, 1990, p. 19)

No matter what challenges you have, it is important that you create an environment that allows you to feel safe and secure. Have you ever imagined what it would feel like to have the stress of the trauma lifted so you could be free to fill your life with your own choices? Begin to explore the possibilities:

- Describe a time when you felt safe.

- What made you feel safe?

- How safe is your environment?

- How safe are you with the people in your life?

Therapist's Guide to Posttraumatic Stress Disorder Intervention

- If you don't feel safe in your home or the people in your life what can you do about it?
- For me to feel safe, I would need ...
  - How can I protect myself?
  - When do I feel safest?
  - How do I manage stressful environments which don't feel safe?
- Am I safe with myself?
  - Do I have thoughts or urges to harm myself?
  - Do I have thoughts or urges to harm someone else?

  Note: If you answered yes to either of those questions talk to your therapist or physician so that you can be validated, supported and helped.

- Make a list of your thoughts or urges and write three thoughts to counter each of them
- Will it be possible for me to ever feel safe?
- Do I believe I have the right to healing and recovery? (why/why not)
- How hard is it for me to give up my shield of fear and distrust and trust myself to feel safe?

Adapted from Davis (1990)

SAFETY AND EMOTIONAL NUMBING

One way of viewing emotional numbing is that it is the reluctance to re-experience trauma, and, therefore, a lack of safety. Avoidance can be useful at times. However, there are also times when avoidance is actually reinforcing the stress reaction because the avoidance is of something or some situation that does not present any danger. Sometimes there is avoidance of thoughts or feelings associated with the traumatic event. Whatever the case, the goal is for you to be in control—to feel in control.

Take a moment to clarify that being in control means choosing to effectively manage the things that potentially could negatively impact your life. To achieve being in control you have to determine the legitimate reasons for choosing to maintain safety from certain people, places, and situations/activities. This requires being authentic, in the moment, and consciously aware of what you are doing and why you are doing it. In other words, to achieve being in control means that you have to actively choose your strategies for being safe. This can be challenging if you have allowed yourself to remain emotionally numb as a means to not think or feel.

Unfortunately, the consequence of allowing emotional numbing to be a coping mechanism for avoidance as a means to feel safe is that numbing is generalized to many, if not all, aspects of your life experience. While this could include choosing to forget different parts of a traumatic experience, it could also leave you feeling detached from people you care about and even detached from experiences that you used to find pleasurable.

Answer the following questions to increase your understanding about emotional numbing and avoidance:

1. What are the people, places and situations/activities you avoid?
   - What are your patterns of avoidance?

2. What are the thoughts, feelings, memories and/or conversations you avoid?
   - What are your patterns of avoidance?

3. What are the once pleasurable activities you are no longer interested in?
   – Describe your feelings of emotional detachment/numbing.

Use the above information to improve coping:

- What have you learned about your coping that needs to be improved or updated?
- Where will be the easiest place to start?
- How are you going to maintain awareness for what you are doing and why?
- How are new ways of thinking and behaving going to benefit you?
- How will it be helpful to use your social support system?

Be not afraid of growing slowly, be afraid only of standing still.

Chinese Proverb

UNDERSTANDING WHERE YOU ARE AT

As part of your journaling, keep track of the time of day/activities/people that contribute to feeling unsafe. The more awareness you develop for those factors the more opportunity you have for problem-solving. Consider:

- How you choose to take care of yourself
- The variation of options you have in how you manage healing and recovery.

Write an explanation for the following statements:

- I am afraid that those close to me will really know what I am thinking/feeling
- I am usually totally overwhelmed before I remove myself from an emotionally disturbing situation
- I am not aware that I am in crisis until I am overwhelmed
- I usually push myself further than I am ready to go
- I usually avoid everything outside of my comfort zone
- I am afraid that I will never be able to deal with the stress of recovery and healing
- I am afraid of moving through my work too quickly and not learning what I need to
- When I get too stressed I space out and go through the motions without feeling anything but numb
- When I get too stressed out I dissociate and don't remember anything
- I space out/dissociate so much that I automatically do things and am not ever aware that I am doing it
- I am afraid that if others knew what I think, feel or do that they would think I am crazy.

To stay focused on healing:

- Write 5–10 activities that are comforting or enjoyable and make the commitment to do 3 of them every day
- Choose a positive emotion you would like to start your day with and then do things that help create that feeling
- Listen to soothing music or do artwork/crafts/be creative
- Create a sanctuary in a garden or in a room (your special place to shut out stress and soothe yourself
- Consider what has been most helpful and supportive of your recovery.

Your last point of safety is associated with your healing and recovery exercises. Initially choose a time frame from beginning to end and give yourself permission to end at any time depending on your own stress level, for example, to bring your work to a close at that time if you exceed a mild level of stress to gain a feeling of control. Were you surprised that you had accomplished some healing and recovery tasks that you had not identified?

Adapted from Davis (1990)

CREATING YOUR OWN SAFE PLACE

There are several factors associated with a safe place that need to be considered along with how you choose to work on recovery while in your safe place:

- It must be an appropriate place that you have easy access to and control of
- When there you must not be distracted by the needs/demands of others or be thinking about other responsibilities
- You must have adequate time in your safe place to reflect on your thoughts and feelings
- If you need to suddenly stop recovery work you are prepared to bookmark it in some way and come back to it
- You give yourself permission to stop if you need a break
- Your safe place is a place you can retreat to if you are feeling distressed.

Establish a regular time or ritual when you go to your safe place. The predictable routine will be reassuring to you and create a positive boundary for others to respect. Other recommendations are to:

- Take a mind vacation. Create a rich visual image of your safe place for times when you can't go there physically. Along with your visualization combine the positive feelings you experience when you are in your safe place
- Select a color that is part of your feeling safe and soothed. Practice seeing that color in your mind
- Make sure that the color you have selected and other objects which are comforting and reassuring are a part of your safe place
- Make a list of daily and weekly routines that are important for you to reinforce the importance of self-care and healing.

1. _____

2. _____

3. _____

4. _____

5. _____

Creating a safe place creates a safe respectable boundary for yourself and for others. It is a statement that I have a right to heal and to recover. It is an affirmation that I am important and will take the time necessary to adequately care for me.

Adapted from Davis (1990)

JOURNALING

Keeping a personal journal is a great tool for venting thoughts and feelings, clarifying areas of confusion in your life experiences, and resulting in deeper self-understanding. Make an effort to describe your thoughts and feelings as thoroughly as possible. Sometimes changes in the self can occur just by recognizing the source of the problem or the consequence(s) of an experience.

An additional benefit of keeping a journal is that it becomes a log of you, how you change and grow as well as areas where you find change to be a challenge difficult to overcome. Other facets of utility in journal writing are that you can ask yourself specific questions, observing how you talk to yourself (maintaining old patterns you want to change), or create goals that you can monitor for change and improvement. Writing is a way to free all of the energy it takes to hold things inside.

Sometimes people think that a journal is just about writing down things that are painful, make them angry, or what they are afraid of. However, a journal is also a place to record:

- Successes
- Good things about yourself (be supportive to yourself to develop or enrich self-esteem)
- Words of hope and encouragement, affirmations (programming new healthy realistic self-talk)
- Forgiveness of self or others. Like self-esteem, forgiveness is one of the keys to successful change. Let go of negatives that take up unnecessary space in your heart and in your mind
- Things you are grateful for.

No excuses:

1. I can't write well so I can't write in a journal. Wrong. Your journal is for your benefit. You will have no trouble reading your own journal and using it in a manner that is helpful to you.

2. I don't want anyone to know what I really think or feel. Your journal is personal, it is not for anyone else to read unless you invite them to. If you cannot trust the people who share your life to respect your privacy there are many questions to be asked regarding those relationships. If necessary, create a special place to keep your journal, or if you have a therapist ask them if you can keep your private journal in your file.

3. I don't have time. Be honest. If you are afraid, not willing, or ready to take responsibility for making your life what you want it to be then be honest about it, and also be honest about what it will take for you to make the commitment to take care of you. Only you can make your life what you want it to be. If you need help or support in getting started, talk to someone you trust to problem-solve what the stumbling block is. You are worth it!

Making the quality of your life a priority is a necessary step toward recovering from the trauma you have experienced.

DEFINING WHAT DOES AND DOESN'T WORK

In order to understand the impact that trauma has had upon you, your view of the world, who you are, and how you live your daily life, take some time to think about the following questions in reference to how you functioned before the trauma. Once you do this you will have began a journey of deciding how you want to manage what has happened to you, who you want to be and what you want to do with your life:

1. How do I describe the core of who I was before the trauma?

   _____
   _____

2. What characteristics describe me?

   _____
   _____

3. What are my values and moral compass composed of?

   _____
   _____

4. Who do I trust to share my thoughts and feelings with regarding what has happened to me and how it has affected me?

   _____
   _____

5. What do I currently fear?

   _____
   _____

6. What thoughts are causing me a problem?

   _____
   _____

7. What feelings are causing me a problem?

   _____
   _____

8. What behaviors are causing me a problem?

   _____
   _____

9. What physical symptoms am I experiencing that I didn't experience before the trauma?

_____

_____

10. What do I do that helps me manage these difficulties?

_____

_____

11. What changes have others observed in me?

_____

_____

12. What am I expecting to change (improve) and what do I need to do to make it happen?

_____

_____

Also consider: What has this exercise clarified about who I was before the trauma, how it has affected me, and how I choose to move forward? (Write an in-depth answer on a separate piece of paper.)

EXPOSURE THERAPY

People with posttraumatic stress disorder (PTSD) tend to avoid things that are upsetting or they fear, even though it is not rational. This avoidance does provide initial relief but over time it actually creates more of a problem and a decreased feeling of being in control. The goal of exposure therapy is to desensitize you, make you less sensitive, to things that are upsetting or provoke feelings of fear but cannot harm you. The thoughts you have become associated to the distressing emotion which leads to avoiding. Exposure therapy decreases these distressing emotions that are associated to the traumatic experience that prevent you from moving on with your life.

How Does Exposure Therapy Work?

You create a list of things that are upsetting or feared from least upsetting to most upsetting (a hierarchy). You will be able to take each thing listed and create a picture of it in your mind with as much detail as possible, using all your senses (what you heard, saw, felt, tasted, and smelled), and first person tense ("I am beginning right now. ..."). This is called imaginal exposure because you are choosing to think about it and create a picture in your mind. You are already in control. You choose when you are going to do it and you will feel ready. If you started with what was most upsetting it may seem too distressing to do. However, with exposure therapy you start with the least upsetting and master each one until you have mastered the most distressing fear on your list. Remember, it starts with what is least upsetting to you on your own list.

What allows you to master or change the experience of fear and distress is that before you start you will be very clear about a type of relaxation technique you will use that allows you to confront the fear while at the same time relaxing your body. This is a big part of the desensitization, because later when you think about the same thing your body will have changed the way it interprets it—it no longer responds with distress and fear. The body and mind will be rational and objective. It will be done slowly so that you are not overwhelmed. It will be a little uncomfortable but you will be in control and know how to manage the emotion that you experience.

At first you might experience an increase in intrusive thoughts and possibly nightmares, but again you will understand why and how you are going to conquer it. You feel assured and are eager to no longer be controlled by your fear and avoidance. You begin to understand, "I have already survived what happened and I don't want it to keep taking away from the good life that I can have."

Exposure therapy teaches you the skills to manage your fear and avoidance now as well as preparing you to manage it should it ever be provoked in the future. Management skills give you control over your own life and exposure therapy is a management skill.

Your therapist will discuss with you the different types of relaxation techniques that will be useful for you to learn and for you to use in eliminating your distress and fear with exposure therapy. Two very common relaxation techniques are progressive muscle relaxation and autogenic breathing. Both focus you on how your body feels when it is relaxed.

WRITING ABOUT YOUR EXPERIENCE

Everything that happens to you becomes a part of who you are. Sometimes the experience(s) is so bad that a person tries to distance themselves from it by avoidance or dissociation. There are times when a person is not emotionally strong enough or resilient enough to deal with the experience and avoidance or dissociation are the only way they can initially cope with it. However, if they continue to use avoidance or dissociation as their means of coping they become less effective in coping not only with that experience but other experiences as well. Therefore, one of the first steps of working through or healing is to make the acknowledgment that this awful experience is now a part of you. When you do this you will also acknowledge that you no longer need to fear it because you have survived it!

To prevent retraumatizing yourself as you begin the working through the process consider the following:

- You have created a safe environment

- Make sure you are aware of where your symptoms come from (the trauma)

- Acknowledge you have the free will/choice to put down your work at any time

- You have a list of safe people you can reach out to if necessary

- You have a list of techniques you can use to calm yourself

- You will rate your level of distress with every step of recovery you make so that you can make the best choice for how you decide to take care of you

- You intermittently take the time to focus on your environment to assure remaining in the present

- You intermittently make an experiential review by going through the awareness of all of your senses

- When you have completed your work at a specific setting, reinforce your thoughts feelings of management and control by acknowledging your accomplishment

- Search for meaning as you progress creating an anchor of accomplishment at every juncture of increased understanding, problem-solving/choices and resolution.

An important point of clarity for anyone choosing to understand how they have been affected by a trauma is the value of recognizing that you may have developed some ways of coping that seem to help you manage emotional distress and physical symptoms that are actually maintaining what you are trying to distance yourself from. You are choosing to engage in the recovery process because you want to face it, understand it, problem-solve, resolve it, and consolidate it so that it no longer controls you. There is a stepwise progression of mastering what has been a problem. It is called graded exposure.

Sometimes graded exposure takes place in your environment through social activities and sometimes it is a mental process which eventually translates to feeling the control you want to experience in any given situation. There are times when a person wants to jump right in and confront the most distressing fear-provoking issue. The reason this is not recommended is because it could result in you feeling so overwhelmed that the fear and avoidance actually increase and you end up in a worse place than when you started.

Graded exposure gives you optimal control. It consists of structured and repeated exposure to the lowest level of whatever it is that anxiety is producing in you, allowing you to conquer the fear or other negative emotions that are associated with that trigger.

This is how it works:

- The structured and repeated exposure gives you the opportunity to disconfirm your fears. You don't move on the next level of stress provocation until the one before it has been challenged and mattered (disconfirmed)

- It also gives you the chance to practice and refine your skills. When you allow yourself to be exposed long enough to the distressing trigger your mind and body has the opportunity to adjust, which changes the message that it is bad and, therefore, needs to be avoided. Remember, whenever the distress is beginning to feel unmanageable that is your cue to cope with it by calming your mind and body. Self-soothing is an important skill. When your self-monitoring skills improve, along with the development of skills for managing experiences of distress, important progress is taking place. Distress merely indicates a need to relax, self-soothe, or to take a break. When this awareness occurs, you are at an important level of change. Associated with this change is the message, "I'm in control."

- The structured and repeated exposure gives you the chance to develop a feeling of comfort and control with situations. By consistently challenging yourself with the progression or small steps of exposure tasks in which you had previously experienced distress or negative symptoms your body and mind begin to respond more calmly. The situations begin to lose their power.

- The repetition of these exercises gives you the chance to improve your confidence. Each step is the opportunity to build upon and expand the personal experience of confidence.

- The exercises are a form of self-responsibility and self-care which state, "I am not willing to allow this to control me anymore, I am taking my life back."

GETTING STARTED

You start by building a progression of small steps that you are prepared to take, from small challenges to bigger challenges which result in:

- Improved coping
- Mastery
- Self-confidence.

Table 5.1 Suggested rating of distress

0	No distress, completely relaxed
1	No distress or minimal distress, relaxed
2	There is no experience of impeding distress, but awareness is up
3	There is mild tension which is keeping you alert
4	There is mild distress and body tension (could feel fear, anxiety, apprehension)
5	Distress is somewhat unpleasant but tolerable
6	Moderate distress, unpleasant feelings, some worry/apprehension
7	Body tension is escalating and unpleasant. However, it is tolerable and you can still think clearly
8	There is a great deal of distress. Associated with it are escalated levels of fear and anxiety. Thoughts of not being able to tolerate much longer take over.
9	Distress becomes so significant it interferes with all other thinking
10	Extreme, intolerable distress, and filled with body tension

First, identify the situations you want to avoid. Remember, since you want to create a stepwise progression from least fear provoking to most fear provoking you will have to spend some time thinking about the things that bother you, that you make excuses for and procrastinate about. Doing so will give you the information you need to create your list for starting your practice leading to mastery for change. For each situation or issue that you choose give it a rating of distress that is experienced in association with it (Table 5.1). In assigning a rating by number, 0 would be completely without distress and 10 would be the most amount of distress. Once the situations are rated then you can organize them from least to most distressing.

Next, make a list of situations or triggers for you and rate them from 0—completely relaxed to 10—extreme, intolerable distress.

Situation	Distress rating

Now that you have identified a number of situations that cause distress, fear, and tension that you want to avoid and have a history of avoiding you can develop the stepwise progression of systematic challenges to conquer. Plan your goals. Decide where it is that you want to get to by planning your goals. Next, you can start thinking about the steps you will need to take to reach those goals. You will be in control of each step, and do not need to move on to the next step until the prior step has been totally mastered and no longer causes distress. You will decide, based upon the level of experienced distress, to keep working or to take a break and then resume your work.

It is important to be as specific and detailed as possible when constructing your progressive list of challenges for change. Keep reminding yourself that no matter what trauma(s) you have experienced, you have survived them, which is a demonstration of the many positive personal characteristics or traits that describe you.

PLANNING GOALS

The goal is to take all the thoughts, feelings, and behaviors that have been the result of trauma and modify them into increasingly less distressing responses. REACH and PRAMS (Center for Clinical Intervention) are the acronyms that will help you plan your goals:

R = Realistic belief in yourself and your ability to make the changes that you desire

E = Expectation of positive changes in how you feel and live your life

A = Acknowledgment of your ability and strength for all you have survived

C = Challenge is the welcomed agent of change

H = Healthy thoughts, feelings and behaviors are the key to the life I want.

P = Personal choice of situations that are most relevant to your identified goals

R = Realistic expectation of experienced distress that can be tolerated while you are making progress and change

A = Achievable goals that you know you can reach with hard work and support

M = Measurable goals that can be accurately assessed as you make progress and change

S = Specific goals that clearly define who, what, when, and/or where.

Go back to the list of situations you developed and rated for level of distress. Choose a couple of those situations and designate them as goals:

1. Choose realistic, achievable, specific, and measurable goals

2. Choose a couple of goals that represent a range of distress levels (on the lower and manageable level of distress so that they are not overwhelming). The idea is to accomplish change

3. Write down specific goals that were previously defined as situations you wanted to avoid

4. Begin to develop a deeper level of understanding associated with your choices of goals and your management skill development

5. Increase your awareness of the manner in which you talk to yourself about your increasing management abilities to improve self-esteem.

It takes courage and perseverance to meet the challenges which will result in you being in control of your life. Healing takes time. Give yourself that time.

Goal	Distress rating

Break each goal into smaller steps and reinforce your ability to achieve the challenge by changing:

- Who is there or participating in a specific activity
- What you do in an effort to achieve your goal
- When you do it (achieving the same goal over a range of time frames)
- Where you do it (achieving the same goal over a range of environments)
- The length of time you do (minutes, hours, etc.).

Now, to complete this homework take one goal and, as practice, write out in detail the issues associated with the problem, exactly how it will be challenged by each step of graded exposure, how you will assure effective emotional management while progressing through the steps of exposure, and what your expectations for change are.

Goal:_____

Issues:_____

_____

_____

_____

_____

_____

DO YOU HAVE PTSD?

The brief summary in Table 5.2 is offered as a review of the physical reactions, emotional reactions, and avoidance involved in an effort to cope with a traumatic experience. As you prepare for work on resolving these areas of disturbance be thoughtful of your needs for safety, quiet, soothing, and support. You will not be asked to expose yourself to all of the details associated with any traumatic experience, but rather can choose specific response patterns that you want to work on to modify or eliminate.

You may feel vulnerable and overwhelmed at any point of this challenging effort that you are committed to. This work will likely be stressful and exhausting, so take breaks whenever you feel you need to, ask for support from someone you trust when you are in need of comfort and soothing, and intermittently practice relaxation exercises (such as deep breathing or meditation) to assure yourself that you are in control of how you choose to move forward. Another helpful gauge of how you are managing would be to use the distress rating scale to monitor your level of personal distress at any time you are working on an assignment, or just do it intermittently so that you become practiced at identifying exactly how you are doing. This increased self-awareness will serve you well in every area of your life.

Remember, one of the most important journeys in life is mastering self-understanding. This must be coupled with basic psychological needs such as safety, trust, control, self-esteem, and intimacy. Be patient and take the time you need for healing.

Someone may have diagnosed you with PTSD or you may have read about it and diagnosed yourself. PTSD is defined by specific symptoms. Table 5.3 shows a symptoms list developed to determine the likelihood that someone has PTSD (Davidson, 2001). The symptoms for diagnosing PTSD are taken from the *Diagnostic and Statistical Manual of Mental Disorders* (DSM-IV) authored and published by the American Psychiatric Association. The major areas of symptoms and their impact are defined by frequency and severity. Think about completing the Davidson Trauma Scale as another means for clarifying and understanding your personal experience and response to surviving a trauma.

If you can't remember, or only vaguely remember what happened to you, know that you are not alone. You may know that you had an experience but your mind chose to block out the memory of images and details to protect you. That will not prevent you from acknowledging

Table 5.2   The four major criteria for the diagnosis of PTSD

1. Re-experiencing the trauma	Intrusive thoughts/mental images (that suddenly pop up in your mind) Increased feelings of anxiety and discomfort in situations that remind you of the trauma Dreaming/nightmare Feelings of reliving the trauma experience Flashback (triggered by a stimulus associated with the trauma such as anniversary date of trauma, same date number, smell, sound, taste) that propels you back into a momentary re-experiencing of the trauma Abreaction or reliving the trauma in real time
2. Emotional numbing	Lack of pleasure in previously pleasurable activities Sense of foreshortened future Absence of emotional responsiveness
3. Avoidance and denial	Suppression of things that remind you of the traumatic event Avoiding people, places, situations that remind you of the trauma Lack of intimacy/desexualization or social isolation Over-controlled emotions Use of substances or addictive behaviors for emotional numbing/escape
4. Physical symptoms	Difficulty falling asleep or staying asleep Feeling irritable/outbursts of anger Difficulty with concentration and/or memory Hypervigilance Easily startled Decreased level of energy or resilience (ability to bounce back)

Table 5.3   Davidson Trauma Scale

Frequency[a]	Severity[b]	Symptom
		1. Painful images, memories, or thoughts of the event
		2. Distressing dreams of the event
		3. Feelings event was recurring, or that you were reliving it
		4. Being upset by something that reminded you of the event
		5. Being physically upset by reminders of the event (including sweating, trembling, racing heart, shortness of breath, nausea, diarrhea)
		6. Avoiding any thoughts or feelings about the event
		7. Avoiding doing things or going into situations that remind you of the event
		8. Inability to recall important parts of the event
		9. Difficulty enjoying things (previously enjoyable)
		10. Feeling distant or cut off from other people
		11. Inability to have sad or loving feelings
		12. Difficulty imaging having a long lifespan and fulfilling your goals
		13. Trouble falling asleep or staying asleep
		14. Irritability or outbursts of anger
		15. Difficulty concentrating
		16. Feeling on edge, being easily distracted, or needing to stay on guard
		17. Being jumpy or easily startled
		TOTAL

[a]Rated as: 0 = none at all; 1 = once only; 2 = 2–3 times; 3 = 4–6 times; 4 = every day.
[b]Rated as: 0 = not at all distressing; 1 = minimally distressing; 2 = moderately distressing; 3 = markedly distressing; 4 = extremely distressing.

the symptoms left as a legacy of the trauma experience. Be practical in choosing to work on what efforts of resolution are going to be beneficial to improving your quality of life.

For each symptom listed, ask yourself how often in the last week the symptom bothered you and how severe your level of distress was. Frequency is rated as: 0 = none at all; 1 = once only; 2 = 2–3 times; 3 = 4–6 times; 4 = every day. Severity is rated as: 0 = not at all distressing; 1 = minimally distressing; 2 = moderately distressing; 3 = markedly distressing; 4 = extremely distressing.

To interpret the impact of the trauma on you add up the numbers in both columns. The higher the score the more likely you have the diagnosis of PTSD. Even though you are able to use this scale for helping to understand your experience of symptoms, only a qualified doctor or therapist can actually render you a diagnosis of PTSD. Using the above scale, you need one or more intrusive symptoms (the first five questions), three or more avoidance symptoms (the next seven questions) and two or more of the somatic or body arousal symptoms (the last five questions).

Now ask yourself three questions:

1. What have you learned about yourself from this review?

   _____

   _____

2. What do you think will be most helpful for you to work on and why?

   _____

   _____

3. If it has taken you a long time to challenge these symptoms, please explain what kept you from taking this step, and why now?

   _____

   _____

WRITING AN OUTLINE OF THE TRAUMA

The next exercise is to write a basic outline of the traumatic event/experience you are choosing to work through and resolve.

1. What was the event?

   _____

   _____

2. How did you feel before the event (level of stress, anxiety, sleeping pattern, ability to cope, etc.)?

   _____

   _____

3. What were you doing during the event?

   _____

   _____

4. What were your reactions during the event?

   _____

   _____

5. How did you feel during the event?

_____

_____

6. What were you in control of during the traumatic event?

_____

_____

7. What did you lack control of during the event?

_____

_____

8. What were your emotional responses to what happened to you?

_____

_____

9. What were you thinking after the traumatic event?

_____

_____

10. What were you physically (body) feeling after the traumatic event?

_____

_____

Now is there anything that you wrote about that you had not thought about until you started this writing assignment? How are you dealing with it or thinking about its importance to your recovery?

_____

_____

DEVELOPING A TRAUMA TIME LINE

A trauma can be recorded in numerous ways. One way is to develop a trauma time line that becomes a visual summary of experience. It is sometimes surprising to see how much you have actually experienced and possibly not resolved. As you look through the outline below you can begin to see that a time line is truly a history of traumatic life experiences from the time of your birth to the present.

A trauma time line should include:

1. Any pre-birth experiences
   – High-risk pregnancy?
   – Confined to bed?
   – Premature delivery?
   – Was your mother in any kind of accident?
   – Did a death occur during the course of the pregnancy?
   – Was she the victim of domestic violence?

2. Accidents

3. Illness

4. Injury

5. Abuse

6. Losses
   – Changes
   – Deaths.

_____

_____

_____

_____

_____

COMMON PTSD THOUGHTS

It is not uncommon to have thoughts of guilt, shame, fear, anger, losing control, etc. Emotional responses vary depending on many factors, including a person's interpretation of a situation. Therefore, if a person changes the way they think, they can change the way they feel.

Why is it beneficial to challenge irrational, negative thoughts?

- What a person thinks influences their feelings and behavior

- Internal thoughts (self-talk) take place 24 hours/day and 7 days/week. However, most people have not chosen to be consciously aware of what they are thinking or if their thoughts are rational:
  – "What am I thinking?"
  – "Why am I thinking it?"
  – "Is it correct thinking?"
  – "Does this type of thinking help me or harm me?" (How/why?)

- Believing a thought is true doesn't mean it is.

To achieve a true change in emotional distress means identifying as many negative thoughts as possible so that you can develop and feel confident about your:

- Ability to manage challenging situations

- Ability to talk yourself through any situation

- Ability and desire to continue to invest yourself in change so that you can resume living a fulfilling life.

Some common PTSD thoughts include:

- The fear will never go away

- The anxiety will never diminish

- I can't deal with the fear and anxiety

- Avoidance is the only way to stay in control

- I can't tolerate feeling overwhelmed

- I will never get better

- I will never enjoy life again

- Nothing will ever be the same.

Take a moment to consider and write your thoughts down. What is your commitment to recovery and healing? What do you need to do?

_____
_____
_____
_____
_____

LEARNING FROM TRAUMA

As previously stated, everything that happens to you becomes a part of who you are. Nothing that happens to you is "wasted," even the really bad experiences. It is a personal responsibility to find or create positives from a negative. If this choice is not made then a traumatic experience is given the power to continually steal precious time and potential positive experience.

Use the journaling that you started to help you set this frame of mind by asking yourself questions about what you have learned:

- What has the traumatic experience taught me about how I see the world?
- What have I learned about me?
  - My strengths
  - My fears
  - My compassion
  - The decisions I make
  - My self-care, or lack of it
  - My feelings of self-worth
  - The trust I have in me
  - My expectations of others
  - How I have chosen to be empowered by what happened to me

(The questions to promote self-understanding are endless)

- What have I accomplished in healing that I did not recognize before?
- What resources have been most useful to me?
- What resources do I need to develop?

Since you can't change anything that has happened to you *choose* to find ways to benefit or be empowered by what is now part of your life history.

CHRONIC PAIN AS PART OF RECURRING TRAUMA

Emotional memories of a traumatic experience get incompletely processed and are then constantly getting reactivated by triggers. Chronic pain is a kind of recurring trauma. Use your answers to the following questions to explore the role of pain in your life.

- Do you have any pain which has not been medically diagnosed? (explain)
- Have you ever been told nothing can be found to be wrong, it is in your head and you need to learn to live with it?
- Have you ever looked for or found the source of pain, outside your body?

- How did your thoughts, feelings, and behaviors influence or reinforce the pain you experience?

- Are you afraid to give up your pain? (explain)

STRATEGIES FOR DEALING WITH RE-EXPERIENCING TRAUMA

Memories, Dreams, Nightmares, Flashbacks, and Other Triggers

Before you begin to work on ways in which you re-experience the trauma, you must acknowledge, accept, and reassure yourself that regardless of what you think and feel you are not currently experiencing the trauma. It is a past event which is a part of your life history. The reassurance comes from knowing that while you re-experience the distress of the trauma, you have already survived it! You are taking back control over your life. It cannot hurt you anymore. Only the way you think about it, feel about, and cope with it can cause you additional harm. The good news is that you have a choice in how you deal with all of those areas.

To thoroughly prepare yourself to deal with this area practice your favorite relaxation techniques. One of the most important aspects of relaxation is the development of an increased awareness for what the body feels like in a totally relaxed state. Such awareness also allows for improved monitoring for even mild changes in heart rate, rate of breathing, and muscle tension, all of which are signals for increased emotional and physiological distress. Another method for grounding is to carefully examine the details of your surroundings. Therefore, if you experience any distress associated with re-experiencing trauma which results in feeling disoriented you can reassert your safety and self-confidence by reaffirming that your environment has remained consistent in the current time frame.

A technique developed by Rothchild (2000) referred to as "dual awareness" allows you to feel secure that you are in your present environment while examining and working on the trauma. The way to determine what degree of ability you have for dual awareness can be achieved by the following exercise:

1. Recall a recent event which was mildly distressing and resulted in minor anxiety

2. What changes do you feel your body experiencing?
   - How does your stomach feel?
   - Are there changes in breathing?
   - Does the rate of your heart beat change (increase/decrease)?
   - Do you feel flushed or chills?
   - Does your body temperature change: all over your body or specific areas of your body?
   - Do you experience muscle tension?

3. Now return fully to being in your present environment
   - Pay attention to all the details in the room: the color of the walls and furniture, the temperature of the room, any specific odors
   - Note the physical changes you experience as your focus of awareness changes

4. For the last step of this exercise, try to maintain awareness of your present surroundings while you recall the mildly distressing event

5. Conclude this exercise with full awareness focused on your present environment.

Understanding and Managing Flashbacks

Meichenbaum (1994) states that flashbacks can be in the form of intrusive thoughts, re-experiences, or intense feelings. The description of this experience has been expanded upon by others, resulting in an enriched view. Flashbacks are understood to be memories of the past that press into the present resulting in a past experience seeming to occur in the here and now. In general, flashbacks are unexpected, with memory, emotional, and sensory aspects of the trauma. In other words, they are sudden and vivid with accompanied strong emotion. There is no escaping the flashback by distraction, blackout, dissociation, or loss of consciousness. However, while experiencing a flashback a person is temporarily not in the here and now. Other characteristics of flashbacks include:

- Fragments of memories
- Entire, detailed memory
- Sensory responses:
  – Visual aspects of trauma
  – Auditory aspects of trauma
  – Olfactory (smell) aspects of trauma
- Muscle memory (such as pain or touch)
- Emotion—intense emotions such as anger, rage, fear, panic, confusion, numbness that comes out of nowhere)
- Behavior (responses/actions) associated with triggers
- Abreaction—a type of flashback where the entire experience happens in the here and now
- Nightmares—flashbacks that occur while sleeping.

The emotional consequences of flashbacks are:

- Feelings of helplessness
- Fear (reinforces feelings of terror, hypervigilance)
- Anger/feeling on edge
- Increased anxiety
- Depression.

The challenges presented by flashbacks are:

- How to separate a flashback from present reality
- Managing a hyperaroused nervous system
- Using appropriate, honest, and helpful self-talk versus fear-based self-talk
- Looking for environmental/emotional connections to ruminative thoughts or repetitive experiences
- Using relaxation techniques for soothing/calming
- Not wasting anything that happens to you (i.e. the choice to take something negative and create positives/learning from it). This is necessary to result in strengthening and empowerment versus further being diminished. It is imperative to ask exploring questions
- Separating short-term from long-term challenges.

Questions Exploring the Experience of Flashbacks

- What is your interpretation of the flashback?
- Will there be different or more information flashbacked?
- How much emotion must be endured?

- What about more sensory experiences?
  - Visual (increased images/increased vividness)
  - Auditory (will there be more or varied sounds than what has been experienced so far?)
  - Somatic (physical symptoms, pain or feeling of pressure/weight)?

- What am I supposed to learn about myself from the trauma?
  - Relative strengths/weaknesses
  - The body's response to intense stress
  - What is helpful for management?

- What needs to be accepted about the trauma?
- How do you experience a flashback without getting caught in it instead of remaining in the moment?
- Can you choose to focus on aspects of the flashback without getting lost in it and losing my place in the here and now?

Hyperarousal

To help put it all together and be prepared to manage the emotional and physical responses of a flashback it is important to understand the physiological mechanism of the adrenal glands. When you are reacting to a flashback or a flashback trigger the adrenal gland is stimulated. With the activation of adrenal activity comes the activation of what feels like the reliving of the event that is remembered. It sounds complicated, and it is. However, as a function of the complexity of these mechanisms there are also numerous and varied opportunities for management. The point at which a person is able to acknowledge and accept that they initially do not have control over how their body reacts to extreme stress is exactly when the opportunity for change is most advantageous.

As frightening and overwhelming as physiological and emotional reactions can be in response to flashbacks and triggers, they are survivable. Remember, you have already survived the trauma. It is now time to challenge and master those difficult responses that limit and negatively impact the quality of your life. One of the things that you may not have realized is the change in the quality of how you interpret what happens around you, how you speak to yourself about it (self-talk), and how those two issues combine create an escalation of negative stressful responding and reinforce negative thoughts, feelings, expectations, and ultimately physical responding.

A tough reality is that in many ways you will get what you expect. In this case you expect the worse and it seems that your experience is indeed in that category. However, as you challenge interpretation and self-talk a de-escalation begins to take hold. Make progress by beginning to think in terms of a decision tree. At each branch you learn to ask yourself and clarify:

- What do I have control over?
- What am I going to do with what I have control over?

THE NEXT LEVEL: MOVING FROM SELF-AWARENESS TO SELF-MANAGEMENT

MANAGING SELF-TALK

The most important conversation anyone will ever have is with themselves. Awareness is used to change self-defeating, negative self-talk into an internal dialogue that is honest, optimistic and useful. What follows is information which will help to refine the impact of your thoughts (self-talk) and what changes can be made to continue your progress toward positive and effective self-talk.

Thinking Distortions

- All-or-nothing thinking. You see things in black and white. If you don't do as well as you think you should, or things don't go as well as you think they should it is experienced as a total failure

- Overgeneralizations. A single negative event is seen as a complete pattern of defeat and failure

- Mental filter. You pick a single negative detail and dwell on it, casting darkness over everything and every possibility

- Disqualifying the positives. You reject positive experiences by insisting that they don't count, or it was a fluke. This is a way to maintain an expectation of negatives and disappointments

- Jumping to conclusions. You make a negative interpretation even though there is no strong, definitive supportive evidence

- Magnification, catastrophizing, or minimizing. You exaggerate the importance of negatives

- Emotional reasoning. You assume that negative emotions reflect the way that things are: "I feel it so it must be true"

- Should statements. You try to motivate yourself with shoulds, shouldn't, and guilt

- Labeling and mislabeling. This is an extreme form of overgeneralization

- Personalization. You see yourself as the cause of some problem, or take on someone's opinion as having more value than it does.

Realistic Self-talk

- This too shall pass and my life will be better

- I am a worthy and good person

- I am doing the best I can

- Look at how much I have accomplished, and I am still working at it

- There are no failures only different degrees of success

- I am not helpless, I can and will take the steps necessary for to get through this

- I know I will be okay no matter what happens

- I am not responsible to make someone else okay

- I don't really need to prove myself to anyone

- Other people's opinions are just their opinions

- I will enjoy myself even when life is hard

- I will respond appropriately, and not be reactive

- I choose to be a happy person

- I cannot control the behavior of others

- My past does not control my future

- Others are responsible for their reactions to me

- I am respectful to others and deserve to be respected by others

- There is less stress being optimistic than pessimistic.

Positive Self-talk = Cognitive Restructuring

Cognitive restructuring decreases negative emotions. People generally do not know when they started thinking that way, but what is known is that it is a habit which has been practiced for a long time. Some people seem to work fast in identifying their negative thinking and creating rational statements to substitute for them. Because the new thoughts are rational they no longer create negative feelings. Sometimes between sessions a person may slip back into the old negative self-talk and feel like they really didn't accomplish the progress they thought they had. Actually, it is not uncommon to experience that slipping back into the old way of thinking—remember it is a habit and habits become kind of automatic. Therefore, you have to practice at being aware of what you are thinking so that you can choose to think in a rational and honest way which is also helpful.

Positive self-talk (cognitive restructuring) allows you to have better control over your feelings. Not only is there the correction of irrational thoughts into rational thought but it also decreases the intensity of emotional reactions by modifying how you think about the things that happen to you.

Remember that you do not always have control over the things that happen to you, but you do have control over how you choose to think about it and what you choose to do about it (problem-solving, management, letting it go, etc.). So, while it is true that experiences affect us in important ways, we can also learn to have more control over our emotional reactions by choosing how we think about what has happened.

Self-talk takes place for 24 hours of every day. We are not always aware of it, but it is always affecting how we feel. Fear and anxiety associated with experiencing a traumatic event shape the way you think, feel, and behave. The result is that after experiencing trauma you may feel a lot of fear that is not necessary and because of it avoid a lot of people, places, and situations that could potentially be wonderful experiences. The consequence is that the event may have in some way harmed you and the way that you have continued to think and respond continues to harm you.

By paying attention to what you are thinking you can begin to identify certain thoughts that are not objective, rational, true, or helpful. As you replace these irrational thoughts with rational ones you will have more positive energy and feel more balanced in living your life, choosing what you want to do instead of being focused on what you want to avoid. Follow these steps:

1. Raise your awareness and identify situations that trigger
   distress = predictability = control

2. Identify emotions and rate their intensity in an effort to identify underlying distressing thoughts (these are often identified as automatic thoughts)

3. Change your automatic thoughts. Create substitute states that are rational

4. Practice challenging negative thoughts with rational substitute thoughts and recognize the positive change in your emotions (less distressing)

5. Keep a journal of your identified negative thoughts, the intense negative emotion they create, and how you feel when you change that way of thinking, reinforcing change.

Challenging
Negative Self-talk

Increasing your awareness of negative self-talk is the cornerstone for controlling those harmful messages that trigger distress. It may seem that whatever triggers your distress pops up out of nowhere, but actually emotional and physical distress are triggered by negative thoughts and interpretations. Therefore, you have to work at carefully choosing thoughts and the interpretation of memories.

Once you identify the thought then you will be able to link to it the reaction it creates and the reason behind that reaction. For example:

Emotional trigger	= Fear
Reaction	= Escape
Reason	= Protect self from danger

Identifying negative thoughts is challenging for someone with PTSD because they invest a lot of energy in trying to not be aware of painful or distressing thoughts (which creates more distress and vulnerability). Unfortunately, this is the opposite of what is helpful. Once you identify the thought and increase your awareness of it and what it provokes then you begin to take control of it because you will be choosing how you are going to deal with it and if there are any associations to triggering it in your environment (people, times, situation that you experience). You are likely more aware of the emotion and reaction than the reason. This is common; now just take the time to refine your awareness about what the reason behind the trigger is and it will help you to determine whether it is associated with the past (traumatic event) or the present and a reasonable/rational response. In other words, if you are feeling the urge to escape due to experiencing fear, is there a safety issue in the present. If yes, take action and make sure you are safe. If not, then change the message to fit the situation. Regardless of how you answer, respond by understanding what is really taking place and problem-solve it rationally, not emotionally. Talk yourself through it.

When you start to develop an understanding of your emotional triggers you begin to think and feel differently about them. Understanding the reason or purpose behind the thoughts (avoidance = protection) allows you to accept your own emotions, not fear them. They lose their power over you because you are facing them. You find yourself more and more prepared to confront them with a response that is helpful to you instead of avoiding it. And the more you are prepared to face it the less you experience it.

Create a template for yourself, as shown below, to monitor your experience so that you can increase your awareness, be in the moment, and respond appropriately and effectively to your experiences using your rational mind. Once you identify the reason, add a rational response that actually matches the situation.

Emotional trigger	Reaction	Reason/What is rational?
e.g. Fear	e.g. Escape	e.g. Protect self from danger

Rational Self-talk and Difficult Anniversaries

It is common for people who have experienced traumatic events to have a difficult time emotionally when the anniversary of a traumatic experience takes place. Sometimes the distress occurs a long time before the anniversary because they are dreading facing the anniversary date; this is called anticipatory anxiety. On the anniversary of traumatic events, there may be an increase in distressing memories, and these memories may be triggered by reminders. An increase in distress around the anniversary date is known as an "anniversary reaction" and it can be mildly distressing for a few days or a more extreme reaction with the reoccurrence of posttraumatic symptoms such as:

- Re-experiencing: A reactivation of physiological responses, and thoughts that occurred at the time of the traumatic event such as fear, and being unsafe. There could be intrusive thoughts, difficulty concentrating, sleep disturbance and nightmares.

- Avoidance: A reactivation to avoid people, places, or situation that are connected to the traumatic event.

- Arousal: The reaction of feeling nervous, on edge, jumpy, and a need to be on guard.

Other types of anniversary reactions could be panic anxiety, specific fears, or phobic reactions, excessive worry, afraid to go certain places, fear for their safety or the safety of their loved ones. Awareness and support are a part of the continuing healing process.

Learning to deal with anniversary dates or time frames is another facet of healing. The emotional distress must be challenged with rational self-talk.

What You Can Do

- Most people feel better within a week or two. Remind yourself. "This will pass." In addition, over time the stress symptoms tend to decrease in frequency and severity.

- Make specific plans so that there are things to look forward to occupy that time frame instead of being isolated and having more time to think about what happened.

- Choose to participate in a manner to help other people such as a charitable donation, volunteering, dedicating a day to spend with family and friends, etc.

- Meet with your therapist or someone else you trust and plan how you want to deal with the anniversary of the event differently.

- If you experience fatigue:
  – Stick to your regular bedtime schedule
  – Remind yourself that you are not in any real danger, calm yourself down, talk to someone

- Difficulty with concentration:
  – Be realistic in the tasks that you can achieve
  – Break down tasks into small, manageable chunks
  – Write lists and slow down

- Increased emotionality:
  – Be grounded, be in the present not in the past. Breathe deeply
  – If you are getting angry, remove yourself from a situation
  – Exercise and take the time to talk to someone you trust.

Coping with an Anniversary Reaction

Anniversary reactions may be based on the way traumatic experiences are represented in memory. Traumatic memories carry with them information specific to the dangerousness of an event. The result could be physical reactiveness, avoidance, and re-experiencing with such a strong feeling of fear that it compels an individual to protect themselves from similar harm. Most people feel better within a couple of weeks after the anniversary of a traumatic event. Others take control by actively choosing to commemorate the anniversary date. Some helpful suggestions for coping are listed in Table 5.4.

Remember, everything that happens to you is a part of your own life history, find a way to honor your life and the lives of loved ones by searching for meaning.

Table 5.4 Tips for coping with anniversary reactions

Do	Plan a way to honor and remember a lost loved one
	Maintain a regular/normal routine
	Reminisce and tell favorite stories/memories about the person who has died
	Create a picture book with photos and associated memories of a lost loved one
	Make a donation to a charitable organization
	Make a toast or say a blessing/prayer at a family meal
	Listen to their favorite music and reminisce about fun memories—honor their life
	Plant a tree or dedicate an area in a park (bench), library, etc.
	Establish a scholarship
	Write cards, letters, or a journal to the loved one to express your feelings
	Create a new tradition
	Plan a distraction such as a weekend or vacation with people you enjoy and care about
	Remember what is still positive about life
	Celebrate the strengths you developed as a survivor of tragedy
	Find some way to turn a tragedy and loss into a way of honoring your lost loved one—don't let the event continue to take away all of the contributions they made while living
	Do something creative, take time to relax, and contemplate constructive ways to rebuild aspects of your life
	Exercise, eat a balanced diet, get adequate rest and utilize your resources
Don't	Drink or use other substances to numb emotions
	Allow yourself the luxury of being immobilized by pain, take it one hour at a time—one day at a time
	Read negative information or distressing news coverage
	Allow yourself to be stuck with anger or other negative emotions; consider attending a grief group or seeking other professional help
	Isolate and ruminate
	Spend time with negative or exploitive people
	Stay up all night or resist sleep to avoid being with normal emotions
	Focus on what wasn't done, wasn't said, or negative and sad experiences

DEALING WITH FEAR WHEN THE DANGER IS PAST

There are many common and normal reactions to danger, two of which are fear and arousal. Sometimes these reactions last for years. When you take the time to understand what causes your reactions to danger to continue when the danger is no longer present, and begin to consider your choices in how you can change both the thoughts and behaviors that have been sustaining it, you will have entered a very important stage of recovery and healing from trauma.

Two factors that maintain those reactions are avoidance and negative self-talk/perceptions. Consider the different ways in which these factors may have affected your recovery and healing.

Avoidance

You may be avoiding people, place, and situations/activities that remind you of your experience of trauma. Initially, avoidance can be a helpful survival mechanism. However, over time it serves to prolong and sustain posttrauma reactions, thus preventing healing and recovery from trauma.

When a person stays with feelings of fear for an extended period of time they misidentify their avoidance as being "safe" and managing their anxiety. Instead, the goal is to decrease anxiety by dealing with fear. Habituation is the process whereby anxiety is decreased on its own by confronting it. This is accomplished by learning relaxation techniques, exposure therapy (extended exposure and systematic desensitization), and positive self-talk/perception (cognitive restructuring/changing internal dialogue).

Negative Self-talk/ Perceptions

Examples of negative self-talk include:

- Catastrophizing
- Excessive worrying
- Self-blame/guilt
- Focus on the negatives instead of the possibilities.

The consequences are that opportunities and quality of life become limited. Fear of losing control often acts to maintain negative self-talk. This false perception is changed by honestly and accurately evaluating and challenging the way you think about yourself and the world. In your evaluation, if it is determined that there is some lingering issue which creates problems then clarify what your choices are for managing it or resolving it so that you can move forward in creating a fulfilling life to be shared with people and activities that are important to you. If you live in the past instead of in the moment, you are cheating yourself from living a full life. Life comprises moments.

Be careful in how you choose to think. Your thoughts will directly influence how you feel and the quality of your life. Use your journal to clarify your thoughts, associated issues, and feelings, how your life is affected, and what it is you are going to do to change it so that your life can be what you want it to be.

Anything unattempted remains impossible.

TALKING YOURSELF THROUGH FEAR

To talk yourself through fear you will first need to identify examples of what you are afraid of and what you choose to avoid (and why). You may be surprised to find that you have organized your entire life around avoidance and fear of:

- Thoughts
- Feelings
- Memories
- People
- Places
- Situations/activities.

Make a list of 10 things you fear that limit opportunities and quality of life, but are not dangerous to you.

1. _____
2. _____
3. _____
4. _____

5. _____

6. _____

7. _____

8. _____

9. _____

10. _____

Coping

Now you are going to decide what your choices are for dealing with each one of the things you fear that are on your list. To successfully accomplish this you will do the following:

1. Decide to face your fear.

2. Approach what you fear. This does not mean placing yourself in danger. It means repeatedly exposing yourself to people, places, or situations that provoke fear, but are not a danger to you.

3. For each issue of fear presented on the list you made, write down three choices for how you could deal with it.

4. Next, write how it will feel to accomplish confronting each point of fear.

5. Identify how confronting each point of fear will have a positive impact on your choices and quality of life.

6. Identify what could be obstructions to change.

7. Identify how you can deal with and overcome these obstructions to change.

8. Who can be an encouraging and reinforcing support system to you in making a decision to face your fears?

9. If you have made previous efforts to challenge your fears, identify what was helpful and what contributed to difficulties.

10. Clarify what is motivating you to make such important changes, "why now."

Destroy procrastination with change.

Og Mandino

FINDING MEANING: BEGINNING TO UNDERSTAND

As previously mentioned, you never waste anything that happens to you. Bad things happen to good people all the time. When something traumatic happens it changes how you feel and see your world, it takes something from you. In other words, experiencing a traumatic event changes you, but in no way does it mean that your life has been shortened, though such a thought is a common experience of those with PTSD. As difficult as it seems to do, if you are to heal you must find meaning from what has happened to you. The bottom line is that the ultimate goal is to transform a traumatic event into a life experience that makes you better, makes you stronger. You choose to learn something that is helpful to you from what started as a life crisis.

TRIGGERS AND FLASHBACKS

Identifying Triggers

Triggers can be an intruding aspect of the trauma or an environmental stimulus which serves as a provocational reminder of the experienced traumatic event. To accomplish this exercise you will need to ask yourself very detailed questions about the traumatic event you experienced. As always, your journal provides your own place to chronicle all things that are important to you. Identifying triggers is one of those things.

1. Write a list of known triggers (senses, people, places, situations) associated with the traumatic experience. If possible list 10 triggers, such as:
   - Senses
     - What did you see?
     - What did you hear?
     - What did you smell?
     - What did you taste?
     - What did you feel (pain, pressure, touch)?

   - People
     - Ages/any developmental issues
     - Attitude
     - Behavior
     - Characteristics
     - How they were dressed

   - Places
     - Details which have served as aspects of a flashback or trigger
     - Include time of day/year/season/weather

   - Situations/activities
     - Events/circumstances

2. Though it may be stressful, take the time to chronicle your responses to the experiences of flashbacks and triggers:
   - Has the manner in which you respond changed over time?
   - When you make that review keep in mind what responses were helpful or had positive results
   - Were there any positive feelings or positive recollections?

3. For a final review, look at each response and ask:
   - Would you like to deal with any of them differently?
   - What kind of responses would diminish the power of the triggers you experience?
   - What kind of responses would empower you?

Managing Flashbacks and Triggers

The more you resist the more it persists. It takes a lot of energy to fear and avoid. It is a miserable and painful existence. When you learn to manage the triggering events and flashbacks the trauma loses its power and you begin to take control. You have already identified your triggers and now you can begin to plan how you are going to deal with them before they happen. Being prepared, by itself, is a management tool. You begin to feel different just because you know that things are going to change—you are going to change.

STRESS MANAGEMENT

Basically, developing a management plan is what a person learns to do in order to neutralize the acute stress they experience. It involves the following:

- Self-care (confronting and managing acute stress requires being in good condition and taking good care of yourself):
  - Adequate sleep/rest
  - Adequate nutrition
  - Positive social support system (make a list of the people who are supportive of your recovery)
  - No substance abuse (including caffeine)
  - Exercise
  - What else is an important part of your self-care plan?
- Self-soothing (learning to enjoy quiet time with yourself)
- Breathing exercises
- Relaxation techniques
- Visualization/imagery of safe and soothing places
- Maintain a list of priorities (know what is important)
- Keep additional stress to a minimum (while working on mastery of managing triggers/flashbacks)
- Engage problem-solving (create choices for dealing with issues)
- Graded exposure (plan what you are to have contact with and what you are not. Start with the easiest to control and manage)
- Journaling for reinforcement
- Medication for mood management and stabilization (consult your physician)
- Self-monitoring—Use your journal to monitor what is most useful to you, how it helps, and the difficulties and/or progress that you are experiencing in your recovery efforts.

Remember that how you deal with everything in your life is *your* choice.

As you can see, there are numerous resources, however, if you do not do anything different nothing is going to be different.

This exercise is a lot of work and can be stressful itself. However, it is work that once completed can change the quality of your life. The goal is to become neutral to the specific triggers that you have identified. When triggers lose their power you no longer have any particular thoughts or feelings about them. What this means is that in accordance with priorities, it is much more important to manage/control what you think you feel (inside) versus all the triggers and other distressing factors (outside); then you are truly able to acknowledge and accept all that is a part of your life history and the power of triggers and flashbacks are diminished.

Warning Signs of Stress

If you lack awareness of the stress that you are experiencing, your emotions and behaviors both give indications of what you are going through, as shown in Table 5.5.

Table 5.5 Emotional and behavioral signs of unacknowledged stress

Emotional signs	Apathy, feelings of sadness
	No longer finding previous activities pleasurable
	Anxiety, easily agitated, restless, excessive worry
	Feelings of guilt and unworthiness
	Irritability, defensiveness, anger, argumentativeness
	Mentally exhausted and preoccupied, lack of flexibility
	Avoidance and denial that you are experiencing problems
Behavioral signs	Avoidant behavior
	Difficulty accepting/neglecting responsibility
	Poor self-care (hygiene)
	Legal problems
	Financial problems
	Difficulty controlling anger or aggressive behavior

Relaxation Techniques

Deep Breathing (5 minutes)

1. Select a comfortable sitting position.

2. Close your eyes and direct your attention to your own breathing process.

3. Think about nothing but your breathing, let it flow in and out of your body.

4. Say to yourself, "I am relaxing, breathing smoothly and rhythmically. Fresh oxygen is flowing in and out of my body, I feel calm, renewed, and refreshed."

5. Continue to focus on your breathing as it flows in and out, in and out, thinking about nothing but the smooth rhythmical process of your own breathing.

6. After 5 minutes, stand up, stretch, smile, and continue with your daily activities.

Mental Relaxation (5–10 minutes)

1. Select a comfortable sitting or reclining position.

2. Close your eyes, and think about a place that you have been before that you found to be a perfect place for mental and physical relaxation. This should be a quiet or soothing environment, such as the ocean, the mountains, a forest, a panoramic view, etc. If you can't think of a real place, then create one.

3. Now imagine that you are in your ideal relaxation place. Imagine that you are seeing all of the colors, hearing all of the sounds, smelling all of the different scents. Just lie back and enjoy your soothing, rejuvenating environment.

4. Feel the peacefulness, the calmness, and imagine your whole body and mind being renewed and refreshed.

5. After 5–10 minutes slowly open your eyes and stretch. You have the realization that you may instantly return to your relaxation place whenever you desire, and experience a peacefulness and calmness in body and mind.

Brief Relaxation

1. Get comfortable.

2. You are going to count backwards from ten to zero.

3. Silently say each number as you exhale.

4. As you count you will relax more deeply and go deeper and deeper into a state of relaxation. When you reach zero, you will be completely relaxed.

5. You feel more and more relaxed, you can feel the tension leave your body.

6. You are becoming as limp as a rag doll, the tension is going away.

7. You are very relaxed.

8. Now drift deeper with each breath, deeper and deeper.

9. Feel the deep relaxation all over and continue relaxation.

10. Now, relaxing deeper you should feel an emotional calm. Tranquil and serene feelings, feelings of safety and security, and a calm peace. Try to get a quiet inner confidence; a good feeling about yourself and relaxation.

11. Study once more the feelings that come with relaxation. Let your muscles switch off, feel good about everything. Calm and serene surroundings make you feel more and more tranquil and peaceful. You will continue to relax for several minutes.

12. When I tell you to start, count from one to three, silently say each number as you take a deep breath.

13. Open your eyes when you get to three. You will be relaxed and alert. When you open your eyes you will find yourself back in the place where you started your relaxation. The environment will seem slower and more calm. You will be more relaxed and peaceful. Now count from one to three.

Brief Progressive Muscle Relaxation

1. Clench both fists, feel the tension. Relax slowly ... feel the tension leave. Feel the difference now that the muscles are relaxed.

2. Tighten the muscles in both arms. Contract the biceps ... now relax the arms slowly.

3. Curl the toes downward until the muscles are tight up through the thigh ... now slowly relax. Feel the tension ease.

4. Curl the toes upward until the muscles in back of the legs are tight ... now relax slowly.

5. Push the stomach muscles out and make it tight. Now slowly ... relax. Your arms are relaxed, your legs are relaxed, and your even breathing gives you a feeling of calmness and releases stress.

6. Pull your stomach in up until your diaphragm feels the pressure. Now ... slowly relax. Feel the tension ease.

7. Pull your shoulders up to your ears. Feel the tension in your back and chest. Now ... slowly relax. Let your arms relax. You are feeling good. Your breathing is easy and restful.

8. Tilt your head backwards as far as you can. Stretch the muscles. Feel the tenseness. Now … slowly relax. Feel the tension go.

9. Wrinkle your forehead. Hold it. Feel the tension. Now … relax. Feel the tension go.

10. Squint your eyes as tight as you can. Hold it. Now … relax.

11. Make a face using all of your face muscles. Hold it. Now relax … slowly … let it go. Your arms are relaxed … your breathing is easy and you feel good all over.

12. In a perfect state of relaxation you are unwilling to move a single muscle in your body. All you feel is peaceful, quiet and relaxed. Continue to relax. When you want to get up, count backward from four to one. You will feel relaxed and refreshed, wide aware and calm.

Mental Imagery (Visualization 10–15 Minutes)
Mental imagery can deepen relaxation when used with other techniques, or may be used by itself. The purpose is to calm your body, thoughts, and emotions. It gives you the opportunity to take a break from tension and stress. Mental imagery uses all of your senses to create and recreate a relaxing place, perhaps a meadow, a walk through the woods, along the beach, or perhaps a special place from your memory.

Prepare your environment so that you can complete this relaxation exercise without interruption. Spend your time getting comfortable. Close your eyes, as you scan your body for any tension. If you find tension release it. Let it go and relax.

- Relax your head and your face
- Relax your shoulders
- Relax your arms and hands
- Relax your chest and lungs
- Relax your back
- Relax your stomach
- Relax your hips, legs, and feet.

1. Experience a peaceful, pleasant, and comfortable feelings of being relaxed as you prepare to make an imaginary trip to a beautiful place.

2. Take a deep breath, and breath out slowly and easily. Take a second deep breath, and slowly breath out. Allow your breathing to become slow and rhythmic.

3. Picture yourself on a mountaintop. It has rained and a warm wind is carrying the clouds away. The sky is clear and blue, and the sun is shining down.

4. Below you see beautiful green trees. You enjoy the fragrance of the forest after the rain. In the distance you see a beautiful white, sandy beach. Beyond that, as far as you can see, is crystal clear, brilliant blue water. A fluffy cloud drifts in the gentle breeze until it is right over you. You experience a very pleasant, delightful feeling. As the fluffy cloud moves down across your face, you feel the cool, moist touch of it on your face. As it moves down your body, all of the tension slips away, and you find yourself completely relaxed and happy.

5. As the soft cloud moves across your body, it gently brings a feeling of total comfort and peace. As it sinks down around you it brings a feeling of deep relaxation. The little cloud sinks beneath you, and you are now sitting on it. The cloud holds you up perfectly and safely. You feel secure. The little cloud begins to move slowly downward and from your secure position on it, you can see the beautiful forest leading down to the beach. There is a gentle rocking motion as you drift along. You feel no cares or concerns in the world, and are completely focused on the relaxed feeling you experience. The cloud can take you any place you want to go, and you choose to go to the beach. As you move to the beach, the cloud gently comes to the ground and stops. You get off the soft cloud onto the beach, and you are at peace.

6. You take some time to look around at the white, sandy beach, and the beautiful blue water. You can hear seagulls and the roar of the waves. As you feel the sun shining on you, you can smell the ocean air. It smells good. As you walk slowly on the beach, you enjoy the warm sand on your feet. Just ahead on the beach is a soft blanket and pillow. You lie down and enjoy the soft material on the back of your legs and arms. As you listen to the waves, the seagulls, and feel the warmth of the sun through the cool breeze, you realize that you are comfortable, relaxed, and at peace.

7. You feel especially happy because you realize that you can return to this special and beautiful place any time you want to. Feeling very relaxed, you choose to go back to the place where you started, knowing that you will take these peaceful and relaxed feelings with you. There is a stairway close by that leads you back to the room where you started. As you climb the five steps, you will become more aware of your surroundings, but you will feel relaxed and refreshed. You are at the bottom of the stairs now, and begin climbing.
   – Step 1 to Step 2: moving upward
   – Step 2 to Step 3: feeling relaxed and more aware
   – Step 3 to Step 4: you are aware of what is around you, and your body is relaxed
   – Step 4 to Step 5: your mind is alert and refreshed, open your eyes and stretch gently.

To fully experience the varying sensations associated with different images meditate on the following topics, adding others to expand your experience if you choose:

- A mountain lake
- A forest
- A happy time in your life or pleasing experience
- Radiating physical health
- White light
- A colorful desert scene.

Using Music
Music can be soothing and relaxing. Make a list of pieces of music that you find calming and meditative. If you are uncertain about the types of music which could be helpful, try classical, instrumental, chanting, and symphony pieces. Most large bookstores and music stores now allow you to listen to a piece of music before you buy it to help you choose. You could

also ask friends or relations who listen to a variety of music who may be able to provide you with some different pieces or artists to try out to give you some idea of how to proceed.

Whatever you choose it must be personal. It needs to be music that would result in the same type of relaxation that you would experience by the mastering of other relaxation techniques. You will be pleasantly surprised by what a wonderful calming resource music can be.

Building Relaxation Techniques into Your Life

You have several options as to how you choose to use these relaxation techniques. You can, through repetition, familiarize yourself with any of the relaxation scripts so that over time you will be able to create the internal dialogue with ease. Alternatively, you can ask someone you trust, who has a soothing voice, to read the script, to guide you though the technique.

If using your own soothing voice, you can make a tape or compact disc (cd) of the script being read by you. An advantage of this is that after a number of repetitions you internalize the script in your own voice. In addition, you find that after a while that you do not need to listen to the recorded script to achieve the relaxed and peaceful results, you simply choose to remove all environmental distractions and take yourself through the relaxation.

If you do not feel that the techniques presented here are useful to you take responsibility to search for a technique that is. Ask those that you trust if they have any ideas or recommendations. Remain focused on the importance of finding all the ways that you can take care of yourself to make your life better.

Most important of all, recognize that there is no limitation placed on what may be relaxing to you. Think in terms of all your senses: serene visuals, relaxing sounds, relaxing smells, soothing taste, and relaxing touch.

DEVELOPING AND UTILIZING SOCIAL SUPPORTS

If you currently lack emotional health it is likely that you are socially withdrawn and not participating in activities that would normally be pleasurable and are thus feeling and being deprived of social support. An essential way to re-establish emotional health and well-being is to develop and utilize appropriate, dependable, and trustworthy social support systems.

Most people need several people to talk to, spend time with, enjoy activities with, and to challenge irrational or narrow/rigid thinking. Whoever the potential candidates are they must be people you care about and want to spend time with. A partner or a family member may be a likely candidate for your support system. You may meet and develop relationships with people through activities or interests that you have in common. Some of these relationships may be strong enough for them to become part of your support system. The common denominator in such relationships is mutual care, positive regard, and trust.

Characteristics of a Supportive Relationship

A supportive relationship will be one with someone who displays the following characteristics:

- Objectivity and open-mindedness. Not judgmental

- They support and affirm your individuality. They respect your strength and do not take advantage of your difficulties

- They empathize with you, making an effort to understand how you think and feel

- They accept you as you are

- They are on your side, appropriately supporting you as you work through difficult issues.

A useful exercise is to list the people who make up your support system:

1. _____
2. _____
3. _____
4. _____
5. _____

If you have a small support system of just one or two people there is no need to feel bad about yourself or think that there is no hope to change it. What you have done is accomplish the first step in understanding what you need to do to change your circumstances.

What Stands in Your Way of Developing your Support System?

Check all that apply:

☐ You have a difficult time reaching out

☐ You have a hard time making and keeping friends

☐ You have low self-esteem

☐ You tend to be needy and draining on others

☐ You become overly dependent and wear people out

☐ You lack the social skills necessary to develop relationships

☐ You have inappropriate behavior which embarrasses yourself and others

☐ You are unreliable.

DEALING WITH ONE TRIGGER AT A TIME: SAFELY EXPOSING YOURSELF TO THE PAST

Without going into distressing details of the traumatic event you experienced, write a brief narrative just as you would to share with someone else. This means having a beginning, middle and end. Remember, this is meant to be a brief but meaningful narrative, not an emotional storm. You are in control and only you know the basics of your experience which can be revealed while maintaining feelings of safety. Considering the following types of information to include in your brief narrative:

- Age
- Time frame of experience (when, how long)
- Environmental details
- Your interpretation of what took place
- Your belief of how it impacted you (then and now).

Actively working on a trigger can be very stressful work. You may be contemplating how you are going to deal with numerous triggers and feeling overwhelmed. The goal is to make this work as manageable as possible. Even dealing with one trigger at a time can stimulate negative emotions, increase body tension, cause physical symptoms, and increase stress in relationships. Therefore, consider the following points for maximizing your feelings of control, diminishing the power of any trigger and bringing issues to resolution.

1. Write out the trigger you are challenging from your list of triggers which have been rated for associated stress level.

2. Remind yourself that you have already survived the real life experience.

3. Rate the triggers by degree of stress and complexity, arranging them in order of when you will focus your efforts and resources on resolving them.

4. Remember that it is in your control to take a break if you feel that you need to put your work aside and soothe or distract yourself in order to come back to the task refreshed.

5. You can choose to ignore the influence of the trigger, thus taking away the power it has held over you.

6. You can choose any technique of distraction from the trigger if you do need a break.

All of these factors highlight the numerous points of control you experience at every step of the work that you are doing.

After each session of work effort dealing with a trigger and increasing your control review the following:

- What was most useful in improving your management and control in dealing with that specific trigger?

- What have you learned that will be helpful in managing other triggers?

- How does it feel to make your healing a priority and begin to master what has controlled you?

Trusting Yourself to Confront Triggers

In trusting yourself to confront triggers you learn to cope more effectively with what you have already survived. Begin to diminish the power of the trigger by writing them down and talking about them. Demystify them.

Start by asking yourself which triggers provoke the most fear and avoidance. Make a list, and for each one, note why it is that it provokes fear.

1. _____
2. _____
3. _____
4. _____
5. _____

For each trigger you identified, offer two ways in which you can effectively manage your responses, and one way that will reinforce your accomplishment (i.e. journaling about it, talking to your therapist, changing thoughts/behaviors that you can feel safe to engage in, etc.).

- Trigger 1_____
  Two ways to manage:

  _____
  _____

One way to reinforce:

_____

- Trigger 2 _____

Two ways to manage:

_____

_____

One way to reinforce:

_____

It is recommended that you record all of your efforts and experiences in working toward resolution in your journal. The information will be helpful to clarify issues and patterns (positive and negative), reinforce change, and aid in problem-solving. As you work on triggers, write about what happened and what you learned by learning to effectively manage triggers.

SELF-MONITORING

From time to time review your working through experience of healing and recovery. Try to think about what you believe would be helpful to review. If you are not able to decide what kinds of questions would offer a helpful review of your recovery experience maybe the following will give you some idea. Self-monitoring is a good tool for every experience of expected self-responsibility, change, growth, and unforeseen challenges.

1. What are your current beliefs associated with the traumatic event?

_____

_____

2. What emotions are you experiencing?

_____

_____

3. What are your physical or somatic experiences (body reactions)?

_____

_____

4. What are your behavioral response(s) to what you are experiencing?

_____

_____

5. What are you denying?

_____

_____

6. What are you avoiding?

_____

_____

7. What do you want?

_____

_____

8. What do you need?

_____

_____

CHALLENGING AVOIDANCE: FACING THE PROBLEM

In general, the longer the avoidance, the longer and more entrenched the issues of avoidance are likely to be. It is not uncommon or abnormal to want to avoid remembering or re-experiencing something traumatic. In the short term, as an initial coping mechanism it seemed to help because it simply felt better to avoid something that caused so much pain and distress. However, it is not the answer because avoidance:

1. Makes the problem more powerful and overwhelming. This often results in chronically being on edge and depressed

2. Can lead to other problems:
   – Undermines self-confidence
   – Increases potential for resentment and other negative emotions
   – Complicates relationships

3. Can lead to overall interference in your life by resulting in lack of joy, lack of trust, lowered expectations, etc.

4. Can increase risk of self-destructive behaviors such as substance abuse and the use of other compulsive behaviors.

Sometimes the reason(s) for avoidance is obvious. However, there may be more of a complicating web of issues that are associated with avoidant behavior. Often, when you acknowledge what you are avoiding there may be the realization that you are also avoiding many other things. It is also common that the internal self-talk message associated with and reinforced by avoidance is that whatever it is must be avoided because it is so stressful, scary, and/or overwhelming. Ultimately, your avoidance prevents you from finding solutions.

Some suggested tactics for dealing with avoidance include:

• Pay attention to your feelings. Do you avoid something because it makes you feel anxious or worried? Perhaps the most important question you could ask yourself about avoidance is, "What would I need to do to feel more comfortable and confident?"

• Self-observation. How do you deal with situations where you feel stuck or immobilized? What do you need to do to get unstuck?

• Self-talk. Do you worry excessively, catastrophize and expect a negative outcome?

• Self-responsibility:
   – What actions do you need to heal?
   – What resources are going to be helpful and supportive of your healing and recovery?
   – How will you keep yourself on track for recovery?

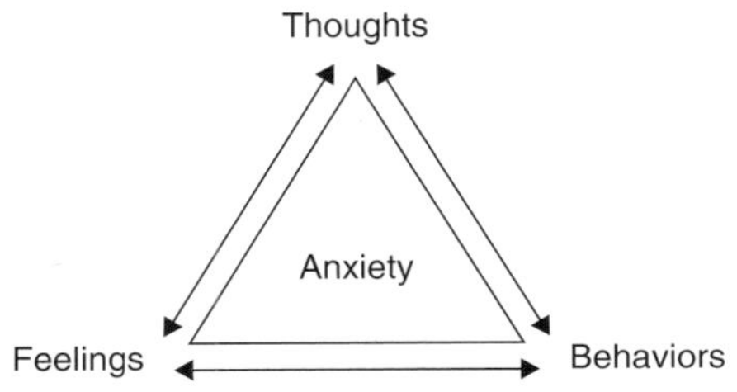

Figure 5.1
Anxiety: a self-perpetuating cycle.

- Self-confidence:
  - How does avoidance erode self-confidence?
  - What types of thoughts would improve self-confidence?
  - What kinds of actions or behaviors would improve self-confidence?
  - How will improved self-confidence improve self-management?

Thoughts, feelings and behavior are all associated with one another and with anxiety (Figure 5.1).

Before pursuing the change you desire, take the time to thoroughly understand what you are doing so that there are no unwanted remnants of old thoughts and behaviors that are going to impede your progress or become woven into your new way of doing things. This exercise will also add clarity to the prioritizing of your focus of recovery and the required efforts for the desired achievement. Matsakis (1998) has acknowledged the numerous behaviors used by trauma survivors to avoid triggers.

The Avoidance Continuum

$$\text{Numb} \Rightarrow \text{Shutdown} \Rightarrow \text{Dissociation}$$

A major consequence is the use of dissociation as a means of protecting the self from the perceived threat, memories, and negative emotions associated with the traumatic event. How many of the following do you experience?

☐ Poor memory	☐ Feeling detached from others
☐ Feeling confused	☐ No interest in sex/sexual dysfunction
☐ Clouded thinking	☐ Lack of emotional/physical control
☐ Unable to concentrate	☐ Lack of energy
☐ Emotional outbursts (rage)	☐ Pulling away from life/isolating
☐ Panic	☐ Separating from your body
☐ Loss of interest in previously pleasurable activities	☐ Out of touch with your surroundings (spectator)
☐ Fall asleep in the presence of others	☐ Stare into space/lose time
☐ Self-mutilation (to release pain or feel alive)	☐ Escaping into fantasy/daydreams
☐ Emptiness	☐ Increase compulsivity (work, substances, sex, gambling, food, etc.)
☐ Increasing need for stimulation	☐ Acting younger than you are
☐ High-risk behaviors (don't care if die, counter emptiness, feel alive)	☐ Magical thinking

The items you checked in this list are a priority to address because they contribute to the foundation of safety, self-care, and emotional well-being. If the basics are not strong you could retraumatize yourself or feel like you take one step forward and two steps back. Work with your therapist and support system to:

- Get stronger
- Be aware of yourself and your surroundings

- Be safe
- Make sure you practice good self-care behaviors.

Rothchild (2000) states that the most common kind of dissociation is varying degrees of amnesia. This is where a person dissociates part of what they have seen or experienced. It is the total repression of memory and physical experience associated with a traumatic event. With dissociation, awareness for surroundings splits off in some manner. Dissociation can take place at the physical, memory/thinking, or emotional level.

It is possible to dissociate at one or all levels at the same time. Dissociation is an extreme defense mechanism for coping with an event which has been interpreted as intolerable. It exists on physical, thinking, and emotional levels:

- Physical level of dissociation: An example would be that you do not feel part of your body during a traumatic experience. There is no sensation of pain
- Thinking level of dissociation: An example would be separating out various aspects of the traumatic experience and only having an awareness of certain memories
- Emotional level of dissociation: For example, when exposed to certain people or situations you feel numb.

Write about your experience and how you are going to begin to challenge it:

_____
_____
_____
_____
_____
_____

OVERCOMING DISSOCIATION

Overcoming dissociation (the continuum of dissociation including amnesia) is important to the resolution of PTSD. Symbolically it connects the dots for the disturbing array of experiences that are disjointed:

- Repetitive dreams/nightmares
- Sleep disturbance
- Symptoms that cannot be related specifically to anything
- Compulsive disorders
- Chronic acute anxiety
- Eating disorders
- Sexual disorders
- Substance abuse.

It is not necessary to recall every detail of a traumatic event to reach resolution, personal growth, and meaning. Instead, envision a box with a lid on it. When there is a troubling or overwhelming distress the lid is slightly ajar and does not fit securely on the box. To make the lid fit does not require that everything be taken out of the box, carefully examined piece by piece and then rearranged in some special order. Instead the goal is to deal with a sufficient

Table 5.6   Implicit and explicit memories

Implicit memory	Sensory images (visual and auditory memory)
	Body sensations (pain/numbness/tingling)
	Emotional reactions (feat/anger/guilt/grief/shame)
	Nervous system responses (parasympathetic–involuntary responses to fear-based stress)
Explicit memory	Psychological (beliefs/meaning)
	Cognitive (facts/sequence of events)

amount of the right issues pushing on the lid so that it is able to fit securely without worry, stress, or pressure. Memory is not perfect. Numerous factors influence the quality of memory and associated emotions. For example, there may not be memory for some aspects of a trauma, there may be fragments or flashbacks.

A significant problem resulting from this phenomenon is memory confusion. What does a fragment mean or what experience is it related to? Are there any distortions or did it actually happen the way it is remembered? How can I bring understanding to the experience of flashbacks? Memory can be visualized as:

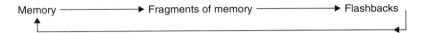

It is possible to simply forget details of traumatizing events. However, in an effort to understand dissociation, keep in mind the vast richness of memory. Memories can be classified as implicit or explicit (Table 5.6).

Levine's (1992) SIBAM model of dissociation (see Chapter 3) offers a simple overview to the central response factors associated with the experience of a traumatic event and resulting dissociation. One or more of the following factors can become dissociated during a traumatic event versus remaining intact as the integration of a "whole memory":

S = Sensation—physical reactions and body (somatic memories)

I = Image—pictures that remain in your mind (visual memories)

B = Behavior—what you did during the trauma

A = Affect—emotional responses (emotional memory)

M = Meaning—how you make sense of what happened (searching for meaning).

Do you dissociate?_____Yes_____No

If yes, in what circumstances or situations do you dissociate?

_____

_____

What dissociative reactions do you experience (Schiraldi, 2000)? When I dissociate, I:

☐ Lie very still

☐ Am slow to respond to others

☐ Seem to move in slow motion

☐ Have flat (muted) emotions

☐ Don't feel pain

☐ Daydream or stare off into space

☐ Tune out

☐ Have lapses in my memory

☐ Feel as if I am on autopilot

☐ Feel as if I am a stranger in my own world

☐ Feel as if I am watching myself from outside my own body

☐ Feel as if I am in a fog.

When do you feel the sensations or do the behaviors you checked?

_____

_____

Understanding Feeling in Control

Write some detailed information about how and when you feel control over the following areas of your life and why.

1. Thoughts

_____

_____

2. Feelings

_____

_____

3. Home

_____

_____

4. Family (parents, marriage, children, relatives)

_____

_____

5. Relationships (friendships, co-workers)

_____

_____

6. Recreation

_____

_____

7. Work/school

_____

_____

8. Religion/spirituality

_____

_____

Dissociation and Three Modes of Memory

According to Bandler and Grinder (1979) there are three primary modes of memory: visual, auditory, and feeling. People think in all of these modes. They think visually (using their mind's eye), they think auditorily (tone of voice and words vocally communicated), and kinesthetically (gut feelings, and physical descriptors such as "she's cold and uncaring," "get a handle on it," "this doesn't feel right," etc.). Recognizing when and why you are dissociated can help you to utilize your grounding techniques to prevent it from occurring.

- Visual:
  - Seeing images of things seen before, as they were seen (remembered)
  - Seeing images of things never seen before (constructed)

- Auditory:
  - Remembered sounds or words
  - Constructed sounds or words

- Feeling:
  - Feeling of emotions and sense of touch.

Bandler and Grinder (1979, 1985) recognized and explored the impact of the statement "everything that happens to you is a part of who you are." While they may not have specifically said that, they demonstrated by the different exercises they developed which explored the parts of the self at varying developmental stages and how those experiences get frozen in time. The following is an adaptation of one of their techniques.

If you recognize that you have dissociated some aspect of a traumatic event:

1. Play the reel in your mind, as if you are watching a movie.

2. Using your safe place as a sanctuary from fear, pain, and distrust, anchor yourself in the here and now. Take in the calming details of the safe place you have created. Use it as verification that nothing can hurt you when you are there.

3. Freeze frame. Freeze all the sensory associations:
   - Seeing
   - Hearing
   - Feeling

Put it in a box, compartmentalize it. Remain in your body, in the present.

4. Take the time to soothe and comfort yourself from what you have survived. If you are struggling emotionally in the here and now as you do this exercise then do what you have learned are the best ways to calm and care for yourself. If you are feeling the pain of the younger you that experienced the trauma, then take the time to be validating, caring, and understanding of how that experience affected you. Care for and comfort that younger you.

5. If necessary, use your grounding techniques to be in the here and now. Remember, this exercise contributes to your management of dissociation, which may have started out as a useful defense mechanism that over time has complicated how you manage your daily life.

What did you learn about you, taking care of yourself, and managing dissociation in this exercise?

Table 5.7   Physiological outcomes commonly related to PTSD

Neurobiological changes	Brainwave activity
	Size of brain structures
	Memory functions
	Fear response
Psychophysiological changes	Hyperarousal of the sympathetic nervous system
	Increased startle response
	Involuntary movement (tics and twitches)
	Sleep disturbances
	Increased neurohormonal changes, resulting in heightened stress/anxiety or increased depression
Physical complaints	Headaches
	Stomachaches
	Body aches
	Digestive problems (diarrhea or irritable bowel syndrome)
	Lack/increase in appetite
	Immune system problems
	Sexual/reproductive problems without identified underlying medical problem
	Asthma or breathing problems
	Dizziness
	Chest pain
	Chronic pain
	Fibromyalgia
	Others?

PROBLEM-SOLVING THE PHYSICAL SYMPTOMS OF PTSD

There are numerous physical symptoms and health issues associated with trauma. If you had a strong physiological reaction to trauma you will need to address these issues in the healing process (van der Kolk, 1997). Create the opportunity to review your lifestyle patterns and self-care behaviors:

1. What are the ways in which you take care of yourself?

2. What self-care behaviors are beneficial as part of a daily and weekly routine?

3. Do you treat your emotional and physical health like a priority?

4. Does your lifestyle routine create a positive balance of productivity and self-care?

5. Are those close to you supportive of your priority of self-care?

What other issues can you identify that are associated with the physical symptoms you experience that are related to PTSD?

Some of the physiological outcomes commonly related to PTSD are listed in Table 5.7.

Following a traumatic event numerous physical systems are agitated. Therefore, the body needs calm, soothing and care for optimal healing. Create a mental and visual image of health and recovery that becomes the life you live.

IDENTIFYING AND MANAGING EMOTION

A range of emotional symptoms of increased arousal are associated with trauma. Check all the responses that you identify with in the following symptoms lists:

DEPRESSION

- ☐ Sad
- ☐ Low energy level fatigued
- ☐ Short-tempered/irritable
- ☐ Apathetic
- ☐ Low self-esteem
- ☐ Body aches (headaches/stomachaches etc.)
- ☐ Anger
- ☐ Negative repetitive thoughts
- ☐ Hopeless
- ☐ Helpless
- ☐ No motivation
- ☐ Social withdrawal/isolation
- ☐ Sleep disturbance
- ☐ Appetite disturbance
- ☐ Lack of pleasure in previously pleasurable activities
- ☐ Memory disturbance
- ☐ Difficulty with concentration and attention
- ☐ Hoping to die/hating your existence
- ☐ Pain so deep it can't be fixed
- ☐ Suicidal thoughts/plan.

Management Choices; the Way Out of Depression

1. If you have a history of depression or are aware that you experience chronic depression consult your physician for medication if you are not currently being prescribed antidepressant medication.

2. Become more aware of the subtleties of your symptoms through education (reading) and charting your moods. This will make you more familiar with the warning signs of depression and allow for earlier intervention.

3. Using the symptom list above, take responsibility for how you think and feel and choose to seek ways to understand, manage, and resolve the disturbance they bring to your life. This is part of your journey in understanding who you are and why.

4. Create a lifestyle which assures taking good care of yourself, including eating well, getting adequate rest/sleep, exercising, quiet time/meditation, spending time with people you enjoy who share your ideas of good self-care choices, continue to work on understanding who you are and why, create an overall positive daily structure which encourages personal growth and meeting goals.

PANIC ANXIETY

Panic attacks are diagnosed when an individual experiences at least four of the following 13 symptoms. The symptoms develop and peak in a short period of time, which results in significant feelings of distress.

- ☐ Palpitations/pounding heart/accelerated heart rate.
- ☐ Chest pain/tightness
- ☐ Sweating
- ☐ Chills/hot flashes
- ☐ Trembling/shaking
- ☐ Feeling short of breath
- ☐ Feeling of choking
- ☐ Nausea/abdominal distress
- ☐ Feeling dizzy/lightheadedness
- ☐ Numbness/tingling in hands or feet
- ☐ Derealization (feelings of unreality)
- ☐ Depersonalization (being detached from oneself)
- ☐ Fear of losing control
- ☐ Fear of going crazy
- ☐ Fear of dying.

Treatment for Panic Anxiety

Possible treatment includes:

- A physical examination to rule out any health-related issues that are causing your symptoms or reinforcing how you are interpreting your symptoms
- Cognitive behavioral therapy
- Medication
- Health behaviors (exercise, decrease or eliminate caffeine and alcohol, positive daily structure, appropriate use of resources and develop a self-care plan)
- Increased understanding of what panic attacks are (relaxation, exercise, challenge negative self-talk, etc.)
- Awareness of painful memories or associations to a traumatic experience.

BEING MINDFUL IN MANAGING ANXIETY

How you choose to think is going to have a significant effect on your recovery experience. Your success in recovery may also depend a lot on the mind-set you have about what you are attempting to accomplish in the therapy process. Expect to experience anxiety as a normal part of recovery, and acknowledge verbally and in writing how you plan to manage it. Anxiety is not always a bad thing. It offers you information about how you are responding, thinking, and feeling in association to what has happened to you. It also is common to experience anxiety when making changes. If you can create ways of thinking that are motivating for you to accomplish your recovery tasks instead of dreading them you will begin to understand how powerful your choice of mind-set truly is.

Anxiety may be uncomfortable, but it also helps us to survive by acting as a warning system. Identify any negative thoughts you have about what you will be working on in your recovery and work toward modifying those thoughts into a useful mind-set that not only accepts anxiety as a normal part of life, but a valuable life experience. Choose to make your recovery efforts a journey of self-understanding and empowerment.

Be A.W.A.R.E.

Adapted from Beck et al. (1985):

- Behave in ways that reinforce your efforts and reinforce a healthy lifestyle and relationship

- Acknowledge and accept your anxiety. Become more familiar with how your level of anxiety goes up and down depending on thoughts, feelings, and experiences. You may increase your awareness for this fluctuation of change by rating the level of your anxiety on a 1–10 scale

- Act in accordance with the anxiety you experience. Use the skills you learn in therapy and from recovery tasks to change your response to anxiety to being "normal" instead of being overwhelmed and fearful. Whatever you have experienced is something you have already survived. Therefore, be in the present with how you think about it and deal with. Do not let it interfere with what you need to be doing in the present

- Repeat acknowledgment and acceptance. Allow yourself to be with your anxiety and allow time to pass. Again, pay attention to the quality of your anxiety experience until it begins to subside

- Expect your fear to continue to resurface. In all likelihood you have repetitively experienced fear for some time, which triggers anxiety. Instead of hoping for fear and anxiety to disappear forever, remind yourself of the skills you are learning which will allow to effectively manage it. Managing fear and anxiety will be the new normal.

Write a list of the skills you have learned that will help you to manage fear and anxiety:

_____

_____

_____

_____

_____

MINDFULNESS

Being mindful refers to being in the present where you choose:

1. To acknowledge the past as what you have already survived

2. To be in the moment by accepting what is actually happening at this moment

3. How you interpret what happens

4. To decide how to think and respond to what you are experiencing in the moment

5. To reframe or rethink what is happening now as an opportunity to manage with new skills and new ways of thinking. Trusting yourself.

The Importance of Mindfulness

The traumatic experience that changed how you think and feel has continued to steal from you. This is seen by the difficulty that those who have experienced trauma have in being in the present moment instead of responding as if they were still stuck in the moment of the trauma. The trauma intrudes in the form of thoughts, flashbacks, and nightmares which are the consequences of fear, avoidance, and hyperarousal. The result is that they are unable to live life fully and have chronic negative thoughts and worry of the past and worry about the future. Mindfulness is the choice to live in the present with all the resources of knowledge, skill, and support that did not exist at the time of the trauma.

Being mindful is the act of being freed from the shackles of the past.

Being Present and Accounted for

When you choose to be in the present you are making a choice to deal with what is happening in your life right now. This requires using all five senses—sight, hearing, touch, smell, taste. Making this choice and learning to live life in the moment allows you to effectively meet the challenges that life brings you. Being in the moment and committing yourself to learn recovery skills puts you in the best position to:

• Solve your problems

• Manage your emotions

• Cope with life.

When you are first practicing living in the present you begin to experience how you are less focused on the past and are free to function fully and enjoy what is happening in your life at this moment. Instead you are focused on the future and all that your life can be.

Getting to the Right State of Mind: the Wise Mind

Being mindful takes you to the right state of mind. It is the right state of mind that encourages and reinforces effective dealing with what is currently happening in your life. It is the right state of mind, the wise mind, where you are able to make choices and decisions that help get you what you want out of life. To get into the right state of mind and out of the reactionary emotional mind requires that you be present and aware of your thoughts and emotions. The right state of mind, the wise mind, is reasonable and logical. When you choose to be in the present and use logic you will be making the choice to manage your life and reach your goals.

Identify the stumbling blocks that stop you living in the moment so that you can get the appropriate supports to develop the skills which will enable you to effectively manage what is happening in your life today.

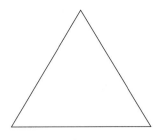

Emotional mind

♦ Thoughts and behaviors are dominated by emotion

♦ Emotions are in charge, feelings rule you

♦ Difficulty thinking clearly

♦ Emotions tend to be overwhelming and intense (positive or negative)

♦ This is viewed negatively socially

Reasonable mind

♦ Thoughts and behaviors are dominated by reason

♦ Emotions are ignored. Feelings are not considered in decisions

♦ Rational, logical, calm

♦ "Numbed out" emotions are suppressed and rationalization is used for coping

♦ This is viewed positively socially

Wise mind

♦ Integrates emotion and reason

♦ Does not ignore or "numb out"

♦ Acknowledging emotion and still thinking clearly

♦ Feeling at peace and centered

Figure 5.2   Right mindedness is wise minded: looking at the right balance. Adapted from Linehan (1993).

Practicing Mindfulness

Traumatic experiences throw you into emotional thinking and responding. If you try to ignore your emotions the result is being "reasonable" without consideration of emotion, which is another extreme. This makes it very hard to get and stay balanced. Healing from trauma involves the decision and commitment to find balance and to maintain it. Mindfulness is choosing to respond to what is happening now, participating in the present, maintaining awareness with what you are doing right now. This requires using your senses of sight, hearing, touch, smell, and taste to be fully aware of the sensations that you are currently experiencing. Using your senses promotes being logical, and being logical promotes effective management. When you are being the moment and getting into the right state of mind you are choosing to create a healthy balance between emotion and reason. Emotion and reason need to become interwoven in a balanced manner, resulting in awareness which prevents "numbing out." You remain responsible for your own life, can make the decisions that are right for you, do not use the words or behaviors of others as an excuse to not do the right thing, and manage your life responsibly and effectively.

The characteristics of the three types of mind—emotional, reasonable, and wise—are illustrated in Figure 5.2.

IDENTIFYING YOUR STATE OF MIND

It is beneficial to be able to identify which state of mind you are in when dealing with emotions, memories and problems. Signs or cues which are an indication of your state of mind can be used to clarify where you are currently functioning as a means to compare if that state of mind is in your best interest for what you are currently needing to deal with.

As an exercise, for a period of one week, maintain a high level of awareness for your state of mind. Identify the connection between what you are thinking, feeling, and experiencing that provokes a particular state of mind. This will give you important information about yourself, how you are influenced and respond, what is helpful to you, and what matches your desired outcome. While you are developing the skill of identifying the cues to your state of mind also begin to think about what you are going to do to get yourself into the state of mind which will be the most useful to you. Below are samples of thinking associated with each state of mind and some ideas about how you will correct this state of mind:

1   **Cues of Being in a Wise State of Mind:**
    - When I am upset or disappointed I can continue to think clearly
    - Even if I am feeling anxious I am able to follow through on what needs to be done
    - I feel that the choices I make are right for me.

2   **Cues of Being in an Emotional State of Mind:**
    - Numbing out and wanting to run away
    - Acting out of control with anger
    - Thoughts or feelings of suicide.

3   **Moving from an Emotional Mind to a Wise Mind:**
    - Going for a walk and being consciously aware of all around you to clear the mind
    - Taking a soothing bath with candles
    - Talking with someone you trust or being in the service of someone less fortunate than you (sometimes it helps to be distracted from our own issues by helping others).

4   **Cues of Being in a Reasonable State of Mind:**
    - Feeling numbed out and detached
    - Pretending everything okay instead of considering feelings in decision-making
    - Rationalizing or intellectualizing.

5   **Moving from a Reasonable Mind to a Wise Mind**
    - Choosing to be aware of current emotions
    - Utilizing your support system to remain mindful
    - Watching children play and allowing yourself to smile.

Using the same outline format as the above, write 3–5 personal answers to each heading: (1) Cues of being in a the wise state of mind, (2) Cues of being in an emotional state of mind, (3) Moving from an emotional mind to a wise mind, (4) Cues of being in a reasonable state of mind, and (5) Moving from a reasonable mind to a wise mind.

DEFENSE MECHANISMS

Defense mechanisms are a way of coping with anxiety, reducing tension, and restoring a sense of balance to a person's emotional experience. Defense mechanisms happen on an unconscious level and tend to distort reality to make it easier for the person to deal with. When defense mechanisms are used to an extreme, they interfere with a person's ability to tell the difference between what is real and what is not.

Defense mechanisms are used independently or in combination with one another. They are used to varying degrees depending on how well they meet a person's need. Review the following defense mechanisms and note which ones you use and under what circumstances.

- Denial: Protecting oneself from unpleasant aspects of life by refusing to perceive, acknowledge, or face them

- Rationalization: Trying to prove one's actions "made sense" or were justified

- Intellectualization: Hiding one's feeling about something painful behind thoughts

- Displacement: Misdirecting pent-up feelings toward something or someone that is less threatening than that which actually triggered the feeling response

- Projection: Blaming. Assuming that someone has a particular quality/qualities that one finds distasteful

- Reaction formation: Adoption actions and beliefs, to an exaggerated degree that are directly opposite to those previously accepted

- Undoing: Trying to superficially repair or make up for an action without dealing with the complex effects of that deed, "magical thinking"

- Withdrawal: Becoming emotionally uninvolved by pulling back or being passive

- Introjection: Adopting someone else's values and standards without exploring whether or not they actually fit oneself, "shoulds" or "ought to"

- Fantasy: Trying to handle problems or frustrations through daydreaming or imaginary solutions

- Repression: Unconsciously blocking out painful thoughts

- Identification: Trying to feel more important by associating oneself with some-one or something that is highly valued

- Acting out: Repeatedly doing actions to keep from being on-edge without weighing the possible results of those actions

- Compensation: Hiding a weakness by stressing too strongly the desirable strength. Overindulging in one area to make up for frustration in another

- Regression: Under stress, re-adopting actions done at a less mature stage of development.

GUILT

A person who is experiencing feelings of guilt is focusing on something that they have done or is embarrassing to them, harmful to another person or some other behavior which has resulted in negative consequences for themselves or someone else. Feelings of guilt and shame are difficult to deal with, mainly because it requires that you forgive yourself for whatever has happened. Self-forgiveness requires honesty and self-acceptance. Challenge your own behavior with appropriate problem-solving and lift that weight off yourself. If you regret your actions, attempt to learn from what has happened. Choose to take responsibility and, as a result, choose to be stronger, smarter and better. Change can be difficult because there is comfort with what is familiar to you. Misery can provide its own kind of insulation from the rest of the world, whereas happiness, in its own way, may be more demanding. Happiness may require more energy, consciousness, commitment, and discipline. There are no excuses when you choose to be happy, live consciously and authentically. Therefore, it takes time and energy and work to liberate yourself from guilt—but it is worth it!

Ask yourself:

- What have I done or said which makes me feel guilty?

- How can I take responsibility for what I have done or choices I have made?

- How can I make peace with what happened, accept and forgive myself and move on?

- How does what has happened help me to understand me and my values?

- If I hide myself through fear, envy, and resentment what will the consequence be?

- What do I feel when my behaviors do not match my values?

- How will my life change if I live it honestly, consciously, and authentically?

BAD MEMORIES AND FEAR

Feeling depressed in combination with feeling overwhelmed by disturbing memories can lead to thoughts of suicide or self-destructive behavior. When a person feels overwhelmed by bad memories from painful experiences it can be a struggle to cope adequately and effectively. Sometimes bad memories include being physically, emotionally, and/or psychologically abused by someone else. One of the most upsetting things about such circumstances is that while you were harmed by someone else in the past you may now be engaging in behavior that continues to harm yourself in some way. It is time to challenge and change these self-harm and self-defeating behaviors.

In addition to haunting memories there may be fears that prevent you from trusting other people. Feeling this way can interfere with using your resources, even when you would like to. However, because you have decided that you no longer want to feel this way there are some things that you can do to initiate a plan of hope and self-recovery. These include the following:

- Therapy: Individual and/or group therapy will be helpful in facilitating the release of the memories, thoughts, and behaviors that have held you hostage.

- Venting your thoughts and feelings: Talking with family members, friends, or a therapist that you trust will help you get out your feelings instead of carrying them around and remaining stuck. It will help you to begin to identify what you need to do to take care of yourself and to heal.

- Journal writing: This is a very helpful strategy. Instead of using emotional energy to hold everything inside, write your feelings and thoughts in a journal. Writing is a constructive way to vent thoughts and feelings, to clarify issues, and to problem-solve what you need to do to take care of yourself. A journal is always there when you need it.

- Creative expression: Being creative or artistic can be helpful for distracting yourself so that you can have a break from painful memories or it can give form and texture to your feelings, emotions and mood.

Consider the following areas and write down:

1. Painful or fearful memories that I need to let go:

_____

_____

2. Things that I have done that have helped me in the past:

_____

_____

3. Resources that I am aware of that would be helpful:

_____

_____

4. My plan for letting go of painful and fearful memories so that they no longer interfere with the quality of my life:

_____

_____

MAPPING AUTONOMIC ACTIVITY

In trauma both the sympathetic and parasympathetic nervous systems are activated. The parasympathetic system often masks the sympathetic nervous system responses. At the apex, the entire system is paralyzed and the experience of the person is one of tonic immobility or freezing. When the autonomic nervous system is out of balance, emotions of depression, anxiety, fear and an overall feeling of a lack of control are provoked.

Signs that the autonomic nervous system are out of balance include effects on:

- Body temperature
- Sleep
- Visual disturbances (or other senses: hearing, smell, taste, touch)
- Heart irregularities
- Muscle tension.

Early signs of trauma reactivation (trauma signals) are combinations of symptoms of the sympathetic (SNS) and parasympathetic nervous systems (PNS) as listed above. Examples are:

- One part of the body being hot (PNS) while another part of the body is cold (SNS)
- Having a normal heart (PNS) rate but sweating (SNS)
- Having constricted pupils (PNS) and a dry tongue/cotton mouth (SNS).

The reactions and responses of the nervous system to posttraumatic stress can be likened to a car that could go out of control at any time until the driver improves their skill and becomes a good driver. The same analogy can be applied to mapping autonomic activity with the use of the accelerator and brakes. The use of the accelerator is good until it starts to feel as if you are losing control, and it is important to learn to use the brakes to prevent

Table 5.8 Examples of using your understanding of the autonomic nervous system to control anxiety

Acceleration (SNS symptoms)	Brakes (Engaging the PNS)
Racing thoughts	Slow down to "digest" the story
Being flooded with images	Focus attention to the body
	Separate the past from the present
Muscle tone/tension awareness	Deliberate muscle tensing and relaxing
	Exercise
Behavior	Journaling: what am I doing?
	Why am I doing it?
Language	Searching for understanding and connections for healing
Transference[a]	Symbolism for points of relationship interpretations, memory and intensity

[a]Transference is defined as a process in therapy where the patient transfers feelings (positive or negative) that have their origin in other key relationships onto the therapist.

you from losing control. In other words, when developing and practicing awareness of the acceleration of sympathetic activation utilize braking and grounding to alleviate anxiety before continuing. Some examples are given in Table 5.8.

This can be illustrated visually by:

Acceleration of the Recovery Process ⇔ Braking or Slowing of the Process

⇓ leads to

Calibration and control of autonomic reactivity

Calibration and control refers to being able to gauge the shifts into and out of sympathetic and parasympathetic activation at a thinking level of understanding instead of fear-based emotional reactivity.

As you refine your understanding of nervous system responses it will begin to open the door to a higher level of self-understanding and the symbolism of the nervous system as it relates to the self, interpretation of environmental stimuli, and psychological defenses (such as denial and rationalization). Becoming aware of the meaning and beliefs attached to a traumatic event diminishes the power that it has had over the quality of life experience. Meaning and beliefs can dominate and restrict a person's life (success/failure, fear of abandonment, aggression, etc.). Understanding who you are and why, along with the recognition of choices, is freeing.

1. What have you learned about your own nervous system responses after having read this?

_____

_____

_____

_____

_____

2. How can you use this information to help you in your recovery and healing?

_____

_____

_____

_____

_____

3. What questions do you have on this topic that need to be answered?

_____

_____

_____

_____

_____

BELIEFS ABOUT POWER AND CONTROL

1. How do you define personal power?

2. Do you think that control of your choices comes from inside of you or outside of you?

3. Have you ever been forced to give up your personal power?

4. If you answered yes to question 3, can you identify by whom, how or in what situations?

5. Can you identify how or in what situations you share power with others?

6. What areas of your life do you have control over?

7. Are there times or situations where you try to control others?

8. Where does your experience of personal power come from (body, size, gender, accomplishments, strength, etc.)?

9. Do you get into power struggles?
   - With who?
   - How do they get resolved?

10. When your personal power is at risk to be taken away or threatened in some way
    - Are you assertive in your response?
    - Are you aggressive in your response?

11. Is the image you have of yourself one of being an independent person?
    - Where?
    - What situations?
    - When?
    - Is there any difference in who is around you?

12. Do you rely on yourself or others?
    - As demonstrated by ...

13. What did you learn about personal power and control from your family?
    - Specifically by who and how?

14. How does gender play a role in your beliefs of power and control?

15. What are your fantasies about power and control?

COPING WITH A DIFFICULT SITUATION

How will you respond if you are expectedly or unexpectedly confronted with a situation that will be a traumatic reaction trigger?

1. Identify some difficult situations that would be extremely uncomfortable or serve as a trigger for a traumatic response.

   _____

   _____

2. What are the triggers that you might have to deal with?

   _____

   _____

3. What types of things would help you cope?
   - An object that serves as a reminder of personal control and choice (what would it be?)
   - Affirmations (create a list)
   - Visualizations
   - Self-talk
   - Safe people/places/thoughts/behaviors
   - Relaxation strategies (list what works best for you).

   _____

   _____

   _____

   _____

4. What are your best coping strategies?

   _____

   _____

5. Take the time to review the last time you were faced with coping with a difficult situation.

   _____

   _____

FORGIVENESS AND SELF-BLAME

Forgiveness is not about another person it is about you changing your internal response to what happened. Forgiving is a coping strategy ranging from the unconditional to conditional, superficial to deep, or a little bit to complete. Forgiveness can be emotional, spiritual, or cognitive (a thinking process). Forgiveness takes time and is a part of internal/emotional healing.

If you blame yourself you could also experience feelings of shame or guilt.

1. Do you blame yourself for what happened?

   _____

   _____

2. Are you angry for yourself for what happened? (If yes, why?)

   _____

   _____

3. What do you need or what would help you forgive yourself?

_____

_____

4. How will forgiving yourself contribute to your healing and recovery?

_____

_____

5. Do you want and need to forgive the offender or person who caused the traumatic event?

_____

_____

IMPACT OF THE TRAUMATIC EVENT ON RELATIONSHIPS

Surviving long-term trauma can lead to numerous problems in how you relate to yourself and others who were not present at the trauma. Check any of the relationship problems listed below:

- ☐ Alienation from others in social areas of life
- ☐ Alienation from others in emotional areas of life
- ☐ Alienation from others in personal areas of life
- ☐ Distrust and being guarded
- ☐ Always waiting for something else bad to happen
- ☐ Difficulty believing that everything will be okay
- ☐ Difficulty believing that you deserve to be happy
- ☐ Detachment
- ☐ Isolation/withdrawal
- ☐ Loss of pleasure in activities previously enjoyed
- ☐ Loss of ability to experience sexual pleasure
- ☐ Loss of ability for healthy attachment or feeling of connection with others
- ☐ Repetitive self-destructive relationships
- ☐ Inability to accept nurturing from yourself or others
- ☐ Difficulty setting and maintaining boundaries
- ☐ Difficulty asserting or advocating for yourself
- ☐ Difficulty communicating want/needs
- ☐ Difficulty communicating feelings/thoughts
- ☐ Abandonment/loss that seem extreme in comparison to the situation.

For every relationship problem you checked write about it in more detail so that you can work on it as part of your healing and recovery. Every problem has numerous parts to it. In an effort to be thorough so that you get the most growth and resolution to everything you work on in your program of healing and recovery consider the following components of detail for each relationship problem statement you identified with:

- What is the specific situation?
- Who do you think of or who is associated with this issue?

- Be specific to place or location.
- Does time of day play a role?
- How have you understood the manner in which you were affected (how did it change you)?
- What is your understanding as to why it happened?
- Were you told to think a certain way about what happened?
- Did you believe that you needed to suffer in silence to protect someone else?
- Did you believe that no one care?
- Did you believe that no one could be trusted?

TRUST

Trust is one of the five basic psychological needs. Depending on the traumatic event, you could find it difficult to trust yourself, others, or the world in general. Use the following questions to clarify your personal and current experience of trust.

1. What does it mean to be able to trust?

   _____
   _____

2. Have you ever been betrayed by someone close to you?

   _____
   _____

3. In what situations or with what people do you trust your own thoughts/behaviors?

   _____
   _____

4. When in certain situations or with particular people are you able to trust your own thoughts/behaviors better than under different circumstances?

   _____
   _____

5. Are there any situations where you trust your judgments about other people or circumstances?

   _____
   _____

6. How would you describe "gut feelings"?

   _____
   _____

7. When do you experience "gut feelings" or instincts?

   _____
   _____

8. What do your gut feelings tell you?

_____

_____

9. What are other ways that you experience awareness of thoughts, feelings, beliefs, or impressions?

_____

_____

10. Are you a person worthy of trust (to self or others)?

_____

_____

11. Do you keep your word (if not, when, why, to whom)?

_____

_____

12. What do you look for that tells you someone is trustworthy?

_____

_____

13. Do you trust early in a relationship before you really get to know a person?

_____

_____

14. Do you trust gradually or all at once?

_____

_____

15. Who/what (groups/organizations/situations) do you trust?

_____

_____

16. When you have to depend on someone else, how does it feel and what do you think?

_____

_____

17. Do you ever have to ask others for help (what situations)?

_____

_____

18. Who has demonstrated that they are worthy of trust (how/why)?

_____

_____

19. What did all the people that you have learned not to trust have in common?

_____

_____

20. What did all the people that you have learned to trust have in common?

_____

_____

INTIMACY SAFETY AND SECURITY

Check all that apply in the following list:

☐ You avoid people (who)

☐ You avoid situations (why)

☐ You avoid social activities (which one(s))

☐ You prefer to be alone

☐ You have no friends

☐ You are afraid to talk to others

☐ You are afraid to be physically close to someone else

☐ You try to make others be physically close to you

☐ Even if you love someone you refuse to be physically sexual with them

☐ You take care of others when you should be taking care of yourself

☐ You have no one to take care of you

☐ You keep others away by being hostile

☐ You are afraid to depend on others

☐ You fear being touched by anyone

☐ You are unable to play and feel carefree

☐ You are unable to make friends

☐ You are unable to maintain friendships

☐ You are unable to be honest about yourself with others

☐ You don't trust or believe that you are alright

☐ You are not able to accept compliments

☐ You find it difficult to make decisions

☐ You are afraid to make decisions because you could make a mistake

☐ You cannot make decisions

☐ You tend to get into terrible relationship situations

☐ You cannot trust people to understand what you have experience.

For every statement that you identified in the above list, write about what role it will play as you proceed with work on your healing and recovery.

_____

_____

_____

_____

_____

BOUNDARIES

A personal boundary simply descries where you end and someone else begins. There are different kinds of boundaries:

- Physical boundaries set the limit of physical space between you and others. They can be too loose or too tight:

Too loose	No boundary
	Trouble setting limits and constantly being enmeshed with others
	Unable to contain your feelings/may overreact
	Trust too quickly
Too tight	Numb
	Trouble setting limits and constantly ending relationships
	Not interested in others

- Emotional boundaries include your rights to safety and security:
  - Overprotection—may not let anyone get close
  - Lacking emotional boundary—not able to see yourself as a separate individual and, therefore, lack personal identity

Check Out Your Physical Boundaries

1. How much space between you and another person is needed for you to feel comfortable?
2. Do you need that amount of space in every relationship?
3. How do you maintain that space?
4. Is it easy or hard for you to maintain that space?
5. Do you let others know if they get too close? (if yes, what feeling does that give you?)

Check Out Your Emotional Boundaries

1. Do you agree to things you really don't want to say "yes" to?
2. Do you tell others too much about yourself?
3. Do you depend on others too much to get your needs met and to be happy?
4. Do you allow others to make comments that hurt your feelings?
5. Do you let people know they have hurt your feelings? (how, and what do you feel?)

To learn more about how you see yourself, write 10 statements that define who you are (for example "I am a good friend")

1. _____
2. _____
3. _____
4. _____
5. _____
6. _____

7. _____

8. _____

9. _____

10. _____

To have healthy boundaries you have to respect your own physical and emotional space and be respectful of the boundaries of others. If your boundaries were invaded and it left you confused you may have to practice to determine what your safe physical space is (generally 45 cm to 1.5 m). Start by answering, "I believe my boundaries are tight, loose, or healthy because …

Physical Boundaries

1. What distance feels comfortable?

2. What makes you uncomfortable in your physical space?

3. What would improve this discomfort and reinforce your feelings of being in control?

4. Practice being assertive. Say what you want from others that would demonstrate their respect for your personal/physical space.

Emotional Boundaries

1. How do you separate your emotions from the emotions of others?

2. Does your mood change based upon the mood of those around you? (Would you like that to change? If yes, how?)

3. Do you allow the rudeness or lack of kindness from others to ruin your day?

4. What do you want to teach people about your emotional boundaries?

AFFIRMING HEALTHY BOUNDARIES

☐ 1. I tell others only what is comfortable to disclose

☐ 2. I will speak honestly about what I want or don't want

☐ 3. I am able to share with others in a direct and appropriate manner

☐ 4. I am able to admit my mistakes and correct them

☐ 5. I am able to accept the opinion of others

☐ 6. I am able to look at the pros and cons of the view of others and decide (not react) how to respond

☐ 7. I am a caring, feeling person

☐ 8. I am empathic and sensitive without being overly distant or overly involved

☐ 9. I don't assume to know what others think or feel

☐ 10. I can ask for help, but don't depend on others to meet my needs

☐ 11. I take the time to know someone before I decide to trust that person

☐ 12. I don't change my thoughts, feelings or beliefs to please others

☐ 13. I don't expect others to know what I want or need without telling them directly

☐ 14. I don't fall apart or have a crisis to get others to take care of me

☐ 15. I am sexual only when I want to be

☐ 16. I make choices about my life

☐ 17. I try to not repeat patterns of pain or abuse (that have happened to me)

☐ 18. I expect realist support/help from others

☐ 19. I respect others and expect them to respect me

☐ 20. I take responsibility for teaching others how to treat me.

Are there any other affirmations that you would add?

_____
_____
_____
_____
_____

Out of the 20 items on the above list, which ones are you currently working on in your healing and recovery program? Also, highlight any that you are struggling with.

_____
_____
_____
_____
_____

FUN GOALS

Under each one write how you incorporate it into daily life, or how you are going to incorporate it.

1. Know what makes you laugh and who makes you laugh.

_____
_____

2. Self-humor. Learn to laugh at yourself. Be more forgiving of the mistakes you make and find humor with what you do. We are all human!

_____
_____

3. Enjoy yourself. Laugh at life. It is true that at another time you will be able to laugh about a crisis you lived through today. Look around, it is not hard to find the ridiculous.

_____
_____

4. Be spontaneous. Take advantage of an opportunity to play. Make the choice to play and have fun. Especially if you have had a bad day.

_____

_____

5. Schedule fun time. That's right. Actually book time to have fun. Create play days when you don't have money for a vacation.

_____

_____

6. Reward achievement. When you complete a goal celebrate. Reinforce feeling good about it!

_____

_____

7. Smile and laugh. You will look and feel more relaxed.

_____

_____

8. Treat yourself to an enjoyable activity and people you like being with: Have lunch with a friend. Take a long bath. Read a good book. You get the idea!

_____

_____

9. Create a collection of fun: Music, crafts, activities, movies, people

_____

_____

10. Live in the moment. Don't wait until tomorrow to be happy, do it today!

_____

_____

COMMUNICATION

There are four central styles of communication (adapted from Miller et al., 1989):

1. _Small Talk_

This is conversation that takes place in social situations that are relaxed and playful. It is used for building rapport and maintaining social relationships.
    Example:

_____

_____

2. _Control Talk_

Shows that you are in charge and can advocate for yourself. It can be forceful, directive, defensive, persuasive and instructive. Associated with control talk is:

- Fight talk: the goal is to justify yourself and hide your own fear and vulnerability
- Spite talk: the goal is to make someone else feel guilty, protect yourself, maintain the status quo and avoid change, getting even etc. In other words taking a self-protective stance in order to avoid distress.

Example:

_____

_____

3. *Exploring Talk* — Demonstrates an effort to evaluate options, increase awareness/insight, clarity feelings/situations. It is an avenue for getting more information, being interested or supportive.

Example:

_____

_____

4. *Straight Talk* — Direct, assertive honest and respectful communication. The goal is to disclose information, collaborate, problem-solve with another, or connecting with someone. It requires observing, active listening and being in the moment.

Example:

_____

_____

THE STEPS OF POSITIVE ASSERTIVENESS

This is especially important if you have been socially withdrawn, fearful, have difficulty being heard or getting your needs met. You are the only one who can make your life be what you want it to be. You have likely been disappointed or hurt numerous times because you expected those close to you to know what you want and need. What you were supposed to learn from that is not to depend on others to read your mind and to take responsibility for effectively communicating your thoughts, feelings, wants, and needs.

The power of change, peace, and personal growth is inside of you. When you accept and acknowledge this fact and cease looking to others to do what you think they should is when your life will begin to move in the direction *you* desire. Use the following:

1. Prepare for a neutral conversation by first diffusing your emotions and by waiting until the other person is likely to be least reactive and most receptive.

2. Deliver your message as briefly and directly as possible, without being angry, sarcastic, condescending, or judgmental. Let your contribution to the interaction be a positive one.

3. Be respectful. Don't offer less than you expect from the person you are speaking to. Allow the other person enough time to respond without feeling pressured.

4. Reflectively listen. If the person becomes defensive, reflect to them what you hear them saying and validate their feelings.

5. Reassert your message. Stay focused on the original issue, and do not be derailed.

6. Reuse this process, utilizing a lot of reflective listening to minimize emotionality, debating, or arguing. It takes two people to escalate a discussion into an argument. Don't participate.

7. Focus on the solution, without demanding that the person respond as you do. Because you brought it up, you have probably been thinking about it and resolved some aspects of the situation. Therefore, it is important that you facilitate their participation in problem-solving the issue so that they don't feel like they have been set up in some way.

Non-verbal behaviors are as important as verbalizing the content of your thoughts and feelings. The signals that a person sends, as well as receives, are crucial to the success of assertive communication. Non-verbal cues include eye contact, body posture, personal space, gestures, facial expressions, tone of voice, inflection of voice, vocal volume, and timing. Other variables include demonstrating listening, head nodding, and appropriate animation.

Entering an ongoing conversation requires the observation of those already involved. As you observe the body language of others, make eye contact, and become part of the group; join in with appropriate statements and comments.

Ending a conversation can take place by initiating a form of closure. "I've really enjoyed this discussion," or "Excuse me, but I need to talk to this person." Other solutions could include a change in content, stating you need to think about what has been said, less self-disclosure, and fewer open-ended statements which encourage ongoing conversation.

Describe several problem situations, determine your goal, and decide how to deal with it.

LISTENING AND GIVING FEEDBACK

Another important aspect of clear and effective communication is being able to listen and to respond or give feedback honestly. You will not be able to listen to what someone else has to say if you are focused on negative emotions or your own agenda.

Listening requires that you focus on the message that another person is trying to express.

1. Describe what you see or observe instead of making an evaluation or giving your judgment.

2. Be specific instead of general. Specifics are helpful.

3. Feedback should provide information about that which can be controlled and changed, otherwise it only adds to frustration.

4. Timing is important: always consider it, but do not use it as an excuse.

5. Check out what the person you were giving feedback to interpreted you as saying. Assumptions cause problems and can lead to hard feelings.

6. Check out the validity of your feedback with others.

7. Encourage feedback, but do not pressure others or impose yourself on them if it is not wanted.

8. Do not overwhelm others with a lot of information. Offer your feedback in small pieces.

9. Own your own feedback and feelings by using "I" statements. After all, it is only your opinion.

10. Share your feedback with others in a way that makes it easy for them to listen to what it is you want to express.

SAYING "NO"

It is not uncommon to feel uncomfortable when saying "no" to a request. Saying "no" can be thought of as part of assertive communication and taking care of oneself. The purpose is not to make another person feel rejected or bad for making a request. To overcome negative feelings when saying "no" ask yourself:

- Is the request reasonable?
- Do you need to ask for more information to clarify all of the facts?
- Would it help to practice saying no when appropriate?

Most importantly, stop apologizing, whether it is something that you just don't want to do or something you can't do.
Ask yourself the consequences of saying "yes:"

- Will you end up angry with yourself for doing something you don't want to do?
- Will it get in the way or distract from things you want to do?

Remember that resentment easily begins to develop and build. And because you are doing something you don't want to do, but are not being honest, it can lead to a lack of communication and dishonest communication.

DEALING WITH UNCOMFORTABLE EMOTIONS

1. **Talk to Someone:**
- Report the facts of the situation. Avoid making the other person defensive by focusing on them instead of the issue or blaming them.

- Use "I" statements. "I feel (angry, happy, afraid, etc.) when this happens or this is said." An "I" statement identifies that you are taking responsibility for your feelings and are speaking assertively with the person to deal with the outcome of any given experience.

- Compromise. Ask "What can we do about this?" This demonstrates respect for the other person's point of view as well as facilitates desired changes, which can benefit both parties.

2. **Take Action:**
- Call a friend or some other person in your support system.

- Go for a drive.

- Write in a journal your feelings and thoughts.

- Write an uncensored letter that you do not intend to send (venting).

- Go to a movie.

- Do something creative (paint, draw, woodwork, needlework, etc.).

- Help someone else, it can distract you from your own distress.

- Read a book that helps to relax and distract you.

- Do something!

3. **Physical Activity:**
- Physical activity is an excellent way to decrease stress and clear your mind so that you can think more rationally and minimize the risk of behavioral and emotional reactiveness. It is a positive way to avoid further complicating an already difficult situation. Emotional distress of any kind creates muscle/body tension. When you feel less distressed you are in a better position to participate in constructive problem-solving. Problems occur or get worse when you ignore or neglect to deal with your emotions, or deal with them in a non-productive pattern. Three common errors:

- Fight. If you know how to argue things through to resolution it can be helpful. However, most people lack this skill. Therefore, they end up causing more problems.

- Flight. Walking out on others and on your own emotions can have negative effects for your emotional and physical well-being.

- Withdrawal. When you don't deal with things they pile up. Things that pile up over time show up as headaches, fatigue, depression, anxiety, panic attacks, etc.

Feelings are spontaneous inner reactions connected to your interpretation of life experiences. Over time you may begin to recognize that how you choose to view or interpret things has a significant impact on how you feel emotionally. It is your responsibility to identify accurate and inaccurate interpretations.

IMPROVING COMMUNICATION SKILLS

Less than 10% of what you communicate to someone will be interpreted based on what you say. Over 40% of interpretation is derived from how it is said, and over 40% is interpreted by how you present yourself physically. An additional problem in communication, which contributes to its ineffectiveness, has to do with non-verbal behaviors or habits that are distracting to the person you are communicating with (such as fidgeting, tapping, smoking, drinking, etc.).

How You Present Yourself: Body Language

1. **Eye Contact:**
- Look directly at the person you are speaking to
- Remain relaxed, spontaneous/normal, serious but not overly intense.

2. **Body Posture:**
- Face the person you are speaking to
- Slightly lean forward toward the person
- Maintain a relaxed, attentive posture
- Keep your hands loosely clasped or on your lap
- The occasional fluid movement of arms or hands is okay
- Keep legs parallel or comfortably crossed
- Avoid being rigid, tense or threatening.

3. Head/Facial Movement:

- Occasionally nod your head affirmatively
- Use appropriate facial responses
- Mirror the person you are talking to.

How to Say It:
Quality of Voice

- Effective tone of voice
- Pleasant
- Interested intonation
- Appropriate loudness
- Moderate rate of speech
- Natural and relaxed conversation
- Simple and precise language
- Fluid speech
- No or minimal use of slang.

Work at increasing your awareness of how others experience you. Do they clearly understand what you intend them to? Do you leave them with the thoughts and feelings about you that you hoped for or expected based upon what you had to say?

Identify what communication skills you effectively demonstrate and what you need to work on. Observe others you feel are skilled communicators, and try to learn from their modeling of effective communication.

FINDING MEANING

It is not uncommon that when a person experiences a traumatic event they are changed and believe that their life will be shortened. This stress and fear actually creates an opportunity. Remember, you cannot afford to waste anything that happens to you. It is an act of self-responsibility to find meaning and knowledge from everything we live through so we gain a greater sense of self and get better at being who we choose to be. This seeking of information and choosing to become better and stronger is referred to as "finding meaning."

What are the benchmarks of finding meaning? Review the list below and check off any that apply to you. For every item you check off, write a brief statement of exactly what you do and for those you don't check off write briefly about what you need to do to accomplish it.

- ☐ Able to sooth yourself when upset or in pain
- ☐ Able to tolerate or somehow decrease the intensity of painful emotions
- ☐ Able to counter thoughts/feelings of self-blame and shame with realistic self-talk
- ☐ Able to be alone without feeling lonely
- ☐ Able to accurately anticipate consequences of choices, actions, and situations
- ☐ Able to effectively and appropriately engage in self-support and mutually supportive relationships
- ☐ Able to be constructive in your connection to a person when they are present and absent

- ☐   Able to set and maintain appropriate boundaries
- ☐   Able to feel secure and laugh at yourself when appropriate/helpful
- ☐   Able to be empathic with others.

HABITS FOR SUCCESS

Stephen Covey's book, *The 7 Habits of Highly Successful People* (Covey, 1999), offers a useful template of baseline behavior and change for everyone. It simply requires that each day you strive to be fully aware and make the best choices possible. It is acknowledging and accepting that you will make mistakes (negative experiences are a common life occurrence) and that you will choose to learn from both of these avenues of information about yourself and the world. It is a way of conceptualizing the experience of finding meaning. Under each of the Seven Habits listed below write briefly about how you incorporate the habit into daily life or how you are going to make it part of how you live your daily life:

1. Be proactive. This means to decide what you want and to make it happen. According to Nike, "Just do it!"

   _____

   _____

2. Personal leadership. In your mind, begin with where you want to end. In other words, create a vision and make it a reality. This way every decision you make and every action you take is incrementally accomplishing your goal.

   _____

   _____

3. Personal management. Appropriately and effectively prioritize and concentrate on what is important. It's not an issue of urgency, but rather staying the course.

   _____

   _____

4. Interpersonal leadership. There is no win or lose there is only win–win. Seek to always be solution focused. You benefit and so does everyone else.

   _____

   _____

5. Empathic communication. Seek first to understand others and then to be understood. The gift of listening to others with the goal of understanding them and their position will more often than not be reflected to you by those who have felt respected by you.

   _____

   _____

6. Creative cooperation. Make things happen through teamwork.

   _____

   _____

7. Balanced self-renewal. Commit to constantly working on improving yourself.

   _____

   _____

COMMITMENT TO HEALING

Healing and recovery are hard work. As a person begins to focus on their healing they begin to recognize that healing really starts to take hold when they develop some power or internal management over their memories and how they respond physically and emotionally to their memories of trauma. Maslow (1954) developed a "Hierarchy of Needs" in association with understanding human motivation:

1. Biological and physiological needs: Basic life needs—air, food, drink, shelter, warmth, sex, sleep, etc.

---

2. Safety needs: Protection, security, order, law, limits, stability, etc.

3. Belongingness and love needs: Family, affection, relationships, work group, etc.

4. Esteem needs: Achievement, status, responsibility, reputation.

5. Self-actualization: Personal growth and fulfillment.

When you allow yourself to be challenged by your beliefs about the five basic needs that give you strength in your pursuit of personal growth you may change some of your beliefs, which is a demonstration of your progress in the journey to find meaning. You will live your life more consciously, authentically, and with intent to advance the healing and recovery process by bringing any intrusive memories, thoughts, or nightmares under more control. Your improved ability to set effective boundaries give you a better ability to contain traumatic experiences, sharing with those you choose to share with because they are worthy of trust and likely a part of your support system.

Power and Dalgeish (1992) provided a number of ways that you could advance the healing process without retraumatizing yourself:

- Choose to be more aware of each choice you make

- Choose to work for the win–win or "common good" that gives you a sense of meaning

- Utilize self-management techniques to control or minimize the impact of flashbacks

- Choose strategies, behaviors, or thoughts that makes you more functional in your daily life

- Seek understanding in why you are resistant to doing your work, and then do something to change it

- Manage your pain in a constructive manner. Maximize benefit, avoid self-harm/injury and be consistent in your efforts of self-care

- Remind yourself consistently that you have already survived the traumatic event. It is now your job to find meaning and learn from what happened. It's not about being diminished it is about being empowered!

- Learn to identify your emotions, where they come from, what they mean, and how to express them honestly and appropriately

- Practice amplifying and calming your feelings. You are in control

- Choose to seek out positive experiences and enjoy them and the positive emotions that come with them.

COMING TO TERMS WITH ASSUMING THE PATIENT ROLE

You may ask, "Why would someone choose the patient role?" The answer is, "the benefits of being sick." Being sick is a presumed legitimate way to get out of being responsible to yourself and your obligations. Unfortunately, the one that is most limited by the patient role is the person being the patient. To better understand yourself and your motivation to change, work through the following exercise, thinking through the issues carefully.

1. List your illnesses, symptoms, and excuses:

   _____

   _____

2. Choose an illness, symptom, or excuse from your list to complete the following statement:

   It happens when _____

   It feels like _____

   It prevents _____

   It results in_____

   It encourages_____

   It demonstrates that I have a deep need for_____

   It benefits me with_____

   An appropriate way to get this need met would be _____

   My plan for dealing with this issue:

   _____

   _____

GUIDELINES FOR COMPLETING YOUR FIRST STEP TOWARD EMOTIONAL HEALTH

The first step is a simple and honest look at how traumatic experiences have affected you and how you live your life. This includes how you perceive things, how you react/respond emotionally and physically to various situations and other people, your coping ability, problem-solving skills, conflict-resolution skills, what motivates you, and the ability to form healthy relationships.

Answer all of the questions that follow as thoroughly as possible, citing specific incidents, the approximate date, how felt, what you thought, and how you responded physically. While it may be an emotional experience for you to review your life experience(s) of trauma, remind yourself that whatever it is, you have already survived it. This writing will help you better understand yourself, clarify the issues to be resolved, and create the opportunity to decide what you are willing to do to resolve these issues.

1. Describe the traumatic life experience(s) you are going to review. Include a description of everyone involved and their behavior and/or responses.

2. How did the experience(s) affect you?

3. How have relationships been affected?

4. What did you learn about yourself?

5. What did you learn about others?

6. How do you function in social relationships?

7. How did the experience(s) affect self-esteem and self-confidence?

8. When did you become aware that you have negative emotional and/or behavioral difficulties associated to the experience(s)?

9. Explain how your difficulties have prevented you from reaching desired goals and having fulfilled relationships.

10. What are your fears and how do they affect your life?

11. Do your difficulties increase during times of stress or discomfort resulting from work/school, family or personal problems?

12. Discuss how your emotional and behavioral difficulties have had a negative impact on significant relationships, intimacy, trust, caused you social problems, loss of friendships, inability to perform sexually, unreasonable demands on others, allowing yourself to be taken advantage of, etc.

13. Have your emotional or behavioral difficulties affected your health?

14. List the emotional and behavioral difficulties that you have attempted to resolve, what you did and what the outcome was.

15. Review all that you have written. Use this information to help make your life what you want it to be. Live consciously, authentically and with awareness for what you do and why. Making things right is an active process not just a thinking exercise.

PSYCHOLOGICAL HEALTH

Creating and reinforcing psychological health is the goal in successfully living a balanced lifestyle. Answer the following questions to clarify where you are in reaching your goals associated with psychological health.

1. What are your values and what is most important to you?

2. What motivates you (and how do you know)?

3. What accomplishments are important to you and what needs to be done to achieve them?

4. What are your personal areas of commitment and life purpose? Are you fully living these areas?

5. Are you pleased/comfortable with your current standard of living? If you desire things to change what is a realistic expectation of change and when?

6. Are you satisfied with the pace of your life? If not, what do you need to do about it?

7. Are you clear about who you are and what you need/want?

8. Are you satisfied with your relationships? (explain)

9. Do you have a sense of purpose in life? (explain)
10. Do you keep balance in all areas of your life? (physical, social, emotional, spiritual, work/school)

REVIEW OF THE IMPACT OF THE TRAUMA ON YOUR LIFE

Check the following statements that you identify with and briefly explain your experience of that issue.

- ☐ What event/experiences do you consider to be traumatic?
- ☐ Do you feel safe at the present time?
- ☐ Do you feel pessimistic or fearful of the future?
- ☐ Have other things happened to you since the original traumatic event?
- ☐ Are you able to trust others?
- ☐ If there is more than one traumatic event can you place them in a hierarchy of most impact to least?
- ☐ Are you more or less emotional than you were prior to the event?
- ☐ Is it difficult for you to sooth/calm yourself when upset?
- ☐ Are things that used to bring you pleasure/joy no longer pleasurable?
- ☐ Do you get more nervous or upset now than you used to?
- ☐ Are you careless or overly cautious when it comes to your safety?
- ☐ Are you obsessive about your safety?
- ☐ Do you engage in self-destructive behavior (cutting, drugs/alcohol, indiscriminate sex, eating disorder, gambling, compulsive spending, etc.)?
- ☐ Have you ever thought about killing yourself?
- ☐ Have you ever tried to kill yourself?
- ☐ Do you have thoughts/plan to harm someone else?
- ☐ Do you feel a lot of anger?
- ☐ Do you find it difficult to control your anger?
- ☐ Are you fearful of losing control or upsetting someone else so you keep your anger inside?
- ☐ Does it bother you to be touched?
- ☐ Does it bother you to have sex or think about having sex?
- ☐ Have you changed how you feel/behave in relationships? (explain)

As you review all of the issues that you identified how would you prioritize them to work on and why?

_____
_____
_____
_____
_____

STRENGTHENING RESILIENCE

The American Psychological Association (2004) recommends the following tips for strengthening resilience (the ability to adapt when confronted with adversity and challenge):

1. **Talk About It:**
   - Utilize your support system
   - Receive care/comfort/reassurances
   - Speak with others who share the experience in an effort to decrease and eliminate negative feelings
   - Acknowledge that everyone experiences distress/trauma and a lack of control in their life in some way.

2. **Strive for Balance:**
   - It is easy for anyone to become overwhelmed by trauma with associated negative or pessimistic view of life and the world
   - Challenge this view and balance this perspective with reminders of other people and situations that are meaningful, comforting, and encouraging
   - Balance is empowering and creates the opportunity for an overall healthier and realistic view of life and the world.

3. **Turn it Off—Take a Break:**
   - Limit the amount of media and information which contribute to or reinforces a negative perspective (only that necessary to remained informed if desired)
   - Avoid overexposure to distressing information that can increase feelings, thoughts and responses to stress
   - Negative images associated with exposure can perpetuate or reawaken feelings of distress
   - Schedule breaks as a distraction from thinking about the event. Choose enjoyable activities with caring sources of support
   - Make the effort to improve your mood and perspective.

4. **Honor Your Feelings:**
   - Start by validating the normal range of emotions experienced following a traumatic event. These could include: intense stress, exhaustion, pain, distraction
   - Be as kind, caring, and non-judgmental with yourself as you would be with a friend.

5. **Take Care of Yourself:**
   - Participate in healthy behaviors to improve the ability to cope with intense stress, such as relaxation techniques (deep breathing, yoga, meditation)
   - Engage in enjoyable activities with people you enjoy
   - Engage in self-care behavior, including good nutrition, adequate sleep, physical activity

- Avoid alcohol and drugs (they can suppress emotions or intensify emotions and pain)
- Maintain normal routines of meals/sleep/work.

6. **Help Others do Something Productive:**
   - Offer support to others who have been affected by the event
   - Volunteer your service in the community.

Grief and general recovery are a long process. Everyone responds in a unique manner. For some it is important to return to work/school and for others it is necessary to create a temporary situation away from work. Trust in a person's ability to deal with the challenges that exist following the experience of a traumatic event are perseverance in staying the course of healing and recovery.

1. What are you currently doing that has been listed?

_____

_____

2. What has been helpful in decreasing negative thoughts and feelings?

_____

_____

3. What do you think would be helpful to do that you are not currently doing?

_____

_____

4. Who is your support system and how available are they?

_____

_____

MANAGING A CRISIS SITUATION

The following is adapted from material developed by the British Red Cross.

Whatever experience you have, it is personal to you. It is important for you to take the time to understand how you have been affected and how you will choose to deal with it.

Normal Feelings/

Emotions to

Experience with

a Crisis

Fear	Of losing control
	Of breaking down
	Of damage to yourself or those you love
	Of being left alone or abandoned
	Of having to leave those they love

	Of experiencing a similar event
Anger	For what has happened to them
	At who caused or allowed it to happen to them
	At the injustice or unfairness of what happened
	At the shame and indignity
	At the lack of understanding of others
	At their perceived deficiencies or inefficiency
Helplessness	The result of experiencing human weakness
	Not being able to protect themselves
	To the change in how they are seen by others
Sadness	For death, injuries and all associated losses
	That things have changed forever
	For the impact to relationships
Grief	For all that has changed
	For all that will never be as expected
Guilt	For surviving
	For being better off than others
	Regrets for whatever had not been done/wish they had done
Shame	For being seen as a victim
	For being seen as helpless
	For emotionally needing others
	For reacting differently than they wished they had
Disappointment	For all the dreams or wishes that will never be fulfilled
	In their own responses
	In the responses of others
Memories	Of loved ones (killed or injured)
	Of losses (what used to be)

All of these feelings or emotions are normal to experience following a personal crisis. However, the intensity will vary, depending on what happened, what you witnessed, or what you endured and for how long.

Physical and Mental Sensations

- Fatigue/tiredness
- Sleep disturbance
- Difficulty with concentration and attention
- Loss of memory
- Dizziness/light headedness
- Palpitations
- Trembling
- Difficulty in breathing/feeling short of breath

- Nausea
- Diarrhea
- Decreased libido
- Muscle tension (which can lead to pain such as headache, neck and backache, abdominal distress/stomachache, menstrual disorders).

Some Helpful Responses and Things to Do

1. **Numbness:**
- Your mind may only allow you to feel your experience emotionally in a slow manner as a protective mechanism. Initially, you might only feel numb
- What happened may seem unreal, either like a dream or like something that hasn't really happened
- This may be misinterpreted by others as being "stoic and strong" or "uncaring."

2. **Activity:**
- Helping others may be a positive distraction from your own pain and distress
- Positive structure and a feeling of purpose always makes a person feel better
- Activity and distraction allows the body and mind to relax from the distress it is experiencing.

3. **Reality:**
- Sometimes facing the reality of what happened can help you to come to terms with the crisis (attending a funeral, going to the scene of the crisis, etc.)
- It is not uncommon, when coming to terms with reality, that there is a lot of thought about what happened and dreams of it too.

4. **Support:**
- Allow others to be caring and supportive of you
- Talking with others who have shared similar experiences can be helpful for venting and for feeling that you are not alone.

5. **Privacy:**
- There may be times when you need to be alone with your thoughts and feelings to work through what has happened and how you have been affected
- It may be beneficial to just spend time with family and close friends who will be more understanding and protective of you.

What Helps

- Take time to sleep, rest, think and be with those who are important to you
- Try to keep your life as normal as possible
- Maintain appropriate attention and caution to normal life activities like driving and completing tasks around your home

- Express your emotions and allow those close to you to share in your grief
- Take the time to review your experience, how it affected you and how you choose to deal with it
- Acknowledge that while you don't necessarily have control over what happens to you, you do have the choice in how you interpret it and deal with it.
- Allow yourself to be part of a group that cares about you.

What Doesn't Help

- Isolating yourself from those who care
- Bottling up your emotions
- Avoiding talking about what happened
- Expecting your memories to go away—the memories and feeling will stay with you for a long time
- Being critical of your reactions to the crisis.

Family and Social Relationships

- Strains and conflicts may develop in existing relationships
- There may be a feeling that those close to you have offered too little support too late or not the kind of support you have needed
- You may avoid those close to you because you feel that you cannot return to them equally what has been given to you.

Remember that accidents are more frequent after experiencing extreme stress. Alcohol and drug use may also increase in an effort to deal with the extra stress.

When to Seek Professional Help

- If sleep disturbance and nightmares continue
- If you feel that emotionally you are not getting back to your old self
- You continue to experience tension, confusion, emptiness, or extreme fatigue.
- You continue to feel numb or you have to stay busy to avoid thinking about it
- If you want to share your thoughts and feelings but have no one to talk to that you trust
- Your personal relationships are being negatively affected by your experience
- If you seem to be having accidents
- If you continue to excessively use substances
- Your work performance is negatively affected.

THE HABIT LOG

Choose a habit that you would really like to change because of the negative impact it has upon other life choices you feel unable to make because of the way the habit interferes with them. Record the occurrence of the habit for 3–4 weeks. Use the following sentence stems to describe what the task was, where it took place, with whom, how you felt, and what the consequences were. Keeping the habit log will help you to develop regular self-monitoring, answering "What am I doing?" and "Why am I doing it?"

Habit to change:_____ Date:_____

I was with_____ at_____

This is what happened _____

_____

_____

Just before then I had been _____

I said to myself _____

And I felt _____

_____

Afterward I said to myself _____

_____

I felt _____

And I did _____

The negative consequences were _____

The positive consequences were _____

DAILY RECOVERY SCHEDULE

Recovery is a dynamic process—things are always changing. Some changes are good and some are challenging, but still part of an overall positive process. This requires awareness and effort to cope with thoughts, feelings, and behaviors that are the focus of change. The chances are that you have been engaging in these habits for a long time. Therefore, once you identify what you need to change, use the following outline to reinforce your efforts.

1. Practice new effective ways of coping.

2. Have adequate support for maintaining change.

3. Self-monitor to maintain awareness.

4. Use journaling to identify what is helpful and what is not helpful.

When trying to change life patterns, it can be helpful to write out a daily plan. This scheduling of daily goals will keep you focused on practicing new skills needed to replace the old habits.

Day	Plan changes (new behaviors/thoughts, use of resources, meetings, positive or negative effects on change)	Rate the day (good/bad and why difficult and why/how you responded)
Monday		
Tuesday		
Wednesday		
Thursday		
Friday		
Saturday		
Sunday		

Make copies of this page for weekly use.

MAINTAINING PROGRESS

Because recovery is new to you, it is important to develop a thorough understanding of yourself, your choices, and the associated consequences of your choices. Seek to understand how and why some sources of support are helpful and reinforcing of the changes you want to make in your life and some are not. Keep the following points in mind to help maintain your progress toward desired change.

1. Always practice good self-care behaviors:
   - Adequate sleep
   - Good nutrition
   - Regular exercise
   - Positive leisure activities
   - Relationships that support your recovery.

2. Positive reinforcement:
   - Positive, rational, and realistic thoughts, "keep your cup half full"
   - Relaxation coupled with positive affirmations
   - Review successful efforts.

3. Positive feedback: Focus on what is right and what works. This can be done by evaluating daily experiences:
   - What was helpful or pleasing?
   - What was learned from approaching things differently?
   - Accept what cannot control or change
   - Do something about things you can change
   - Positive use of feedback from those you trust, meetings/support group.

4. Develop realistic expectations and limitations:
   - Acknowledge what you do not know and need to learn
   - Take responsibility to learn and make appropriate changes
   - Accept that personal growth continues throughout your life.

5. Acknowledge and accept that there are a lot of resources available to support your desired life changes, but that you are responsible for you.

Keep a journal to maintain a log of experiences, how you respond, and what you learn from each experience. This is helpful skill for building a strong recovery.
Make a list of your trusted resources:

_____
_____
_____
_____

REINFORCING THE PROGRESS OF TREATMENT GOALS

HELPING WAYS OF THINKING AND DOING

Take the time to review your treatment goals and what has been achieved in reaching those goals.

1. Identify the strategies that have been most helpful to you in decreasing or eliminating symptoms:
   - Write a list of specific skills you developed and the steps you used

   _____

   _____

   - What was the rationale or reason for each skill you developed?

   _____

   _____

2. If there are posttraumatic symptoms that are still a problem, how could you use the skills/methods listed above to continue your efforts for alleviating or eliminating symptoms?

   _____

   _____

You have accomplished a lot and have good reason to feel very positive about your effort and commitment to healthy coping and personal growth. In order to successfully maintain all of the benefits of your hard work you need to be prepared to deal with any sign of re-emerging symptoms. Often, a re-experiencing of symptoms is related to going back to old ways of thinking and behaving. Keep in mind, a normal life is full of ups and downs. There will be times when anxiety is experienced. This is not a reason for fear or alarm, but a potential opportunity to practice using the skills that have been developed to manage PTSD symptoms and self-care.

An experience of any symptoms is not a relapse. It does not necessarily mean that your hard work is lost, it is just a reminder to practice the skills you know work. Choose to see it as an opportunity to review self-care lifestyle and use of skills as well as resources.

Now write out a maintenance plan:

1. Make a list of coping strategies and exercises (ways to practice)

   _____

   _____

   _____

2. Make a list of high-risk situations, people, places (e.g. trauma anniversary)

   _____

   _____

   _____

3. If a situation does take place, break down every step of what has happened and to identify faulty thinking or other contributing factors

   _____

   _____

   _____

4. What is your plan for dealing with these potential ups and downs associated with the traumatic experience?

   _____

   _____

   _____

PTSD RELAPSE PREVENTION

Relapse prevention is very important to maintain symptom management and recovery from the symptoms of PTSD. It is a way of taking all of the skills that you have learned and matching them up to the people, places, memories, and situations that trigger fear, avoidance, and being emotionally overwhelmed. You can then reinforce the evidence of your changes in thinking and behaving that has allowed you to manage your experiences resulting from being traumatized. Effective management provides an opportunity to relearn safety and to rethink all that you have been through.

When you are in therapy there is the feeling of safety created by the therapist and therapy framework. When therapy ends it is not uncommon that new fears may arise in the form of distressing thoughts, memories, and feelings. Think of this as a test for simply reviewing and using the skills that you have learned. This preparation is what is known as "relapse prevention."

If you are feeling stressed and emotionally uncomfortable, the chances are that you are being confronted with a trigger. However, you have been working hard to develop management skills and are prepared to effectively deal with this trigger. Think of it as an opportunity to practice improved coping. This practicing is important for preventing a lapse or relapse and will contribute to feelings of self-efficacy ("I can deal with this"). The best defense is an offense. In other words, take for granted that you will be confronted with triggers and because you are prepared for coping with the associated challenging emotions and physical symptoms you will prevent a recovery setback. The coping strategies that you have learned can overcome setbacks. Therefore, think of all that you have learned in therapy and with your motivated efforts to heal. When you put together all the management skills you have learned for coping with triggers you have a "relapse prevention plan."

Effective Coping

Write down five triggers and effective management skills for coping with each one.

1. Trigger: _____

Coping skills: _____

_____

_____

2. Trigger: _____

Coping skills: _____

_____

_____

3. Trigger: _____

Coping skills: _____

_____

_____

4. Trigger: _____

Coping skills: _____

_____

_____

5. Trigger: _____

Coping skills: _____

_____

_____

If you have any questions or concerns about how you will cope with a specific trigger give yourself permission to use your resources for problem-solving, such as talking to your therapist or another trusted person about your concern(s).

Note: "Lapse" refers to the return of some PTSD symptoms; "relapse" refers to full return of PTSD symptoms.

Strengthening
Relapse Prevention

The best way to prepare or inoculate yourself against relapse is by developing your personalized relapse prevention plan. Actually, taking this step of thinking about the return of symptoms and how you will deal with them is the first step of a relapse prevention plan. The following steps will prepare you to manage any setbacks that are experienced.

1. What have you learned about PTSD and what causes it?

    _____

    _____

2. What are some ways of coping that you have used which seem to help at first, but over time make the problem worse (such as avoidance, isolating, dissociation)?

    _____

    _____

3. What skills did you learn to help you manage and eliminate your posttraumatic symptoms? For example, ways of thinking or specific behaviours.

    _____

    _____

Psychological First
Aid for Coping with
a Lapse

Forewarned is forearmed. You should be prepared with strategies for dealing with relapse should it occur. This means that if you begin to experience PTSD symptoms (fear, anxiety, nightmares, avoidance) you will have a plan of action. This homework will challenge you to identify faulty thinking or negative self-talk which may influence your interpretation of and coping with difficult situations.

1. Is a lapse/relapse a catastrophe or an opportunity?

    _____

    _____

2. Explain why a lapse/relapse is a temporary problem in coping (interpretation and responding) and not a catastrophe.

    _____

    _____

3. Break it down: Learn why the lapse/relapse occurred. Examine every possibility of what interfered with your coping, and what you have learned.

    _____

    _____

4. Review the skills that you have learned for coping with such a situation (for example, challenging rational versus irrational).

    _____

    _____

5. Write down all of the stress management skills that you have learned, then practice them and write down how you felt.

_____

_____

6. Containment: Write down the things that you are trying to prevent an escalation of such as anxiety, fear, and avoidance.

_____

_____

7. Make a list of people, places, or situations that you have been avoiding due to fear and then write how you will gradually challenge each one of them (using rational self-talk, gradual exposure, etc.).

_____

_____

8. Write what you have learned about your skill and strengths as well as areas that need to be worked on for improving your resilience to acute stress and triggers.

_____

_____

Remind yourself that life is full of ups and downs and that it is normal to feel anxious and overwhelmed at times. When this happens it is merely an opportunity to practice the skills that you learned in therapy. In the writing that you have done in this exercise you have prepared yourself for facing any re-emergence of PTSD symptoms.

All you will need to do is to slow things down, be thoughtful about the skills you have and choose a useful way to interpret what you are experiencing and how you choose to respond.

Interrupting a Potential Relapse

The exercises you have completed on relapse prevention have made you aware of potential risks and your ability to manage them. Now you are going to take it a step further by thinking about changing the possible course of events by interrupting a potential relapse. The goal is to maintain and extend gains made during your recovery. If you have had thoughts of other aspects of recovery and risk of relapse which are unique to you during the course of these exercises write them down.

An important aspect of recovery is changing patterns of behavior, feelings, and thinking as well as problem-solving situations that lead to feeling and acting like you did before you started your recovery process. Once you have identified such patterns, there are a number of ways to prepare yourself to think and behave as you want to:

1. Generate a list of thoughts, feelings, behaviors and situations that places your recovery progress at risk.

2. Write out the stepwise progression of events that increases your risk of relapse to increase your understanding of what takes place.

3. Visualization can be used to mentally practice successful ways of thinking and behaving.

4. Learn from modeling the successful behaviors of others.

5. Present the situations you identified to those you trust so that you can go over your plan and get feedback.

Utilize as many of your new coping skills and resources as you can to increase the potential for the change(s) you desire by increasing your awareness and being prepared. Begin practicing now by writing out new choices for managing thoughts, feelings and behaviors:

_____
_____
_____
_____
_____

What presents the greatest problem to change and how can it be overcome?:

_____
_____

PRACTICING CHANGE

If you have been working on developing new skills, probably one of the most important changes has been assertive communication skills. Developing assertive behaviors and improved communication requires practicing the changes you desire. Make a list of social situations to which you would like to respond differently. Then write out how you normally have dealt with each situation and how you would like to deal with it. The following are some of the techniques that can be used for practicing change:

1. Role-playing. If you are anticipating a specific situation, ask someone you trust to role-play the part opposite you. Role-play every possibility to see which one works best for you. Practice with your therapist or someone else you trust.

2. Self-talk. Affirmations, rational substitute statements, and rational thinking.

3. Empty chair. Imagine that the individual you are anticipating dealing with is sitting in a chair and play out the interaction.

4. Talk to yourself in a mirror.

All of these techniques should help to give you the feeling of having successfully done what you are wanting to do. Practice is helping and reinforcing of change.

Practice
_____

Identify some situations for practicing change. Practice will allow you to feel more comfortable about trying the change in an actual situation. Be patient with and encouraging of yourself.

1._____
Old response:_____
New response:_____
2._____
Old response:_____
New response:_____
3._____
Old response:_____
New response:_____

ANTICIPATING HOW TO COPE WITH AN EMERGENCY

An emergency means different things to different people. Use this as an opportunity to think about what would be considered an emergency situation to you and what would feel like a crisis to your progress of recovery. After careful thought used in identifying a potential emergency situation(s), take the time to think out a plan of how to respond so that you could get back on track as quickly as possible. PLAN: Use your resources. Immediately journal about the crisis, and talk with your therapist or another trusted individual who is supportive of your healing and recovery efforts.

If you find yourself in an emergency situation, choose to do the following:

1. Remove yourself from the situation.

2. Take 15–30 minutes to engage in a relaxation techniques (deep breathing, meditation, etc.).

3. Challenge negative self-talk (catastrophizing, fear-provoking talk). That didn't help before and it won't help if you are in crisis. Instead, choose to think in terms of what the options are and what you are responsible to do in taking care of yourself.

4. Choose to focus on something else to distract yourself briefly. This will prevent an unnecessary escalation of negative emotions and give you time to collect yourself so that you can choose how you want to respond.

5. Review your plan for self-care.

6. Call someone who is supportive of your healing and recovery efforts.

7. Go to a safe place.

8. Use your journal to discharge fear and stress and to problem-solve what you need to do for the moment.

Emergency contacts	Phone number
1. _____	_____
2. _____	_____
3. _____	_____
4. _____	_____
5. _____	_____

What do you think will be most helpful for getting through a crisis?

1. _____

2. _____

3. _____

GETTING UNSTUCK

U = Understanding

N = Nurture yourself

S = Self-acceptance

T = Truthfulness

U = Utilization of resources

C = Choices

K = Keep doing what works in your efforts of healing and recovery toward gaining desired control over your life.

If you have experienced negative thoughts about yourself and how you responded to past experiences, take the time to write about the details of what took place and what skills you have learned that have improved your coping and understanding of your limitations at that time. It is important, throughout the course of healing and recovery, that you intermittently review the changes that you have made and give yourself credit for skill development and personal growth.

1. Learn to accept yourself, both your strengths and your weaknesses. We aren't good at everything. The strengths help us all deal with our weaknesses.

2. Continue to learn new skills for how to decrease self-defeating, unhealthy thoughts, behaviors, and emotions. Substitute rational and believable thinking, feelings and behaviors.

3. Learn to tolerate normal negative emotions like feelings of sadness and loss. These feelings change, but not immediately because they are connected to experiences that are often resolvable, where other choices for closure must be pursued.

How can you use the acronym "UNSTUCK" to help you stay on course for healing and recovery?

_____

_____

_____

_____

_____

RELAXING WITHOUT SUBSTANCES

Everyone needs to relax and get adequate respite from daily stressors. There are also times when people have difficulty sleeping. Take the time to think about different choices that you have access to when you need rest, relaxation, and sleep. If you have used substances in the past because you didn't know what else to do or it was an abusive habit and you are choosing to do things differently consider the following:

Rest and Relaxation

- Meditate
- Read a book
- Take the time to appreciate the beauty of the outdoors:
  - Take a walk in a pretty place
  - Watch the clouds
  - Birdwatching

– Just spending time in a natural settings/park
– Star gazing

- Take an art class and develop a skill
- Get a massage
- Listen to classical music or the sounds of nature
- Reflective moments of gratitude.

Sleep

- Get adequate exercise/yoga
  – Activities you do with other people or a group
  – Activities you do on your own

- Develop a ritual for unwinding to help prepare your body for sleep. Choose pleasant or soothing activities that help to relax the body and mind.
  – Hot bath or shower
  – Herbal tea
  – Meditation
  – Progressive muscle relaxation
  – Relaxing sound (sounds of the surf or waterfall)
  – Prayer
  – No stimulating conversation, stimulating TV etc.

- Closing the day with reflection/journaling of gratitude.

Write down your plans for improving rest/relaxation and sleep:

Rest

1. _____
2. _____
3. _____

Sleep

1. _____
2. _____
3. _____

Approximately half of those who have PTSD experience a sleep disturbance or insomnia and nightmares. It may be important to target nightmare vigilance and fear of sleep if there is a history of sleep difficulty that has not been overcome. Keep a journal of your thoughts, feelings, memories and behaviors associated with sleep to help determine what the underlying problem is. One technique for dealing with nightmares is to use imaginal exposure to the content of the nightmare and then intentionally alter it using image rehearsal. If you experience nightmares talk to your therapist about changing the content and taking control.

If the bedroom is perceived as a dangerous place then problem-solve with your therapist things that you can do to feel safe (such as leaving the television/radio/stereo on or sleeping with a night light on). Also, be prepared to modify any behaviors which may be contributing to sleep-related problems.

SELF-CONTROL

Self-control is an important social skill. If you have given yourself permission to be reactive for a long time, it will be a challenge to practice self-control. However, the positive consequences, especially the way you feel about yourself, will reinforce your efforts. It is important to work toward increasing your awareness about how you respond and what choices you can make in responding in a more effective manner. Consider the following steps for achieving self-control.

1. Stop to think
2. Pay attention to how you feel inside and what you need to do to be in the best frame of mind to make a good choice
3. Decide whether you are losing self-control. In other words, learn and decide on what appropriate behaviors are
4. Think about your choices
5. Relax and calm yourself
6. Make a choice
7. Do not react to another person's response
8. Review in your mind whether you made the best choice for you
9. Learn from every experience of practicing self-control
10. Be honest with yourself and feel good about your efforts.

Describe three experiences where you have not demonstrated self-control and then identify what you would do differently:

1. _____
2. _____
3. _____

COPING WITH DISAPPOINTMENT

Everyone has hopes and dreams for the future. Sometimes things don't work out the way they expected, even when they have been working very hard toward a specific accomplishment. Sometimes things don't work out because the right decisions and actions were not taken, and other things just did not work out. Whatever the case, you have the choice to get so frustrated and disappointed that you want to give up and use the disappointment to better understand what has happened and work at having a different outcome in the future.

The Meaning and Value of Disappointment

When you have been planning and hoping for something that does not happen, it is normal to feel disappointed. Generally, you accept the loss and move on. Be careful to not use a disappointment as an excuse to fall back into old ways of coping that are not a part of your plans for healing and recovery. Instead use it as an opportunity to learn and reinforce desired change. Expectations need to be realistic. Take an honest look at how things really are. There are different kinds of disappointments.

1. Simple disappointments (with an entire range of how you experience it):
   – Small and easy to forget
   – Happens to everybody
   – Deep and painful
   – Could be the result of poor decision-making
   – Could be the result of being in the wrong place at the wrong tine, i.e. not personal
   – Could have been an unrealistic expectation

2. Chronic disappointments: tend to be a lifestyle pattern associated with not learning from experience or having unrealistic expectations

3. Life stages:
   – Expectations that certain accomplishments will be made at specific time of life (security, job position, accomplishments, etc.)
   – Children growing up, loss of parents, etc.
   – Changes in health or physical functioning.

How to Decrease Disappointment

1. Develop realistic expectations and limitations

2. Be flexible. There are a lot of things that are outside of your control

3. Recognize disappointments, talk about them, and learn from them

4. Work hard at making your plans a reality

5. Accept when you cannot influence a situation.

What role has disappointment played in your feelings of control over your life, self-esteem and motivation to work toward goals?

_____

_____

SELF-CONFIDENCE

An important part of healing and recovery is learning more about yourself and your abilities. List positive statements about yourself to each of the following questions.

• What can I do now that seemed difficult or impossible before?

   1. _____
   2. _____
   3. _____

• What can I accomplish if I make a commitment and put my mind to work on it?

   1. _____
   2. _____

3. _____

- What personality traits am I working on acquiring?

    1. _____
    2. _____
    3. _____

- What are the long-term goals I am working on that will add to my feelings of being successful?

    1. _____
    2. _____
    3. _____

You can see that building self-confidence is an active process that requires

1. Taking action

2. Choosing to think in a positive and productive way

3. Observing others who are successful at what they do

4. Developing and using resources

5. Developing goals and breaking them down into manageable steps.

SELF-CARE BEHAVIORS (JOHNSON, 2004)

It is very important to have patterns of self-care behaviors as part of your lifestyle. It is expected that some self-care behaviors are part of a daily routine, where other behaviors may be part of a weekly regimen, etc. If you do not practice self-care behavior you will never reach the optimal results for your efforts because there is a lack of boundaries, self-nurture, and effective prioritizing. Make a commitment to emotional and physical health. You may even want to start with a medical exam to make sure everything is in order. Consider the following in developing your self-care plan:

1. Utilize relaxation techniques to decrease body tension, clear your mind, and leave you with an overall sense of well-being.

2. Choose to be around people who are supportive, caring and kind. Schedule time for pleasurable relationships and activities.

3. Process difficult experiences by:

    - Utilizing your support system. Talk about your experiences with people you trust. Be careful to not isolate and withdraw. Instead spend time with people who offer a feeling of comfort and care.

    - Initiating a journal. Instead of keeping thoughts and feelings inside where they have the potential to build up or cause increased confusion, get them down on paper. Some individuals have difficulty expressing themselves to others, or are afraid of being judged.

    - Remembering that therapy is a resource. It is a safe, non-judgmental environment with a safe person where you can speak freely about your thoughts and feelings without concern for how others may judge you. Therapy can be very helpful for resolving a crisis or problem-solving.

4. Regular, moderate exercise. Aerobic exercise, such as brisk walking, is beneficial for alleviating and maintaining decreased body tension, clearing your mind, and leaving you with an overall sense of well-being. Approach each day with a purpose. Be productive by outlining daily structure which includes adequate sleep, good nutrition, exercise, relaxation, utilization of resources, and task accomplishment.

5. Avoid anxiety-provoking conversations or making significant life decisions when you are experiencing significant stress. Instead create a feeling of calm to center yourself so that you can decide what is the best way to move forward and to identify the resources you need to do it.

6. Avoid being self-critical. Be as kind and understanding to yourself as you would be to another. Use positive self-talk to reassure yourself that the symptoms you are currently experiencing will subside with effort, personal growth, and time.

7. Get adequate rest and sleep. Positive thinking requires energy.

8. Take responsibility for your own life. Life is about choices. Understand yourself, your behaviors, your thoughts/beliefs, and your motivations.

What are some additional things you would find useful in adding to your self-care plan.

RESOURCES AND FURTHER READING

American Psychiatric Association (2000) *Diagnostic and Statistical Manual of Mental Disorders*, 4th edn, text revised. Washington, DC: American Psychiatric Association.

American Psychological Association (2004) The APA Help Center. The American Psychological Association website. www.apahelpcenter.org

Astin MC, Rothbaum B (2000) Exposure therapy for the treatment of post-traumatic stress disorder. *Clin Q* 9: 52–55.

Baker GR, Salston M (1993) *Management of Intrusion and Arousal Symptoms in PTSD*. San Diego: Association of Traumatic Stress Specialists (International Association of Trauma Counselors).

Bandler R, Grinder J (1979) *Frogs into Princes*. Moab, UT: Real People Press.

Bandler R, Grinder J (1985) *Using your Brain for a Change*. Moab, UT: Real People Press.

Beck AT (1976) *Cognitive Therapy and the Emotional Disorders*. New York: International Universities Press.

Beck AT, Emery G, Greenberg RL (1985) *Anxiety Disorders and Phobias: A cognitive perspective*. New York: Basic Books.

Bourne E (2001) *Beyond Anxiety & Phobias: A step by step guide to lifetime recovery*. Oakland, CA: New Harbinger Publications.

Busuttil W (2000) The development of a 90 day residential program for the treatment of complex PTSD. In: *Strategies for Comprehensive Treatment in Clinical Practice* (Williams MB, Sommer JF, eds). Binghampton, NY: Haworth Press.

Covey S (1999) *The 7 Habits of Highly Successful People*. New York: Simon & Schuster.

Davidson J (2001) Recognition and treatment of posttraumatic stress disorder. *JAMA* 286: 584–588.

Davis (1990) The Courage to Heal Workbook.

Enright RD, Fitzgibbons RO (2000) *Helping Clients Forgive: An empirical guide for resolving anger and restoring hope*. Washington, DC: American Psychological Association.

Friedman MJ (2000) *Post-Traumatic Stress Disorder: the latest assessment and treatment strategies*. Kansas City, MO: Compact Clinicals.

Grand LC (2000) *The Life Skills Presentation Guide*. New York: John Wiley & Sons.

Greenberger D, Pacoly CA (1995) *Mind over Mood: A cognitive therapy treatment manual for clients*. New York: Guilford Press.

Herman JL (1992) *Trauma and Recovery*. New York: Basic Books.

Ilardo J (1992) *Taking Risks for Personal Growth: A step by step workbook*. Oakland, CA: New Harbinger.

Johnson SL (2004) *The Therapist's Guide to Clinical Intervention*, 2nd edn. San Diego: Academic Press.

Levine P (1992) *The Body as Healer: Transforming Trauma and Anxiety*. Lyons, CO: USA.

Levine P, Frederick A (1997) *Walking the Tiger: Healing trauma*. Berkeley, CA: North Atlantic Books.

Linehan MM (1993) *Skills Training Manual for Treatment of Posttraumatic Borderline Personality Disorder*. New York: Guilford Press.

Linehan MM (1996) *Cognitive Behavioral Treatment of Borderline Personality Disorder*. New York: Guilford Press.

Maslow AH (1954) *Motivation and Personality*. New York: Harper and Row.

Matsakis A (1994) *Post-traumatic Stress Disorder: A complete treatment guide*. Oakland, CA: New Harbinger Publications.

Matsakis A (1998) *Trust after Trauma: A Guide to Relationships for Survivors and those who Love Them*. Oakland, CA: New Harbinger Publications.

Meichenbaum D (1994) *A Clinical Handbook/Practical Therapist Manual: For assessing and treating adults with post-traumatic stress disorder*. Waterloo, Ontario: Institute Press.

Pennebaker JW (1997) *Opening Up: The healing power of expressing emotions*. New York: Guilford Press.

Power M, Dalgleish T (1992) *Cognition and Emotion: From Order to Disorder*. Hove, Sussex: Psychology Press.

Rothchild B (2000) *The Body Remembers: The psychophysiology of trauma and trauma treatment*. New York: WW Norton.

Schab LM (1996) *The Coping Skills Workbook*. King of Prussia, PA: The Center for Applied Psychology.

Schiraldi GR (2000) *The Post-traumatic Stress Disorder Sourcebook*. Los Angeles: Lowell.

Smyth LD (1999) *Client's Manual for the Cognitive-Behavioral Treatment of Anxiety Disorders*. Havre de Grace, MD: The Red Toad Company.

Tedeschi RG, Park CL, Calhoun LG (eds) (1998) *Post-traumatic Growth: Positive changes in the aftermath of crisis*. Mahweh, NJ: Lawrence Erlbaum Associates.

van der Kolk B (1997) The body keeps score: Memory and the evolving psychobiology of post-traumatic stress. In: *Essential Papers on Post-Traumatic Stress Disorder* (Horowitz M, ed.). New York: New York University Press.

Wilson JP, Friedman MJ, Lindy JD (2001) *Treating Psychological Trauma and PTSD*. New York: Guilford Press.

Zampelli SO (2000) *From Sabotage to Success: Ways to overcome self-defeating behavior and reach your true potential*. Oakland, CA: New Harbinger Publications.

INDEX

Self-care
   behaviors, 344–345
   grief therapy goal, 221
   improvement, 215
   plan, 180
Self-confidence, strategies, 343–344
Self-control, *see also* Impulse control
   improvement in substance abuse, 232–233
   strategies, 342
Self-esteem, improvement, 199, 210, 216, 234
Self-monitoring, traumatic event recovery,
      289–290
Self-mutilation, PTSD risks, 30
Self-regulation therapy, PTSD management, 134
Self-talk
   fear coping, 278–279
   negative talk
      challenging, 275
      perceptions, 278
   positive talk and cognitive restructuring, 274
   rational talk and difficult anniversaries,
      275–277
   realistic talk, 273–274
   thinking distortions, 273
Serotonergic system, PTSD, 97–100
Sertraline, PTSD management, 159
Sex differences
   PTSD frequency, 19–21
   PTSD risks
      cultural differences, 27
      military service personnel, 27–28
      summary of studies, 25–26
      trauma exposure, 26
Shame, challenging in therapy, 193
Shiatsu, PTSD management, 162
SIBAM, dissociation model, 293
SIP, *see* Structured Interview for PTSD
SIT, *see* Stress inoculation therapy
Skin level boundary exercises, somatic
      treatment, 146
Sleep
   depression management, 211
   hyperarousal
      disturbances, 97
      management, 201–202
   insomnia management, 148, 158
   optimization, 341–342
Social support
   barriers, 287
   supportive relationship characteristics,
      286–287
Sociocultural factors, PTSD risks, 33
Somatic experiencing, PTSD management, 163
Somatic memory
   implicit memory, 293
   pain dimensions, 17
   physical complaints following trauma, 17
Somatic treatment, PTSD
   autonomic nervous system responses, 144–145
   body awareness exercises, 146–150
   boundary exercises, 146–150

stress inoculation therapy, *see* Stress
      inoculation therapy
Somatization disorders, PTSD comorbidity, 34
Spiritual/religious counseling, PTSD
      management, 161
SSRIs, *see* Selective serotonin reuptake inhibitors
Stress
   neurobiological pathways, 91–93
   noradrenergic system, 93–95
   pathology, 80–81
   response *see* specific components
Stress inoculation therapy (SIT)
   overview, 136–137
   phases
      application training, 138
      conceptualization, 137
      skills acquisition, consolidation, and
         rehearsal, 137–138
Stress management
   anxiety management, 217
   dissociation treatment, 206
   mental processing aspects, 222
   relaxation techniques, 282–286
   self-management, 281
   warning signs of stress, 281–282
Structured Clinical Interview for DSM-IV
      (SCID), 59
Structured Interview for PTSD (SIP), 59
Substance abuse
   maternal, 107
   PTSD risks, 30–31, 34, 37–41
   screening, 57–58
   therapy goals
      abstinence, 232
      assessments, 231–232
      communication improvement, 233
      coping improvement, 234
      family interactions, 234
      motivation, 232
      problem-solving improvement, 234
      rational thinking, 232
      refusal skills, 233
      self-control improvement, 232–233
      self-esteem improvement, 234
      social skills, 233
Subthreshold PTSD
   diagnosis, 9–10
   resiliency, 12
   traumatic stress response, 10–11
Successful habits, 322
Suicide
   anger, 223–227
   anxiety, 213–218
   avoidance, 196–200
   communication assertiveness, 229–231
   complex PTSD, 239–240
   depression, 207–213
   dissociation, 205–206
   eating disorders, 235
   first responders, 242–243
   grief, 218–221